PIERCE
GENEALOGY

BEING
THE RECORD
OF
THE POSTERITY OF

CAPT. MICHAEL,
JOHN AND
CAPT. WILLIAM PIERCE

WHO CAME TO THIS COUNTRY FROM ENGLAND

Frederick Clifton Pierce

HERITAGE BOOKS
2008

HERITAGE BOOKS

AN IMPRINT OF HERITAGE BOOKS, INC.

Books, CDs, and more—Worldwide

For our listing of thousands of titles see our website
at
www.HeritageBooks.com

Published 2008 by
HERITAGE BOOKS, INC.
Publishing Division
100 Railroad Ave. #104
Westminster, Maryland 21157

International Standard Book Numbers
Paperbound: 978-0-7884-2104-4
Clothbound: 978-0-7884-7010-3

TO

MY PARENTS,

MR. AND MRS. SILAS A. PIERCE,

THIS WORK IS

MOST RESPECTFULLY DEDICATED

BY THEIR SON,

THE AUTHOR.

Concerning this nebular history, then; is it a human invention or is it a divine record? Is it "a tale told by an idiot signifying nothing," or is it a plan of infinite imagination signifying immortality?

Prof. BENJAMIN PEIRCE, of Harvard University.

AUTHOR'S PREFACE.

Fifteen years ago while at work compiling data for the History and Genealogy of the Pierce family (my own branch), considerable information was obtained of the family of Captain Michael Pierce, an early inhabitant of Plymouth Colony, who moved from Weymouth to Scituate. Having been urged by numerous members of this family to complete the work as far as possible, the attempt was made, with what success the reader of this volume can judge. Thousands of letters were written, and in nearly every instance prompt, full and complete replies received, varying in length from a single page of note paper to over twenty pages of foolscap. It required considerable work to arrange all this matter in a presentable shape. The form adopted by the New England Historical and Genealogical Society in the publication of their *Register* has been used as the best and simplest arrangement. It is the habit of some persons to depreciate genealogical studies and labor, and in some instances even to ridicule the efforts of those so engaged. It is a matter of extreme indifference to them whether they ever had any ancestors or not, and in nearly every case of this kind the persons only care for themselves. They are so wrapt up in self, that all other matters dwindle into utter insignificance.

Of the numerous Pierce, Peirce and Pearce genealogies which I have published, there are none in which the emigrant ancestors were so active and prominent in the early history of the Massachusetts and Plymouth colonies as in this particular branch. Three brothers, John, Captain William and Captain Michael, took a leading part in the early struggle of the infant colonies in New England.

ABBREVIATIONS AND EXPLANATIONS.—Æ. for aged; abt. for about; b. for born; bap. for baptised; bef., before; ch., children; d., died; dau., daughter; dec'd, deceased; m., married; unm., unmarried; inv., inventory; rep., representative; res., resided, resides or residence; w., wife; wid., widow; yr., year; s. p., without issue. There are other abbreviations, of such common use, that the meaning will be obvious. A name in parenthesis, thus, Sarah Pierce, dau. of John and Maria (Scott) Pierce, indicates the maiden name of the mother. An interrogation mark implies doubt or want of absolute certainty. Birthplaces are not always given, but they can be ascertained by reference to the person's father and his residence at the time of his birth.

OLD AND NEW STYLE.— In computing time, the solar year is reckoned 365¼ days, but this is too much by eleven minutes and a fraction. If this excess be neglected, in the course of centuries first of January would fall back toward midsummer, and in 1582, the time of Pope Gregory XIII, it was found that the vernal equinox which in A. D. 325, happened on the 21st of March, actually occurred on the 10th of March. For the purpose of rectifying the calendar, the Pope ordered that ten days be dropped from that year. This was called "New Style," and the former calendar "Old Style." The new calendar was soon adopted by all Catholic countries, but in England and her colonies, it was disregarded till 1752, when the error of the old calendar amounted to eleven days, and by an Act of Parliament, they were dropped from September of that year. If the year began the 25th of March, the date would be February 9, 1684, if the year began the 1st of January, the date would be February 9, 1685, and changed to New Style by addition of 11 days would be February 16, 1685.

Origin of the Name.— One of the most common methods of bestowing surnames was from the place or residence. Not only countries but counties and towns were a fruitful source of surnames. John from Cornwall became John Cornwall or Cornish. Richard, who lived near a piece of woodland was spoken of as Richard at or near the wood, originating the surname Atwood, or John living near a hill became John Hill. So with Underhill, Atwell, etc. John living near a clump of oaks was John atten oaks, abbreviated into Noakes, or William who had pitched his tent or cabin near a notable ash tree was known as William at the ash or William atten ash, which easily drifted into Nash. So, too, Thomas who lived near a small stream (or in Anglo-Saxon *a becket*) was Thomas at the becket, and thus was named the martyr Thomas a'Becket. The most common terminations of English surnames taken from places are *ford, ham, lea* and *ton*. *Ford* is from the Saxon *faran*, to go, signifying the place where a stream could be crossed.

In the name of Shakespeare's birthplace we have a memento of three different eras of English history, viz., the period of the occupancy of the old Britons, the Romans and the Saxons. *Strat* is an abbreviation of *strata* (street), the name by which the great Roman roads were known. *Ford* tells us that one of these roads crossed a stream, and *Avon* is the name which the old Britons or Celts gave to the streams.

The word *lea, leah* or *leigh* signifying a partially wooden field, served as the ending for many surnames, such as Horsley, Cowley, Ashley, Oakley, Lindley and Berkley, or Birchley, *Hay* or *haw* means a hedge, and this has given us Hayes, Haynes, Haley, Haywood, Hawes, Haworth, Hawthorn, Haughton or Houghton.

Occupations, too, have afforded an endless array of surnames. This method was used by the Romans in such names as Fabricus (smith), Pistor (painter), Agricola (farmer). In England a skillful hunter would adopt that as his surname, and equally so with the carpenter, joiner, sawyer, baker or butcher.

Personal traits and complexions, too, gave rise to surnames. From the former we have the names Stout, Strong, Long, Longman, Longfellow; and from the latter, Brown, Black, etc. Some mental and moral traits were also used to denote surnames. Richard the First, of England, was better known as Richard of the lion heart. The next step would be to derive from this quality the surname Lion.

The name of Pierce is a common one in England, being undoubtedly derived from the baptismal name, Peter or Pirse, or Pierse, as it was called after the Conquest and while French was still the court language, and has been variously called or written Pieres, Pierse, Pierce, Pearce, Piers, Peires, Peirce, Peirse, Pearse, Peers, and families of the same name settled in the counties of Gloucester, Kent, Devon, Norfolk, Bedford, Somerset, Suffolk, England. Percy, Piercy, Percey, Pierce, Pearce, etc., local. The renowned family of Northumberland, England, derived their name from Percy Forest, in the province of Maen, Normandy, whence they came, which signifies a stony place, from *pierre*. It may signify a hunting place from *pirsen*, Teutonic, to hunt; *percer*, French, to penetrate, to force one's way. [Arthur's Etymological Dictionary of Christian Names, 1857.]

The following are the different ways the name is spelled in several countries:

English.	French.	Swedish.	Danish.	Dutch.	Italian.	Spanish.	Portuguese.
Peter.	Pierre.	Per.	Pedeo.	Pieter.	Pietro.	Pedro.	Pedro.
Piers.	Pierrot.			Piet.	Pier.		Pedrinho.
Pierce.	Perrin.				Piero.		
	Peire.				Pietruccio.		

[From History of Christian Names, England, 1863.]

ARRANGEMENT OF THE BOOK.— The plan adopted, as stated previously, is that of the *Genealogical Register* which is by far the most intelligible. The small figure over a name to the right, thus Fred.[6], indicates the generation to which the person belongs, reckoning from the original ancestor in this country, Capt. Michael Pierce. The descendants for several generations belonged to the agricultural class and were characterized by good sense, sound judgment and christian excellence. They helped swell the ranks of honest New England yeomanry, with an ancestry not often great, but always virtuous, filling with fidelity and honor the stations they were called upon to fill, the descendants can well be proud of their ancestors and learn from them that "the richest bequest which any man can make, for the benefit of posterity, is that of a shining and spotless example."

FRED. C. PIERCE.

ROCKFORD, ILL., *July* 30, 1889.

NOTE ON THE SPELLING AND PRONUNCIATION OF THE NAME OF PIERCE, BY PROF. JAMES M. PEIRCE OF HARVARD UNIVERSITY, TAKEN FROM THE GENEALOGICAL REGISTER.

The *spelling* of the name of Pierce is generally supposed to have no significance in determining relationships. Certainly a great variety in this regard will be found in printed and written documents, from the settlement of New England until now. But my observation leads me to believe that a high degree of uniformity exists in the spelling, *as used by persons bearing the name*, in any one family connection. Thus the descendants of Robert of Woburn, and I believe nearly the whole body of the descendants of John of Watertown, from the beginning to the present day, almost everywhere use the spelling *Peirce;* though John himself appears to sign his will *Pers* or *Perss* in an antiquated hand resembling German *Schrift*. The spelling Pearse in the will of his wife Elizabeth is not written by the testator, who signs only by *mark*. On the other hand, the descendants of Samuel of Charlestown and of Sergt. Thomas of Woburn most commonly employ the spelling *Pierce*, which is also, I *think*, that of the signature of the will of Thomas, senior, of Charlestown, which may, however, be *Peirce* or *Peerce*. In the old *pronunciation* of the name, according to the tradition prevalent in several branches of the family of John of

Watertown, the vowel-sound was the same that we now hear in the words *pear*, *heir* and *their*; and this pronunciation is remembered by living persons as having been sometimes used by old-fashioned people. This was probably quite independent of the spelling. The same sound was, according to A. J. Ellis, used in the verb *to pierce*, in the seventeenth century, and by some in the eighteenth century. On the other hand, the verb may be occasionally heard with the pronunciation *perce* (or *purse*), which is now the prevalent pronunciation of all forms of the surname in the neighborhood of Boston.

Let me add that the great number of families of this name among the early settlers of New England makes it exceedingly difficult to trace the different lines. Savage is guilty of many omissions under this name, and has committed some decided mistakes. The perplexity in which all printed authorities leave the subject make the matter very difficult for the author.

JAMES MILLS PEIRCE.

CAMBRIDGE, MASS.

PIERCE PROCLIVITIES.— A prominent and distinguishing trait of character in the Pierce family is casually exposed to view by the Historian Babson, in his description of the tumultuous proceedings occasioned by the violent party spirit that prevailed in the country after the embargo of President Jefferson in 1806. "At a town meeting held in Gloucester, the two political parties struggled for the mastery through the day and amid darkness until half-past ten at night, and the floor of the church wherein the meeting was held he describes as presenting a scene of wild confusion and discord worthy of Pandemonium itself. The leaders of each party entertained their friends with unbounded hospitality, and each had its own place of refreshment for general resort." But he adds: — "The Democrats not unreasonably expected success, as they had the influence of the Pierce family." Young ducks do not take to the water more naturally than the Pierce family throughout the country to Democratic principles. Indomitable perseverance is also a trait that marks their character in every department of life, and has generally crowned their efforts with ultimate success, though attained after repeated and sometimes very mortifying failures.— Gen. E. W. PEIRCE, Freetown, Mass.

THE THREE EMIGRANTS.

John Pierce,* born in England, brother of Captain Michael and Captain William, secured a patent for New England, February 12, 1620, which superseded the Wincob patent. Pierce was one of the adventurers, and the patent conveyed with self-governing powers a tract of land to be selected by the planters near the mouth of the Hudson. So little did the body of adventurers know of the Pilgrims, that they long termed them "Mr. Pierce's Company."

This patent is still at Plymouth in good condition and bears the seals and signatures of the Duke of Lennox, the Marquis of Hamilton, the Earl of Warwick, Sir Ferdinando Gorges, and another whose name cannot now be deciphered.† With the incredible carelessness formerly shown as to historical documents and relics, this

---

* Citizen and clothworker of London.

† See Landmarks of Plymouth, p. 40.

patent was once lost. Years after it had been supposed to have disappeared forever, it was accidentally found among the papers of the late Judge Davis, to whom it seems to have been lent by some official, who neither made a note of the transaction nor took the trouble to remember it. This patent is now given in the Mass. His. Soc. Coll., Vol. IV, series ii, p. 156, with valuable notes by Charles Davis.

As stated above, it gave to Pierce no boundaries, but to him and each of his associates one hundred acres of land. At the end of four years they were to have one hundred acres for each emigrant. Rent was to be paid after seven years, at the rate of two shillings for each one hundred acres. Each "undertaker" was to have fifteen hundred acres for the support of churches, schools and hospitals. The colonists were to devote themselves chiefly to planting, selling, making and producing staples, such as corn, silk-grass, hemp, flax, pitch, tar, soap, ashes, potash, iron, clapboards, etc. This patent remained in force for only one year, and was supplemented by another under which Pierce ineffectually sought to make the Plymouth people his vassals.

In 1622, the above patent was changed for another (a "deed-pole") to him, his heirs, associates and assigns. His plan was to take no associates, but to set himself up as the sole proprietor of the country, the settlers becoming his tenants, subject to him as their lord-paramount, and under his laws and courts, the adventurers tried to buy Pierce's claim. The patent had cost him £50, but as he would not sell for less than £500, the trade was not made.

In December, 1621, John Pierce equipped the "Paragon," and set out to take possession of his principality. He was hired to take along many passengers and much freight for Plymouth. In fourteen days the "Paragon" returned to London badly damaged by a storm, but the next February he again started out with additional passengers and freight crowded by the owner to cover his recent losses. In mid-ocean a perfect tempest beat upon her for two weeks. Her upper works were torn off, her mainmast cut away, and her escape from sinking was the narrowest; but finally she found her way back to England, where she was at once repaired and again started under command of Captain William Pierce, the owner's brother.

The adventurers had expended for goods, passage-money and subsistence £640, for most of which they had a claim on Pierce. His losses had much reduced his property, and in settlement he purchased his stock as an adventurer and assigned his patent to the Plymouth Company.

2

CAPTAIN WILLIAM PIERCE.

Born in England abt. 1590, m. Jane————, res. Boston,* Salem, Mass. He was killed in the Bahamas, at New Providence, July 13, 1641.

Captain William Pierce in the early history of the colonies was the most celebrated master of ships that came into the waters of New England. He was on very intimate terms with all the leading colonists, and was a warm friend of Winslow and Bradford. He was first noticed in the early records of the colony in 1622, when he was master of the "Paragon," the owner of which ship was his brother John Pierce of London. In 1623, Capt. Pierce brought over to Plymouth the "Anne" with her noteworthy company. In 1624, he came in the "Charity," conveying Winslow, with his cattle which were the first brought into New England. In 1625 he was at Plymouth in the "Jacob," again bringing Winslow and more cattle.

In 1629, he commanded the renowned "Mayflower," and in her he took a company from Holland as far as the Bay on their way to Plymouth; and in the next year, Feb., 1630, he came with the "Lion" from Bristol, England,† which was a part of Winthrop's fleet. Owing to the destitution at the Bay, he was hurried back for provisions, with which he returned November 22,‡ just as

---

* 1634 he owned a house and lot in Boston.

† Arrived in Salem May, 1630.

‡ April 10, 1633, arrives at Boston Mr. Hodges, one of Mr. Pierce's mates, in a shallop from Virginia; and brings news that Mr. Pierce's ship was cast away on a shoal four miles from Feak Isle, ten leagues to the north of the mouth of Virginia Bay, November 2, about five in the morning, the wind south-west, through the negligence of one of his mates who had the watch, and kept not his lead a sounding as he was appointed; they had a shallop and a boat aboard; all who went into the shallop came safe ashore; but the boat sunk by the ship's side, and twelve were drowned

the crisis of the famine had arrived. He also brought sixty passengers, including Roger Williams and his wife Mary. November 29, 1631,* he came over again in the "Lion," and with him John Elliot and Governor Winthrop's wife. In 1632 he sailed once more to Boston and Plymouth in the "Lion;" but after carrying Winthrop to Weymouth lost his ship on the Virginia coast, for which place he sailed October 27, 1632.† In 1634 he was gathering Oldham's corn in the "Rebecca,"‡ and taking observations in the "Narragansett," and the next year commanded the defense of London, and was first in the West Indies, and then later on in the

---

in her and ten taken up in the shallop. There were in ship twenty-eight seamen and ten passengers; of these were drowned, seven seamen and five passengers, and all the goods lost except one hogshead of beaver. Next day the ship was broken to pieces. They were nine days in much distress before they found any English. Plymouth men lost nine hundred weight of beaver and fish. Many others lost beaver, and Mr. Humphrey fish.

April 7, Pierce's letter came to hand at Plymouth. It was dated Virginia, December 25, 1632, and was as follows:

Dear Friends, etc.—The Brint of this fatal Stroke that the Lord has bro't on me and you all, will come to your Ears before this comes to your Hand, it is like; and therefore I shall not need to enlarge. My whole Estate for the most Part is taken away; and yours in a great measure by this and your former Losses [He means by the French and Mr. Allarton]. It is Time to look about us before the Wrath of the Lord brake forth to utter destruction. The Good Lord gave us all Grace to search our Hearts and try our Ways, and turn to the Lord and humble ourselves under his mighty Hand, and seek Atonement etc. Dear Friends, you may know that all your Beaver [the Ht loss we sustain of this kind], and the books of your accounts are swallowed up in the Sea. But what should I more say? Have we lost our outward Estates; yet a happy loss if our souls may gain; there is yet more in the Lord Jehovah than ever we had in the world. O, that our foolish Hearts could yet be weaned from the Things here below, which are Vanity and Vexation of Spirit; and yet we fools catch after Shadows that fly away and are gone in a moment etc. Thus with my continued Remembrance of you in my poor Desires to the Throne of Grace, beseeching God to renew his Love and Favor to you all in and through the Lord Jesus Christ, both in Spiritual and Temporal Good things, as may be most to the Glory and Praise of his name and your everlasting good.

So I rest your afflicted Brother in Christ,

WILLIAM PIERCE.

* This ship left Salem April 1, and arrived in Bristol April 29.

† A fast had been ordered, but on his arrival it was changed to one of Thanksgiving.

‡ 1633 Pierce's "Rebecca" of sixty tons was built at Medford.

ice, rescuing refugees from the Connecticut Valley and returning them to Boston. In 1636, with the fine new ship "Desire," one hundred and twenty tons, built for him at Marblehead, he went with Endicott's force to Block Island. In 1637, he carried supplies from Boston for the soldiers of the Pequod War and acted as tender. In 1638, he sailed between Boston and the West Indies; and it is sad to relate that according to the usage of the times, he took out several Pequod prisoners as bondmen, and returned with a few negro slaves, though even then some leading citizens condemned this traffic. At this time he seems to have presented Winthrop with what the latter calls an *aligarto*—an animal which much interested the grave Bostonians. In 1638, he cleared the "Desire." from London with passengers for Boston; the English officers writing his name "Piers." From Boston he kept on to the West Indies. In 1639, he sailed the "Desire"* from Boston to the Thames in twenty-three days — a passage which would even now reflect much credit on such a craft and its captain.

It is well known that Pierce's Almanack for 1639 was the first thing in book form printed in the English colonies.†

In 1641, he carried a party of dissenters to settle in the West Indies; but owing to the hostility of the Spaniards, turned back with his passengers, and put into New Providence to bring away a congregation living there. Though finding the Spaniards already in possession, he stood gallantly in, hoping to rescue his countrymen. When the enemy opened upon him with cannon, he sent his people into the hold for safety, retaining on deck but one man to aid in working the ship. While lying in the caboose watching the sails, the captain and this sailor were fatally wounded by the same shot. The "Desire" was then headed for home; her noble master

---

* 1636 Pierce's "Desire," one hundred and twenty tons, was built at Marblehead.

† In 1638, Mr. Glover, an English clergyman, sailed with his wife for Boston, bringing a printing-press and an exceedingly illiterate printer named Stephen Day. Glover died on his voyage, but his widow, who had property, bought a house at Cambridge. There the press was set up by Day, and some printing done, and the first bound work issued in the colonies was issued in 1639, calculated for New England by William "Peirse," mariner, former captain of the "Anne," "Lion," and "Mayflower."

finding a fitting grave in the blue sea upon which so much of his life had been spent. His death was much lamented in the two colonies, which had so long known him as a skilful navigator and a Christian gentleman.

In 1632, he was one of the one hundred and fifty-one members of the Charlestown Church which removed to Boston.

Prince, in his annual, part II, sec. 2, p. 69, says: William Pierce, captain of the "Lion," was the ancestor of the Rev. James Pierce of Cambridge, and Exeter in England.

In 1636, Capt. Wm. Pierce brought the first sweet potatoes into New England from the West Indies; he brought fifteen tons, and sold them in Boston at two pence a pound.

In 1633, Capt. Wm. Pierce brought the first cotton into New England from West Indies.

In Winthrop's Journal, under date of Saturday (12th June, 1630), we find the following: "About four in the morning we were near our port. We shot off two pieces of ordnance and sent our skiff to Mr. Pierce, his ship (which lay in the harbour and had been there [blank] days). About an hour after Mr. Allarton came on board us, in a shallop, as he was sailing to Pemaquid." Brave Allarton, therefore, must have been the first person who welcomed Mr. Winthrop and his associates to New England.

The muster of Capt. Wm. Pierce, June 23, 1624. He then resided in James city, Virginia. It was as follows:

Capt. Wm. Pierce came in "Sea Venture."

Mrs. Jane Pierce, his wife, in the "Blessings."

SERVANTS.

Thomas Smith, æ. 17 years, in the "Abigaill."

Henry Bradford, æ. 35 years, in the "Abigaill."

Esther Ederife, a maid-servant, in the "Jonathan."

Angelo, a negro woman, in the "Treasuror."

The rest of Capt. William's servants, provisions, armes, munition, etc., are at Mulberry Island.

The muster of the inhabitants at Mulberry Island, Virginia, taken June 25, 1624:

The Muster of Capt. Wm. Pierce's Servants.

Richard Attkins, æ. 24, came in "London Marchamst."
Abigail, his wife, came in "Abigaill."
Wm. Barker, æ. 20, came in "Abigaill."
Robert Ashton, æ. 29, came in the "Treasuror."
Hugh Wing, æ. 30, came in "George," 1620.
Robert Lathoun, æ. 20, came in "George," 1620.
Richard Aldon, æ. 19, came in "George," 1620.
Thomas Wood, æ. 30, came in "George," 1620.
Roger Ruce, came in "Charles."
Alexander Gill, æ. 20, came in "Bonny Bess."
Samuel Morris, æ. 20, came in "Abigaill."
Thomas Rose, æ. 35, came in "Jonathan."
Robert Hedges, æ. 40, came in the ———.
John Virgo, came in "Treasuror."
Susan, his wife, in the same ship.
John Gatter, came in "George," 1620.
William Richardson, came in "Edwine."
Richard Fine, came in "Neptune."
John Nowell, came in "Margaret and Jane."
Richard Downes, came in "Jonathan."
John Cranich, came in "Marygold."
Percevall Wood, came in "George."
Ann, his wife, came in "George."
William Raymont, came in "Neptune."
William Bullock, came in "Jonathan."
Anthony Baram, came in "Abigail."
Elizabeth, his wife, came in "William and Thomas."
Thomas Harwood, came in "Margaret and Jane," 1622.
Grace, his wife, came in "George."
Thomas Read, æ. 65 years.

Children.

Edward, b. 1633, d. 1673. Edward Pearse, who Dr. Calamy styles "a most affectionate and useful preacher," was ejected from St. Margaret's, Westminster, when the "Act of Uniformity" took place. He was the author of several practical treatises, the most noted of which is entitled, " The Great Canaan, or a Serious Warning to the Timely and Thorough Preparation for Death," etc., which was frequently distributed at funerals. It has been reprinted about twenty times. He earnestly prayed, in his last illness, that something of his might be useful after his decease. "Which prayer," says Dr. Calamy, "was remarkably answered in the signal success of his little book." He was born in 1633, and died in 1673. There was another Edward Pearse, who was author of " The Conformist's Plea for the Non-Conformists," who has been confounded with the person above mentioned. I take this to be the minister of Cottesbrook, in Northamptonshire; whom the " Plea " really confirmed is apparent from South's " Sermons," Vol. VI, p. 33; from Kennet's Register and Chronicle, p. 755, and from Neale's " History of the Puritans," Vol. IV, p. 508.

JAMES, b. and d. in England.

WILLIAM, b. in England, m. Esther Webb. She was the daughter of Richard Webb, who died in Boston in July, 1659. In his will he says, I give to Esther Pearce, and mentions her two children, Moses and Esther. He d. January, 1661. Res. Boston, Mass.

The administration of the estate of William Pierce, mariner of Boston, was granted to his widow, Esther Pierce, 31st January, 1661. He left four sons and one daughter, most of them being very small. The estate was divided 3d June, 1672, by agreement of Esther Pierce, William Pierce, Nathaniel Pierce, Roger Clapp, guardian to Moses Pierce, Joseph Webb, guardian to Ebenezer Pierce, Phineas Upham, guardian to Esther Pierce. The estate was valued at £228, and approved by John Martin, Joseph Webb. The house and land on the "backside of Boston," being worth £180. Ch.— *Esther*, b.   . She d. unm. In 1679, Oct. 30th, she sold land to Nathaniel Pierce of Boston, bounded on the south with the alley leading into the land of Esther Pierce, the elder; on the east with land of Ebenezer Pierce. The witnesses were Nathaniel Thayer, Moses Pierce and Esther Pierce. At this time she was called a spinster and of Boston. *William*, b.   ; m. Elizabeth ———. They resided in Boston a short time, and a son, William, was born, and died Jan. 4, 1661. They subsequently removed to Newport, R. I. From the Boston records, we learn that William Pierce of Newport, R. I., eldest son of William Pierce of Boston, mariner, deceased, and his wife, Elizabeth, release to Thomas Carter of Boston, his interest in land in Boston. The father died intestate leaving Esther his relict widow and five children his estate. The estate was afterward divided. This is dated 14th Dec., 1688, and is witnessed by Christian Peirse. William, Jr. resided in Boston, and later Newport, R. I. *Nathaniel*, b.　　　; m. Christian Stoddard; res. Boston. She was b. Mar. 22, 1657; the dau. of Anthony Stoddard. *Moses*, a Moses Pierce m. Eliza, and had Moses, b. May 23, 1709; John, b. Mar. 27, 1713; Elizabeth, b. Nov. 11, 1714; John, b. Mar. 4, 1726; Edward, b. Oct. 10, 1728; Elizabeth, b. Mar. 30, 1730; Edward, b. Apr. 27, 1734. *Ebenezer*, b. Mar. 16, 1661, unm., d. before. As per agreement of William, his brother, " Ebenezer died intestate and without issue." *Mary. Martha*, b. May 16, 1659, both d. young. *Mary*, b. Dec. 10, 1656, d. young.

CAPTAIN MICHAEL PIERCE.

Captain * Michael Pierce, who was born in England, emigrated to America not far from 1645. Locating first in Higham in 1646, the following year he removed to Scituate, where he resided when he met his untimely death. Savage says of Higham, 1646. Farmer locates him in Scituate in 1647.

In Scituate he purchased land in the Conihassett in 1647. His house was on the Cohasset road, one mile from the present North Meeting-house, at the well-known place formerly owned by Elijah Pierce, of the sixth generation that has possessed it. There is no record of Captain Pierce's family in Scituate. Hobart's Journal records, " Persis, daughter of Michael Pierce, baptized 1646," also, " Michael Pierce's daughter born 1662, and Michael Pierce's

---

* Michael Pierce was commissioned captain by the Colony court in 1669.

3

wife died 1662." His first child may have been born at Higham.
Persis married Richard Garrett, 3d, 1695. Abigail married Samuel Holbrook, 1682. He had a son Ephraim, who removed.
Benjamin married Martha, daughter of James Adams, 1678, and
succeeded to his father's residence. His children, Martha, Jerusha, Benjamin, Ebenezer, Persis, Caleb, Thomas, Adams, Jeremiah, Elisha, born from 1679 to 1699. John (also son of Captain
Michael), settled north of the Conihassett burying-ground. He
married Patience, daughter of Anthony Dodson, 1683; his children,
Michael, John, Jonathan, Ruth, Jael, David, Clothier, born from
1684 to 1698. Hayward Pierce, Esq., late of Scituate, descended
from Captain Michael, through Benjamin (who married Martha
Adams), Benjamin (who married Mary Cowen and Elizabeth
Perry), Benjamin, who married Charity Howard, and Jane Howard of Bridgewater, 1742 and 1750, daughters of Thomas. The
sons of Hayward, Esq., were Hayward, of New Orleans; Waldo
and Bailey, of Frankfort (Maine); Elijah of Scituate (on the
paternal residence); Silas of Boston, — and his daughters, the
wives of Mr. Lincoln of Cohasset, Mr. Nathaniel Cushing, and
Mr. Walter Foster of Scituate. Benjamin and Jonathan, brothers
of Hayward, Esq., removed to Chesterfield. Captain Michael
has left evidence on record, in the town of his usefulness in public
affairs. But his memory is to be forever honored for the brave
manner in which he fell in defense of his country.

He was in the Narragansett fight in Dec., 1675, and escaped with his life, but to fall in a more terrible conflict in
Mar. following. His will is dated 1675, and the preamble is in
these impressive words: "Being, by the appointment of God,
going out to war against the Indians, I do ordain this my last will
and Testament: and first, I commit my ways to the Eternal God,"
&c. He then gives "to wife Ann [she was a second wife] the
house which I last built, &c. To son Benjamin my present dwelling-house. To son John all my lands in Higham; to son Ephraim,
£5; to daughter Abigail Holbrook, £5; to daughters Elizabeth,
Deborah, Ann, Abiah, Ruth, Persis, £50 each." [Deane's History
of Scituate.]

Captain Michael Pierce of Scituate was a brother of Captain William Pierce of London. [Drake's Indian Chronicle, pp. 307, in News from New England, 1676.]

In 1666, the military of Scituate elected their officers, and made return to the Colony Court for ratification, viz.: Jas. Cudworth, Captain; Michael Pierce, Lieutenant. The Court returned an answer as follows: " As to Mr. Cudworth, it is directly against the advice of the Court, and as to Mr. Pierce, he is a stranger to us, therefore Sergt. John Daman is directed to take the command till further orders." The matter was adjusted in 1669, and the Court, having become better acquainted with Mr. Pierce, commissioned him Captain.

In 1673, the Colony Council ordered that, when a town shall be in distress, the chief officer of the next town shall send such aid as they may think proper; and that power be given them to press men. Toward the latter part of the year (Dec. 17) this Court was called together, on an " extraordinary occasion," on account of the war with the Dutch. Taking into consideration the repeated demonstrations of hostility on the part of the enemy, their intended invasion of Long Island, their large army of armed vessels, which were very prejudicial, they determined to endeavor to undertake this removal, thinking all this a just ground for war; and notwithstanding the lateness of the season, hearing that the Dutch would have recruits early in the spring, they judged it best to make an immediate attack. Though they considered that they were " apparently overrated," in the proportion of the Confederate colonies, they determined to raise their quota by one hundred men, if sufficient provision could be obtained for their voyage and march. Their officers on the expedition were Captain, James Cudworth (pay per day, six shillings); Lieutenant, John Gorham (five shillings); Ensign, Michael Pierce (four shillings).

The Narragansetts early in the spring of 1676 had committed ravages in Rhode Island; parties had even penetrated to Plymouth and killed a number of inhabitants. On this alarm, Capt. Michael Pierce of Scituate, with a company of fifty Englishmen and twenty friendly Indians from Cape Cod, was ordered to pursue the Indians toward Rhode Island. He proceeded without any rencounter near to Pawtucket, in that part which has been called Attleboro Gore, when he discovered that there were Indians near him, but not suspecting that Canonchett was there. He, therefore, ventured to cross the river and commence the attack, but soon found himself in the presence of an overwhelming force. To fly was impossible, and to retreat in order, before such an enemy, was equally desperate. His only resource was to fall back to the river's bank, in order to avoid being surrounded, and make the sacrifice of himself and of his brave men as costly as possible to the foe. But the Indians, having a large force, soon sent a party across the river to attack in the rear. This surprise only induced the captain to change the front of his company, and place them back to back; and in this position they fought until nearly every man fell, and with a bravery like that at Thermopylæ, and deserving of as great success.

Capt. Pierce fell earlier than many others; and it is due to the honor of one of his friendly Indians, called Amos, that he continued to stand by his commander and fight, until affairs were utterly desperate, and that then he escaped by blacking his face with powder as he saw the enemy had done, and so passing through their army without notice.

Mather and others relate also pleasing anecdotes of two or three other of Capt. Pierce's friendly Indians, who escaped by equally curious artifices and presence of mind. One who was flying and closely pressed by a hostile Indian sought the shelter of a large rock. Thus the two waiting in awful suspense to shoot each other. Capt. Pierce's Indian putting his cap on the end of a stick or his gun, gently raised it to the view of his enemy, who immediately discharged his gun at the cap, and the next moment was shot dead by the friendly Indian. Another in his flight pretended to pursue an Englishman, with hostile demonstrations, and thus escaped; this was a disastrous blow to Scituate. It was generally believed that every Englishman was killed, but such was not the case.

The following is a letter from Rev. Noah Newman of Rehoboth, dated the day of the battle, to a friend, the Rev. John Cotton of Plymouth.

REVEREND AND DEAR SIR.— I received yours, dated the 20th of this instant, wherein you gave me a doleful relation of what happened with you, and what a distressing Sabbath you had past. I have now, according to the words of your letter, an opportunity to retaliate your account with a relation of what yesterday happened to the great saddening of our hearts, filling us with an awful expectation of what further evils it may be antecedaneous to, both respecting ourselves and you. Upon the 25th of this instant, Capt. Pierce went forth with a small party of his men and Indians with him, and upon discovering the enemy, fought him, without damage to himself, and judged that he had considerably damnified them. Yet he being of no great force, chose rather to retreat and go out the next morning with a recruit of men; and accordingly he did, taking Pilots from us, that were acquainted with the ground. But it pleased the Sovereign God so to order it, that they were enclosed with a great multitude of the enemy which hath slain fifty-two of our Englishmen and eleven Indians — 18 from Scituate, encluding Capt. Pierce; Marshfield, 9; Duxbury, 4; Sandwich, 5; Barnstable, 6; Yarmouth, 5; Eastham, 4. Thomas Mann is just returned with a sore wound. Thus, sir, you have a sad account of the continuance of God's displeasure against us; yet still I desire steadfastly to look unto him who is not only able but willing to save all such as are fit for his Salvation.

It may be pleasing to the reader to be informed that Canonchett was taken prisoner a few days after by Capt. Denison of Stonington. A young soldier of the company, Robart Staunton, put some questions to the Sachem, when he received this proud and disdainful answer: "You too much child — no understand matters of war — let your captain come — him I will answer," and when he was informed that it was determined to put him to death, he said: "I like it well — I shall die before my heart is soft, or before I have spoken any thing unworthy of myself." Canonchett was son of the famous Miantonomoh, Chief Sachem of the Narragansetts.

July 15, 1653, Michael Pierce of Higham, receives John Read as an apprentice for nine years. Witness, Samuel Norten and Nathaniel Sarther.

Sunday the 26th of March, 1676, was sadly remarkable to us for the tidings of a very deplorable disaster brought into Boston about five o'clock that afternoon, by a post from Dedham, viz., that Captain Pierce of Scituate in Plymouth Colony, having intelligence in his garrison at Seaconicke, that a party of the enemy lay near Mr. Blackstone's, went forth with sixty-three English and twenty of the Cape Indians (who had all along continued faithful, and joyned with them), and upon their march discovered rambling in an obscure woody place, four or five Indians, who, in getting away from us halted as if they had been lame or wounded. But our men had pursued them but a little way into the woods before they found them to be only decoys to draw them into their ambuscade; for on a sudden, they discovered above five hundred Indians, who in very good order, furiously attacked them, being as readily received by ours; so that the fight began to be very fierce and dubious, and our men had made the enemy begin to retreat, but so slowly that it scarce deserved the name, when a fresh company of about four hundred Indians came in; so that the English and their few Indian friends were quite surrounded and beset on every side. Yet they made a brave resistance for about two hours; during which time they did great execution upon their enemy, whom they kept at a distance and themselves in order. For Captain Pierce cast his sixty-three English and twenty Indians into a ring, and six fought back to back, and were double — double distance all in one ring, whilst the Indians were as thick as they could stand, thirty deep. Overpowered with whose numbers, the said Captain and fifty-five of his English and ten of their Indian friends were slain upon the place, which in such a cause and upon such disadvantages may certainly be titled *The Bed of Honor*. However, they sold their worthy lives at a gallant rate, it being affirmed by those few that not without wonderful difficulty and many wounds made their escape, that the Indians lost as many fighting men (not counting women and children), in this engagement as were killed in the battle in the swamp near Narragansett, mentioned in our last letter, which were generally computed to be above three hundred.* [Drake's Indian Chronicle, pp. 220–2.]

---

* See Bliss' History of Rehoboth, and Daggett's History of Attlebro.

1676, March the 26th. We had news of the defeat of Captain Pearse with about forty English and eleven of our Indian friends near Seconck alias Rehoboth, who were surrounded with a great party of the Indians and overpowered; yet God was pleased to rescue several of them, who made a safe escape. [Same, p. 253.]

Captain Pierse, brother of Captain Pierce, of London, with fifty-five men and twenty Christian Indians went to seek out their enemies, the Indians whom according to their intelligence they found rambling in an obscure wood; upon his approach they drew into order and received his onset with much difficulty, being in the end forced to retreat, but it was so slowly that it scarcely deserved that name, when a fresh company of Indians came into their assistance, beset the Christian friends, killed Captain Pierce and forty-eight of his men, besides eight of the Christian Indians. The fight continued for two hours, the enemy buying the victory very dearly, but at last obtained it so absolutely that they deprived us of all means of learning of their loss. This was one of the most desperate fights of the war, and perhaps the most bloody.* [Same, pp. 307-8.]

The Indians having carried their whirlwind of war to the very doors of Plymouth, causing the sending out of Capt. Pierce (or as his name is uniformly in the records, Peirse) to divert them from these ravages, and destroy as many of them as he was able. He had a large company, consisting of seventy men, twenty of whom were friendly Indians. With these, no doubt, Peirse thought himself safe against any power of the Indians in that region.

Meanwhile this most valiant chief captain of the Narragansetts, Nanuntenoo† learning, we presume by his spies, the direction the English were taking, assembled his warriors at a crossing place on Pawtucket river, at a point adjacent to a place then called Attle-

---

* See Hubbard, and the notes 1, 173-8.

† That Nanuntenoo commanded in person in the fight with the force under Capt. Peirse has been a question; indeed, our only authority is not very explicit upon the matter (Hubbard Postscript, 7), who observes that when Dennison surprised him he "was, at that moment, diverting himself with a recital of Capt. Peirse's slaughter; surprised by his men a few days before."

borough-Gore, and not far distant from Pawtucket Falls. It is judged that Nanuntenoo was upon an expedition to attack Plymouth, or some of the adjacent towns, for his force was estimated at upwards of three hundred men.

On arriving at this fatal spot some of Nanuntenoo's men showed themselves retiring, on the opposite side of the river. This stratagem succeeded — Peirse followed.* No sooner was he upon the western side than the warriors of Nanuntenoo, like an avalanche from a mountain, rushed down upon him; nor striving for coverts from which to fight, more than their foes fought them face to face with the most determined bravery.

A part of Nanuntenoo's force remained on the east side of the river to prevent the retreat of the English, which they most effectively did, as in the event will appear. When Capt. Peirse saw himself hemmed in by numbers on every side, he drew up his men upon the margin of the river in two ranks, back to back,† and in this manner fought until nearly all of them were slain. Peirse had timely sent a messenger to Providence for assistance, and although the distance could not have been more than six or eight miles, from inexplicable cause, no succor arrived; and Mr. Hubbard‡ adds, "as Solomon saith, a faithful messenger is as snow in harvest."

This dreadful fight was on Sunday, 26 March, 1676, when as Dr. Mather says: "Captain Peirse was slain and forty and nine English with him and eight (or more) Indians, who did assist the English." The Rev. Mr. Newman of Rehoboth wrote a letter to Plymouth, dated the day after the slaughter, in which he says: "Fifty-two of our English and eleven Indians" were slain.§ The company was, no doubt, increased by some who volunteered as they marched through the country, or by such as were taken for pilots.

---

* Dr. Mather (Brief Hist. 24) says: "A small number of the enemy who, in desperate subtlety, ran away from them, and they went limping to make the English believe they were lame," and thus effected their object.

† Deane's History of Scituate, p. 121.

‡ Hubbard's Narrative, 64.

§ See the letter giving the names of the company in Deane's Scituate, 122-3.

Nanuntenoo's victory was complete, but, as usual on such occasions, the English consoled themselves by making the loss of the Indians appear as large as possible. Dr. Mather says that some of the Indians that were afterward taken confessed they lost one hundred and forty, which, no doubt, is not far from the truth.*

An Englishman, and perhaps the only who escaped from this disastrous fight, was saved by one of the friendly Indians in this manner. The friendly Indian being taken for a Narragansett, as he was pursuing, with an uplifted tomahawk, the English soldier, no one interfered, leaving him to pursue an unarmed Englishman at such great advantage. In this manner, covering themselves in the woods, they escaped.

A friendly Indian, being pursued by one of Nanuntenoo's men, got behind the roots of a fallen tree. Thus screened by the earth raised upon them, the Indian that pursued waited for him to run from his natural fort, knowing he would not dare to maintain it long. The other soon thought of an expedient, which was to make a port-hole in his breast-work, which was easily done by digging through the dirt. When this was done he put his gun through and shot his pursuer and then fled in perfect safety.

Another escaped in a manner very similar. In his flight he got behind a large rock. This afforded him a good shelter, but in the end he saw nothing but certain disaster, and the longer he held out the more misery he must suffer. In this deplorable situation he bethought himself to try the following device: Putting his cap upon his gun, he raised it very gradually above the rock, as though to discover the position of the enemy; it had the desired effect — he fired upon it. The one behind the rock now rushed upon him, before he could reload his gun, and despatched him. Thus, as Mr. Hubbard says, "it is worth the noting what faithfulness and courage some of the Christian Indians showed in this fight." That this most excellent author did not approve of the severity exercised toward those who appeared friendly is abundantly proved by his writings. In another place he says: "Possibly, if some of the English had not been too shy in making use of such of them as

---

* Mr. Hubbard's account is the same.

4 ·

were well affected to their interest, they never need have suffered so much from their enemies."

A notice may reasonably be expected of the unfortunate Capt. Michael Pierce of Scituate. He was one of those adventurous spirits, "who never knew fear," and who sought rather than shrank from dangers. He was like his great antagonist, in the Narragansett fight; and in 1673, when the government of Plymouth raised a force to go against the Dutch, who had encroached upon them in Connecticut, he was appointed ensign in one of the companies. He resided in several places before going to Scituate. Mr. Deane, in his History of Scituate, gives a genealogical account of his family, from which we learn that he had a second wife and several sons and daughters; of what family he was there is no mention.* He possessed considerable estate and made his will on engaging in the war with the Indians.

The "sore defeat" of Captain Peirse, and the tide of the Indian successes about that time, caused the united colonies to send out almost their whole strength. [Biography and History of the North American Indians by Drake, book 3, pp. 231–2; Daggett's History of Attleboro, Mass., 1834.]

The courage and resolution displayed on the occasion of Pierce's fight in 1676 deserves commendation. These brave soldiers were entitled to the gratitude of the colony, for whose defense they had thus sacrificed their lives. They were taken by surprise and completely surrounded by a force ten times their superior. Pierce was a bold and adventurous man—fear formed no part of his character. His men partook of his courage. They pushed forward — perhaps imprudently — and thus fell into the snare which their enemy had prepared for them. Considering the number engaged, it was doubtless the most warmly and closely contested of all the engagements which took place, during that eventful

---

*In the records of Plymouth, under date March, 1669, there is an entry as follows: "Miche. Peirse, of Scituate, was presented at the court for unseemly carriages toward Sarah Nichols of Scituate," and forasmuch as there appeared but one testimony to the presentment, and that the testimony was written and not read unto the deponent, the court saw cause to remit the said presentment.

period, between the red and white men. Nearly four hundred were killed on both sides. History has recorded, with applause, every feat of bravery, when performed on a more conspicuous station, whilst it has often overlooked the humble, though equally meritorious exploit. It requires more true courage to die on such a field with such a foe, than on the plains of Waterloo, amid the ' pomp and circumstance of glorious war."

Quinsniket and " Nine Men's Misery," A Legend of the Indians. The story of Pierce's fight, and the capture of Canonchet near Pawtucket. From the Providence *Journal*, July 19, 1873.

Some five or six miles to the northward of Providence, lying in the old town of Smithfield, but in what is now Lincoln, between the Louisquisset and the Smithfield turnpikes, is a spot known in the dialect of the Narragansetts, by the name of " Quinsniket," meaning rock house. This name arose from the immense over-hanging rock which rests on the apex of the hill under which slept Nanuntenoo the night before he destroyed Captain Pierce and nearly all his men. On the green sward to the southward of this immense rock he built his council fire, and planned the fatal am-buscade, and right well he executed it. Here, on beautiful Quin-sniket, the bountiful hand of nature had brought together every thing which could delight the eye of the Indian — a splendid view, security from enemies, luxuriant foliage, rare plants, and the waters of the bright Moshassuck for his beverage.

> " Again Moshassuck's silver tide
> Reflects each green bush on its side,
> Each tasselled wreath and angling vine,
> Whose tendrils o' er its margin twine."

So sang a Rhode Island poet, and to-day the same bright, glit-tering brook runs by us that run by Nanuntenoo two centuries ago.

> " For men may come, and men may go,
> But I go on forever."

The great rocks protected the Indian from the cold north winds, while the southern sun warmed the opening of his wigwam. (Quinsniket is a hill, wild and beautiful as the Trossachs, but less large, and lacks its poet. A rudely constructed dam turns the watery marsh on the hill-top into a lovely pond, sheltered on every side, and fringed with wild woods and flowers, a pretty rivulet finds its way from the pond, among the rocks, to join the waters of the Moshassuck below.) Years ago, Mr. Stephen H. Smith stocked this pond with golden carp, and to-day they continue to delight the eye of the visitor. Mr. Smith now sleeps in the old Quaker burying-ground hard by, in the long row of his ancestry; a blue slate slab, in keeping with all the others, marks his resting-place. He was a man filled with the wisdom which only experience and observation bring — more faithful to the cares and interests of others than to his own, a true mark of unselfish generosity; he lent the helping hand to nature, and that with no stint. In the neighborhood, he built a fine stone mansion, and planted trees and shrubs and flowers about it, and now its ivy-mantled front accords beautifully with the landscape. On Quinsniket he planted lilies and ferns and beautiful shrubs, that they might delight his own eyes as well as those who were to come after him. Let us carry some flowers from his favorite hill and lay them upon the grave of him, who, when living, was more generous to others than just to himself.

Many years since, a laborer sent on the hill to obtain a load of stones, removed, without knowing it, the remains of the last wigwam left by the Indians. It had been preserved for a memorial of its former inhabitants by Mr. Smith, the father of Stephen, and to mark the spot, he set out a honey locust just by the spot where the Indian built his fire; this tree is now large and vigorous. It can be seen near the cluster of pines with a hemlock among them, just below the great rock. Mr. Smith remembered the remains of other wigwams along the western borders of the swamp, which now forms the pond, but these have long since ceased to form the residence of a Wampanoag.

A few days ago, with a parcel of bright boys and girls, we visited again Quinsniket, and while the party wandered about, we told them the Indian legend connected with the spot. Verily it was bravely planned and skillfully executed, and exhibits one of the most striking specimens of Indian war, an ambuscade laid with

Indian subtlety, an assault under cover of the original forest, an absolute extinction of the enemy, and then a retreat to the fastnesses of Quinsniket to revel in songs of victory. Let us tell again the story of Pierce's fight, one of the bloodiest battles fought in Phillip's war, one of the last and greatest victories won by the Indians in Rhode Island, and, on the side of the English, if not fought with prudence, then at least with valor unsurpassed.

The Indians, after their final defeats in attacking the Massachusetts towns of Deerfield, Springfield, Hadley and Hatfield, fled in various directions and in bands of different numbers to their native shores of the Narragansett. Tradition says that the last of the Wampanoags made Quinsniket a resting place in their retreat from Massachusetts.

It was near Quinsniket, which point probably formed the base of operations for the Indians, that Pierce's fight took place. The precise locality can still be pointed out between Valley Falls and Central Falls, on territory then known as the Attleborough Gore. Capt. Pierce was at Rehoboth, with sixty-three English soldiers and twenty friendly Indians, when he learned that there were Indian enemies in the neighborhood of Pawtucket Falls, and determined to attack them. He wrote a letter to Capt. Andrew Edmunds, of Providence, to meet him at a spot on the Pawtucket river and assist him in this attack. The messenger who carried the letter attended divine service (for it was Sunday) before delivering the letter. Thus left to his fate, Capt. Pierce slowly and steadily pushed his company forward until the advance had crossed to the west side of the Blackstone river at the point before designated. Here he discovered a few Indians, who fled at his approach into the woods, limping as they ran. This led Pierce's men to suppose them to be some band of infirm stragglers. They accordingly gave chase, and the entire company fell into an ambush, with the river in their rear and a thousand savage and enraged Indians encompassing them on all other sides. The fight was on Sunday morning, March 26, 1676, almost two hundred years ago. It was of short duration, scarcely more than a couple of hours. Capt. Pierce and nearly all the English were slain. Of sixty-three Englishmen, fifty were slain on the field, and also eleven of the twenty friendly Indians. Few lived to tell the story of the defenders.

Upon discovering the nature of the attack, Capt. Pierce formed his company into a circle, and in this form continued to fire upon his enemies, his circle of fire continually contracting. The battle begun on the east side of the river, but Capt. Pierce took his company over to the west side, when encountering another band of perhaps four hundred Indians, he found himself no better situated, and here the main battle was fought. Several anecdotes illustrative of Indian strategy in battle having attached themselves to this affair, we will relate a few. An Englishman and a friendly Indian agreed that the latter should pursue the former with uplifted tomahawk, through the bands of hostile Indians, the Englishman apparently using every exertion to escape, and the Indian every endeavor to capture or kill. The ruse was successful and both escaped. Another stratagem now related in many stories of the Indians, here originated.

A friendly Indian was pursued by an enemy and took refuge behind a rock. The enemy keeping the closest watch on the rock presently perceived what he supposed to be the head of the friendly Indian appearing gradually above the rock, and fired upon the supposed head. Having thus drawn the fire of his enemy, the friendly Indian instantly sprang up and shot his antagonist without further trouble, and escaped. Thus this ruse also succeeded.

One of Captain Pierce's friendly Indians, named Amos, who had continued the fight until affairs were utterly desperate, having discovered that many of the enemy had blackened their faces with powder, tried it on his own, and escaped among them without suspicion. Thus this ruse also succeeded. Still another friendly Indian, being pursued by an enemy, took refuge behind the roots of a large tree, which had been blown down, here carefully boring a small hole through the earth which still clung to the roots and gave him shelter, he fired upon his enemy, killed him and escaped. Thus this ruse also succeeded.

After the fight was over, the victors with nine prisoners whom they had captured, proceeded to a spot among the hills of Cumberland, near a house but lately owned by Elisha Waterman, where seating the prisoners upon a rock they commenced the war dance preparatory to the torture, and the final dispatching of the prisoners. From this circumstance has arisen the present name of the locality, "Nine Men's Misery."

We recently, in company with some friends, hunted up this once famous locality. Its position is precisely defined on the maps, but we defy the most resolute antiquarian to read the accounts of the place and then find it without a guide. The old chroniclers describe it as a natural amphitheatre surrounded with rocks, in which the Indians took their prisoners, and differing among themselves as to the mode of torture, slew them with their tomahawks, and thus put an end to their misery; but in truth, there is no amphitheatre at all; there is a ledge of rocks just by Camp Swamp, near which the prisoners were probably slain. After their friends found the bodies, they probably took them to the top of the little knoll, buried them and built the rude monument to mark their resting-place. During the War of the Revolution some physicians from Providence opened the graves, and more recently some hunters in chase of a rabbit, which sought refuge within the monumental pile, pulled it down to capture the animal. Thus the rude hand of the destroyer treated the resting-place of some of the bravest of our earliest soldiers. Camp Swamp is within a few rods of the locality. Here the Indians, when hard pressed, sought an asylum. Hence its name.

Our search for "Nine Men's Misery" would have been in vain had we not accidentally fallen in with Mr. Jason N. Sprague, who has long lived in the neighborhood and is perfectly familiar with the history. He took us over the Elisha Waterman place — once a splendid farm — now a wilderness — once a rich man's residence — now a ruin. In favorable seasons its former owner made from its immense orchards more than a thousand barrels of cider; kept hundreds of sheep and cattle, and horses in abundance; now a couple of cows and perhaps a dozen hens are its only tenants.

Capt. Pierce killed in this battle a hundred and forty of his enemies, but he left enough to proceed the day after the battle to

Rehoboth, where they burned forty houses, and on the twenty-ninth, two days after the battle, twenty-nine more in Providence. Tradition says that when the Indians appeared on the highlands to the northward of the town, Roger Williams took his staff and went to meet them, in the hopes of pacifying them, as he had often done before. The chiefs met him in a friendly way, and told him that those who had long known him would not injure him, but the young men were so enraged that they would probably kill him if he ventured among them, whereupon he returned to the garrison.

Nanuntenoo, or as he is now better known as Canonchet, son of Miantonomi, was chief of the Indians who fought this battle, still lingered in the neighborhood. His visit in this part of the country was to obtain seed corn which he expected to plant in the little settlements along the banks of the Connecticut. Scarcely had the exultant shouts for his victory ceased before the now thoroughly aroused English were again in pursuit of their enemies. George Denison, of Westerly, a resolute and able man, commanded the English. In the course of their march they shot an Indian and captured two squaws, from whom they learned the whereabouts of their Indian enemies, and immediately laid their plans for their capture. Canonchet had placed two sentinels upon a high hill to watch the approach of his enemies. They saw the approach of the English, but were so alarmed at their numbers that they ran away without notifying Canonchet, but he soon learned of the approach of the English, and fled. He was seen and followed, and in the race threw away his blanket, belt, and finally a laced coat which the English had given him. By these articles his identity became known to his pursuers, who now redoubled their exertions. Canonchet came to the Blackstone, which he undertook to cross, but his foot slipping on a stone, he fell partially into the water, wetting his gun and giving his enemies time to come up with him, when one of them, an Indian much smaller than Canonchet (who was a very large and powerful man, and one withal whose bravery was unimpeached), seized Canonchet, who surrendered without any further trouble. The first Englishman who came up was a young man named Robert

Stanton. He asked Canonchet some questions. Canonchet at first took no notice of his inquiries, but finally with a look of scorn turned to Stanton and said: " You too much child — no understand matters of war — let your chief come — him will I answer." Canonchet was delivered to Denison, by whom he was carried to Stonington, where he was put to death, his head cut off and sent to Hartford, and his body burned. When informed of the disposition to be made of him, without an emotion he said to them, " I like it well. I shall die before my heart is soft, or I have said any thing unworthy of myself." Thus died one of the greatest of the Rhode Island aborigines.

1. **Captain Michael Pierce,** b. abt. 1615, m. ————, she d. 1662; m. 2nd, Mrs. Annah James; res. Hingham and Scituate, Mass.; killed by Indians Sunday, Mar. 26, 1676.

Widow Anna James and family resided in Marshfield in 1650. She m. Capt. Michael Pierce abt. 1663. She had a son Mark, and her daughter Abigail m. Charles Stockbridge, b. 1638, son of John.

Scituate was incorporated Oct. 5, 1636, and so called from *Satuit*, meaning " Cold Brook," and applied to a little pure and cold stream running into the harbor. The town was settled as early as 1628 by several men who came from Kent, England.

Capt. Pierce resided in that part of Scituate which was incorporated as South Scituate, Feb. 14, 1849. It was near the house of Cornet Robert Stetson that he resided, on a beautiful plain near the North river and not far from Herring brook. He assisted in erecting the first saw-mill which was burned by the Indians May 20, 1676. This mill was the first one erected in the colony. It was only a short distance from this place that Samuel Woodworth wrote " The Old Oaken Bucket." The scene so vividly described in his charming lyric, is a little valley through which Herring brook pursues its devious course to meet the tidal waters of North river. The view from Coleman Heights, with its neat cottages, its maple groves and apple orchards, is remarkably beautiful. " The wide spreading pond," " the mill that stood by it," " the dairy-house," " the rock where the cataract fell," and even " the old well," if not " the moss-covered bucket " itself, may still be seen just as the poet has described them.

5

WILL OF MICHAEL PIERCE OF SCITUATE.

Dated *January*, 1675.

Scituate, in the government of New Plymouth, 1675, }
January the 15. }

I, Michael Pierce of Scituate, in the government of New Plymouth in America, being now by the appointment of God going out to war, against the Indians, doe make this my last will and testament: First I do committ myself and wayes unto the Eternal God; nextly concerning that estate which God has blessed me with, I thus dispose.   First I give unto my beloved wife Annah Pierce, during her life, the westward end of my now dwelling house, in Scituate aforesaid which I last built to dwell in, and the bed in it, with what appurtenances to it, to use and dispose of, as she shall see cause, and the one half of my other household stuff for her use during her life, and then to be disposed of to my children as she shall see cause.   Also my will is that for my wifes yearly maintenance, that my son Benjamin Pierce shall pay unto her twelve pounds per year, one half in money and the other half in provisions, and also sufficient firewood for her use in the house during her life; And I give unto my son Benjamin aforesaid my now dwelling house and barn in Scituate aforesaid, and all the land which I have in Scituate excepting that I bought of Benjamin Bates of Hingham, and that which I bought of William James of Scituate and excepting the abovesaid westerly end of my abovesaid house, during my wife's life as abovesaid, out of which abovesaid Estate in house and lands given to my son Benjamin, he shall pay unto my aforesaid wife for her maintenance twelve pounds a year, as abovesaid during her life, and sufficient firewood also as abovesaid.   And I give unto my son, John Pierce all my lands in Hingham, in the Massachusetts, and my land in Scituate which I bought of William James, of Scituate, paying out of it to my son Ephraim's two children Eserikum Pierce and Ephraim Pierce, to each of them fifteen pounds at the age of twenty and one years; provided that neither my son Ephraim aforesaid, nor either of his after him, or any by or under him, shall go about to molest my said son John of or upon the attempt of the three or four acres of meadow land in Hingham aforesaid which my father James gave unto my said son Ephraim which is not yet so fully confirmed to me as by my son Ephraim's promise it should have been.

Also I give unto my aforesaid son Benjamin all my movable estate in cattle and boats, and household goods, and such like, excepting that which I have disposed of to my wife as abovesaid, out of which said moveable estate my said son Benjamin shall pay these legacies which I give to my children as followeth :

first I give unto my son Ephraim Pierce, five pounds.

2 I give unto my daughter, Abigail Holbrook five pounds.

3 I give unto my daughter Elizabeth Peirce, thirty pounds.

4 I give unto my daughter Sarah Pierce, thirty pounds.

5 I give unto my daughter Anna Pierce, fifty pounds.

6 I give unto my daughter Mary Holbrook, twenty pounds.

7 I give unto my daughter Abiah Pierce, thirty pounds.

8 I give unto my daughter Ruth Pierce, thirty pounds.

9 I give unto my daughter Peirsis Pierce, fifty pounds.

Also I give unto my grandchild Elizabeth Holbrook five pounds to be paid her by my son Benjamin aforesaid at her day of marriage or 21 years old.

Also I give to my grandchild Abigail Holbrook five pounds, to be paid her by my son John Pierce aforesaid at her day of marriage, or twenty-one years of age.

Also my will is, that if it should please God that my beloved wife aforesaid should be afflicted with lameness or sickness so that the abovesaid 12 income be not sufficient to maintain her in comfortable manner, that then what shall be meet by my overseers to be added for her comfortable maintainance shall be equally payed her yearly by my son Benjamin Pierce and my son John of that estate which I have given them as aforesaid.

Also I make my   abovesaid my executrix and my son Benjamin Pierce abovesaid my executor of my last will and testament, and also I the abovesaid Michael Pierce my truly and well beloved friends Cornett Robert Stetson* and Isaac —— and my brother Mark Jennes and my brother Charles Stockbridge overseers or witnesses of this my abovesaid last will and testament. In witness whereof I set my hand and seal this fifteenth of January 1675   MICHAEL ———

Witnesses   BENJAMIN WOODWORTH
    CHARLES STOCKBRIDGE

By reason of the dangerousness of the times there wilbe a court in July next, and the parties

---

* Cornet Stetson was an enterprising and useful man in his day. He was many years deputy for Scituate — a commissioner in 1664 to run the line between Plymouth and Massachusetts colonies, and a member of the Board of War. He d. 1702, æ 90.

that delays may be prejudicial to the estate
Benjamin Woodward gave oath before me
unto Michael Pierce signing sealing and
this was testified upon oath the fift of Ju   [Mutilated]
    The foregoing is a copy of the will of Michael Pierce, recorded
in Vol. 3, Part 2, page 8 of Plymouth Colony Record of Wills.

CHILDREN.

    I. PERSIS, bap. 1646; m. Dec. 3, 1695, Richard Garrett
        3rd, b. 1659; res. Scituate, Mass. Ch., John, b.
        1706, and Anna, Deborah.
2.   II. BENJAMIN, b. 1646; m. Martha Adams and Mrs.
        Elizabeth Adams Perry.
3. III. JOHN, m. Patience Dobson.
4.   IV. EPHRAIM, m. Hannah Holbrook.
     V. ELIZA.
    VI. DEBORAH.
   VII. ANNA.
  VIII. ABIAH.
    IX. RUTH.
     X. ABIGAIL, b. ——; m. John Holbrook; res. Scituate,
        Mass. Ch., Thomas, b. Jan. 15, 1672; John, b.
        Nov. 19, 1686, and six daughters.

   2. **Capt. Benjamin**[2] **Pierce** (Michael[1]), b. 1646; m. Feb. 5,
1678, Martha Adams, the daughter of James Adams; m. 2nd, July
21, 1718, Mrs. Elizabeth (Adams) Perry.
    He d. in 1730; his will being probated Oct. 15, of that year;
resides Scituate, Mass.

WILL OF BENJAMIN PIERCE.— In the name of God Amen.
This fourth day of November Anno Domini, One Thousand Seven
hundred and twenty nine. In the third year of his Majesties
Reign, &c.
    I Benjamin Pierce of Scituate in ye County of Plymouth in
New England, Gent. being of sound mind, and memory (Blessed
be God for it) Do make and ordain this my last will and testament
in manner and form following, viz.

First of all I commend my soul to God that gave it and my body to decent Burial at the Discretion of my executor hereafter named.

And as touching my worldly Estate which God hath allowed me.

All my just debts and funeral charges being first and fully paid. I give devise and dispose of ye same in manner and form following viz.

Imprimis. I give and bequeath unto my beloved wife Elizabeth Pierce all that estate or goods which she brought to me in marriage which shall remain att my Decease. I also give to my wife thirty pounds in Bills of Credit or in Goods equivalent thereto in value, as by covenant agreed upon before marriage. I also give her a cow and its keeping winter and summer to be done and performed by my son Elisha one of my Executors. I also give unto my wife five pounds in Bills of Credit or other pay equivalent to be paid to her yearly and every year during her natural life after my decease to be paid by ye aforesaid Executor.

Now in case she quits all claim to the thirty pounds above mentioned I give her for her use as long as she shall remain my widow ye particulars hereafter mentioned viz. I give her ye use of that room in my house wherein we now dwell togather with all the furniture thereunto belonging — Except ye Trundle bed my Chest — the Doggs of Iron ye fire shovels and tongs and my small box — I also give her convenient cellar room likewise all the meat and corn and such like provisions as shall be in store for the subsistence of my Family att my Decease, also five bushels of Indian corn and two bushels of Rye to be paid to her yearly, and five cords of good burning solid wood for Fuel to be brought to her door every year so long as she continues to dwell in the Room afore allowed her. I also give her out of my orchard as many apples as she shall need in the summer and about six bushels for winter. I also give her one hundred weight of good Pork and a quarter of Beef yearly and a convenient horse to ride to meeting on, all which are to be paid and performed by my son Elisha, one of the Executors. Furthermore I give my wife freely my little irish spinning wheel to dispose of as she pleaseth.

Item. I give to my son Benjamin all that Estate of Housings and Lands whereon he now dwells and the meadows thereunto belonging which said Estate I have already given him by Deed, as also one lot of land containing ten acres called meeting House which I took up in said Benjas Right provided the said Benja does pay or cause to be paid out of the sixty pounds in the aforesaid deed conditioned to be paid by him the sum of twenty-five pounds in manner and form following viz. Fifteen pounds to my son Ebenezer within one year after my decease. Five pounds to my son Jeremiah within two years after my Decease, and five pounds to my Daughter Jerusha Bailey within three years after my Decease all which payments to be made in Bills of Credit or Goods equal in value.

Item. I give to my son Ebenezer one hundred and ten pounds in specie as aforesaid over and above what Estate I have already given him. Fifteen Pounds to be paid by Benjamin as aforesaid and the remainder being ninety five Pounds to be paid by my son Elisha one of my executors in four several yearly purportional payments after my decease.

I give to my son Ebenezer all my wearing clothes.

Item. I give to my son Caleb Peirce over and above what I have already given him fifty Pounds to be paid to him by son Thomas. Thirty Pounds to be paid in a year after my decease and the other twenty in two years.

Item. I give to son Thomas all my lands lying on each side of the way where his house stands also three acres and a quarter of salt meadow lying near ye widow Lincoln also two acres more of salt meadow lying on the southerly side of farm neck so called which I bought Will and Jonathan Peirce. he yealding and pay-ing the Fifty Pounds aforesaid to my son Caleb, and Thirty Pounds to my daughter Jerusha Bailey. Mind ye 50 pounds are to be paid in three several yearly proportional payments and ye Thirty to be paid thus Fifteen within a year and ye other Fifteen at ye end of two years after my decease. Mind I give all ye land and meadow mentioned in ye article to my son Thomas his heirs executors and assigns forever.

Item. I give to my son Jeremiah two thirds of ye lands I have not already disposed of lying in ye beech woods joining to ye patent line at a place known by ye name of Mt. Hope, also ye other two acres Will and John Peirce which salt meadow mind I give it to him his heirs and assigns forever. moreover I give to my son Jeremiah Twenty Pounds to be paid in four yearly pro-portional payments by my son Elisha one of my Executors.

Item. I give to my son Elisha all my Estate of Housings and Lands and meadows and all my other estates both real and per-sonal of every sort and kind whatsoever and wheresoever lying either in Scituate or elsewhere that is not otherwise hereby devised and disposed of. He the said Elisha paying and performing all ye several duties, services and legacies above and beneath required of him. mind I give them to him his heirs, executors and assigns forever.

Item. I give to my Daughter Jerusha Bailey Ninety Five Pounds besides what I formerly gave her. Thirty pounds to be paid by Thomas and five by Benjamin as above mentioned and the other sixty to be paid by my Son Elisha in four yearly proportionate payments after my Decease.

Item. I give to my grandson Benjamin Pierce ye eldest son of my son Ebenezer ten pounds to be paid in Bills of Credit or Goods equal in value by my son Elisha aforesaid when he shall be arrived to ye age of twenty and one years. But in case ye said Benjamin should die before that time then the said ten pounds to be paid in equal proportion among his Brethren and Sisters.

Item. I give to my Grandsons Benjamin and Ebenezer Bailey a certain firelock they now have in custody or the value of it in Bills of Credit to be paid by my son Elisha if he should see fit to take the firelock to himself.

Item. I give to my Grandson Benjamin Pierce son of my son Benjamin a certain firelock which his father hath in custody.

Lastly. I do hereby nominate and appoint my two Sons Thomas and Elisha Pierce to be ye sole executors to this my last will and testament.

In witness whereof I have hereunto set my hand and Seal the day and year first above written.

BENJAMIN PEIRCE. [SEAL.]

Signed sealed pronounced and declared by said Benjamin Peirce to be his last will and testament in presence of us. Witnesses

EPHRAIM LITTLE,
NATHL. ELLS, JR.
KEZIA PENY.

October ye 13th 1730.

The above named Ephraim Little, Nathaniel Ells Jr. and Kezia Peny made oaths that they saw the above named Benjamin Peirce sign seal and declare the above and within written to be his last will and testament and that they are the same time in ye presence of ye said testator set to their hands as witnesses and that according to ye best of there observation he was of a sound and disposing mind and memory before Issac Winslow Judge of Probate.

CHILDREN.

I. MARTHA, b. Nov. 14, 1679; d. before 1730. Not mentioned in Benjamin's will.

II. JERUSHA, b. Feb. 13, 1681; m. —— Bailey. Ch., Benjamin and Ebenezer.

5.   III. BENJAMIN, b. Mar. 11, 1683; m. Mary Cowen and
      Elizabeth Perry.
6.   IV. EBENEZER, b. Apr. 2, 1686; m. —— ——.
      V. PERSIS, b. June 6, 1688. She d. before 1730. Not
      mentioned in her father's will.
6½.   VI. CALEB, b. June 12, 1690; m. —— ——.
7.   VII. THOMAS, b. Nov. 14, 1692 ; m. Mary Booth.
      VIII. ADAMS, b. June 11, 1695. He d. before 1730. Not
      mentioned in father's will.
8.   IX. JEREMIAH, b. Sept. 17, 1697; m. Bethsheba Little-
      field.
9.   X. ELISHA, b. Nov. 24, 1699; m. Sarah Edson and Mary
      Field.

3. **John² Pierce** (Michael¹), m. 1683, Patience Dobson. She
was the daughter of Anthony and Mary (Williams) Dobson, b. abt.
1660, in Scituate. Res. Scituate and Swansey, Mass. He d. June,
1738. His will is dated June 6, 1738, and was proved at Taunton,
Nov. 6, 1750, from Swansey. Witnesses, Jonathan Slead, Sibil
Slead and William Hart. His son David was executor.

CHILDREN.

10.   I. MIAL, b. Sept. 24, 1684; m. Mary Wood.
11.   II. JOHN, b. Apr. 12, 1686 ; m. Abigal Vinton.
      III. JONATHAN, b. Feb. 24, 1688.
      IV. RUTH, b. Sept. 6, 1689; m. June 18, 1719, Stephen
      Cornell.
      V. JAEL, b. Feb. 24, 1692 ; m. July 24, 1717, Hezekiah
      Chace.
      VI. DAVID, b. Jan. 1, 1695. He was ex.of his father's will.
12.   VII. CLOTHIER, b. May 5, 1698; m. Hannah Sherman.
      VIII. MARY, b. ——; m. —— Norton.
12½. IX. SAMUEL, b. abt. 1702; m. Polly Barber.

4. **Ephraim² Pierce** (Michael¹), m. Hannah Holbrook.* He
moved to Warwick, R. I., from Weymouth, Mass., where his first child

---

*Dau. of John of Weymouth.

was born, and according to the town records, was called Isricum. May 3, 1681, he was made freeman of the colony from Providence. His will is dated July 18, 1718, and was proved in Warwick, Sept. 23, 1719. He d. Sept. 14, 1719, and his wife also died the same year. Warwick is one of the oldest towns in Rhode Island. In 1642, it was the shire town of the Colony of Warwick, which, however, in 1643 was united with the Colony of Acquidnick. Its Indian name was Shawomet, and it was incorporated in 1647.

The story of the trials endured by the original purchasers of Warwick has been so recently brought to mind by the publication of Judge Brayton's "Defense of Samuel Gorton,"* that little needs to be said by way of explanation of the following document. Unable to find a peaceful home in the older settlements "the Gortonoges" had in 1641 withdrawn to Pawtuxet and settled upon land bought of Robert Cole. The hostility of the Arnolds impelled them to recede to Shawomet in the winter of 1642–3. In the following autumn an invading force from Massachusetts captured nine of them, imprisoned seven during the next winter, and in March, 1644, on giving them release banished the whole number from Massachusetts and from their own possessions in Warwick. Though relieved from this interdiction, as they thought, by the patent from the Earl of Warwick and his assistant Commissioners, which was brought by Roger Williams the next September, and emboldened thereby to return to their homes in Warwick, they were, nevertheless, harassed by warrants from the General Court of Massachusetts, and as late as 1650 were informed of the passage of an act to annex their lands and make them part of Suffolk county, receiving at the same time a summons to send people to Boston for trial. The immediate effect of all these harsh experiences seems to have been to fire the settlers with "indignant energy," yet their hardships must have had, withal, a depressing influence.

Among the numerous enemies which the outspoken course of Gorton had made, one of the most powerful at this time was William Coddington. Even when in 1644 the colonists upon the Island disregarding their former trouble with Gorton and his friends, were giving them shelter during their banishment, Coddington had written to Winthrop in this strain: "Gorton came before I knew it, is here against my mind, and shall not be protected by me."† Now in July, 1651, news arrived in Warwick

---

* R. I. Historical Tracts, No. 17.

† Defense of Samuel Gorton.

that on the 3d of the previous April this very Coddington had
been commissioned Governor for life of Rhode Island and Con-
anicut.* It seems to have been admitted on every hand that this
commission had in effect vacated the charter under which Providence, Warwick, Newport and Portsmouth had been united in
1647, though the first two towns were not included within Coddington's jurisdiction. William Arnold wrote about it on September
1, 1651, as follows: "Whereas Mr. Coddington have gotten a
charter of Road Island and Conimacuke Island to himselfe, he
have thereby broken the force of their charter that went under the
name of Providence, because he have gotten away the greater
parte of that colonie."† The Gortonists indicated their opinion
by contributing of their poverty £100 to send, in connection with Providence, an agent to England in quest of a new
charter. Roger Williams sailed in October for that purpose and
with him John Clarke, the agent of the Island towns, to effect, if
possible, a revocation of the detested commission. At the date of
the offer of sale they had been gone five months without success
and it could not be foreseen that the following autumn would bring
them complete victory.

Meanwhile Plymouth and Massachusetts were having a friendly
dispute before the Commissioners of the United Colonies concerning the ownership of the Shawomet lands, and in September, 1651,
Plymouth was advised to take possession of them by force if the
inhabitants would not willingly submit themselves to its jurisdiction.

To the settlers the political situation must have appeared very
dark. Without an undisputed charter they were well nigh de-
fenseless against their rapacious persecutors from the other colonies, while unfriendly neighbors were ever on their borders. Local
dissensions increased their discomfort, and their relations with
the Indians seem to have been unsatisfactory. There is no reason
for wonder that the signers of the paper were ready to sell their
lands and depart to some new home in search of peace and quiet.

The language upon the document suggests as the persons ad-
dressed the General Court of Commissioners for the main-land
towns; but this Court held no meeting, of which we have any
record, in the month named, either in Warwick or elsewhere. It
met at Pawtuxet on the 25th of February preceding, and also at
Warwick on the 18th of May following. There was on the 1st of
March an "Assemblie of yᵉ Colonie at Portsmouth."‡

It seems very probable that the movement for the sale of the

---

* Greene's Short History of R. I. incorrectly says "Connecticut."

† R. I. Colonial Records, Vol. I.

‡ R. I. Colonial Records, Vol. I.

lands had reached the stage indicated by this tender of sale, when for some cause it was interrupted before the names of all the owners of the lots had been secured. There are the signatures of seven of the original purchasers. Of the other five, Weston was certainly, and Shotton, probably, dead; while Power, Waterman and Waddell were not then residents of Shawomet if they ever had been. Only four of the other landholders, of whom there had been thirty-one as early as June, 1648,* seem to have affixed their signatures, and three of these were sons of John Greene, another signer. All this points to quite a narrow range for the desire to effect a sale, or, more probably, to some interruption of the process of obtaining signatures. What led to this interruption?

There was, it is possible, a political change within the town which encouraged the signers and checked their ardor for emigration. At the February General Court not one of them was in office, but at the May meeting four of them were Commissioners. At this latter meeting Gorton's popularity was conspicuously shown, for he was chosen Moderator for the day, and General Assistant for his town.†

It is probable, however, that the chief occasion for delay was furnished by the famous quarrel that sprang up not long after this very 22d of March between one of these signers, John Warner, and his fellow magistrates and townspeople.‡ This began, it will be remembered, about a disputed bill for the board of certain Dutch sailors, but led to such high feeling and bitter words that on the 24th of April Warner was disfranchised by vote of the town. Considerable interest was excited throughout the colony. Against the final vote, passed in June, restoring to Warner his house and land, which had been attached, Gorton and Holden earnestly protested.

Doubtless before the embittered feelings of the landholders had become sufficiently soothed to allow of an united effort to sell their lands, September§ had come with the glad news that the authorities in London had granted to the colonists the temporary use of their old charter; and when, in October, it was known that Coddington's commission had been absolutely revoked and the charter permanently restored, the chief reason for the proposed sale having been removed, the whole matter seems to have been dropped.‖

* Fuller's History of Warwick.
† R. I. Colonial Records, Vol. I.
‡ Fuller's History of Warwick.
§ Greene's Short History of R. I.
‖ R. G. Huling in *Narragansett Register.*

CHILDREN.

13.   I. AZRIKIM, b. Jan. 4, 1671; m. Sarah Heywood and
            Elizabeth Esten.
14.   II. EPHRAIM, b. 1674; m. Mary Low.
       III. MICHAEL, b. 1676.
       IV. RACHEL, b. 1678; m. —— Peet.
        V. HANNAH, b. 1680; m. —— Martin.
       VI. EXPERIENCE, b. 1682; m. —— Wheaton.
15.   VII. JOHN, b. 1684; m. —— —.—.
      VIII. BENJAMIN, b. 1686; d. Aug. 9, 1698.

5. **Benjamin³ Pierce, Jr.** (Benjamin², Michael¹), b. Mar. 11,
1683; m. Feb. 5, 1711, Mary Cowan; d. Feb. 10, 1724; m. 2nd, Elizabeth Perry. She d. bef. her husband. He d. Dec., 1772; res.
Scituate, Mass. His will was proved Dec. 27, 1772, and mentions
children Martha Forbes, Mary Keith and Benjamin.

CHILDREN.

16.   I. BENJAMIN, b. Dec. 4, 1721; m. Charity Howard and
            Jane Howard.
       II. MARTHA, b. Jan. 5, 1712; m. Oct. 19, 1735, John Fobes
            (John, Edward, John); b. 1714 in Bridgewater.
            Ch., Edward, b. 1739, rem. to Lake Champlain;
            Martha, b. 1741, m. 1762 Eliab Haywood; Libeus,
            b. 1743. He d. 1783, and she d. 1795.
       III. MARY, b. Feb. 4, 1717; m. Mar. 18, 1741, Ebenezer
            Keith, b. 1716 in Bridgewater; res. Scituate. Ch.,
            Luther, b. 1743; Rachel, b. 1744; Mary, b. 1745;
            Ebenezer, b. 1747; Amos, b. 1750; Lucy, b. 1751;
            Susannah, b. 1753; Caleb, b. 1755; Calvin, b. 1757.
            Mary d. 1758, and he m. for a second wife Mrs
            Hepzibah (Perkins) Carver by whom he had sev-
            eral ch. He was a son of Samuel and gr. s. of Rev.
            James Keith, a Scotchman, who was the first minis-
            ter in Bridgewater; he was educated in Aberdeen,
            Scotland, and came over in 1662. His first sermon
            was preached from a rock.

6. **Ebenezer**[3] **Pierce** (Benjamin[2], Michael[1]), b. Apr. 2, 1686;
m. —— ——.

Ebenezer was born in Scituate, Mass., but moved to Attleboro,
where he was a member of the Second Congregational Church in
1749. Attleboro was first settled in 1669 by John Woodcock,
his house was the garrison and licensed in 1670. Many of the
first settlers were from Rehoboth and Scituate, Mass. The town
was originally called the "North Purchase," and incorporated in
1694.

CHILDREN.

17.   I. BENJAMIN, b. —— (eldest son), m. Eliza ——, and Rebecca Blanding.

18.   II. EBENEZER, b. ——; m. Elizabeth Darby.

6½. **Caleb**[3] **Pierce** (Benjamin[2], Michael[1]), b. June 12, 1690 ; m.
——; res. Scituate, Mass.

CHILDREN.

18½.   I. BENJAMIN, b. ——; m. Sarah Pope.
     II. CALEB, b. ——.
     III. JOSHUA, b. ——.
     IV. NEHEMIAH, b. ——.

7. **Thomas**[3] **Pierce** (Benjamin[2], Michael[1]), b. Nov. 14, 1692;
m. Nov. 27, 1717 Mary Booth.

His will is dated Apr. 24, 1774, and proved at Plymouth, July
22, 1775. Her will was dated June 10, 1776, proved Mar. 28,
1786. Witnesses, Lawrence Litchfield, Ezekiel Hayden and John
Mott. Res. Scituate, Mass.

CHILDREN.

19.   I. EZEKIEL, b. Nov. 13, 1718; m. —— ——.
     II. THOMAS, b. June 25, 1720; m. July 2, 1750, Mary
Nicholson; res. Scituate, Mass.
     III. LYDIA, b. Aug. 26, 1726; d. before 1786.
20.   IV. SETH B., b. Sept. 7, 1728 ; m. Jemima Turner.
     V. MARY, b. Feb. 9, 1734.
     VI. DESIRE, b. May 10, 1742; d. unm., May 9, 1825.

8. **Jeremiah³ Pierce** (Benjamin², Michael¹), b. Sept. 17, 1697; m. July 1, 1732, Bethsheba Littlefield.

According to the will of his father, Jeremiah was given lands at Mt. Hope, and it is supposed he moved there. Mount Hope is regarded as a corruption or rather the English of the Indian *Montaup*, which word was used by the aborigines to designate the hill in the town of Bristol, Bristol county, R. I. The epithet Mount Hope or Montaup has from time immemorial been applied to the historic hill in Bristol. This town (Bristol including the hill) was transferred, with four other towns, from Massachusetts to Rhode Island, February 27, 1746–7. There is now a Mt. Hope swamp where Philip was killed August 12, 1676, O. S.; also, Mt. Hope bay. Residence, Scituate, Mass., and Mt. Hope.

9. **Elisha³ Pierce** (Benjamin², Michael¹), b. Nov. 24, 1699; m. Feb. 2, 1731, in Bridgewater, Sarah Edson, dau. of Capt. Josiah Edson. He was a deacon and often rep. for his town. He was b. 1705, and d. abt. 1735; m. 2nd, Apr. 29, 1738, Mrs. Mary Field, b. 1707. She was the daughter of Ephraim Howard of Bridgewater, and was m. to John Field, son of Capt. John, in 1726. He died in 1729, leaving John, b. 1727; m. 1760, Hannah Blackman; and James, b. 1729. Elisha Pierce d. in Aug., 1770. The will was allowed that year. Res. Scituate.

CHILDREN.

I. SARAH, b. Jan. 12, 1732; m. Aug. 30, 1751, Samuel Holbrook, Jr.; m. 2nd, —— Park; res. Scituate, Mass.

II. ELISHA, b. Apr. 9, 1739; d. bef. 1770.

21. III. CALVIN, b. Apr. 14, 1742; m. Huldah Howard and Abigail Bailey.

IV. MARY, b. May 5, 1746; d. bef. 1770. Not mentioned in father's will.

V. PERSIS, b. July 2, 1748; m. Aug. 22, 1772, Barnabas Litchfield. Ch., Warren, Barnabas, dau. Molly m. Seth Stoder; Lydia d. unm.; Freelove d. unm.; Persis m. —— Sprague; Lucy m. Wm. Studley. Res. Scituate.

10. **Mial³ Pierce** (John², Michael¹), b. Sept. 24, 1684; m. Oct. 15, 1719, Mary Wood; d. Jan. 1, 1770. He d. 1764; res. Swansey, Mass. His will was dated 1748, and proved 1764, and Emet and Barnaby Chase and Stephen Cornell were witnesses. Her will was dated 1764 and proved 1770, Jan. 1. Witnesses, Benjamin Buffington, Moses Buffington and David Peirce.

Swansey is one of the oldest towns in Massachusetts. It is on the Rhode Island line. The Indian names of the place were Mattapoiset, Wannamoiset and Ashuelot. It was incorporated Oct. 30, 1667, and derived its name from Swansea, Wales. The town is memorable as being the spot where the first blood was shed in King Philip's war. June 24, 1675, the alarm of war was first sounded in Plymouth colony, when eight or nine were killed in and about Swansey. Six men were also murdered in a dwelling-house the same day.

CHILDREN.

    I. ELIZABETH, b. Apr. 7, 1725; m. —— Lawton.

    II. FREELOVE, b. Feb. 5, 1730; m. Apr. 1, 1767, John Monrow; res. Swansey.

    III. MARY, b. Oct. 26, 1721; m. July 30, 1747, Stephen Manchester; res. Swansey.

22.   IV. MIAL, b. Sept. 25, 1728; m. Hepsibeth Mason.

    V. PHEBE, b. Feb. 16, 1723; m. Sept. 19, 1751, Jonathan Wheaton; res. Swansey.

    VI. SARAH, b. Sept. 13, 1720; m. May 3, 1744, Jared Born; res. Swansey.

    VII. BETHIA, b. ——; m. Dec. 2, 1759, David Wilson; res. Swansey, Mass.

11. **John³ Pierce** (John², Michael¹), b. Apr. 12, 1686; m. Oct. 26, 1712, Abigail Vinton. He d. Apr., 1766; res. Scituate and Dighton, Mass. Dighton was originally a part of Taunton, and was incorporated May 30, 1712. The first church was organized in 1710. His will was proved May 5, 1766. Witnesses, Abiel Terry, Henry Tew and John Crane. Ebenezer Pierce and Ebenezer Phillips were executors.

CHILDREN.

23.   I. JOHN, b. abt. 1713; m. Anna Burt.
24.   II. ELISHA, m. ——.
     III. EBENEZER, m. Mar. 21, 1752, Ruth Tilden; res. Scituate.
     IV. OBADIAH.
     V. LYDIA, m. Mar. 20, 1734, Abial Simmons of Dighton, Mass.
     VI. SYBIL, m. Ebenezer Phillips.
     VII. MARTHA, m. —— Eddy.
     VIII. ABIGAIL, m. —— Burt. She d. bef. 1766, leaving Clothier and Gordon; res. Dighton, Mass.

12. **Clothier³ Pierce** (John², Michael¹), b. May 5, 1698; m. Nov. 19, 1718, Hannah Sherman; res. Swansey, Mass. I think he m. 2nd, Mrs. Mary (Allen) Coffin. See Thurston Genealogy, p. 270–5622.*

CHILDREN.

     I. DAVID, b. 1730.
25.   II. CLOTHIER, b. Feb. 24, 1720; m. ——.
     III. ELIZABETH, b. Oct. 28, 1724; m. Dec. 13, 1741, Joel Howbeed; res. Swansey.
     IV. FREELOVE, b. July 4, 1727.
     V. HANNAH, b. Feb. 16, 1722.

12½. **Samuel³ Pierce** (John², Michael¹), b. abt. 1702; m. Polly Barber. He d. ——. Res. Plymouth Co., Mass., and Putnam Co., N. Y.

CHILDREN.

26.   I. DANIEL, b. 1742; m. Mehitable Carver.
     II. There was one other child, a daughter.

13. **Azrikim³ Pierce** (Ephraim², Michael¹), b. Jan. 4, 1671; m. Dec. 31, 1696, Sarah Heywood (Swansey records say Howard), b. Mar. 2 1676; d. Aug. 12, 1712; m. 2nd, May 6, 1713, Elizabeth Esten, b. Apr. 8, 1683, dau. of Henry and Elizabeth (Martin) Esten; d. May 18, 1718. I think he married again, but to whom, I cannot

---

* A Clothier Pierce was married to Mary Hill in Newport, R. I., Dec. 26, 1764.

tell. Res. Warwick, R. I., and moved to Rehoboth, Mass., before 1721.

Rehoboth was incorporated in 1645. Its Indian name was Seconet, and the first white settler was William Blackstone. The Rev. Samuel Newman, author of a "Concordance of the Bible," removed here with a part of his church from Weymouth in 1644. He selected the Hebrew name Rehoboth for the place, because, as he remarked, "*The Lord hath made room for us.*" In 1646, forty of its dwellings were burned to ashes by the Indians.

CHILDREN.

I. SARAH, b. Oct. 2, 1707; d. July 23, 1725.

27.   II. SAMUEL, b. —— ; m. Rebecca Budlong.

III. AZRIKIM, b. Dec. 3, 1697; d. Feb. 28, 1698, in Swansea.

28.   IV. BENJAMIN, b. —— ; m. Mary Budlong.

28½.   V. ISAAC, b. abt. 1702; m. Esther ——.

VI. TABITHA, b. Aug. 27, 1717; m. Jan. 8, 1730, John Budlong, Jr., b. 1698; d. Jan., 1763. She d. abt. 1746. Res. Warwick, R. I.

John Budlong, Jr., m. for his second wife Mrs. Renew Moon. She d. 1779. John was a freeman in 1724. His will was proved Mar. 14, 1763. Son John was executor. He gave to John all lands at Brush Neck, Warwick; to Nathan house and land now occupied by his son John; to Pearce Budlong land on Rockey Hill; to John Pearce, William and James £500 each. Joseph, a son by the second wife was blind. His inventory was £14,269 11s. 6d. The widow's inventory £2,541 9s. 8d. Her will was proved Sept. 13, 1779. Ch., Isabel, b. Apr. 10, 1731; m. Elisha Green, Jr.; John, b. Aug. 25, 1733; Sarah, b. Jan. 10, 1735; Nathan, b. Apr. 12, 1739; Pearce, b. —— ; Tabitha, b. ——.

29.   VII. JOSEPH, b. Apr. 7, 1714; m. Mary Martin.

VIII. HOPESTILL, ⎱ b. Aug. 14, 1716.
IX. ELIZABETH, ⎰

14. **Ephraim³ Pierce, Jr.** (Ephraim², Michael¹), b. 1674; m. Mary Low. Res. Rehoboth and Swansey, Mass.

7

CHILDREN.

30.   I. MIAL, b. Apr. 24, 1693; m. Judith Ellis.
31.   II. DAVID, b. July 26, 1701; m. Mary Wood.
       III. ELIZABETH, b. May 30, 1703; m. July 30, 1724, Jeremiah Eddy; res. Swansey.
       IV. MARY, b. Nov. 16, 1697; m. Jan. 14, 1723, Benjamin Norton; res. Swansey.
       V. CLOTHIER, b. May 24, 1728.
32.   VI. EPHRAIM, b. ——; m. Mary Stevenson.

15. **John³ Pierce** (Ephraim², Michael¹), b. 1684; m. 1705. Res. Rehoboth, Mass.

CHILDREN.

33.   I. JOHN, b. abt. 1706; m. Mary ——.

16. **Benjamin⁴ Pierce, Jr.** (Benjamin³, Benjamin², Michael¹), b. Dec. 4, 1721; m. 1742, Charity Howard of Bridgewater, dau. of Jonathan, Jr., b. 1721; m. 2nd, May 13, 1750, Jane Haywood of B., dau. of Dea. Thomas, and gr.-dau. of Dea. Joseph, b. 1720. He d. June, 1768. From the records at Plymouth, Mass., in the office of the probate court, the following data is obtained relating to Benjamin Pierce:

1768, July 14, Jane Peirce of Scituate, was appointed administratrix of Benj. Peirce.

1768, Dec. 6, Jane Peirce was appointed guar. of Thomas Peirce, son of Benj. Peirce.

1768, Dec. 6, Benjamin Peirce, Jr., appointed guar. of Jonathan Peirce (minor) above 14 years.

1768, Dec. 6, Jane Peirce appointed guar. of Caleb Peirce, under 14.

In a division of Benjamin Peirce's estate in Plymouth records, I find mentioned the name of Benjamin Peirce, eldest son; Jonathan Peirce, 2nd son; Thomas Peirce, 3rd son; Caleb Peirce, 4th son. Res. Scituate, Mass.

CHILDREN.

34.   I. BENJAMIN, b. Mar. 1, 1746; m. Mrs. Priscilla (Merritt) Wade.

35.   II. JONATHAN, b. Feb. 18, 1748; m. Mary Litchfield.
36.   III. HAYWOOD, b. June 22, 1753 ; m. Judith Bailey.
37.   IV. CALEB, b. Aug. 7, 1755 ; m. Abigail Bailey.
      V. THOMAS, b. abt. 1750; m. before 1768.

17. **Benjamin⁴ Pierce** (Ebenezer³, Benjamin², Michael¹), b.
——; m. Eliza ——, b. ——; d. Apr. 18, 1772; m. 2nd, June 16,
1773, Rebecca Blanding, b. ——; d. June 28, 1784. He d. July 23,
1793. Res. Scituate, Attleboro, Mass., and Westmoreland, N. H.
Benjamin was born either in Scituate or Attleboro, Mass. He
was a member of the Second Congregational Church of the latter
place in 1749, and moved to Westmoreland, N. H., about 1764,
where he died twenty years afterward.

CHILDREN.

38.   I. EZRA, b. Feb. 1, 1752; m. Rebecca ——.
      II. LYDIA, b. Dec. 18, 1753; d. young.
      III. LYDIA, b. Aug. 22, 1756; m. Jan. 22, 1776, Capt. Daniel
              Carlisle ; d. Sept. 12, 1856, at Westmoreland, N. H
              She reached the great age of one hundred years,
              and the occasion was duly celebrated by her rela-
              tives and townspeople. Their children were David,
              George, Sarah, Shubal, Mary, Eunice and Gratia.
39.   IV. NEHEMIAH, b. Dec. 2, 1759; m. Phebe Lawrence.
40.   V. BENJAMIN, b. Feb. 13, 1761; m. Lucinda Cobb.
      VI. EUNICE, b. 1746; m. Silas Barrett, and d. 1838.
              They res. in Hinsdale, N. H., and then moved to
              New York State.

18. **Ebenezer⁴ Pierce** (Ebenezer³, Benjamin², Michael¹) b.
—— ; m. Apr. 11, 1751, Elizabeth Darby, of Berkley.
Ebenezer was born in either Scituate or Attleboro, Mass. He
resided in Rehoboth, where he was married, and later moved to
Attleboro and subsequently to Somerset. All the children unite
in deed of June 1, 1790, to brother David, on file in the registry
office at Taunton.
He d. Oct. 10, 1783. Res. Somerset, Mass.

CHILDREN.

41.　 I. EBENEZER, b. ——; m. Keziah Butterfield.
　　　II. OBADIAH.　He was a mariner.
　　　III. LYDIA, m. —— Chace.
　　　IV. ELIZABETH, m. Joshua Brown.
　　　V. MARY, d. unm., Oct. 17, 1795.
　　　VI. PATIENCE, m. Sylvester Perry.
　　　VII. DAVID, living in 1790.

18½. **Benjamin⁴ Pierce** (Caleb³, Benjamin², Michael¹), b. ——;
m. Mar. 1, 1738, Sarah Pope.　He d. s. p. Aug., 1756.　Res. Dartmouth, Mass., Aug. 23, 1756.　At the probate office in Taunton,
Sarah was appointed executor.　He gave his negro girl Phylis
to his widow, and then after her death she has her freedom.

Benjamin Peirce, of Dartmouth.　His will dated July 26, 1756,
proved Sept. 15, 1756.　Witnesses, Samuel Perry, Elisha Parker,
Thomas West, wife Sarah.　Children, none mentioned, but brothers Caleb, Joshua and Nehemiah.

19. **Ezekiel⁴ Pierce** (Thomas³, Benjamin², Michael¹), b. Nov. 13,
1718; m. ——.　Res. Scituate, Mass.

CHILDREN.

42.　 I. EZEKIEL, b. abt. 1739; m. —— McCourter.
　　　II. JOSEPH, b. ——.

20. **Seth B.⁴ Pierce** (Thomas³, Benjamin², Michael¹), b. Sept. 7,
1728; m. Sept. 6, 1766, Jemima Turner; d. Apr. 19, 1814.　He
d. Dec. 9, 1810.　Res. Scituate, Mass.

CHILDREN.

43.　 I. THOMAS, b. Aug. 26, 1767; m. Anna Beales and Mrs.
　　　　　John Pierce.
44.　 II. JOSEPH, b. Apr., 1769; m. Sally Hatch.
　　　III. WILLIAM, b. ——; m. Dec. 4, 1793, Molly Curtis.
45.　 IV. NATHANIEL, b. Feb. 7, 1773; m. Winnet Otis, Nabby
　　　　　Bailey and Sophia Briggs.

46.   V. JOHN, b. Oct. 29, 1776; m. Mercy Merritt.
     VI. DESIRE, b. March 6, 1779; m. Dec. 11, 1802, Wm.
       Peaks; res. Scituate, Mass. Ch., William, b. Aug.
       28, 1803; Martin F., b. July 2, 1805; Diantha, b.
       June 21, 1807; Hannah W., b. Aug. 26, 1809.

21. **Calvin⁴ Pierce** (Elisha³, Benjamin², Michael¹), b. Apr. 14,
1742; m. Sept. 19, 1767, Huldah Howard; m. 2nd, Sept. 27, 1778,
Abigail Bailey. Res. Scituate, Mass. He d. Dec. 2, 1817.

CHILDREN.
     I. MARY, b. Oct. 15, 1768.
    II. HULDAH, b. Sept. 19, 1770.
   III. HANNAH, b. Sept. 15, 1779; d. Aug. 21, 1811.
47.   IV. CALVIN, b. Mar. 16, 1782; m. Alice Otis.
      V. ELISHA, b. Mar. 8, 1783.

22. **Capt. Mial⁴ Pierce** (Mial³, John², Michael¹), b. Sept. 25,
1728; m. Mar. 26, 1752, Hepsibeth Mason. He d. Nov., 1810. His
will was proved Nov. 6, 1810. Theop. Luther, Jonathan Slead,
Job Slead and Theop. Shore were witnesses. His son Asa was
executor. Res. Swansey and Somerset, Mass.

CHILDREN.
48.   I. MIAL, b. 1752; m. Mehitable Wheeler.
      II. ANNA.
     III. SARAH, m. —— Jones.
      IV. BETHANY, m. July 29, 1781, David Jones in Swansey.
       V. HANNAH, m. Mar. 18, 1784, Baker Slead, in Swansey.
      VI. LYDIA, m. —— Martin.
     VII. PHEBE, m. Oct. 4, 1798, John Slead; res. Somerset.
49. VIII. ASA, b. Mar., 1761; m. Nancy Hathaway.

23. **John⁴ Pierce** (John³, John², Michael¹), b. abt. 1713; m.
May 18, 1737, Anna Burt, of Beverly. He d. Sept., 1798. His
will is dated Sept. 2, 1795, and proved in 1798. James Smith,
David Andrews and John Whitmash, witnesses. Benamuel Bowers, executor. Don't mention children. Res. Dighton, Mass.

CHILDREN.

I. ZEPHENIAH, b. Dec. 20, 1738.

50. II. JOHN, b. Oct. 16, 1740; m. Rebecca Snell.

24. **Elisha**[4] **Pierce** (John[3], John[2], Michael[1]), b. ——; m. ——.
Res. Dighton, Mass.

CHILDREN.

51. I. BETHUEL, b. 1754; m. Sybil Phillips.

II. LEVI, b. 1759; d. unm., Nov. 26, 1847.

52. III. ELISHA, b. 1746; m. Elizabeth Kane.

25. **Clothier**[4] **Pierce** (Clothier[3], John[2], Michael[1]), b. Feb. 24,
1720; m. ——. Res. Dartmouth, Mass., and Newport, R. I.

CHILDREN.

53. I. DANIEL, b. 1746; m. Mary Hix.

II. PERRY. He m. and res. in New York State. His
son Cromwell m. Anne ——, who later m. her
cousin, Rev. Isaac Pierce.

54. III. CLOTHIER, b. 1753; m. Chole Chace.

26. **Col. Daniel**[4] **Pierce** (Samuel[3], John[2], Michael[1]), b. 1742;
m. 1768, Mehitable Carver, b. Dec. 12, 1753; d. Apr. 16, 1837.
He served in the Revolutionary army, and was a colonel. He d.
Apr. 20, 1812. Res. Carmel, Putnam Co., N. Y.

CHILDREN.

I. ORPHA, b. June 19, 1769; d. æ. ——, 1836.

II. RUTH, b. June 21, 1771; m. Benjamin Fuller. Ch.,
Hetta, m. Jarvis Washburn. He d. Feb. 21, 1870.
She d. Sept. 3, 1848. Nathan, Jerry, Daniel, Alva
m. Eliza Ferris; Elijah, Harry, Betsey m. Jonathan
Goodridge; Julia A., Jane, b. Jan. 17, 1809; m.
Aug. 19, 1826, Wm. Houghteline, b. Oct. 20, 1801;
d. Sept. 15, 1855, Dayton, O.; Sally A. m. Dr. J.
A. Gore.

III. CLOE, b. June 1, 1773; d. 1854.

IV. SAMUEL, b. Feb. 8, 1775; d. 1863.

V. TIMOTHY, b. Feb. 8, 1775; m. and d. s. p.
55¼.	VI. ABIZER, b. Dec. 1, 1779; m. Jane Hopkins.
VII. DANIEL, b. 1779; d. middle aged.
55½.	VIII. JONATHAN, b. 1781; m. Betsey Crossman.
55¾.	IX. WILLIAM, b. Feb. 22, 1783; m. Elizabeth Badeau.
X. HESTER, b. 1786.
55.	XI. BARNABAS C., b. Sept. 30, 1792; m. Nancy P. Wildman.
XII. POLLY, b. Sept. 11, 1795; m. Barnabas Carver; d. s. p. 1872.
XIII. MEHITABLE, m. —— Jones.

27. **Samuel⁴ Pierce** (Azrikim³, Ephraim², Michael¹), b. ——; m. Nov. 26, 1721, Rebecca Budlong, b. 1700, dau. of John Budlong. He res. in Warwick, R. I., and was made a freeman there, May 6, 1729. In 1760 he was a resident of that place.

CHILDREN, BORN IN WARWICK.

56.	I. AZRIKIM, b. May 27, 1723; m. Bethsheba Millard and Sarah Bliss.
II. SARAH, b. Oct. 12, 1725.
III. SAMUEL, b. Mar. 16, 1728.
IV. REBECCA, b. June 17, 1734.
V. FREELOVE, b. Jan. 14, 1735; m. June 30, 1760, William Ross; res. Newport, R. I.

28. **Elder Benjamin⁴ Pierce** (Azrikim³, Ephraim², Michael¹), b. ——; m. Jan. 8, 1730, Mary Budlong, b. 1706. Res. Warwick, R. I. He d. bef. 1763.

She was a daughter of John and Isabel (Potter) Budlong. John was taken captive by the Indians in Nov., 1675, at the same time with his father and mother, and the remainder of the family were killed. John was returned by his captors, and lived with his uncle Moses Lippitt.

THE OLD BAPTIST CHURCH AT APPONAUG.— At a church meeting held in old Warwick, R. I., of which Elder Manassah Martin was pastor, Dec. 6, 1744, Benjamin Pierce and wife, Ezrikham Pierce and wife, Edward Case and wife, John Budlong and such others as wished to form a church at the Fulling mill, of the same faith and order, were granted leave. Several members from East Greenwich united with them, and the church was duly organized; Benjamin Peirce was ordained their minister. They eventually erected a meeting-house on an eminence east of the village of Apponaug, which commanded an extensive prospect of this village, river, islands, and surrounding country. There is a tradition that it was built at the suggestion of Elder Peter Worden, who, in 1758–9, built a house of worship in Coventry, twenty-eight feet long and twenty-six feet wide, and two stories high, and preached in it many years, and afterward settled in Apponaug. It is said that this house was of the same dimensions as the one in Coventry, which became known in later times as the Elder Charles Stone meeting-house ; Elder Stone having been the successor of Elder Worden. The church became involved in difficulty owing to some change in the religious sentiments of Elder Pierce, and diminished in numbers, and was finally dissolved, and "their meeting-house went to decay for many years." At what precise period this occurred does not appear, but it was previous to the Revolutionary war.

Elder Knight, in his history, makes no mention of any other pastor than Elder Pierce in connection with this church, and it is probable that the connection of Elder Worden was of short duration. Of the subsequent history of Elder Pierce, the writer has no knowledge. The Pierces furnished a number of Elders to the church in different places. Elder Nathan Pierce was settled over the Rehoboth many years, and till his death in 1794. Elders Preserved and Phillip Pierce, brothers, were ordained in the same church about the year 1800. The latter soon after went West. [Fuller's History of Warwick, R. I.]

The Warwick, R. I., record has this to say of his marriage: These are to certify all ministers of Justice, that Benjamin Perce, now residing in ye Town of Warwick, in ye Colony of Rhode Island and Providence Plantations, and Mary Budlong, daughter of Mr. John Budlong of town and Colony aforesaid, was lawfully married this 8th day of January, 1729–30, by me.

JOHN WARNER, *Justice.*

CHILDREN, BORN IN WARWICK.

I. BENJAMIN, b. June 1, 1732; d. June 28, 1736.

II. PARDON, b. Aug. 5, 1735; m. Mary ——; res. Warwick, R. I.

III. MARY, b. Oct. 29, 1737.

57.   IV. AZRIKIM, b. ——; m. Louis Warner.

28½. **Isaac[4] Pierce** (Azrikim[3], Ephraim[2], Michael[1]), b. abt. 1702;
m. 1724, Esther ——. He d. June, 1747. Res. Welfleet, Mass.
The will of Isaac Pierce of Eastham, dated Dec. 9, 1746, proved
Jan. 13, 1747, at Plymouth, Mass., mentions Esther Pierce, his
wife, and sons Joshua, Silas, Isaac and Joseph; daughter "Hannah, the wife of Stephen King." His son Joseph was sole
executor.

CHILDREN.

57b.   I. JOSEPH, b. 1725; m. Oct. 8, 1747, Susannah Newcomb, b. 1725. Susannah was the daughter of
Simon Newcomb, who was born in Eastham, Nov.
30, 1699; he lived in that part which was set off
as Wellfleet in 1763. At his death he gave his
daughter Susannah half of his sheep.

II. ISAAC, b. ——; m. Feb. 18, 1744, Esther Cowell.

57c.   III. JOSHUA, b. ——; m. Elizabeth Newcomb.

IV. SILAS, b. ——; m. Nov. 27, 1737, Eunice Cole.

V. HANNAH, b. ——; m. Stephen King.

29. **Dea. Joseph[4] Pierce** (Azrikim[3], Ephraim[2], Michael[1]), b.
Apr. 7, 1714; m. Oct. 3, 1734, Mary Martin, b. 1718; d. Oct.
16, 1803. He d. May 5, 1787. His will was proved Jan. 5, 1787,
and his son Joseph was executor. Res. Rehoboth, Mass.

CHILDREN.

58.   I. NATHANIEL, b. July 9, 1735; m. Sarah Pierce and
——.

59.   II. STEPHEN, b. Aug. 7, 1739; m. Anna Wheeler.

8

III. Elizabeth, b. Jan. 21, 1742; m. Mar. 20, 1758, James Gilmore, Jr., of Rehoboth.

IV. Mary, b. Feb. 23, 1743; m. Jan. 12, 1759, William Gilmore of Rehoboth.

V. Ann, b. June 10, 1746; m. Feb. 24, 1765, Levi Chaffee of Rehoboth. He d. and she m. —— Horton.

60. VI. Noah, b. Feb. 11, 1752; m. Patience Rounds, Elizabeth Hail and Sabary Wood.

VII. Joseph, b. Dec. 1, 1752; d. young.

VIII. Amy, b. Nov. 19, 1754; d. young.

IX. Rhobey, b. Feb. 17, 1757; m. Nov. 3, 1776, Joseph Waldron of Rehoboth.

61. X. Joseph, b. Dec. 5, 1759; m. Mary Pierce and Lydia (Pierce) Horton (see).

XI. Hannah, b. Apr. 18, 1762; m. Capt. Israel Pierce (see).

XII. Rhoda, b. Aug. 18, 1764; d. bef. 1787.

30. **Dea. Mial⁴ Pierce** (Ephraim³, Ephraim², Michael¹), b. Apr. 24, 1692; m. Judith Ellis, daughter of Judge Ellis. She was b. 1686; d. Oct. 6, 1744. He d. Oct. 18, 1786, æ. 94. Res. Warwick, R. I., Swansey and Rehoboth, Mass.

CHILDREN.

I. Ephraim, b. Nov. 9, 1712; d. Nov. 1, 1789.

62. II. Wheeler, b. July 11, 1714; m. Elizabeth Allen.

63. III. Nathan, b. Feb. 21, 1716; m. Lydia Martin.

IV. Mary, b. Oct. 18, 1718; m. Dea. Martin.

V. Judith, b. Oct. 21, 1720; m. Apr. 26, 1736, Wm. Tibbett ?

64. VI. Mial, b. Mar. 24, 1722; m. Elizabeth —— and Patience Martin.

65. VII. Jobe, b. Apr. 25, 1723; m. Abigail Pratt.

66. VIII. Caleb, b. June 8, 1726; m. Mary Rowland.

67. IX. Joshua, b. —— ; m. Mary Horton.

31. **David⁴ Pierce** (Ephraim³, Ephraim², Michael¹), b. July 26,
1701; m. Nov. 26, 1719, Mary Wood. She d. in Aug., 1768. He
d. Jan., 1767. Res. Swansey, Mass. His will was proved Jan.
26, 1767. It was witnessed by Cobb Arnold, Brooks Mason and
Russell Mason. David, Jr., was the administrator. He had two
negro slaves named " Cato " and " Tillis." Her will is dated
Aug. 8, 1768. Witnesses, Benj. Weaver, Clark Purrington and
Russell Mason. John Mason was executor.

CHILDREN.

68.   I. DAVID, b. Jan. 14, 1726; m. Elizabeth Baker.
    II. ELIZABETH, b. Jan. 2, 1734; m. Jan. 1, 1756, Thomas
       Thurston; res. Swansey.
    III. HANNAH, b. Jan. 1, 1730; m. Feb. 14, 1754, Samuel
       Law.
69.   IV. JONATHAN, b. Apr. 7, 1725 ; m. Susannah Moott.
    V. MARY, b. Feb. 22, 1727; m. Aug. 28, 1748, John Law.
    VI. PATIENCE, b. Oct. 10, 1720; m. Feb. 26, 1741, Oba-
       diah Baker and Russell Mason.
70.   VII. PRESERVED, b. Aug. 17, 1736; m. Hannah Case and
       Lydia Simmons.
    VIII. PHEBE, b. Jan. 27, 1739; m. Dec. 30, 1763, Isaac
       Upton ; res. Swansey.

32. **Ephraim⁴ Pierce** (Ephraim³, Ephraim², Michael¹), b. ——— ;
m. Sept. 2, 1733, Mary Stevenson. Res. Swansey, Mass.

CHILDREN.

    I. MARY, b. Aug. 27, 1745.
    II. PELEG, b. Jan. 13, 1742.
    III. RICHARD, b. Jan. 1, 1734.

33. **John⁴ Pierce** (John³, Ephraim², Michael¹), b. abt. 1706;
m. Mary ———. He d. Mar., 1768. His will was proved at Taunton, and Mary was admr. Res. Rehoboth, Mass.
In 1733 the Rehoboth town record has this:

John Pierce brought a wild cat's head before the town, and *his* ears were cut off by the constable in the presence of two select-men. *Prima facie* — a rather painful assertion.

CHILDREN.

I. MARY, b. June 6, 1727 ; m. —— Allyn.
II. LYDIA, b. Oct. 16, 1729; d. bef. 1768.
III. ROBIE, b. Oct. 5, 1731 ; d. bef. 1768.
70½. IV. NATHANIEL, b. abt. 1732. Mentioned in father's will.
V. CLOTHIER, b. Oct. 3, 1734. Mentioned in father's will.
VI. CLOTILDE.
VII. SARAH, b. Nov. 1, 1736; unm. in 1768.
71. VIII. COMFORT, b. Mar. 26, 1741 ; m. Betsey Allen.
IX. REBECCA, b. —— ; m. Oct. 5, 1766, Elkanah Ingalls.

34. **Dea. Benjamin**[5] **Pierce** (Benjamin[4], Benjamin[3], Benjamin[2], Michael[1]), b. Mar. 1, 1746 ; m. Mar. 2, 1769, Mrs. Priscilla (Merritt) Wade, b. June 26, 1743 ; d. Jan. 30, 1837. He d. May 4, 1809. Res. Scituate and Chesterfield, Mass. He was a deacon in the Congregational church.

CHILDREN.

72. I. BENJAMIN, b. July 8, 1777 ; m. Deborah James.
II. ISRAEL, b. —— ; d. unm., Mar. 4, 1810. He was a cripple, and walked with crutches. Was a splendid penman and good accountant, and for some years was a clerk in a wholesale house in Albany, N. Y., and later clerked for his brother in his stores in Chesterfield and Westhampton, Mass. Benj. was appointed administrator. (See Northampton [Mass.] Records, Vol. 26, p. 248.)
III. CHARITY, b. —— ; m. Hon. Sylvanus Clapp. He was the son of Ebenezer and Catharine (Catlin) Clapp of Northampton, and was b. 1764; m. Jan. 6, 1792, and settled in Westhampton, Mass. He was a very popular man, and though a Democrat

in politics, was at various times chosen to the State Legislature by a union of both political parties. He was of a remarkably pleasant disposition, possessed fine conversational powers, and could indulge in story telling to universal acceptance. He d. Apr. 14, 1847. Ch., Bela P., b. Nov. 6, 1792; d. Sept. 4, 1856; Ralph, b. Aug. 11, 1795; d. Mar. 6, 1850.

   IV. PRISCILLA, d. bef. 1809.
    V. JANE, d. bef. 1809.
   VI. MABEL, d. young.
  VII. ANNIE, m. —— Stebbins.
 VIII. ZERIAH, d. bef. 1809.
   IX. TIRZAH, b. ——; m. —— Parsons.
    X. PARNEL, d. bef. 1809.

35. **Jonathan⁵ Pierce** (Benjamin⁴, Benjamin³, Benjamin², Michael¹), b. in Scituate, Mass., Feb. 18, 1748; m. Feb. 13, 1773, Mary Litchfield in Scituate. He d. in Canton, N. Y., b. Dec. 6, 1807. Res. Scituate and Chesterfield, Mass.

Jonathan Pierce was born in Scituate, Mass., and toward the close of the eighteenth century, moved to Vermont.

CHILDREN.

    I. ISAAC, b. ——.
   II. PENELOPE, b. ——; m. Josiah Fisk.
  III. TABITHA, b. Mar. 1, 1782; m. 1803, Samuel Stiles, b. May 8, 1777; d. Oct. 5, 1872. She d. Dec. 3, 1811. Ch., Orpha, b. July 28, 1804; m. July 4, 1821, Admiral Nelson Risley, and d. Dec. 27, 1883; Pierce, b. Dec. 27, 1806; d. unm., Nov., 1827; Samuel S., b. June 26, 1811; m. May, 1834, Charlotte Sternberg, and d. Feb. 13, 1880; Silvanus, b. Aug. 2, 1809; m. Oct. 4, 1832, Susanna Green, and Nov. 11, 1886, Mary A. Gordon; res. Shoreham, Vt., and Hermon, N. Y.

IV. BARNABAS, b. ——; m. Sally Stone.
V. CALEB, b. ——; m. Hannah Parker.
VI. PHILLIPPI, b. ——.
VII. NAOMI, b. ——.
VIII. MABEL, b. Feb. 11, 1792; m. at Potsdam, N. Y., Elijah Ames, b. Apr. 19, 1790; d. July 17, 1860, in Canton, N. Y. Ch., Philemon, b. June 11, 1811; d. July 2, 1881; Harrison, b. Aug. 21, 1813; m. Feb. 23, 1837, and Oct. 23, 1849; he d. Oct. 11, 1854; Almon, b. Oct. 4, 1815; d. Feb. 2, 1823; Naoma, b. June 5, 1817; m. Jan. 14, 1844, —— Ames; Thirman, b. Dec. 16, 1819; Julius, b. Mar. 7, 1821; m. Apr. 14, 1852; res. Canton, N. Y.; Orpha M., b. Apr. 27, 1822; Sarah L., b. June 19, 1824; m. 1845; d. May 4, 1879; Salmon, b. Mar. 27, 1826; d. Feb. 27, 1827; Bethana, b. Aug. 27, 1828; d. Dec. 20, 1842; Eurany, b. Feb. 27, 1830; d. May 14, 1831; Mary A., b. Oct. 4, 1834; res. Canton, N. Y.
73. IX. LIBBEUS, b. 1774; m. Vesta Bailey and Mariam Ames.
74. X. HOWARD J., b. June 18, 1775; m. Bridget House.

36. **Capt. Haywood[5] Pierce** (Benjamin[4], Benjamin[3], Benjamin[2], Michael[1]), b. June 22, 1753; m. Nov. 2, 1777, Judith Bailey, dau. of Amasa and Elizabeth (Bourn) Bailey. Res. Scituate, Mass. He d. Oct. 18, 1826. He was a rep. in 1792–1809–1812–3–4.

Hayward Pierce, Esq., late of Scituate, descended from Capt. Michael through Benjamin, who married Martha Adams, Benjamin, who married Mary Cowen and Elizabeth Perry, Benjamin, who married Charity Howard and Jane Howard of Bridgewater, 1742 and 1750, daughters of Thomas.

The sons of Hayward, Esq., were Hayward of New Orleans, Waldo and Bailey of Frankfort (Maine), Elijah of Scituate, on the paternal residence, Silas of Boston, and the daughters, the wives of William Lincoln of Cohassett, Nathaniel Cushing, and Walter Foster of Scituate. Benjamin and Jonathan, brothers of Hayward, Esq., removed to Chesterfield, Mass. [Hist. of Scituate.]

CHILDREN.

75.　　I. HAYWOOD, b. Mar. 24, 1782; m. ——.
76.　　II. WALDO, b Feb. 21, 1778; m. Catherine Treat.
77.　　III. BAILEV, b. Aug. 29, 1787; m. Ann Somerby and Eliza Tobey.
78.　　IV. ELIJAH, b. July 30, 1789; m. Rebecca Bailey and Lucy P. Litchfield.
79.　　V. SILAS, b. Feb. 15, 1793; m. Hannah Lopez.
　　　　VI. BECKEY, b. Apr. 3, 1785; m. Sept. 25, 1813, Wm. Lincoln; res. Cohassett, Mass.
　　　　VII. JANE, b. Dec. 14, 1780; m. Nov. 30, 1807, Nathaniel Cushing, b. Oct. 25, 1779; d. May, 1862; she d. May 19, 1838. Ch., Jane, b. Sept. 26, 1808; Nathaniel, b. Dec. 19, 1809; d. May, 1857; Haywood P., b. May 3, 1812; m. Maria Pierce; Nathan, b. May 29, 1814; m. Oct., 1863, Carrie E. Kelley; she d. Apr., 1864; res. Boston, Mass.
　　　　VIII. BETSEY, b. Nov. 25, 1795; m. Oct. 1, 1817, Walter Foster; res. Scituate, Mass. He was son of Dea. Elisha and Grace (Barstow) Foster, b. 1789.

37. **Caleb[5] Pierce** (Benjamin[4], Benjamin[3], Benjamin[2], Michael[1]), b. Aug. 7, 1755; m. Abigail Bailey, dau. of Amasa and Elizabeth (Bourn) Bailey. Res. Scituate, Mass.

CHILDREN.

　　　　I. CALEB, b. ——.

38. **Hon. Ezra[5] Pierce** (Benjamin[4], Ebenezer[3], Ebenezer[2], Michael[1]), b. Feb. 1, 1752; m. Rebecca ——, 1746; d. Apr. 4, 1821. Res. Westmoreland, N. H., d. Sept. 16, 1808. He was a deacon in the church; served several years as a selectman; was two years representative to the General Court, and two years a State senator.

CHILDREN.

  I. ELIZABETH, b. 1774; d. Mar. 20, 1823.
  II. REBEKAH, b. ——; m. Dec. 31, 1812, Zenas Veazey,
    and d. Sept. 1, 1843; res. Westmoreland, N. H.
  III. SALLY, b. Apr. 14, 1795; d. Feb. 16, 1798.
80. IV. ARTEMAS, b. July 10, 1779; m. Hannah Goodridge.
  V. LAWRENCE, b. ——.

39. **Nehemiah**[5] **Pierce** (Benjamin[4], Ebenezer[3], Ebenezer[2], Michael[1]), b. Dec. 2, 1759; m. Dec. 6, 1791, Phebe Lawrence, b. Oct. 17, 1755; d. Jan. 30, 1823. He d. Aug. 22, 1818. Res. Westmoreland, N. H., and 1813, rem. to Windham, Vt. He was in the Revolutionary war.

CHILDREN.

  I. NATHAN, b. Feb. 8, 1784; d. Sept. 22, 1798.
  II. LUCY, b. Nov. 17, 1785; m. May 30, 1804, Joseph
    Covey of Wardsboro, Vt. She d. Dec. 26, 1882.
    He was b. Oct. 11, 1775; d. Dec. 8, 1863. They
    had ten children.
82. III. EZRA, b. Dec. 6, 1788; m. Polly Farr.
83. IV. SEM, b. July 8, 1794; m. Lydia Moses, Joanna Brown,
    and Mrs. Myra Olds French.
  V. ROLAND, b. July 8, 1782; d. Aug. 4, 1783.
  VI. PHEBE, b. Feb. 10, 1792; d. May 28, 1815.
  VII. NEHEMIAH, b. Dec. 2, 1797; d. Sept. 30, 1798.

40. **Benjamin**[5] **Pierce** (Benjamin[4], Ebenezer[3], Ebenezer[2], Michael[1]), b. Feb. 13, 1761; m. Feb. 17, 1788, Lucinda Cobb, b. Oct. 11, 1768, d. June 3, 1858. He d. May 23, 1847. Res. Westmoreland, N. H., and Windham, Vt.

He was born in Westmoreland, N. H. During the Revolutionary war he served his country. Benjamin belonged to the Baptist church, and on several different occasions was a member of the State Legislature. A strong, successful man, he was respected by all who knew him.

CHILDREN.

I. ZILPHIA, b. Nov. 10, 1789; m. Oct. 5, 1813, Dr. John Butterfield, b. July 14, 1781; d. Oct. 15, 1827. She d. May 22, 1848; res. Grafton, Vt. Ch., Mary P., b. Aug. 27, 1815, d. Nov. 12, 1827; John Lewis, b. Aug. 29, 1820, m. Oct. 17, 1850, Jane Smith; res. Grafton. For many years he was engaged quite extensively in the business of quarrying soapstone at Cambridge, Vt. As early as 1844, when only 24, he was a delegate from Vermont to the convention which nominated Henry Clay for president. Since then he has filled various and many offices of trust and honor. Devotedly attached to his native State and town, he has served them faithfully in both branches of the State Legislature, s. p.; Sophia C., b. Aug. 24, 1826, m. Sept. 18, 1849, James Duncan; res. Boston, Mass.

II. MARY, b. Jan. 24, 1792; m. Jan. 24, 1822, Timothy Burton, b. July 25, 1786, d. Dec. 22, 1859. She d. Aug. 5, 1866. Res. Windham, Vt., and Iowa. Ch., Sarah, b. Dec. 9, 1822; d. Dec. 26, 1841; Lucinda C., b. Feb. 21, 1824; d. May 8, 1884; Dr. Elijah P., b. Jan. 8, 1826; m. Jan. 31, 1854, Harriet L. Caldwell; res. New York, Iowa; Maria, b. Oct. 9, 1827; m. Dec. 7, 1852, Henry Pierce, and d. Apr. 30, 1870; Mary P., b. July 14, 1829; d. Feb. 22, 1833; William B., b. Sept. 2, 1831; m. Sept. 22, 1858, Mary A. Upham; res. New York, Iowa; Orlando C., b. Sept. 27, 1833; m. Jan. 18, 1860, Mary W. Jennison, and Addie A. Congdon; res. Webster City, Iowa.

84. III. ALSON, b. June 21, 1794; m. Sylvia Corbin.

IV. BENJAMIN, b. Nov. 4, 1796; d. Oct. 17, 1804.

V. SARAH, b. Dec. 20, 1798; m. May 10, 1835, Simeon Barrett, b. Mar. 6, 1796; d. Jan. 22, 1876. She d. July 2, 1883. Res. Northampton, Mass. Ch.,

9

Argenette E., b. Aug. 21, 1836; m. May 18, 1862, Henry Jones; res. Northampton; Sarah L., b. Dec. 21, 1837; d. Feb. 18, 1838; Cortez P., b. Oct. 18, 1839; m. July 14, 1874, Julia V. Howe; d. June 23, 1886; res. West Townsend, Vt.

85.   VI. NATHAN, b. Mar. 1, 1801; m. Anna H. Burnap.
86.   VII. SINSON, b. Feb. 15, 1803; m. Dorcas Andrew.
      VIII. EUNICE, b. Apr. 7, 1805; m. Oct. 11, 1845, Liba Chapin, b. Aug. 17, 1794; d. Apr. 12, 1866. She d. Jan. 2, 1849. Res. Jamaica, Vt. Ch., Ellen A., b. June 30, 1846. A teacher in the public schools of Boston; res. Charlestown, Mass.; George P., b. Dec. 2, 1848; d. Sept. 21, 1851.
      IX. BENJAMIN M., b. Mar. 5, 1809; m. Nov. 4, 1868, Martha Howard. Res. South Windham, Vt., s. p.

41. **Ebenezer[5] Pierce** (Ebenezer[4], Ebenezer[3], Benjamin[2], Michael[1]), b. Rehoboth, Mass., Apr. 7, 1759; m. Keziah Butterfield, b. Aug. 28, 1761, at Harvard, Mass.; d. Aug., 1840. He d. Dec. 7, 1832. Res. Rehoboth, Mass., Westmoreland, N. H., and Wardsborough, Vt.

1752. June 4. Ebenezer Pierce of Rehoboth deeded to Samuel Darby, land in Rehoboth on south side of Cedar Swamp for £13 6s. 8d.

1752. Feb. 27. Ebenezer Pierce of Attleboro bought homestead of Ebenezer Saulsbury — 30 acres, bounded by Samuel Darby, Bullock, Briggs, &c.

1767. March 26. Ebenezer Pierce and his wife, Elizabeth, of Rehoboth, for 30 pounds convey to Timothy Bullock of Wrentham 20 acres and dwelling where they live. Same they bought of Saulsbury.

1767. May 7. Ebenezer Pierce of Rehoboth buys of Samuel Atherton of Attleboro, land and house on road leading from Nathan Willmarth to Noah Blandin's, 30 acres.

1772. Sept. 30. Ebenezer and wife Elizabeth deed the above to Dan Willmarth, for 170 pounds.

1790. June 1. Ebenezer Pierce, trader; Obediah Pierce, mariner; Lydia Chase, widow; Joshua Brown, mariner; Elizabeth, his wife; Mary Pierce, spinster, all of Somerset, and Sylvester Parry, Patience Parry of Dighton, deed land in Somerset, of which their late mother, Elizabeth Pierce, died seized, to their brother, David Pierce.

CHILDREN.

87.   I. LEMUEL, b. Jan. 6, 1781; m. Hannah ———.
88.   II. EBENEZER, b. Jan. 27, 1783; m. Julia Miller.
      III. ELIZABETH, b. May 25, 1786; d. Oct. 17, 1876, s. p.
89.   IV. ADOLPHUS, b. Oct. 19, 1789; m. Mehitable Wight.
      V. KEZIAH, b. Oct. 6, 1791; unm.

42. **Ezekiel[5] Pierce** (Ezekiel[4], Thomas[3], Benjamin[2], Michael[1]), b. abt. 1739; m. —— McCourter. Res. Scituate, Mass.

Ezekiel Pierce lived and died in Scituate, Mass. He was a teacher and made a specialty of instructing youths in the art of navigation, and fitting young men for seafaring life. At his time of life Scituate was a seafaring town and had quite a harbor for light vessels. He claimed descent from three brothers who came over from England. His wife died soon after the birth of his son Solon.

CHILDREN.

90.   I. SOLON, b. Dec., 1764; m. Betsey Jones.
      II. AUGUSTUS, b. ———; was in Revolutionary war, and last res. at Conhocton, N. Y.
      III. ROLLIN, b. ———; he was in the navy during the Revolutionary war, and d. at sea.
      IV. EZEKIEL, b. ———.
      V. LYDIA, b. ———.

43. **Capt. Thomas[5] Pierce** (Seth B.[4], Thomas[3], Benjamin[2], Michael[1]), b. Aug. 26, 1767; m. June 2, 1793, Anna Beales, b. Oct. 4, 1771; d. Feb. 28, 1827; m. 2nd, Jan. 23, 1833, Mrs. John Pierce, *nee* Mercy Merritt, b. Jan. 24, 1784; d. Apr. 4, 1838.

Capt. Thomas Pierce was born in Scituate, Mass., Aug. 26, 1767. The writer knows little of his early days, only that he was a sea-going man, and was probably master of some vessel or vessels, as he was accustomed to spin "sea yarns," and was familiar with foreign parts, thus it is presumed he came by the title of captain.

He married Anna Beal, but the date of his marriage is not at hand.*

The earliest child was born in 1796.

In November, 1800, he moved from Scituate to Durham, Maine, and was there a farmer, and was much employed in town affairs. He was land surveyor and conveyancer, and, in short, was the "squire" of that region.

A very long list of marriages in his handwriting, running from 1812 to 1831, shows that the marriage service was performed by him for many of the young men and maidens of that time.

His diary, which would have afforded much information about himself and the family, was lost, excepting two tiny pamphlets of a few pages each, written in the most delicate characters, without flourish or blot, and with the greatest economy of space. His account books of later date, familiar to many, exhibit the same characteristics, always bearing an aspect of extreme neatness.

February 28, 1827, his wife died in Durham, and January, 1833, he married in Scituate Mrs. Mercy Pierce (whose maiden name was Merritt), the widow of his brother John, and engaged in farming.

April 4, 1838, his second wife died in Scituate, and in 1839 he returned to Maine, and joined his son-in-law, James Booker, at "Little River" in Lisbon, in a business partnership, dealing in the usual variety of merchandise in a country store. The business was successful, but years began to tell on him, and in 1844 the partnership was terminated.

He continued to live in the family of this son-in-law, and died at his house June 21, 1850.

Captain Peirce was a member of the Masonic order, and was a careful and upright business man, respected wherever he was known.

---

* In Scituate town records, the *intentions* of marriage is dated June 2, 1793.

He had a vein of pleasant humor, and was intelligent and companionable.

The last one of his children (Mrs. Booker) having died just prior to the preparation of this sketch, much of interest, especially relating to his early years, is lost.

Res. Scituate, Mass., and Durham, Me.

CHILDREN.

I. SETH, b. June 3, 1796; d. Durham, Me., May 5, 1826.

II. LUCY B., b. June 30, 1798; m. Solomon Crossman. She d. Apr. 12, 1868. He d. Aug. 1, 1862; res. Lisbon, Me.; one son, Seth P., res. Lisbon Falls, Me.

III. EMILY, b. Dec. 30, 1804; m. Nov. 28, 1824, James Booker, b. Oct. 8, 1798; d. June 25, 1882. Res. Lisbon Falls, Me. Ch., Ira P., b. Nov. 28, 1832; m. Nov. 21, 1855, Clara W. Whittemore; res. Brunswick, Me.; Laura A., b. June 31, 1827; m. Jan. 4, 1851, Edmund Berry; res. Lisbon Falls, Me.

91. IV. IRA, b. Aug. 14, 1807; m. Phebe Stevens and Julia B. Townsend.

V. ANNA B., b. Apr. 3, 1806; m. Dec. 21, 1829, Joseph Moore, b. Dec. 3, 1803; d. Sept. 9, 1855. She d. Apr. 25, 1880. Res. Lisbon, Me. Joseph Moore, born in Newfield, Me., in 1803. He was one of triplets (the others, Asenith and Benjamin, died in infancy). I don't know month and day of birth, but will have it sent you.

Joseph Moore moved to Durham when a young man, and married there Anna B. Pierce, and was in trade there. He subsequently moved to Lisbon, and owned mills and lands and carried on both, and became prominent in Whig politics. His brothers were Democrats until the Republican party was formed, when two became Republicans.

He held town offices and chairman of board of selectmen eight years in succession, occasionally odd years. Was in the Maine Legislature as representative two years, I think (one certain). He

died at age of 51, Sept. 9, 1855. Was a very prominent man, of stern habits and character, about six
feet in height, dark; noted for the positiveness of
his nature.

Ch., Elvira D., b. Apr. 22, 1831; m. July 5,
1852, Julius M. Corbett; res. Lisbon, Me.; Eliza
J., b. Nov. 17, 1833; res. Auburn, Me.; Alonzo
P., b. Apr. 15, 1836; m. Albertina Curtice; res.
Boston, box 2517; Geo. B., b. Nov. 18, 1838;
res. Auburn, Neb.; Jos. E., b. Mar. 14, 1841; res.
Thomaston, Me.; Augustus, b. June 4, 1843; res.
S. Auburn, Neb.; Thos. A., b. Aug. 12, 1847;
res. Boston, address, box 2517.

Moore, Joseph E., Thomaston. Democrat, in
religion a member of the pulpit committee of the
Baptist church, and agent of Baptist parsonage;
lawyer, married; age 43. Born in Lisbon, educated at Westbrook Seminary and Maine State
Seminary (now Bates College), and graduated at
Bowdoin College, class '65. Closed his law partnership with A. P. Gould in 1878, when he went to
Europe and spent a year in study and travel, and
has practiced his profession in Thomaston since.
Member of school committee; was delegate to
Democratic National Convention at Cincinnati in
1880, and attended the National Democratic Convention at Chicago in 1884. Member of the House
in 1878 and 1883, the latter year member of commission on revision of the statutes. Always a
Democrat, and was Democratic candidate for
speaker, and was the one relied upon on that side
of the house.

Ella Maud Moore (wife of Joseph E.), born in
Warren, Me., July 22, 1849; moved to Thomaston,
Me., with her parents, December, 1851. Her father
was Samuel E. Smith, and graduated at Bowdoin
College, 1834, at the age of 17, and said to have
been the best classical scholar there. She is a
member of the Smith family of Wiscasset, Me.,
who were all prominent and furnished judges and
governors.

Mrs. Moore inherited from her father delicate health, and a literary taste. She was noted as a scholar and writer, and has written simply for amusement. Has published a book of poems, "Songs of Sunshine and Shadow." Wrote a story for *Youths' Companion*, and among some 7,000 competitors took first prize of $500 for best story for girls. This was the first story she ever wrote for publication. She has never written as a labor, but simply for her own amusement.

44. **Capt. Joseph[5] Pierce** (Seth B.[4], Thomas[3], Benjamin[2], Michael[1]), b. Apr., 1769; m. July 23, 1808, Sally Hatch. Res. Scituate and Boston, Mass.

CHILDREN.

I. JOSEPH, b. Mar. 27, 1809.

II. SALLY A., b. Mar. 21, 1811; d. June 30, 1822.

45. **Nathaniel[5] Pierce** (Seth B.[4], Thomas[3], Benjamin[2], Michael[1]), b. Feb. 7, 1773; m. Feb. 8, 1800, Winnet Otis, b. June 20, 1780; d. Sept. 3, 1804; m. 2nd, Sept. 27, 1806, Nabby Bailey, b. Dec. 31, 1778; d. Mar. 13, 1825; m. 3rd, Feb. 2, 1831, Sophia Briggs, b. Apr. 24, 1791. He d. Aug. 17, 1838. Res. Scituate, Mass.

CHILDREN.

I. OTIS, b. June 27, 1801; d. Scituate, July 7, 1861.

92. II. WILLIAM, b. Dec. 27, 1802; m. Sarah L. Willard.

93. III. MARTIN B., b. July 17, 1807; m. Mary E. Wellman.

IV. WINNETT O., b. Apr. 18, 1809; d. May 6, 1832.

V. ABIGAIL, b. Oct. 8, 1811; d. Apr. 14, 1858.

VI. NATHANIEL, b. June 28, 1814; d. Aug. 17, 1838.

VII. LOUISA, b. July 23, 1816; m. Albert Lane; res. Rockland, Mass.

94. VIII. JOHN B., b. July 22, 1832; m. Martha W. Litchfield.

46. **John[5] Pierce** (Seth B.[4], Thomas[3], Benjamin[2], Michael[1]), b. Oct. 29, 1776; m. Nov. 10, 1810, Mercy Merritt, b. Jan. 24,

1784; d. Apr. 4, 1838. He d. May 16, 1816, at sea. Res. Scituate, Mass.

CHILDREN.

95. I. JOHN W., b. Dec. 4, 1811; m. Mary A. Whiton.
96. II. HENRY T., b. Sept. 29, 1813; m. Ella A. Hulse and Mary E. Chapman.
97. III. JOSEPH D., b. Nov. 15, 1815; m. Martha S. Price.

47. **Calvin**[5] **Pierce** (Calvin[4], Elisha[3], Benjamin[2], Michael[1]), b. Mar. 16, 1782; m. July 9, 1807, Alice Otis. Res. Scituate, Mass.

CHILDREN.

   I. ALICE, b. Feb. 10, 1808.
  II. MERCY, b. Apr. 2, 1810.
 III. CALVIN, b. Mar. 6, 1812.
  IV. MARY L., b. Aug. 13, 1814.
   V. ANNA O., b. May 19, 1817.
  VI. ELISHA, b. Nov. 23, 1820.

48. **Mial**[5] **Pierce** (Mial[4], Mial[3], John[2], Michael[1]), b. 1752; m. Oct. 20, 1773, Mehitable Wheeler, b. 1755; d. 1800. He d. Mar., 1839. Res. Rehoboth and Swansey, Mass.

CHILDREN.

98.   I. MASON W., b. Sept. 1, 1794; m. Lucinda C. Davis.
      II. NOAH, b. Nov. 20, 1785. ⎱ *
     III. AARON, b. Nov. 20, 1785. ⎰
      IV. MIAL, d. unm.
99.   V. DARIUS, m. Mary Hapgood and Lucinda Walker.
      VI. MARY, m. Mar. 12, 1807, Edward Mason. She d. Mar., 1874; a son, Oliver, res. Nebraska City, Neb.
     VII. HOPESTILL, m. Nov. 26, 1797, John West; res. Ithaca, N. Y.
    VIII. MARY, m. —— Ware; res. Superior St., Car Ware, Providence, R. I.

---

* Both died of yellow fever on the Island of St. Thomas in the West Indies, in 1815, and both were sea captains.

49. **Asa**[5] **Pierce** (Mial[4], Mial[3], John[2], Michael[1]), b. Mar., 1761; m. Sept., 1785, Nancy Hathaway, b. Oct., 1763; d. Feb., 1842. He d. Mar., 1842. Res. Somerset, Mass.

CHILDREN.

100.   I. ISAAC, b. Oct. 11, 1790; m. Anna M. Chace.
101.   II. JOHN H., b. May 23, 1792; m. Content Bowen.
102.   III. ASA, b. Sept. 16, 1787; m. Theolotia Perrin.

50. **John**[5] **Pierce** (John[4], John[3], John[2], Michael[1]), b. Oct. 16, 1740; m. Oct. 30, 1783, Rebecca Snell. He d. Feb. 6, 1825. Res. Dighton, Mass.

CHILDREN.

    I. REBECCA, b. June 20, 1785; m. 1810, William Case, b. Mar. 11, 1785; d. Aug. 9, 1872, and res. in Cortland county, N. Y. Ch., Joseph, b. Nov. 29, 1812; m. Jan. 25, 1841; d. Sept. 11, 1865; Anthony, b. Sept. 19, 1814; m. Feb. 28, 1840; d. Apr. 5, 1863; Lorrina, b. Sept. 18, 1816; m. Feb. 28, 1840, Seth Shearer; res. McGrawville, N. Y.; Jane, b. June 3, 1820; m. May, 1842; d. Apr. 26, 1877.

    II. SALLY, b. Jan. 7, 1788.

103.   III. JOHN, b. Mar. 27, 1790; m. Alice Pitts.

    IV. LOVINA, b. May 13, 1792; m. Apr., 1812, Dea. Aaron Case, b. Aug. 6, 1788; d. Mar. 27, 1871. She d. Mar. 5, 1870. Ch., Frederick P., b. Feb. 18, 1813; m. Angeline Lewis; res. Dighton, Mass.; John, b. Apr. 27, 1815, unm.; res. Swansey, Mass.; Joseph, b. Apr. 15, 1817; m. Eliza Gray, res. Swansey, Mass.; Alfred, b. Apr. 27, 1820; m. Eleanor Macomber, and d. Oct. 5, 1862; Isaac, b. Apr. 25, 1823; m. Mercy Ann Kelton and Mrs. Hannah Wilmorth; res. 22 Marshall St., Providence, R. I.; Rebecca Jane, b. Nov. 10, 1830; m. Zenas Knapp, s. p.; res. 83 Spring St., Newport, R. I.; Rev. William, b. Dec. 27, 1832; m. Martha Dibble and Emily Allan; res. West Oneonta, Otsego Co., N.Y.

10

104. V. ANTHONY, b. July 16, 1795; m. Olive Lee and Deborah (Pierce) Brightman.

VI. NANCY, b. Apr. 30, 1797; m. Oct. 3, 1815, Stephen
Manchester; res. Dighton, Mass.; b. 1790; d.
Preble, N. Y., 1875. She d. 1872. Ch., Nancy,
b. 1818; m. Silas Baldwin; res. Tully, N. Y.;
Anthony Pierce, b. 1820; m. Evaline Trass; res.
Preble, N. Y.; David, b. 1822; d. 1824. Whit-
comb T., b. 1826; m. June 12, 1851, Lucelia G.
Burling, b. Nov. 13, 1837; d. Oct. 5, 1869, and
Emily Seber; res. Ogdensburg, Kansas; Ch.,
Frances E., b. Solon, N. Y., May 21, 1852; m.
May 31, 1876, Hon. John B. Finch; res. Evans-
ton, Ill.

Like many women of our land who have attained
influence and prominence in literary circles, on the
platform, and as leaders of charitable, missionary
and temperance work, Frances had but little to
depend upon in early life, in obtaining an education from books, save her own resources. The
premature death of her mother laid almost insur-
mountable obstacles in her pathway, but with that
energy characteristic of her life work, she obtained
sufficient education at the home district school and
by private study to become a teacher at the age of
nineteen. For five terms thereafter she taught
school in the vicinity of her home, took a course
of study in the Cortland State Normal School in
1875, and further prepared herself for the teacher's
vocation in the McGrawville Academy. In May,
1876, she was united in marriage to Hon. John B.
Finch. This event opened a new era before her,
and presented a wide and varied field of labor
seemingly suited to her ambition. From that time
until the death of Mr. Finch, her work was insep-
arably connected with that of her husband. She
joined the Good Templars soon after her marriage,
and for three years following traveled with her
husband, interested herself in temperance work,
and acquainted herself with many of the best

authors. In 1879 she was elected General Superintendent of Juvenile Temples of Nebraska, and during that year organized a number of temples. In 1880 she did some work in connection with the Woman Suffrage Reform, began the study of elocution, and gave many select readings and valuable papers and poems before appreciative audiences throughout the country. Encouraged in these endeavors, and desirous of making her efforts of greater value to others, she, in 1883, entered the School of Oratory, North-Western University, at Evanston, Ill., from which she was graduated in June, 1884. In 1886 Mrs. Finch extended the greeting of the world's Good Templars to the National W. C. T. U. Convention at Minneapolis, and during the past two years she has been officially connected with the Good Templars of the district of which Chicago is the center. Mrs. Finch is a woman of broad views and unprejudiced opinion. She possesses that versatility and adaptability to society and circumstances that well fit her for the great work of temperance reform. The death of her husband has placed upon her new and grave responsibilities, so that, in whatever field of labor she may be engaged, her many friends will follow her with their sympathies, and welcome her success in all her undertakings. [Written by Prof. R. J. Peck of Cortland, N. Y.]

The following sketch of the life of the late Hon. John B. Finch was prepared by his widow:

John B. Finch was born in Lincklaen, Chenango county, New York, March 17, 1852.

Frances E. Willard said: "He was the son of a mechanic, and the third boy in a family of eight children. He had the happy heritage of these hard conditions, obscurity and poverty; but, passing by the palace with its cradled princes, fortune paused within his humble home and emptied out her horn of plenty upon that royal head. The child was so ethereal, of a spirit so sportive, and an alertness so surprising, that they called him " Bird," and this was his only name until, at three years of age, he rebelled against it as not fit for a boy, and said,

"My name is John," to which he steadily adhered. We who now learn for the first time what B stood for in his name can see in it a prophecy of that multitudinous nature of which we were so proud, in which the flashing eagle of argument did not dismay the full-voiced nightingale of rhetoric or the winsome dove of pathos." At three years of age, John suffered a severe attack of scarlet fever, which caused a serious disease of the heart. He developed physical vigor so slowly that he was too fragile to endure the labors and restraints of the school-room, or the rude sports of the play-ground; he early learned to depend upon himself for amusement, and to find in the books his mother taught him to read, companionship which he always enjoyed. At the age of ten years, John began attending district school; but the foundation for his education had been laid by his loving mother's teaching, and the recitation was but a minor incident in the search for that knowledge which he was bound to win. Until he was twenty, all these years were occupied in the quietude of farm life among the rugged hills of Chenango county, with but few opportunities to learn of this great world and its mysteries. The rudiments of his education were obtained in the district school, academy and university. His great knowledge and broad culture were obtained from reading the best literature, and his study of nature, and inspiration from nature's God.

John began teaching in the common school when he was but fifteen years of age; he taught his last term when he was twenty-four. During that time he studied law and medicine, and did many kinds of work to pay for his education; often borrowed books of classmates and learned his lessons while "the boys were asleep." With patched clothes and ragged shoes, he carried off the prizes of the schools with inspired courage, as he rested under the benediction of his mother's words, "Johnnie, people will look at your head, not at your feet."

In 1871 John B. Finch and Kittie L. Coy were united in marriage; during the four years of their wedded life, they taught school and studied together. He guarded and protected her, loving her with all the strength of his boyhood. When silently the angels carried her home he stood by her lifeless body feeling that utter desolation which no language can express, no artist picture, no painter put upon canvas.

In March, 1876, Mr. Finch began active temperance work. The following May he was married to Miss Frances E. Manchester, at her home in McGrawville, N. Y. From 1876 to 1887 Mr. Finch was in public life, and his subsequent history is an open book that the world has read. In 1867 he joined the Good Templars; in the work of that order he won his first victories, and proved his great powers as an orator and organizer. He received his first recognition from the supreme officer in the Good Templars in 1876. The three years following Mr. Finch averaged more than one lecture each day, and thousands of people signed his iron-clad temperance pledge. In 1884 he was elected to the highest position in the international body of Good Templars, which position he held while he lived. When he was placed at the head of Good Templary, that body was divided into two great sections, but principally through his efforts, in 1887, the sections were united, and he was the leader of six hundred thousand Good Templars.

At Pittsburg, Pa., June, 1884, Mr. Finch was made chairman of the National Committee of the Prohibition party. He led that party through the struggle of '84, to triumphant victory. A party that had been growing slowly for about twelve years, with no organization in many of the States, unheard of by many people, through the leadership of John B. Finch, was thrown upon the political horizon and recognized in every home in this country as a mighty political factor.

The evening of October 3, 1887, at Lynn, Mass , John B. Finch delivered his last lecture, and before he reached the hotel, without a moment's warning, he entered eternity. At the early age of thirty-five, he had accomplished the work of a long life. He knew if he did not rest, heart failure was inevitable, but he said, "I will wear out, not rust out."

We close this sketch with a tribute from Joseph Cook:

"John B. Finch fell dead in Boston, which has seen many historic deaths; but since Warren, in his early manhood, fell at Bunker Hill, there is no death of a young man more pathetic than that of this reformer and hero. The soil of this city is henceforth the more sacred for having been an altar on which so costly a sacrifice was laid.

"So much fervor is rarely found combined with so much caution as his; so much impetuosity with so much gentleness; so much restlessness and daring with so much sagacity and patience. His speech was a mirror of his soul. His epigrams had marvelous force. His eloquence was a combination of thunderbolt and sunbeam. He was a prophetic ray of the dawn of a better age than ours, which will place his name among the jewels of its morning stars."

Sarah Lavina, b. 1828, m. Elisha B. Crosby; res. Preble, N. Y.; Olivia Jane, b. 1831, m. Abraham H. Hollenbeck; res. Ness, Kansas; Edgar, b. 1833, d. 1833; William Allen, b. 1837; m. Eliza Chair and ——; Amanda, b. 1839, m. Melvin Burlingham; res. Cortland, N. Y.

105.   VII. Gamaliel, b. Dec. 15, 1799; m. Persis Baker.

        VIII. Simeon Burt, b. Mar. 12, 1802; lost at sea, Sept. 3, 1821.

        IX. Polly, b. Apr. 12, 1804; d. June 2, 1804.

51. **Bethuel[5] Pierce** (Elisha[4], John[3], John[2], Michael[1]), b. 1754; m. Sybil Phillips, b. Dec. 16, 1757; d. Apr. 25, 1841. He d. Dec. 15, 1827. Res. Freetown, Mass.

Children.

106.   I. Bethuel, b. Aug. 6, 1784; m. Elizabeth Goff.

107.   II. Nathan, b. Nov. 20, 1794; m. Mary A. Chase.

       III. Hampton, b, Mar. 6, 1786; d. Sept. 7, 1854.

IV. ARNOLD, b. May 21, 1787 ; d. Nov. 25, 1840; res.
Berkley, Mass.

V. SYBIL, b. Feb. 14, 1782; m. 1804, Ezra Bliss, b. June
17, 1780; d. May 11, 1857. She d. July 18, 1858;
res. Rehoboth, Mass. He was a justice of the
peace for fourteen consecutive years. Ch., Pascha,
b. Dec. 2, 1805; d. Dec., 1805 ; George E., b. Feb.
27, 1807 ; d. May 11, 1879; Caroline M., b. Sept.
16, 1808; d. June, 1850; Lucina W., b. Nov. 30,
1810; m. Squire Goff; Ezra L., b. Oct. 24, 1812 ;
d. Dec. 13, 1836; Julina, b. June 8, 1815 ; m. Geo.
C. Pierce (see); Nathan P., b. Jan. 19, 1817; d.
Apr. 22, 1863; Mary I., b. May 29, 1819; d. Apr.
14, 1863; Martha D., b. Dec. 15, 1822; m. Francis
Moore; res. Bristol, R. I.; Francis A., b. Mar. 26,
1829; m. Rachel H. Goff; res. Taunton, Mass.

108. VI. GEORGE, b. Dec. 24, 1792 ; m. Lucinda Chace, Melitta
Chace and Betsey M. Hathaway.

109. VII. JOHN, b. July 9, 1798; m. Lydia Clark.

VIII. ABIGAIL, b. Dec. 21, 1801; d. ——, R. I.

52. Elisha[5] Pierce (Elisha[4], John[3], John[2], Michael[1]), b. 1746;
m. Elizabeth Kane, b. 1747; d. 1840. He d. 1839. Res. Dighton,
Mass., Providence, R. I., and Taunton, Mass.

CHILDREN.

I. HANNAH, b. July 23, 1768; m. 1786, Abial Farring-
ton, b. July 12, 1765 ; d. Feb. 9, 1853. She d.
Oct. 10, 1849. Ch., Abial, b. Apr. 1, 1789; d.
Nov. 1, 1871, in Brattleboro, Vt.; Hannah, b.
Nov. 4, 1791; m. Perley Sherman ; d. Springfield,
Mass., July 23, 1880.

110. II. SUBBINUS, b. Jan. 12, 1772 ; m. Elsie Ballou.

III. MERRIBAY, b. May 15, 1776; m. George Shores; res.
Taunton. (?)

IV. ELIZABETH, b. Feb. 13, 1770 ; m. Peter Harvey and
Josiah Perry ; res. Brimfield, Mass. She d. 1856.

They moved to Freetown, N. Y. It was near the Catskill mountains, forty miles from Canajoharie, where they had to go two miles on horseback. At the death of her husband, being left with the farm and six children, she soon came back, bought a farm in Brimfield, Mass., and with the help of her boys carried it on. She done her own spinning and weaving; her house always in perfect order, she had time to spin and weave for others. While at Freetown the bears used to often come near the house. One night her husband having gone to mill she saw one in a tree near the house. Dressing herself and boys to spend the night, she built a fire and kept the bear until her husband came in the morning. She was called very courageous after that. She was always happy, thoughtful of all around her. She had such a love for fun that one had to laugh, if with her long. She was eighty-seven years old when she died, but her mind was just the same.

V. NANCY, b. Feb., 1774; m. 1795, Richard Sanderson; d. May, 1796. She d. Nov. 18, 1859; res. Providence, R. I. Ch., William B., b. Feb. 2, 1796; m. Ruth A. Allen; res. New Bedford.

In 1886, a New Bedford newspaper said: " Yesterday was the ninetieth birthday of Mr. William B. Sanderson of this city, and during the day and evening his children and their children's children to the fourth generations, besides friends, called on him to extend their congratulations and speak words of cheer to the aged gentleman, and he was substantially remembered by them also. Mr. Sanderson enjoys very good health for a person of his age and retains his faculties to a remarkable degree. He was much pleased to receive the callers, and seemed to take delight in speaking of the scenes of his younger days. His wife, Mrs. Ruth A. Sanderson, who has been blind for some twenty-five years, also enjoys pretty good health, and the aged couple are living in the house built by him many years ago. They have five children, fifteen grandchildren and thirteen great grandchildren living.

VI. MARY, b. May 21, 1780; m. Samuel Phillips. She d.
    1844. He d. Jan. 22, 1853; res. Taunton, Mass.

VII. WELTHY, b. Apr. 20, 1778; m. Sulvanus Macomber;
    d. Mar. 6, 1859. She d. May 11, 1859; res. Taunton, Mass.

111. VIII. ELIPHALET, b. June 3, 1782; m. Anise Mitchell.

IX. SARAH, b. Oct. 9, 1784; m. —— Pettes.

X. ELISHA, b. Apr. 14, 1787; m. and d. 1842 in the South.

XI. PELEG, b. Feb. 12, 1789.

> Peleg went to Canada and married there, but in
> the war of 1812 had to leave in the night. They
> had to leave so that none of the neighbors would
> suspect. They built up a large fire, set the table
> and had their supper cooking. They crossed the
> river each in a canoe, and went to Brimfield, Mass.
> A writer says about him, that he came to her
> father's, and she remembers what a handsome man
> he was. They had one child, his name was Emery
> and he was drowned. They must have gone back
> after the war, as no one seems to remember them.

XII. MARY, b. Sept. 20, 1792; m. Samuel Phillips. He
    d. Jan. 22, 1853. She d. Oct. 6, 1844.

53. **Daniel**[5] **Pierce** (Clothier[4], Clothier[3], John[2], Michael[1]), b.
1746; m. Feb. 13, 1773, Mary Hix of Rehoboth, b. 1748; d. 1844.
He d. in Castile, N. Y., in 1839. Res. Rehoboth, Mass., Vermont,
Ogdensburg and Castile, N. Y.

CHILDREN.

112.
    I. ISAAC, b. Nov. 14, 1776; m. Elizabeth Taylor.

    II. PATIENCE, b. ——; m. Jerry Comstock.

    III. DYER, b. ——.

    IV. HULDAH, b. ——; m. Samuel Havens, b. Mar. 27,
        1785. He was murdered on the Ogdensburg, N.
        Y., bridge by three Irishmen, Brields, Raney and
        Abby, who were hung. Ch., Nelson, b. Aug. 6,
        1811; res. Henry, Dakota; Horace, Samuel, Geo.
        W., Jay and Clarissa.

11

V. POLLY, b. ——; m. James Carr.
VI. TRUMAN, b. ——; m. Lucy Harris; a daughter res.
in E. Delavan, Wis.
VII. MIAL, b. ——.
113. VIII. DANIEL, b. Jan. 17, 1793; m. Levina Clark.
IX. CLARISSA, b. ——; m. Charles Jurtince.

54. **Clothier⁵ Pierce** (Clothier⁴, Clothier³, John², Michael¹),
b. 1753; m. June 24, 1781, Chloe Chace, b. 1756; d. 1816. He
d. 1813. Res. Dartmouth, Mass.

CHILDREN.

114.   I. CLOTHIER, b. Sept. 4, 1784; m. Bethia C. Cleveland.
II. One other child, a son, who died young.

55. **Barnabas C.⁵ Pierce** (Daniel⁴, Samuel³, John², Michael¹),
b. Sept. 30. 1792; m. May 1, 1819, Nancy P. Wildman, b. Feb. 5,
1803; d. Apr. 2, 1885. He d. Sept. 12, 1878. Res. Sparta, Ohio.

Barnabas Carver Pierce was born in the year 1792, in the county
of Putnam, State of New York. Was raised a farmer. At the call
to defend the country in the war of 1812, he was among the number that fought bravely to sustain the American flag, for which service he drew a pension until the time of his death. At the age of
28, he was married to Nancy P. Wildman, daughter of Eld. Wildman of the State of Connecticut. In 1820 emigrated to Ohio;
endured all the hardships of a pioneer life, was a Baptist in principle, and peacefully fell asleep Sept. 12, 1878.

CHILDREN.

115.   I. THOS. Q., b. Dec. 26, 1820; m. Fidelia Watrous.
II. NATHAN W., b. Mar. 10, 1825; d. Mar. 13, 1825.
III. MARY E., b. May 12, 1823; d. infant.
IV. PERRY N., b. Dec. 5, 1827; m. in 1864; a doctor,
and res. in Andrews, Ohio.
V. BETSEY Q., b. Apr. 1, 1831; m. Sept. 20, 1865, Rev.
Jas. Webster. She d. Aug. 20, 1868. Ch., Chever,
b. July 25, 1866; Ida S., b. Aug. 12, 1868; m. ——
Sharp; res. Galion, Ohio.

117.   VI. DANIEL H., b. Aug. 1, 1837 ; m. Mariah Hartman.
116.   VII. Columbus D., b. Nov. 1, 1839 ; m. Hortense Price.

55¼. **Abizer⁵ Pierce** (Daniel⁴, Samuel³, John², Michael¹), b.
Dec. 1, 1779 ; m. Jane Hopkins, b. Dec. 1, 1777.

CHILDREN.

118.   I. EDWARD H., b. Apr. 13, 1803 ; m. Betsey Field.
There were five other children, but all are now
gone.

55½. **Jonathan⁵ Pierce** (Daniel⁴, Samuel³, John², Michael¹), b.
1781; m. Betsey Crossman.   Res. Putney, N. Y.

CHILDREN.

I. PHEBE J., m. and res. Monticello, N. Y.
II. HENRY, b. Mar. 9, 1809 ; m. Dec. 12, 1835, Salome
M. Badeau, b. June 9, 1818 ; res. s. p., Putney,
N. Y.
III. BETSEY A., m. —— Halstead; res. Newburgh, N. Y.
IV. DANIEL.
V. MARIA, d. ——.
VI. HANNAH, m. Albert Scott.   She d. 1840 ; res. New-
burgh, N. Y.
VII. JOHN.
VIII. CATHERINE, b. 1825 ; m. Lewis Tenney.   She d.
Nov. 1, 1885 ; res. Carmel, N. Y.
IX. HATTIE M., d. ——.
X. WILLIAM, b. ——.

55¾. **William⁵ Pierce** (Daniel⁴, Samuel³, John², Michael¹), b.
Feb. 22, 1783; m. Feb. 4, 1813, Elizabeth Badeau, b. Oct. 10,
1787; d. Dec. 17, 1858. He d. Dec. 13, 1858. Res. Carmel,
N. Y.

CHILDREN.

I. WILLIAM H., b. Dec. 8, 1813 ; d. unm., Mar. 6, 1863.
120.   II. ISAAC B., b. Apr. 29, 1816 ; m. Mary J. Hazleton.

III. CORDELIA R., b. Mar. 13, 1821; m. Nov. 1, 1860,
   John H. Badeau, b. Feb. 28, 1808; res. s. p., Mahopac Falls, N. Y.

IV. SUSANNAH, b. Mar. 27, 1818; d. Oct. 5, 1820.

V. HANNAH H., b. Apr. 7, 1823; m. Oct. 24, 1843, John
   J. H. Jackson, d. 1845; m. 2nd, 1855, Rev. Jos.
   C. Foster. He d. s. p., 1860. Ch., Catherine E.,
   b. Nov. 24, 1844; m. Joshua F. Dean.

56. **Azrikim**[5] **Pierce** (Samuel[4], Azrikim[3], Ephraim[2], Mi-
chael[1]), b. May 27, 1723; m. Nov. 6, 1751, Bethsheba Millerd, d.
Oct. 19, 1765; m. 2nd, May 6, 1766, Sarah Bliss, b. Nov. 28, 1732.
His estate was probated Nov. 27, 1775. His wife Sarah was
admr. Oct. 20, 1776; the widow Sarah was appointed guardian to
Abraham, Pardon and Isaac, minors. He d. Nov., 1775. Res.
Rehoboth, Mass.

CHILDREN.

121. I. JOHN, b. July 31, 1756; m. Mary Gilmore.
     II. ISRAEL, b. May 22, 1754; res. Providence, R. I.; a
         tailor. (See Prov. records.)
122. III. SQUIRE, b. Aug. 27, 1758; m. Freelove Wood and
         Betsey Goff.
123. IV. JOSEPH, b. Dec. 15, 1752; m. Freelove Wood.
      V. RUTH, b. Oct. 18, 1756; m. Nathan Pierce. (?)
     VI. BETHSHEBA, b. Apr. 15, 1763; d. young. (?)
    VII. AZRIKIM, b. Oct. 9, 1765; d. young. (?)
   VIII. PARDON, b. ——; m. Susan West, and had Chester,
         Mary, Frank and Alice.
124. IX. ABRAHAM, b. Feb. 18, 1770; m. Lavina Stoddard and
         Eliza Wood.
      X. ISAAC, b. 1761; m. in Newport, R. I., Mar. 14, 1785,
         Sarah Bliss, b. 1764; d. Sept. 22, 1799, the dau. of
         Henry. He d. Nov. 21, 1788, in Newport, R. I.
         Ch., Mary, b. Feb. 4, 1786; Isaac, b. June 30, 1788.
         Both are buried in the Bliss burying-ground in
         Newport, R. I.

57. **Azrikim**[5] **Pierce** (Benjamin[4], Azrikim[3], Ephraim[2], Michael[1]), b. ——; m. Feb. 13, 1763, Lois Warner, dau. of William Warner, formerly of Warwick, R. I. She died and he married again. Res. Warwick, R. I., and ——.

CHILDREN.

126.   I. BENJAMIN, b. ——; m. Sarah Carpenter.
127.   II. JARED, b. 1765; m. Elsa Gorton.
       III. WILLIAM, b. ——.
       IV. LOIS, b. ——; m. Russell Warren of Otsego, N. Y.

57b. **Joseph**[5] **Pierce** (Isaac[4], Azrikim[3], Ephraim[2], Michael[1]), b. 1725; m. Oct. 8, 1747, Susannah Newcomb, b. 1725; d. before 1801. He d. 1803. Res. Welfleet, Mass. His will was dated Aug. 11, 1801, and proved Aug. 9, 1803.

Rich's History of Truro. — The brig Resolution, an American privateer, was taken by an English vessel Nov. 20, 1770, and her crew committed to old Mill Prison Jan. 22, 1771. Among the crew was Joseph Pierce of Welfleet. The following were his only children and his wife was then dead.

CHILDREN.

127[1].   I. JOSEPH, b. Nov. 10, 1759; m. Joanna Young.
127[2].   II. ISAAC, b. May 13, 1754; m. Drusilla Cole.
       III. MARTHA, b. 1749; m. Oct. 20, 1768, Nathaniel Rider.
       IV. THANKFUL, b. 1751; m. Nov. 13, 1767, Noah Sweet.

57c. **Joshua**[5] **Pierce** (Isaac[4], Azrikim[3], Ephraim[2], Michael[1]), b. abt. 1707; m. July 24, 1729, Elizabeth Newcomb, b. 1708.

Elizabeth was the daughter of Thomas Newcomb, who was born in Kittery, Me., in 1668, and m. in 1693, Elizabeth Cook. They first resided in the north part of Eastham. His name is on the petition from the inhabitants of North Eastham in 1723. He d. 1760. Res. Eastham, Mass.

CHILDREN.

127a.   I. SAMUEL, b. 1730; m. Vashti Cole and Mercy Ryder.

II. DAU. b. ——; m. Eleazer Atwood.

127b.　III. JOSHUA, b. abt. 1740 ; m. Thankful —— and Hepsibeth ——.

58. **Nathaniel[5] Pierce** (Joseph[4], Azrikim[3], Ephraim[2], Michael[1]), b. July 9, 1735; m. June 24, 1756, Sarah Pierce, b. 1733; d. May 3, 1800; m. 2nd, ——, b. 1754; d. May 11, 1822. He d. Feb. 26, 1821. Res. Rehoboth, Mass.

CHILDREN.

128.　I. NATHAN, b. 1756; m. Rhoda Giles.
129.　II. JONATHAN, m. Rebecca Giles and Betsey Bowen.
　　III. SARAH, b. Sept. 6, 1759.
　　IV. LYDIA, b. Aug. 2, 1763.
130.　V. AARON, b. Sept. 20, 1765; m. Elipha Bliss and Nancy Rounds.
131.　VI. NATHANIEL, b. Nov. 30, 1766; m. Rachel Moulton.
　　VII. ISRAEL.

59. **Stephen[5] Pierce** (Joseph[4], Azrikim[3], Ephraim[2], Michael[1]), b. Aug. 7, 1739; m. Mar. 20, 1758, Anna Wheeler, b. Oct. 15, 1737 ; d. June, 1824. She was daughter of James Wheeler. He d. Jan. 28, 1805. His will was proved Mar. 5, 1805. Calvin Pierce was executor. The witnesses to the instrument were Jonathan Hix, Simeon Bliss and David Perry, Jr. Res. Rehoboth, Mass.

CHILDREN.

I. RUTH, b. Dec. 7, 1758 ; m. Dec. 9, 1780, James Bunt.
II. MARY, b. Aug. 23, 1760; d. young, Rehoboth, Mass.
III. ZILPHA, b. Sept. 15, 1762; m. Solomon Garry ; res. Cabot, Vt. She d. May 17, 1830. Ch., Burt, res. Cabot; Eli P., m. Sarah A. Bartlett.
IV. ANNA, b. Jan. 1, 1764; m. June 4, 1792, Capt. Jonathan Walker ; res. Rehoboth and Dighton, Mass. He was in Capt. Elijah Walker's company, and went to Rhode Island, Dec. 1, 1776, 16 days. He was afterward a corporal, and went to Tiverton,

Aug. 2, 1780. Ch., Robert, b. Dec. 10, 1792; m. Oct. 6, 1816, Lydia, dau. of Elder Sylvester Rounds of Rehoboth; rem. to Allen, N. Y., in 1820, and d. in Placer Co., Col., Dec. 16, 1850; they had ten ch.; Polly, b. Sept. 21, 1794; m. Mar. 6, 1811, Sylvester Rounds; res. Angelica, N. Y., and had thirteen ch.; Joseph, b. Jan. 2, 1800, m. Aug. 9, 1823, Emergency Rounds, sister of Robert's wife and Polly's husband; res. Hickory Grove, Grant Co., Wis., and had seven ch.; Abigail, m. Jacob Ostrander, and d. 1856, Grant Co., Wis.

V. STEPHEN, b. June 24, 1766; m. Mrs. Mary Sloan Southwick, and d. 1841; res. East Calais, Vt. She d. Feb. 26, 1878, æ. 90 y. 4 m. and 16 d. Ch., Joseph W., b. July 6, 1816; m. June 2, 1847, Miranda Goodenough, b. Mar. 12, 1823. He d. Sept. 20, 1878. Ch., Joseph B., b. Jan. 7, 1848; m. Mar. 4, 1876, Clarissa A. Blake, b. Apr. 16, 1845; res. Lower Cabot, Vt. Ch., Vera W., b. Mar. 2, 1877; Archie B., b. Feb. 19, 1880; d. Oct. 6, 1881; Flora L., b. Feb. 11, 1851; d. Sept. 7, 1864; Melvin W., b. Sept. 2, 1852; m. Nov. 23, 1873; res. W. Medford, Mass.

132.   VI. BACKUS, b. Mar. 13, 1768; m. Lucy Goodenough.
133.   VII. ASAHEL, b. Apr. 7, 1771; m. Clarissa Peck.
134.   VIII. NOAH, b. Jan. 26, 1773; m. Ruth Gerry.
       IX. MARTHA, b. Apr. 22, 1775; m. Abijah Commins, and d. 1823.
135.   X. CALVIN, b. Dec. 2, 1780; m. Constant Bulroomb.
       XI. ROBA, b. Feb. 5, 1783; d. unm., Apr. 16, 1865.

60. **Noah**[5] **Pierce** (Joseph[4], Azrikim[3], Ephraim[2], Michael[1]), b. Feb. 11, 1752; m. Sept. 4, 1774, Patience Rounds, b. ——; d. ——; m. 2nd, Oct. 2, 1796, Elizabeth Hail, b. ——; d. ——; m. 3rd, Apr., 1813, Sabary Wood, b. ——. He d. Mar. 16, 1829. Res. Rehoboth, Mass., and Bristol, R. I.

CHILDREN.

     I. REUBEN, b. Aug. 5, 1775; d. young.

136.   II. NOAH, b. Feb. 26, 1776; m. Betsey Besagade.

137.   III. APPOLLOS, b. Apr. 6, 1779; m. Hannah Brown.

138.   IV. PEREZ, b. June 24, 1789; m. ——.

     V. ROBY, b. ——.

     VI. RACHEL, b. ——.

     VII. LAVINA, b. ——.

    VIII. WILLIAM H., b. 1799.

     IX. BETSEY, b. 1797; m. —— Mason; res. Warren, R. I., and d. May 2, 1871, Swansey, Mass.

     X. MARY, b. ——; m. —— Butterworth.

     XI. CLARISSA, b. ——; m. —— Bishop. She d. in Barrington.

61. **Joseph⁵ Pierce** (Joseph⁴, Azrikim³, Ephraim², Michael¹), b. Dec. 5, 1759; m. Dec. 2, 1779, Mary Pierce, who d. s. p.; m. 2nd, Jan. 30, 1811, Mrs. Lydia (Pierce) Horton, b. 1781; d. Sept. 3, 1824. He d. July 20, 1840. Res. Rehoboth, Mass.

CHILDREN.

     I. MARY A., b. Sept. 11, 1811; m. Oct. 30, 1830, Peleg F. Walker, b. Dec. 11, 1803; d. Feb. 27, 1858; res. Taunton, Mass. Ch., Mary A. F., b. Oct. 27, 1831; m. Chas. H. Briggs; res. Taunton, Mass.; Samantha J., b. Apr. 1, 1838; m. Alex. H. Root and —— Swan; res. Bristol, R. I.; Lydia B., b. Mar. 3, 1840; m. Geo. D. Cowen; res. Taunton; Betsey J., b. July 14, 1843; m. Richard L. Hewett; res. Taunton.

139.   II. JOSEPH H., b. Dec. 29, 1813; m. Rachael P. Jones.

     III. LYDIA M., b. July 23, 1817; m. July 3, 1835, Nelson D. Baker, b. June 19, 1816; res. 18 Pleasant St., Providence, R. I. Ch., Chas. W., b. Dec. 6, 1836; m. Philma Rathburn; Edwin G., b. June 8, 1839; m. Maggie Dean; Jos. W., b. June 17, 1843;

m. Julia Weaver; Geo. E., b. Oct. 17, 1847; m.
Ruth 'A. Burney; Saml. D., b. July 2, 1855; m.
Minnie Lee.

IV. JAMES L., b. Mar. 13, 1825; m. Aug. 16, 1840, Sarah
M. Bryant, b. Feb. 1, 1820, s. p. He is a clergyman ; res. Rehoboth, Mass.

62. **Wheeler**[5] **Pierce** (Mial[4], Ephraim[3], Ephraim[2], Michael[1]),
b. July 11, 1714; m. Apr. 8, 1737, Elizabeth Allen. Res. Swansey, Mass., and Scituate, R. I. In 1760, Wheeler Pierce, then of
Scituate, R. I., deeded 89 acres of land to his brother, Capt. Mial
Pierce of Swansey, Mass.

CHILDREN.

140.   I. WHEELER, b. ——; m. Mrs. Elizabeth Bosworth.

63. **Rev. Nathan**[5] **Pierce** (Mial[4], Ephraim[3], Ephraim[2], Michael[1]), b. Feb. 21, 1716; m. Oct. 6, 1736, Lydia Martin, b. July
17, 1718; d. Dec. 21, 1798. She was a daughter of Ephraim
Martin, and "a remarkably smart woman." He d. Apr. 14, 1793.
She was from Barrington, R. I. Lydia Martin was a short, black-
eyed, round-faced, handsome woman, who was noted for her
learning and the assistance she gave her husband. They res.
Rehoboth and Swansey, Mass. His will was proved June 4, 1793.
Hezekiah Martin was executor, Stephen Bullock, Judith Martin
and Freelove Horton, witnesses. Her will was proven Jan. 18,
1798. The witnesses were Nathaniel Miller, Jacob Saunders and
Hezekiah Martin; the latter was also executor. He spelt his name
Perce, and she Pierce. He was a Baptist minister, and for forty
years he preached in one church. He was succeeded by his son,
Rev. Preserved, who also preached in the same pulpit for forty
years. The meeting-house is still standing, and is now known as
the Pierce meeting-house. Elder Daniel Martin, son of Dea.
Melatiah, was born in Swansey, Sept. 23, 1702, and was ordained
pastor of Pierce or the Second Baptist Church in Rehoboth, Feb.
8, 1753. This church at first consisted of between thirty and forty
members under the pastoral care of Elder Martin; a few years

after Nathan Pierce was ordained, his colleague, Elder Martin, d. Nov. 18, 1781, æ. 79.

CHILDREN.

I. FREELOVE, b. Oct. 8, 1742; m. July 29, 1764, Lt. James Horton. He was in the Revolutionary war.

141. II. NATHAN, b. Jan. 22, 1745; m. Sarah Davis.

142. III. BENJAMIN, b. Jan. 29, 1747; m. Content Luther and Fanny ——.

143. IV. PARDON, b. Oct. 23, 1749; m. —— and Elizabeth ——.

V. MARY, b. Mar. 23, 1750; m. Dec. 23, 1770, Dea. Hezekiah Martin, b. Rehoboth, Mass., Mar. 22, 1748. He was ordained a deacon. Representative from Rehoboth to the General Court in the years 1812–3. He resided on the same farm on Rock river, where his father and grandfather had lived before him, and which is now in the possession of his grandson. He d. Nov. 16, 1834; she d. Sept. 22, 1827; res. Rehoboth, Mass. Ch., Huldah, b. Sept. 8, 1771; m. Jonathan Martin of Swansey; Gideon, b. Apr. 19, 1773; lost on the coast of Africa, a sailor, d. s. p., Jan. 11, 1800; Lydia, b. Mar. 25, 1775; m. July 27, 1794, Jacob Sanders; Hannah, b. Feb. 12, 1777; m. Jenks Wheeler and James Sanders; Hezekiah, b. Mar. 25, 1779; m. Patience Mason and Emily Ann Mason; Pearcy, b. Oct. 23, 1780; m. Cromwell Horton; Ambrose, b. Nov. 29, 1782; m. Phebe Martin and Polly Miller; Polly, b. Feb. 24, 1785; m. Silas Bailey; Luther, b. May 21, 1787; m. Nancy Wheeler; Darius, b. Oct. 26, 1789; m. Hannah Horton; Angier, b. Apr. 21, 1795; m. Sarah Simmons.

144. VI. MARTIN, b. Feb. 15, 1752; m. Keziah Wheeler.

VII. JUDAH, b. Oct. 23, 1754; m. Dec. 1, 1782, Nehemiah Cole. She d. in Bristol, R. I., July 17, 1806.

VIII. HEZEKIAH, b. Jan. 25, 1755; rem. to Vermont.

145. IX. PELEG, b. Nov. 15, 1756; had many wives.

146. X. PRESERVED, b. July 28, 1758; m. Sarah Lewis and Nancy Cushing.

147. XI. ISAAC, b. Sept. 22, 1763; m. Ann Fitch, Polly Bowen and Elizabeth Carpenter.

    XII. CHLOE, b. Nov. 18, 1765; m. Jan. 18, 1787, Darius Bullock; res. Rehoboth, Mass. He was the son of Judge Bullock of Rehoboth. Soon after their marriage they moved to Smithfield, Pa., and had five children, Dr. Darius and Jesse; Chloe, m. —— Johnson; Lydia, m. James Martin; Eunice, m. —— Niles; res. Halifax, Vt.

    XIII. LYDIA, b. Apr. 1, 1741; d. bef. 1793. Not mentioned in father's will.

148. XIV. DAVID, b. Apr. 11, 1739; m. Mary ——.

    XV. JOSEPH, b. Sept. 7, 1746; d. bef. 1793; not mentioned in father's will.

64. **Capt. Mial[5] Pierce** (Mial[4], Ephraim[3], Ephraim[2], Michael[1]), b. Mar. 24, 1722; m. Elizabeth, b. ——; d. ——; m. 2nd, Nov. 6, 1740, Patience Martin, b. 1718; d. Aug. 12, 1770. He d. Mar. 15, 1792. Res. So. Rehoboth, Mass., near Hornbine Meeting-House.

65. **Lt. Jobe[5] Pierce** (Mial[4], Ephraim[3], Ephraim[2], Michael[1]), b. Apr. 25, 1723; m. Abigail Pratt, dau. of Dr. Micah of Taunton, Mass., b. Nov. 28, 1725; d. May 3, 1813. He d. Oct. 4, 1791. Res. Rehoboth, Mass.

CHILDREN.

149.   I. JOBE, b. Aug. 7, 1753; m. Hannah Bullock.

    II. ISAAC, b. ——.

    III. JOHN, b. ——.

150.   IV. SAMUEL, b. ——; m. Phebe ——.

66. **Caleb[5] Pierce** (Mial[4], Ephraim[3], Ephraim[2], Michael[1]), b. Jan. 8, 1726; m. Mar. 20, 1748, Mary Rowland. His will is dated Aug. 19, 1775, and proved June 30, 1776. Witnesses, John West, Susanna Burt, and David Pierce. His wife Mary was executor. He d. 1776. Res. Rehoboth and Swansey, Mass.

CHILDREN.

151.   I. SYLVESTER, b. 1749; m. Patience Wheeler.
        II. LYDIA, m. —— Horton.
        III. JOHN.
        IV. REUBEN, res. Providence, R. I.
152.   V. CALEB, b. 1753; m. Mercy Wheeler.
        VI. SIMEON, m. and res. Hall's Hollow, N. Y.
        VII. MARY.
        VIII. LEVI, res. Buffalo, N. Y. He had two sons, Allen
and Dr. Reuben, who rem. to New Buffalo, Mich.

67. **Joshua⁵ Pierce** (Mial⁴, Ephraim³, Ephraim², Michael¹),
b. ——; m. Mar. 24, 1748, Mary Horton. Res. Rehoboth and
Swansey, Mass.

CHILDREN.

154.   I. SHUBAL, m. Abigail Mason.
155.   II. ISRAEL, m. ——.
156.   III. HENRY, b. 1750; m. Lydia Mason.
157.   IV. BARNARD, b. Feb. 4, 1764; m. Mary Rounds.
        V. WILLIAM, d. æ. 21.
158.   VI. JOSHUA, b. ——; m. Susannah Rounds.
        VII. SARAH.
        VIII. SILENE, m. June 24, 1803, Capt. Nathan Pierce;
                res. Dighton, Mass.
        IX. HANNAH.
        X. MARY, m. Joseph Pierce.

68. **David⁵ Pierce** (David⁴, Ephraim³, Ephraim², Michael¹), b.
Jan. 14, 1726; m. Oct. 31, 1754, Elizabeth Baker. Res. Swansey
and Somerset, Mass. He d. July, 1801. His will is proved July
7, 1801. His wife was dead at that time. His oldest son, Ebenezer, was executor. Witnesses to will, Asa Chase, Jonathan
Pierce and David Brayton.

CHILDREN.

159.   I. OBIDIAH, b. Feb. 12, 1762; m. Susannah Luther.
160.   II. DAVID, b. Feb. 14, 1766; m. Lydia G. Gibbs.

III. EBENEZER.
IV. LYDIA, m. ——— Chase.
V. ELIZABETH, m. Oct. 15, 1786, Joshua Brown.
VI. PATIENCE, m. ——— Perry.
VII. MARTHA, m. ——— Gibbs.

69. **Jonathan**[5] **Pierce** (David[4], Ephraim[3], Ephraim[2], Michael[1]),
b. Apr. 2, 1725; m. Apr. 11, 1745, Susannah Moott; m. 2nd, ———.
He d. 1820. Res. Somerset, Mass.

CHILDREN.

161. I. JOHN, b. 1768; m. Annie Chase.

70. **Preserved**[5] **Pierce** (David[4], Ephraim[3], Ephraim[2],
Michael[1]), b. Aug. 17, 1736; m. Apr. 23, 1761, Hannah Case; m.
2nd, Feb. 27, 1788, Lydia Simmons. He d. 1798. Res. Swansey
and Somerset, Mass. May 1, 1798, in Probate Court at Taunton,
the widow Lydia was appointed guardian to all the children that
were minors.

CHILDREN.

    I. ELIZABETH.
   II. MARY.
  III. MERCY.
   IV. ABRAHAM.
    V. JOB.
   VI. POLLY.
  VII. BETSEY.
 VIII. CYNTHIA.

70½. **Nathaniel**[5] **Pierce** (John[4], John[3], Ephraim[2], Michael[1]),
b. abt. 1732; m. ——— Olive ———. Res. Rehoboth, Mass.

CHILDREN.

    I. DOROTHY, b. Dec. 6, 1775; d. ———.
   II. ROSE, b. May 25, 1777.
  III. OLIVE, b. Apr. 27, 1780.
   IV. DOROTHY, b. Feb. 2, 1782.

V. JOHN, b. Apr. 5, 1784; d. ——.
VI. JOHN, b. Sept. 7, 1786.
VII. LUCINDA, b. Apr. 14, 1788.
VIII. COMFORT, b. May 25, 1790.
IX. CYRENE, b. Aug. 28, 1792.
X. NATHANIEL, b. Aug. 6, 1794.
XI. PASCHAL, b. June 7, 1796.

71. **Comfort⁵ Pierce** (John⁴, John³, Ephraim², Michael¹), b. Mar. 26, 1741; m. Mar. 26, 1761, Betsey Allen. He d. ——. Res. Rehoboth, Mass.

CHILDREN.

161½.   I. JOHN, b. May 16, 1762; m. Betsey Bowen.
      II. BETTY, b. Dec. 8, 1765.
161¾.   III. COMFORT, b. Nov. 30, 1768; m. ——.
     IV. PATIENCE, b. Apr. 14, 1769.

72. **Benjamin⁶ Pierce** (Benjamin⁵, Benjamin⁴, Benjamin³, Benjamin², Michael¹), b. July 8, 1777; m. 1799, Deborah Jones, b. Jan. 6, 1777; d. May 7, 1844. He d. Dec. 5, 1838. Res. Chesterfield, Mass.

Benjamin Pierce was born in Scituate, Mass., in 1777; he resided there until after his marriage, when he moved to Chesterfield, Mass. He was a business man in Massachusetts, had a farm of some 400 acres; had flouring and saw-mills, hotel, and ran two stores, and like many others failed and started for Ohio, but meeting misfortune on the way, stopped in New York, and bought a farm in Constantia, Oswego county, where he lived a good many years. In moving to Indiana he was taken sick and died on the way, at Miamitown, Ohio, Dec. 5, 1838. He was a Congregationalist in Massachusetts, but when he went to New York in Feb., 1818, there was no church of that denomination near, and he went into the Presbyterian church and worshipped with them ever after.

CHILDREN.

162.   I. HENRY, b. Dec. 29, 1806; m. Rebecca Tompkins and Mary Fraser.

163. II. BENJAMIN, b. May 26, 1812; m. Lusinai Jenkins.
164. III. JOHN J., b. Apr. 14, 1801; m. Fanny Harwood.
  IV. LOIS, b. Apr. 10, 1802; m. Feb. 19, 1826, Clark
   Bentley, b. June 1, 1801; d. Oct. 28, 1867. She
   d. Apr. 6, 1859; res. Chesterfield, Mass. Ch.,
   Mary C., b. Sept. 18, 1828; m. Feb. 9, 1849, ——
   Merrill; res. Marcellus, N. Y.; Martha L., b. Jan.
   28, 1827; d. Sept. 13, 1843; Lois I., b. Dec. 20,
   1830; m. June 12, 1848; d. July 9, 1861; Cyrus
   H., b. Oct. 25, 1832; m. Jan. 18, 1860; res.
   O'Neil, Neb.; Eliza P., b. May 8, 1835; m. Jan.
   12, 1862; d. Feb. 14, 1869; Clark G., b. June 23,
   1837; m. Dec. 10, 1867; d. Apr. 9, 1873; Benja-
   min P., b. Sept. 12, 1840; m. Oct. 22, 1868; res.
   Ft. Dodge, Iowa; Martha J., b. Apr. 26, 1846; m.
   Apr., 1864, W. G. Perkins; res. Oakland, Ill.
165. V. HARVEY, b. Sept. 26, 1804; m. Sarah Dickerson.
  VI. NANCY, b. Aug. 30, 1808; m. Henry M. Hewett; res.
   California. She d. s. p., Oct. 19, 1866.
  VII. JANE, b. Jan. 20, 1810; m. Dr. John B. Davis. She
   d. Aug. 5, 1844; a dau., Sarah J., m. Daniel V.
   Johnston; res. Brookville, Indiana.
  VIII. DEBORAH, b. May 3, 1814; m. Aug. 3, 1836, John
   W. McNaime, b. Dec. 23, 1814; d. Sept. 13, 1877.
   She d. Feb. 16, 1876; res. Porkdale, Ontario. Ch.,
   James H., b. Aug. 15, 1837; m. Dec. 11, 1861;
   res. Toronto, Canada; Jane A., b. Mar. 27, 1839;
   m. Feb. 16, 1861, Albert McIntosh, and d. Aug.
   18, 1885; Mary C., b. May 16, 1841; m. Aug. 4,
   1862, Thomas H. Miller, and d. Aug. 4, 1862;
   Edgar B., b. Sept. 25, 1843; m. Sept. 6, 1870; res.
   Denver, Col.; Lois A., b. Sept. 6, 1849.

73. **Libbeus**[6] **Pierce** (Jonathan[5], Benjamin[4], Benjamin[3], Benjamin[2], Michael[1]), b. 1774; m. Vesta Bailey, b. 1781; d. June,
1825; m. 2nd, Mariam Ames. He d. Mar. 2, 1845. Res. Scituate,
Mass., Sudbury, Vt., Chesterfield, Mass., and Canton, N. Y.

CHILDREN.

166.   I. PAUL, b. Apr. 24, 1801; m. Emeline Mead.
167.   II. WILLIAM, b. Jan. 29, 1799; m. Patty Fuller.
      III. PARMELIA, b. Jan. 7, 1820; m. July 19, 1854, Harrison White, b. Nov. 30, 1814; res. Leicester Junction, Vt. Ch., Julia P., b. Oct. 31, 1855; m. Sept. 10, 1879, —— Cushman; res. Middlebury, Vt.
       IV. CELINDA V., b. Sept. 9, 1822; m. July 29, 1845, Henry Lawrence, res. Griswoldville, Mass. He was b. Dec. 2, 1812; d. Aug. 20, 1870. Ch., William H., b. July 9, 1846; d. Dec. 16, 1881; Franklin D., b. Mar. 7, 1848; res. New York city; Hartwell E. L., b. Oct. 7, 1850; d. June, 1853.
        V. MASON, b. ——; at one time he res. in Lenawee, Mich.
       VI. ORLANDO, b. 1802; killed by kick of a horse in 1822.
      VII. MELVIN, b. ——; m. and d. in Illinois.
     VIII. JONATHAN, b. 1806; m. Marium Carpenter in April and died in a few months in 1834 in his twenty-eighth year. No children.
       IX. ALLEN, b. 1810; d. æ. 24.
        X. BENJAMIN, b. ——; d. 1840 in Florida. He went to Texas as a soldier and was on his way home when he died.
       XI. CHARLES, b. 1816; d. of a fever in his eighteenth year in 1834. He and his brother Jonathan and Allen all died within six weeks of each other of fever.
      XII. NANCY MARIA, b. May 18, 1809. (The first white child born in Canton, N. Y.); m. Feb. 13, 1831, Col. Josiah Barber, b. Aug. 27, 1807, d. June 5, 1887. She d. Mar. 29, 1881. Res. Canton, N. Y. Ch., Elizabeth M., b. Feb. 21, 1832; m. June 1860, Lorenzo Lawrence, and d. Mar. 31, 1865; res. Canton, N. Y.; Celestia S., b. Oct. 19, 1833;

m. July 25, 1852, S. E. Corbyn and d. Aug. 21,
1856; Phebe Jane, b. June 26, 1835; d. Sept. 9,
1852; Chas. B., b. June 12, 1837, M. D.; m. Mary
Wilson; res. Keeseville, N. Y.; Julia A., b. Mar.
30, 1839; m. Dec. 6, 1857, S. E. Corbyn; res.
Black River, N. Y.; Harriett P., b. July 7, 1841;
m. Myron Nickerson; res. Canton, N. Y.; Ellen
E., b. Apr. 21, 1843; m. Oct. 13, 1866, Wm. H.
Allen; res. Pierpont, N. Y.; Gilbert R., b. Oct.
21, 1845; m. Dec. 1, 1869, Rhoda Smith; res.
Watertown, N. Y.; Pliny W., b. June 27, 1849, M.
D., m. Kate Newell; res. 320 Broadway, New
York city, N. Y.

74. **Howard J.**[6] **Pierce** (Jonathan[5], Benjamin[4], Benjamin[3],
Benjamin[2], Michael[1]), b. June 18, 1775; m. Jan. 25, 1801, Bridget
House, b. 1785; d. in Potsdam, Aug. 23, 1830.   He d. at Madrid,
N. Y., Oct. 20, 1848.   Res. Rutland, Vt., and Madrid, N. Y.

Jonathan Pierce, Howard J.'s father, moved from Massachusetts to Vermont toward the close of the eighteenth century.
Howard Jonathan emigrated from Vermont to Potsdam, N. Y., in
1803 with his family.   He and Barney Hogey and Captain Bailey
were the three first settlers in Potsdam.   His wife's maiden name
was Bridget House.   Their family increased to six sons and three
daughters.   He passed away at Madrid, N. Y.

CHILDREN.

168.   I. HOSEA H., b. Oct. 1, 1801; m. Harriett Bernathy
            and ——.
169.   II. ONEASMUS O., b. Aug. 16, 1809; m. Catherine Blue.
170.   III. DENNIS D., b. Aug. 7, 1811; m. Phila M. Gibbons.
171.   IV. JOHN J., b. July 19, 1813; m. Catherine Rogain.
172.   V. HIRAM H., b. July 5, 1818; m. Prudence Sackett
            and Eliza Fisher.
        VI. SILOMA S., b. Aug. 5, 1816; m. Edward Jones.
    13

VII. Polly C., b. ——.

173. VIII. Artimus A., b. Mar. 18, 1805; m. Celinda Carter.

IX. Mary M., b. ——; m. John H. Wait. Their son, Orvill, b. July 2, 1828; m. Sept. 5, 1852, Mary Conroy; res. Novi, Mich.

X. Laura J., b. Nov. 18, 1807; m. Mar. 3, 1826, Luther Wait, b. Apr. 22, 1806; d. Apr. 11, 1841; m. 2nd, July 29, 1845, Daniel M. Arbor, b. Feb. 18, 1816; d. Dec. 21, 1873; res. Bell Branch, Mich. Ch., Luther P., b. Apr. 15, 1841; m. Apr. 4, 1867, and June 15, 1881; res. Beech, Mich.; Laura J., b. Dec. 24, 1846; m. Alvin C. Pierce; res. Bell Branch, Mich.

XI. Henry.

XII. Matilda.

XIII. Harson.

XIV. Jane.

XV. Diana.

XVI. Hamel.

75. **Haywood[6] Pierce** (Haywood[5], Benjamin[4], Benjamin[3], Benjamin[2], Michael[1]), b. Mar. 24, 1782; m. Dec., 1812, Mary Mills; d. 1817. He d. in South America, Apr., 1840.

Haywood Pierce was born in Scituate, Mass., in 1782. While yet a young man he went to New Orleans, finally engaged in business, and became very wealthy. After many years, and at an advanced age he again returned to the North, and visited his relations, by whom he was received with much joy. His only child was a daughter. Mr. Pierce died while on a visit in South America. Res. New Orleans, La.

CHILDREN.

I. Julia, b. 1815; m. 1831, E. Rouvert, b. ——; d. Apr., 1841; res. Thibodeaux, La. Ch., Julia R., b. ——; m. —— Breen, b. ——; Edmund, d. 1862; res. Thibodeaux, La.

76. **Waldo**[6] **Pierce** (Haywood[5], Benjamin[4], Benjamin[3], Benjamin[2], Michael[1]), b. in Scituate, Mass., Feb. 22, 1778; m. Dec. 4, 1803, Catherine Treat, b. in Haverhill, Mass., Dec. 2, 1782; d. Aug., 1863. He d. Sunday morning, Oct. 10, 1841. Res. Frankfort, Me.

Waldo Pierce, son of Haywood, was born at Scituate, Mass., in the year 1778.

When a young man he settled in Maine, town of Frankfort, lower village, which is situated upon a branch of the Penobscot, called Marsh river, affording fine facilities for mills and shipping; a picturesque little valley surrounded by forest-covered hills, and connected with the upper village by bridge and an enchanting road three miles in length, which sixty years ago ran through the forest primeval.

Here Waldo Pierce married Catharine Treat, " a noble woman, nobly planned," whose father, Joshua Treat, was a pioneer in this wilderness, and had built a saw and grist-mill, and entered the first wedge of civilization, about one century ago.

The mills and a store formed a little nucleus of trade for the people scattered in the back districts, who were extremely poor, but brought here their little " grist to grind."

He enlarged this business, was an active, enterprising man, and in later years was in possession of a large property. His eldest sons, who settled in Bangor, eighteen miles distant, were among the most influential men in that city, and there the father invested largely the slow gains of many years.

At about the age of sixty he made, in connection with Mr. Albert L. Keller, an extensive purchase from Thorndike, Sears, and Prescott, of Boston, of what was known as " Ten Proprietors' Land," a portion of Waldo patent, of which they were residuary owners.

The explorations and care consequent upon this heavy purchase proved too much for his strength, and heart disease was developed, which, after a painful illness of three years, caused his death.

Mr. Pierce was in stature somewhat above medium height, rather stout and strongly built, blue eyes, light hair, and ruddy complexion, of dignified mien, a fine specimen of the New England type.

He was most exemplary in his life, and guarded well the morals of his numerous family, was strenuous and firm on the point of education, and though schools in those days were of the " stone for bread " order, yet once a day every child of sufficient age must go up to the little one-storied seat of learning upon the miniature Acropolis of the village.   Here in winter a Solon — presumably — and a Minerva in summer, dispensed the rudiments of the three R's.— with perhaps a few other letters thrown in — to the eight benches on a side, slanting upward, similar to modern theaters, with aisle in center, girls upon one side and boys opposite.

In this same building were held religious services, and Mr. Pierce was just as strenuous in attendance upon these.   A Methodist minister, quite superannuated, here preached sermons each Sabbath, that it would seem would make the very stones cry out, so long, so dull and dreary were they — at least to the juvenile mind, but the subject of this sketch must have gained something from them, or else he had the spirit of a martyr, for he never failed to be present with his children at these solemnities.   The old Puritan spirit was predominant in him, and education and religion were to him the foundation stones of character.

His house was always open to the poor and distressed.   It was nothing unusual to see half a dozen at a time of this class sitting around the old and ample kitchen hearth, and to "feed the hungry and clothe the naked" was his kind wife's daily business in those early times of poverty and destitution.   For all these solid traits of character, his children tenderly revere his memory.

"In Frankfort, Me., Oct. 10, 1841, Waldo Pierce died of organic disease of the heart, aged 63.   He was a man of clear, strong and vigorous mind, of stern republican simplicity of habits and manner. He emigrated from Scituate, the place of his birth, and came to Frankfort, then a wilderness.

In early life he was a mechanic, but as his means increased, he engaged in mercantile pursuits which gave full scope to the exercise of his forecast and sagacity.   He was a pattern of economy, industry and perseverance, entered upon his plans with ardor, and pursued them with untiring zeal.   His labors were immense; the result was that with his single and unaided hand, he acquired a large estate.

The venerable divine who performed his funeral rites, said of him, "I have known that man for forty years, in all of the relations of life, and I have never known him to exhibit resentment, anger or ill-will.   I have never known him to wrong any man. He was honest, benevolent and kind-hearted.   His house was the home of the poor, and our whole vicinity is in mourning."   [Copied from the Waldo *Signal.*]

CHILDREN.

I. HAYWOOD, b. July 5, 1808; m. Feb. 17, 1834, Mary
    Ann Greenwood, s. p.; res. Frankfort. He d.
    Dec. 16, 1854.

II. NANCY VALERIA, b. Jan. 15, 1824; d. Mar. 4, 1828.

III. ARTEMUS, b. Nov. 13, 1820; unm.; res. Frankfort.

IV. LUCILLA S., b. Jan. 1, 1819; m. Aug. 24, 1842, Israel
    Webster Kelley; she res. at 37 East Springfield
    street, Boston, Mass. Ch., Israel Webster Kelley,
    the son of Israel W. and Rebecca (Fletcher)
    Kelley, was b. Jan. 5, 1804; graduated at Dart-
    mouth College, 1824. " Webster Kelley, after his
    graduation at college, began the study of law at
    Frankfort, Me., and in due time went into prac-
    tice with his brother, Albert L. He rose rapidly
    in his profession. Removing not long after to
    Belfast, he formed a partnership with Albert John-
    son. In 1841, he was appointed deputy collector
    of customs under President Harrison, and went
    back to Frankfort. He was an earnest advocate
    of the Whig party in politics. He was highly
    esteemed for his integrity and professional ability."
    After a course of legal practice in Maine, he
    removed to Boston. Some time subsequent to
    this he was called to argue an important case in
    Amherst, N. H. It was a case which had already
    been tried three times, no jury having been found
    who could agree on a verdict. He gained the case
    for his client, to the surprise and admiration of his
    friends, and the dismay of his opponents; but
    before he could reach his home he was struck
    down with a fatal attack of pleurisy. He d. in
    Henrietta, N. H., July 3 1855. Ch., Howard
    Webster, b. Feb. 19, 1844. Howard Webster re-
    turning from Fayal, at the age of twenty, was lost
    at sea from barque Eschol, which went down with
    several hundred on board in 1865; Catherine Peirce,
    b.——; Grace Fletcher, b. ——; Allston, b. 1854;
    d. Sept. 19, 1856; Webster, b. Mar. 17, 1856, gradu-
    ated from Latin School, Boston, and Harvard Col-
    lege, 1879, with honors. Taking Bowdoin Prize,
    completed his course in Harvard Law School.
    Admitted to practice, Boston Bar, 1887.

174.   V. GEORGE A., b. Mar. 4, 1812 ; m. Louisa T. Pike.
       VI. HARRIETT MARIA, b. Aug. 11, 1817; m. May 26,
            1852, Hayward Pierce Cushing, b. May 3, 1812;
            d. Oct. 13, 1870; res. 8 Walnut street, Boston,
            Mass. Ch., Florence M., b. Apr. 24, 1853 ; grad.
            Vassar, 1874; Haywood W., b. Sept. 22, 1854;
            grad. Harvard, 1877; Livingston, b. June 29, 1856;
            grad. Harvard, 1879; m. Oct. 18, 1882, Ada
            Thomas; Jennie, b. Jan. 19, 1858; grad. Vassar,
            1880; m. May 21, 1884, H. O. Underwood; res.
            Belmont, Mass.; Ida, b. Aug. 28, 1860; grad. Vas-
            sar, 1883 ; m. Nov. 16, 1887, Wm. L. Underwood;
            res. Belmont, Mass.
175.   VII. WALDO T., b. Sept. 16, 1804; m. Hannah Jane Hills.
      VIII. CAROLINE H., b. Aug. 31, 1806 ; m. Feb. 15, 1829,
            Albert L. Kelley.

       Albert Livingston Kelley, the son of Israel W.
and Rebecca (Fletcher) Kelley, was born in Bristol, N. H., Aug. 17, 1802, graduated at Dartmouth
College, 1821, and married Caroline H. Pierce,
Feb. 15, 1829. Mr. Kelley was fitted for Dartmouth College at Atkinson's Academy. On the
completion of his college course he went to Portland, Maine, and there read law with Hon. Stephen
Longfellow. He was admitted to the bar in
Cumberland county, Maine, in 1825. By the appointment of the municipal authorities at Portland,
he gave the oration at the celebration of the 4th
of July of that year. On the recommendation of
Daniel Webster, he was appointed agent for the
"Ten Proprietors' Tracts," so called, in Eastern
Maine, a property then owned by David Sears,
William Prescott and Israel Thorndike. He established his residence at Frankfort, Me., in September, 1825, and began the practice of his profession,
and the discharge of the duties of his agency. His
legal practice soon became extensive, and he took
at once and ever afterward retained a high position at the bar. One writer says of Mr. Kelley:
"I think I never knew a man of such absolute in-
dependence of thought and action." He is further
characterized as "an extensive reader, a fine
writer, an able and eloquent speaker, a wise and

sagacious counselor, and an accomplished gentleman." He d. Aug. 18, 1885; res. Winterport, Me. Ch., Edward Albert, b. May 30, 1831, at Winterport. Fitted for college at the military school, Lieut. Whiting, Ellsworth, Me., at Foxcroft's Academy, Me., and at North Yarmouth Classical Academy. Entered Bowdoin College and remained there until the middle of the junior year. He began the study of law with the eminent lawyer, George F. Farley of Groton, Mass., in 1851. In 1853, he was admitted to the bar and practiced in partnership with Mr. Farley until 1855. Remained in Groton until 1861; then moved to Boston, where he still resides, and of whose bar he is a prominent member, making a specialty of will cases and the care of trust property; m. Nov. 15, 1854, Mary Farley of Groton. Ch., Elizabeth. He was given the honorary degree of A. M. by Bowdoin College. He is a man of refinement, of strong character and unswerving principle; Caroline Ellen, b. Apr. 22, 1833; m. Oct. 9, 1863, Nathan Cushing of Boston, and d. Apr. 9, 1864; Julia C., b. June 3, 1835; m. Nov. 11, 1856, Dr. Wm. R. Stanley of Lahaska, Pa.; Alburtic R., b. Aug. 9, 1837; d. Dec. 30, 1837; Waldo P., b. Feb. 5, 1839; d. Aug. 29, 1842; Frank W., b. Mar. 20, 1841; attorney at law; res. Winterport, Me. ; Waldo C., b. June, 1843; d. Aug. 2, 1861; Silas Pierce, b. May 24, 1845; res. Winterport; Fitzroy, b. Dec. 14, 1847, member of the firm of wholesale grocers, "Silas Pierce & Co.", in Boston; m. Feb. 24, 1875, Amanda Marble.

176. IX. CHARLES H., b. Apr. 1, 1810; m. Ellen W. Kelley.

X. JANE, b. Nov. 3, 1813; d. Apr. 10, 1815.

XI. EMILY J., b. Sept. 3, 1815 ; m. Sept. 12, 1833, Hon. Charles Stetson; res. Bangor, Me.

Hon. Charles Stetson was born in New Ipswich, New Hampshire, in November, 1801; graduated at Yale College in 1823 ; practiced law at Hampden, Maine, for some years, and removed to Bangor; was judge of the Municipal Court of that city in 1834, and held that office until 1837, when he was ap-

pointed clerk of the Supreme Court of Maine.
He was a member of the Governor's Council four
years from 1845 to 1848. He was elected to
Congress from the Fifth congressional district of
Maine in 1849, and served in the Thirty-first
Congress. He continued to reside in Bangor
until the time of his death, March, 1883. He
was married in 1833, to Emily J. Pierce, daughter
of Waldo Pierce of Frankfort, who is now living
at Bangor — eight children survived him. He
was b. Nov. 7, 1801; d. Mar. 27, 1883. Ch.,
Charles P., b. May 24, 1835; m. May 24, 1875,
address, Bangor, Me.; Emily, b. Nov. 28, 1837;
m. May 30, 1865, to James S. Brown, Milwaukee, Wis.; Anna M., b. May 28, 1839; Amasa
S., b. July 21, 1841; d. July 29, 1842; Caroline
P., b. May 30, 1843; m. Oct. 12, 1871, Franklin
A. Wilson of Bangor; Frances A., b. Jan. 4, 1847;
Frederick, b. Dec. 30, 1848; d. June 10, 1850;
Franklin, b. Dec. 11, 1850; m. Dec. 5, 1877, ad-
dress, St. Johns, N. B.; Ada P., b. Mar. 31, 1853;
m. Sept. 7, 1880, John C. Holman of Boston; d.
Aug. 27, 1884; Hayward, b. May 30, 1857.

177.   XII. SILAS F., b. Dec. 18, 1825; m. Frances L. Griffin.

XIII. NANCY A., b. May 20, 1822; d. Aug. 5, 1822.

77. **Bailey[6] Pierce** (Haywood[5], Benjamin[4], Benjamin[3], Benjamin[2], Michael[1]), b. Aug. 29, 1787; m. Dec. 13, 1812, Ann Somerby,
b. Sept. 22, 1788; d. June 30, 1818; m. 2nd, June 16, 1819, Eliza
Tobey, b. Mar. 11, 1795; d. Feb. 14, 1865. He d. Apr. 4, 1844.
Res. Frankfort and Belfast, Me.

CHILDREN.

I. ELIZA T., b. Sept. 30, 1813; m. Dec. 31, 1845, James
Arcy; m. 2nd, June 14, 1860, John Burrill of
Newburyport. She d. Nov. 14, 1884.

II. ANN MARIA, b. June 12, 1815; m. Dec. 8, 1836,
Amos B. Treat. She d. June 11, 1837; res.
Frankfort.

III. SARAH S., b. Oct. 31, 1817; m. Sept. 4, 1844, John Cole; res. 442 Cumberland street, Portland, Me.

IV. ABBY COX, b. Sept. 11, 1824; res. 8 Walnut street, Boston, Mass.

78. **Elijah**[6] **Pierce** (Haywood[5], Benjamin[4], Benjamin[3], Benjamin[2], Michael[1]), b. July 30, 1789; m. Nov. 16, 1816, Rebecca Bailey; d. Aug. 7, 1819; m. 2nd, Oct. 1, 1825, Lucy P. Litchfield. Res. Scituate, Mass.

CHILDREN.

I. HAYWOOD, b. Sept. 6, 1817; d. unm. 1855.

II. SILAS, b. July 26, 1826; res. Boston, Mass.

178.   III. ELIJAH F., b. July 1, 1827; m. Sarah A. Perry.

IV. SARAH B., b. June 10, 1829; d. unm. Oct. 28, 1882.

V. BENJAMIN, b. May 23, 1831.

VI. ELIZABETH B., b. May 9, 1833; d. unm. Aug., 1876.

79. **Silas**[6] **Pierce** (Haywood[5], Benjamin[4], Benjamin[3], Benjamin[2], Michael[1]), b. Feb. 15, 1793; m. Hannah Lopez of Boston, Mass. She d. Nov. 27, 1884. He d. s. p., Aug. 27, 1879. Res. Boston, Mass.

80. **Artemas**[6] **Pierce** (Ezra[5], Benjamin[4], Ebenezer[3], Ebenezer[2], Michael[1]), b. July 10, 1779; m. Feb. 28, 1804, Hannah Goodridge, b. Oct. 2, 1782; d. Feb. 25, 1869. He d. July 28, 1867. Res. Londonderry, Vt.

CHILDREN.

I. EVELINE, b. Sept. 15, 1805; m. Dec. 18, 1825, Jason Buxton, b. Dec. 21, 1799. Ch., Sylvia, b. Aug. 17, 1826; m. Apr. 10, 1849, John M. Rockwell, and d. July 21, 1854; Emily, b. Dec. 18, 1830; m. Nov. 10, 1855, William Rockwell; res. Woonsocket.

II. MARY R., b. Sept. 20, 1807; m. Dec. 1, 1840, Joshua D. Parker, b. Mar. 19, 1805; d. Sept. 23, 1887. Ch., Mary E., b. May, 1844; m. John Thompson; res. Londonderry, Vt.; Emily A., b. Oct. 21, 1851; Mary R., d. Mar. 19, 1871; res. Londonderry, Vt.

14

III. Rebecca L., b. July 9, 1810; m. Sept. 26, 1837,
Oliver Clapp, b. June 2, 1797; d. Sept. 19, 1859.
Ch., Hannah E., b. Apr. 24, 1840; d. Nov. 9,
1860; Annah J., b. Nov. 4, 1841; d. Dec. 19, 1849;
Harriett I., b. Feb. 13, 1848; d. Aug. 13, 1848;
res. Blackstone, Mass.; m. 2nd, July 20, 1862,
Libeus Gaskill, b. July 22, 1808; d. Jan. 19, 1868.

IV. Hannah, b. July 14, 1812; m. Mar. 19, 1835, William Barrows, b. Apr. 4, 1810; d. Feb. 27, 1841.
Ch., Gilbert, b. Jan. 27, 1836; m. Leora Moulton
and Rosa L. Burt; res. Woonsocket, R. I.; Gilman, b. Jan. 27, 1836; m. Ellen Prescott; res.
Groton; William G., b. Sept. 23, 1887; m. Lydia
S. Willard; res. Providence, R. I. Hannah m.
2nd, Sept. 26, 1846, Peter Nutting, d. May 17,
1876; res. Windham, Vt., and Groton, Mass.

V. Jerusha H., b. Dec. 20, 1814; m. May 22, 1836,
Emery Melendy, b. Jan. 2, 1800; d. Jan. 21, 1877.
She d. Sept. 23, 1888. Ch., Emery W., b. May
20, 1841; m. Dec. 16, 1868, Constantia A. Newell,
b. Jan. 18, 1845; d. May 15, 1881; m. 2nd, Sept.
20, 1883, Lucy E. Rider, b. July 16, 1850; Jonathan W., b. Nov. 18, 1845; m. Nov. 26, 1868;
Caroline L. Arnold, b. June 29, 1845; res. Londonderry, Vt.

179. VI. Gilman G., b. May 4, 1817; m. Elizabeth Woodworth.

180. VII. William, b. Nov. 26, 1819; m. Malinda Abbott
and Mary V. Hesleton.

VIII. Amarilla R., b. May 13, 1822; m. July 18, 1843,
George M. Pratt, b. Feb. 22, 1816. Ch., George
A., b. May 17, 1845; m. Oct. 4, 1873, Mina M.
Cone; Frank P., b. Nov. 6, 1852; m. Aug. 8, 1875,
Mary J. Harvy; res. Chicago, Ill.

IX. Ezra, b. Oct. 22, 1824; m. Oct. 28, 1851, Ellen
Abbott. She d. s. p., May, 1881; res. Chester, Vt.

82. **Ezra**[6] **Pierce** (Nehemiah[5], Benjamin[4], Ebenezer[3], Ebenezer[2], Michael[1]), b. Dec. 6, 1788; m. Dec. 5, 1810, Polly Farr. He d. June 23, 1869. Res. Windham, Vt.

CHILDREN.

I. MARY, b. June 30, 1814; m. Horace Austin, and d. Nov. 29, 1842, leaving two daughters.

II. EZRA, b. Dec. 14, 1815; m. Mar. 13, 1838, Betsey J. Hastings; res. Windham, s. p.

III. PHŒBE, b. Jan. 22, 1818; m. Dec. 1, 1842, Nathan Hastings; res. Townshend. One son, Edwin.

IV. NELSON, b. Mar. 19, 1821 ; d. Aug. 28, 1822.

V. WILLIAM H., b. Apr. 8, 1824; m. Dec. 8, 1852, Maria Burton, dau. of Timothy and Mary (Pierce) Burton who d. s. p. and ——.

VI. CHARLES N., b. Mar. 26, 1826.

VII. ANGELINE C., b. May 26, 1828; d. Apr. 19, 1853.

181. VIII. MERRILL, b. Feb. 18, 1830; m. Amanda Robbins.

IX. FLORINDA, b. Sept. 18, 1832; m. Aug. 15, 1858, Oscar Howe of Townsend, and d. Oct. 16, 1867.

83. **Rev. Sem**[6] **Pierce** (Nehemiah[5], Benjamin[4], Ebenezer[3], Ebenezer[2], Michael[1]), b. July 8, 1794; m. Sept. 3, 1815, Lydia Moses, b. Mar. 28, 1793; m. 2nd, Joanna Brown, b. Nov. 15, 1808; d. Oct. 30, 1859; m. 3rd, Mrs. Myra Olds French, b. ——. He d. Oct. 15, 1865. Res. Londonderry, Vt.

Rev. Sem Pierce was born in Windham, Vermont, July 8, 1794. Until he was twenty-one years of age he worked on his father's farm. After his conversion he began to preach, or as he called it, to talk in small assemblies, and from that he gradually worked his way up the ladder by close application and studious efforts until he received a regular call to preach in the Baptist Church in South Londonderry, Vermont. He was the pastor there for more than twenty years, and ably discharged his pastoral duties. He was then called to Plymouth, later to Cavendish and other places. He was a man of strong, sterling integrity, one whose word was as good as his bond any time. Always a friend of the poor, the downcast and the oppressed. Those in sickness or in trouble instinctively turned to him for help and kindly sympathy, sure always of getting what they looked for. He represented the town in the Legislature a number of times, and there, as in every other place, his voice was always heard on the side of right. It is, perhaps, enough to say of him, that those who knew him best loved him most.

CHILDREN.

I. NEHEMIAH, b. May 3, 1816; d. young.

182. II. JOSIAH, b. Feb. 6, 1818; m. Adeline Whitman.

III. PHYLITTA, b. Feb. 16, 1820; m. Jan. 8, 1839, Merrick Woods, son of Dea. Amos Woods, b. Sept. 1, 1811; d. Apr. 24, 1881. She d. Nov. 6, 1852. Ch., Nellie L., b. Aug. 3, 1841; m. Feb. 21, 1865, John Warren Rand, son of Jasper and Sally (Pierce) Rand. [See Peirce Genealogy, p. 69.] Ch., John W., b. July 1, 1866; res. Fitchburg, Mass. He is superintendent of the fire alarm telegraph.

183. IV. SEM, b. Dec. 21, 1825; m. Eliza Howard.

V. JOHN, b. Apr. 23, 1828; d. Apr. 25, 1828.

184. VI. WILLIAM W., b. Mar. 14, 1836; m. Lizzie A. Stone.

VII. LYDIA, b. Mar. 20, 1824; d. young.

VIII. LELAND, b. ——; d. young.

185. IX. NEHEMIAH, b. Nov. 5, 1837; m. Jane A. Shumway and Marcia A. Eddy.

X. MARION IDA, b. July 19, 1840; m. June 30, 1872, Thomas K. Hamilton, b. June 30, 1844. Ch., Helen P., b. Apr. 26, 1878; res. Merrimac, Mass.

XI. MARIA, b. ——; d. æ. 12.

XII. EDWARD W., b. ——; } both d. in infancy.
XIII. EDWARD O., b. ——; }

XIV. AURILLA, b. Oct. 10, 1829; m. Dec. 12, 1849, John C. Cutter, b. Aug. 21, 1827. She d. Oct. 21, 1888; res. Winchendon, Mass. He was at one time the proprietor of a summer resort. In 1862, he entered the Thirty-sixth Regiment of Massachusetts Volunteers as second lieutenant of Company D. In June, 1863, he was promoted first lieutenant and regimental quartermaster, in which office he continued until the close of the war. Ch., Nelson S., b. Sept. 13, 1850; d. Aug. 25, 1854; John M., b. Mar. 4, 1852; add. 76 Monroe street, Chicago, Ill.; Sarah A., b. Dec. 2, 1860; m. Sidney E. White; res. Winchendon.

84. **Dea. Alson**[6] **Pierce** (Benjamin[5], Benjamin[4], Ebenezer[3], Ebenezer[2], Michael[1]), b. June 21, 1794, in Windham, Vt.; m. Aug. 27, 1819, Sylvia Corbin, b. Feb. 23, 1794; d. Mar. 18, 1865. Res. Painted Post, N. Y.

CHILDREN.

I. BENJAMIN C., b. Oct. 14, 1820; d. Aug. 10, 1844.

II. MARY A., b. May 21, 1823; m. Dec. 30, 1849, Dr. Floyd Morse, b. Apr. 11, 1825; d. Sept. 20, 1858; res. Painted Post, N. Y. Ch., Emma P., b. Oct. 31, 1850; m. Sept., 1875, Rev. Giles H. Hubbard; Benjamin R., b. Oct. 21, 1852; m. Feb. 27, 1885, Emma Clapp; res. Ridgefield, Ill.; Floyd H., b. Aug. 31, 1854; Annie L., b. May 23, 1856.

III. MARTHA A., b. Oct. 25, 1824; m. Sept. 15, 1846, Charles J. Cooper, b. Mar. 13, 1823; d. Nov. 4, 1883; res. Cooper's Plains, N. Y. Ch., Charles J., b. July 9, 1847; d. Sept. 25, 1872; Benjamin P., b. Jan. 14, 1849; m. July 16, 1874, Callie T. Owens; Mary E., b. Dec. 12, 1850; m. May 10, 1876, Dr. E. A. Overhiser; John E., b. Sept. 27, 1852; m. June 30, 1872, Mary Frieslater; Frank, b. Dec. 11, 1854; m. Oct. 7, 1886, Mary A. Kingsbury; res. Castile Rock, Cal.

186. IV. STEPHEN BYRON, b. Apr. 15, 1839; m. Sophia E. Stilson.

85. **Dea. Nathan**[6] **Pierce** (Benjamin[5], Benjamin[4], Ebenezer[3], Ebenezer[2], Michael[1]), b. Mar. 1, 1801; m. Mar. 17, 1830, Anna H. Burnap, b. Oct, 29, 1807. He was born in Windham, Vt., but removed in early life to West Townsend, Vt. For many years he was deacon of the Congregational Church. He was successful in business and honored and respected by all. In his eighty-fourth year he moved to Suffield, Conn. Res. West Townsend, Vt., and Suffield, Conn.

CHILDREN.

I. LUCIA A., b. June 9, 1831 ; m. May 5, 1858, Jeremiah Baldwin, b. Dec., 1827; res. Northfield, Minn. Ch., Willis P., b. Feb. 28, 1859; Horace, b. Nov. 13, 1860; James A., b. Sept. 16, 1865; Minnie A., b. Jan. 20, 1868.

II. MARIA L., b. Nov. 19, 1832; m. Aug. 24, 1860, Jonas C. Kendall ; res. Dunstable, Mass. Ch., Frederick L., b. July 30, 1861 ; Caroline E., b. Aug. 27, 1864; Anna L., b. Aug. 2, 1867; James E., b. Sept. 4, 1870; Evangeline, b. Apr. 30, 1873.

III. CHARLES N., b. June 19, 1835; d. June 27, 1869.

187.   IV. ALBERT R., b. Feb. 16, 1837; m. Eliza S. Phelps.

188.   V. JAMES E., b. Aug. 12, 1839; m. Francis Hall.

VI. JULIA, b. June 10, 1841; m. Oct. 28, 1877, Gardner S. Washburn; res. Plainview, Minn.

VII. MARY E., b. Mar. 9, 1843 ; m. Mar., 1885, Willis H. Taft. She d. Apr. 19, 1888; res. Jamaica, Vt.

86. **Simeon**[6] **Pierce** (Benjamin[5], Benjamin[4], Ebenezer[3], Ebenezer[2], Michael[1]), b. Feb. 15, 1803; m. Dec. 9, 1835, Dorcas Andrews, b. May 28, 1813; d. ——. He d. Dec. 23, 1879. Res. South Windham, Vt.

CHILDREN.

189.   I. JEROME W., b. Nov. 29, 1836; m. Eugenie L. Stark and Anna E. Brooks.

* II. MARGARET A., b. Dec. 12, 1837; m. Jan. 31, 1866,
William H. Haywood; res. Troy, O.

III. ALSON, b. Mar. 19, 1837; d. Jan. 10, 1838.

IV. MARTHA A., b. Mar. 19, 1840; m. Jan. 31, 1860,
Gilbert I. Francis, b. Dec. 6, 1831; res. South
Windham, Vt. Ch., Charles G., b. Nov. 29, 1860;
res. Providence, R. I.; Sim P., b. July 28, 1862;
res. San Angelo, Texas; James H., b. June 1,
1872.

V. ELLA C., b. Jan. 29, 1846; d. Feb. 21, 1865.

87. **Lemuel⁶ Pierce** (Ebenezer⁵, Ebenezer⁴, Ebenezer³, Benjamin², Michael¹), b. Westmoreland, N. H., Jan. 6, 1781; m. Hannah
——, b. Jan. 31, 1787; d. May 26, 1855. He d. Jan. 25, 1852.
Res. Wardsboro, Vt.

CHILDREN.

I. MINERVA, b. June 29, 1810; d. Feb. 4, 1872.

II. ZEBINA, b. Oct. 20, 1813; d. Oct. 26, 1868.

III. NANCY, b. Jan. 15, 1815; d. May 24, 1872.

IV. CURTIS R., b. June 25, 1817.

V. FRANKLIN, b. May 12, 1819; d. Oct. 5, 1820.

VI. EMERSON F., b. Apr. 21, 1821.

VII. WINSLOW, b. May 15, 1823; d. Mar. 3, 1849.

VIII. IRA O., b. Aug. 7, 1826.

IX. SARAH, b. Apr. 17, 1829; d. July 8, 1863.

X. MATE, b. Apr. 17, 1829; d. Apr., 1829.

88. **Ebenezer⁶ Pierce** (Ebenezer⁵, Ebenezer⁴, Ebenezer³, Benjamin², Michael¹), b. ——; m. Julia Millen, b. ——; d. ——. He
d. ——. Res. ——.

CHILDREN.

I. SERAPHINE, d. s. p.

II. CHARLES, m. Lydia Robbins.

190. III. WARREN, b. ——; m. Sarah Williams.

IV. JULIA.

V. PUAH.

* Adopted.

89. **Adolphus**[6] **Pierce** (Ebenezer[5], Ebenezer[4], Ebenezer[3], Benjamin[2], Michael [1]), b. Oct. 19, 1789; m. Dec. 3, 1812, in Windham, Vt., Mehitable Wright, b. Oct. 13, 1790, in Thompson, Ct.; d. May 12, 1868. He d. July 7, 1864. Res. Windham, Vt., and Garrettsville, O.

CHILDREN.

191.   I. HIRAM, b. Feb. 22, 1815; m. Mary M. Messenger.

90. **Rev. Solon**[6] **Pierce** (Ezekiel[5], Ezekiel[4], Thomas[3], Benjamin[2], Michael[1]), b. Dec., 1764, in Scituate, Mass.; m. 1790, Betsey Jones, b. Jan., 1773; d. Aug., 1857. He d. Mar. 25, 1830, at Yorkshire, N. Y. Res. Penfield, N. Y.

Rev. Solon Pierce was the son of Ezekiel Pierce, who lived and died in Scituate, Mass. Solon was born in December, 1764, and was the youngest child of his parents. His mother died when he was a mere infant, and he continued to reside with his father until fourteen years of age, when he went to live with his uncle Joseph, a very rich farmer. His uncle studied New England economy, and lived on pork, beans and brown bread, crust coffee and bean porridge. While young he took three trips to sea in a fishing vessel, each trip consuming a year. He married at twenty-six, Betsey Jones, and settled at Whitestown, N. Y., one mile from Utica, N. Y. He was a prosperous farmer, owned one-hundred-acre farm, which was well improved and stocked and paid for. A company claimed his farm and began suit to recover it by ejectment. Solon lost his farm, and the cost of the suit left him with but little cash. At this time he had a family of seven children. Moving to Penfield, Monroe county, N. Y., he began preaching. He was well read, had a good education and was a fine speaker. He excelled all others in that section in preaching funeral sermons, and was very often sent for to perform this service. In March, 1826, he removed to Yorkshire, N. Y., where his earthly labors were closed, March 25, 1830, in his sixty-seventh year. He was an uncompromising patriot, and two of his brothers were in the Revolutionary war, one died at sea, and the other served through the war, and died at Conhocton, N. Y. In the rebellion of '61 to

'65, Solon had one son, eight grandsons, and two great grandsons in the war, two of whom were killed in the army.

CHILDREN.

I. SOLON, b. Aug. 4, 1791; m. ——; d. 1850, and has a son, Wesley; res. Allen, Mich.

II. POLLY, b. May 8, 1793.

III. JANE, b. July 11, 1795 ; d. 1861; a son, Daniel Fuller, res. Roxana, Eaton Co., Mich.

IV. BETSEY, b. May 23, 1797; d. unm.

V. LYDIA, b. July 19, 1799.

VI. DANIEL, b. Oct. 19, 1801; has a son Solon W., an attorney, residing in Friendship, Wis. He was born Mar. 7, 1831; m. Apr. 16, 1866, Harriet E. Waterman, b. Mar. 9, 1838. Ch., Harrie S., b. July 17, 1877; Katie L., b. Feb. 18, 1867 ; Jennie May, b. Mar. 1, 1868; Nellie L., b. Mar. 17, 1872; Jessie W., b. Nov. 26, 1874; res. Friendship, Wis.

VII. FANNY, b. Sept. 13, 1803.

VIII. JOSHUA, b. Aug. 7, 1805.

192.   IX. EZEKIEL, b. June 19, 1809; m. Phebe Thornton.

X. JOHN J., b. Aug. 29, 1811; has a dau. Estel; res. Fremont, Ind.

XI. OLIVE, b. Aug. 24, 1813.

193.   XII. WILLIAM B., b. May 23, 1816 ; m. Clarissa J. Doty and Jane M. Butterfield.

194.   XIII. ELVAH F., b. Aug. 21, 1818; m. Merana N. Nye.

91. **Ira[6] Pierce** (Thomas[5], Seth B.[4], Thomas[3], Benjamin[2], Michael[1]), b. Aug. 14, 1807; m. 1837, Phebe Stevens; d. 1844; m. 2nd, June 2, 1846, Julia B. Townsend, b. Jan. 1, 1825. He d. Jan. 18, 1864. Res. Racine and Pleasant Prairie, Wis.

CHILDREN.

I. EUGENE, b. May 10, 1850; m. Aug. 10, 1882 ; res. Fort Atkinson, Wis.

15

195.   II. ALONZO B., b. May 10, 1838; m. Phebe Vaughn and
             Louisa Gamble.
        III. SERENO, b. June 17, 1847; d. July 15, 1847.
        IV. ANGELINE L., b. July 25, 1848; m. Feb. 10, 1885,
             Addison Gardner; res. Brockport, N. Y.
         V. ELLA BELLE, b. Aug. 6, 1854.
        VI. GENEVIEVE, b. Oct. 30, 1856; m. Dec. 19, 1882,
             Frank Shuart, b. June 2, 1856; res. s. p., Pleasant
             Prairie, Wis.
       VII. NELLIE B., b. Aug. 9, 1859.

92. **William**[6] **Pierce** (Nathaniel[5], Seth B.[4], Thomas[3], Benja-
min[2], Michael[1]), b. Dec. 27, 1802; m. Nov. 23, 1826, Sarah L.
Willard, b. Mar. 18, 1809; d. 1834. He d. Dec. 7, 1849. Res.
Lowell, Mass.

CHILDREN.

       I. JOHN O., b. Nov. 16, 1829; m. July 2, 1867; res.
           Philadelphia, Pa.
      II. ANN W., b. Dec. 4, 1833; d. infant.
     III. WILLIAM H., b. Oct. 15, 1827; m. Aug. 18, 1850,
           Charlotte B. Temple, b. Mar. 16, 1831; res. Abing-
           ton, Mass. Ch., Ellen M., b. Aug. 8, 1851.

93. **Martin B.**[6] **Pierce** (Nathaniel[5], Seth B.[4], Thomas[3], Benjamin[2], Michael[1]), b. July 17, 1807; m. Mary E. Wellman, b. Jan.
29, 1815. He d. Dec. 25, 1876. Res. Duxbury and Abington,
Mass.

CHILDREN.

196.   I. HENRY B., b. Aug. 6, 1841; m. C. Elvira Carew,
             Augusta Arnold and Fanny B. Pease.

94. **John B.**[6] **Pierce** (Nathaniel[5], Seth B.[4], Thomas[3], Benjamin[2], Michael[1]), b. July 22, 1832; m. Jan. 10, 1856, Martha W.
Litchfield, b. Oct. 24, 1833. Res. North Scituate, Mass.

CHILDREN.

I. WILLIAM Z., b. Mar. 11, 1857.
II. GEORGE E., b. June 3, 1860; d. Dec. 23, 1863.
III. JOHN C., b. Oct. 31, 1869.

95. **John W.**[6] **Pierce** (John[5], Seth B.[4], Thomas[3], Benjamin[2], Michael[1]), b. Dec. 4, 1811; m. Feb. 11, 1841, Mary A. Whiton, b. June 8, 1816; d. Feb. 5, 1884. Res. Higham, Mass.

CHILDREN.

I. M. ANN, b. Oct. 7, 1843.

96. **Henry T.**[6] **Pierce** (John[5], Seth B.[4], Thomas[3], Benjamin[2], Michael[1]), b. Sept. 29, 1813; m. Sept. 6, 1849, Ella A. Hulse, b. Oct. 30, 1828; d. Sept. 18, 1854; m. 2nd, Apr. 14, 1857, Mary E. Chapman, b. Feb. 22, 1837. Res. Newburgh, N. Y. He d. 1888.

A friend sends the following of Mr. Henry T. Pierce, who has just deceased from cancer in the stomach. He deserves notice for two things: Through all his life he acted upon the charge given by a dying mother, of being uniformly just to every one; and such was the testimony of several persons to me during his distressing illness, that he had never wished to take advantage of anybody, but had acted always to others as he desired they should act to him. It seems to me only a necessary result of such practical righteousness, that an agonizing disease did not disturb the serenity of his last hours. I always felt cheered by entering his sick-chamber. I knew how much he had to endure, having had several friends removed by this fearful malady. But none of them bore it more bravely than he, knowing as he said, that it came from the Father's hand, was part of his spiritual education, making him even glad to leave a world where he had so much to love, and dear ones who had so much right to love him.

> They say he died; it seemed to me
> That after months of pain and strife,
> He slept one evening peacefully,
> And woke in everlasting life.

I. FRANK H., b. Oct. 25, 1850; m. Mary Stocker.

II. THEODORE W., b. June 10, 1852; unm.; res. 189 Duane St., N. Y. City.

III. J. DEXTER, b. Dec. 5, 1858; unm.; res. Larimore, Dakota.

IV. ALBERT S., b. Mar. 8, 1860; m. June 10, 1886, Edith Heard; b. Apr. 20, 1863; res. Newburgh, N. Y.

V. EMMA C., b. Dec. 23, 1862; m. Dec. 24, 1884, Wm. Coldwell; b. May 6, 1863; res. s. p., Newburgh, N. Y.

97. **Rev. Joseph D.**[6] **Pierce** (John[5], Seth B.[4], Thomas[3], Benjamin[2], Michael[1]), b. Nov. 15, 1815; m. Nov. 30, 1858, Martha S. Price; b. 1830, d. Dec., 1885. He d. Nov. 16, 1880. Res. North Attleboro, Mass.

No sadder funeral service, at which there was more of heartfelt sorrow, was ever attended in Attleboro than that solemnized from the First Universalist Church in North Attleboro on a November afternoon in 1880. The life of the Rev. J. D. Peirce had been such as to cause universal regret and sorrow at his death. This esteem for him in life and sorrow at his dying were attested by the large congregation of his fellow townsmen who came to pay the last tribute of respect, and by the many beautiful floral offerings.

The church wherein he had ministered for more than a quarter of a century's time, was most appropriately prepared for the final service. The pulpit was heavily draped in black with festoons of smilax overhanging it. Upon the walls immediately back and to the side of the pulpit were heavy folds of black, and festoons of the same were arranged upon the side walls, encircled the chandelier and formed the draperies for the singers' gallery. The contributions of flowers were beautiful and bounteous.

Preceding the service at the church there was prayer at the house, Rev. Mr. Goodrich, of Pawtucket, officiating. To those who were in waiting at the church, the tolling bell and mournful dirge told of the approach of the solemn procession. The body was borne from the house to the church, escorted by Aurora Lodge. Members from Howard Encampment, I. O. O. F., and a delegation from Orient Lodge were also in attendance. A delegation from Bristol Lodge, F. & A. M., were in waiting at the church.

Rev. Mr. Hill in his address referred to the special and public interest in this death, and spoke of the unusual mark of respect, alluding to the fact that stores, shops, all places of business and the schools were closed and that business was generally suspended; that among those present were ministers of and representatives from every church; men representing all classes; and delegations from different orders. These testified that a good man had died. He spoke of the departed as a good minister of Jesus Christ, and quoted from St. Paul's first Epistle to Timothy, the qualifications necessary to the perfect minister. There were none of the virtues named in that text which the departed had not thoughtfully considered, and he came as near the standard as it ever is in the power of man to come. The speaker devoted a brief space to an outline of his biography, giving the facts contained in the obituary elsewhere published. But it was upon his excellence as a good citizen and faithful Christian minister, whereby he won the esteem of all his fellow men and of all ministers, of whatever faith, that he dwelt. He was a disinterested, faithful laborer, seldom thinking of himself. He found his work for Christ where Christ found it; in the street, the store, the shops, public places, the school; he loved all, prayed for all and worked for all, and for the good and moral interests of the town. He had unbounded sympathy for those in trouble and went about ministering to the sick and afflicted. In schools and public life and in the fraternal orders he took an active part, but it was in the church and Sunday school he loved most to work. As a preacher he stood high with his brothers in the ministry, but sought to teach by his example rather than to lead by his eloquence. The speaker exhorted those who had enjoyed . the fellowship and social influence of this good man to emulate the example he had made for them, and closed with the words of consolation and sympathy for the bereaved family and friends, trusting that they might be sustained in this the hour of trial, by the same faith with which he had been sustained in sickness and in death.

After the services in the church the remains were borne to their final resting place in Mount Hope cemetery, where the last sad rites were performed in the simple service of Odd Fellows.

During the service in the church an unfortunate interruption occurred, caused by the giving way of support beneath, and the settling of the floor for about six inches. A most disastrous accident was avoided by the timely discovery of this. It was necessary to clear the church of nearly half the people in it, and a panic was prevented by presence of mind and a skillful management of the affair. Order was restored in a few moments and the service proceeded.

Another paper says:

Attleboro has lost this week her oldest settled clergyman and her most esteemed citizen. Rev. Joseph Dexter Peirce, for twenty-eight years pastor of the First Universalist Church, died Tuesday, after a brief illness of one week, of typhoid pneumonia. The deceased was born in Scituate, Mass., November 15, 1815, and, therefore, at his death was sixty-five years and one day old. His father died while the subject of this notice was in early youth and he was brought to manhood by a mother's care. Fortunately, she was a woman of rare strength and tenderness of character, and nobly fulfilled the mission which devolved upon her. In his pulpit services, the son often testified to the fidelity and strength of a mother's love. Who doubts that the picture was drawn in tender remembrance of the days when mother and son lived and toiled, rejoiced and suffered, at the same fireside?

Joseph Dexter was the youngest of three sons. John, the eldest, now lives in Hingham, Mass. Henry, the other brother, entered into rest a few years ago, at Newburgh, N. Y., where his family now reside. Joseph was apprenticed in his youthful days as a carpenter. At this time he was an eager reader of biography, travels and history, and what he then read he spoke of with zest in recent years. His taste for intellectual pursuits was so far gratified that he obtained, at his own expense, a thorough academic education, and entered upon the work of studying for the ministry with Rev. Dr. Hosea Ballou, 2nd, the first president of Tufts College, at Medford, Mass. He was ordained in 1839, and after preaching a few months in East Boston, he was settled for five years in Hartland, Vermont, where he engaged in both teaching and preaching. In 1844, at the age of twenty-nine, he was called to the pastorate of the First Universalist Church, at North Attleboro. But after three years' successful service he was obliged to resign his ministry on account of ill-health. He then became principal of the old academy which stood in the rear of Kendall's block, and not a few of our men and women, now in the prime of life, enjoyed here the benefit of his instructions.

In 1850 he was called to the First Universalist parish of Claremont, New Hampshire, where for five years he performed the work of school committee, teacher and clergyman, with such acceptance that a deacon of the Baptist church there declared, in view of his returning here, "We cannot get along without him." He was often called to attend funerals in the surrounding towns, and, to this day, there are people there who remember with grateful emotion the words of sympathy which fell from his lips, as

some loved one was borne from their home to return no more forever. And to-day there are friends in Claremont whose eyes will
moisten with tears as they read that his work is ended.

In June, 1855, he received a unanimous call to return to the
First Universalist Church at North Attleboro, and accepted it.
Here for more than a quarter of a century he labored unceasingly
in the Master's vineyard, until called to receive the reward of those
who love their fellowmen. With the exception of Rev. Dr. Miner,
he had, at the time of his death, been settled longer over the same
church than any other pastor of the denomination in Massachusetts.

During this period he became identified with all the interests of
the town. He served as a member of the school committee about
twenty years, and was chairman of the board at the time of his
death. In this work he felt it his duty to be engaged, and he loved
it. His convictions of the common school and his principle of
action were well expressed in his report for 1857. " The specific
object of the district school is the cultivation of the intellect;
but it is also the duty of those who are intrusted with the public
education of the young, to watch the development of their moral
natures, to guard them, as far as may be practicable, against the
contagion of evil, to impress righteous principles upon their minds
and hearts, in fine, to inspire them with reverence to God and
good-will to his children. It richly deserves the fostering care of
the patriot, the generous support of the philanthropist, and the
fervent prayer of the Christian."

In November, 1868, he was elected to represent the town in the
General Court, and he served his constituents faithfully and cred-
itably. As the first president of the North Attleboro Library
Association, he was instrumental in establishing the public library,
now supported by the Union Improvement District.

As a member of that worthy body, representing " Friendship,
Love and Truth," his heart was in ministries of mercy and relief.
He was one of the eight charter members of Aurora Lodge, of
whom, in his own words, "seven have now fallen asleep." No
man more thoroughly understood and appreciated the spirit and
principles of the institution, and, all along his connection with
the great brotherhood, are tablets of honor to his wisdom, until
he came to be universally loved by his brethren. He was a worthy
member of Bristol Lodge, Free and Accepted Masons, and at his
death Deputy Grand Patriarch of Howard Encampment, I. O. O. F.

But it was as a minister of the Gospel that he loved best to be
known. He felt, as he himself said, that he had a natural gift
for preaching. It is not the place here to analyze his doctrines.

The church which he walked before so long will have to go a great way to find his equal, and still further to find a better man than he, one who so conscientiously carried out, in his daily life, the spirit and teachings of the Divine Master.

Mr. Peirce was married November 30, 1858, to Martha S. Price, daughter of George Price, Esq., who, with his four daughters, his beloved household, are now called, in deep bereavement, to breathe the prayer, " Thy will, O God, be done ! "

The death of one who so long lived and wrought in every good work, and who spoke words of consolation in so many bereaved households, is a public loss. He was, in all the higher and grander elements of character, an almost exceptional man. His life took the hue of heaven, and no man ever lived in the town, certainly not in the memory of the present generation, who had more friends and fewer enemies as he passed to his needed rest. Of feeble health — he once said that he had not known a waking hour free from pain for fifteen years — he yet night and day devoted his time and talents to the works he loved with tireless zeal. He demonstrated by his example the loftier qualities of man, and his departure has caused a void which it will be hard to fill.

Children.

I. AGNES, b. June 3, 1860 ; m. May 22, 1886, Hon. John D. Long of Hingham, Mass., b. Oct. 27, 1838. Of this marriage a paper has this: Congressman and ex-Governor John D. Long of Massachusetts was married in the Universalist Church, at North Attleboro, to Miss Agnes Pierce. Miss Pierce was the daughter of the Rev. Joseph E. Pierce, who was for many years pastor of that church, and who died in 1880. Her mother died last December, and for that reason the wedding was very private, the only person present besides the immediate families of the contracting parties being Miss Fanny Barrows of North Attleboro, a friend of the bride. There were no groomsmen or bridesmaids, and the entire party numbered only thirty-five. Gov. Long's two daughters were present. The ceremony was performed by the Rev. Henry A. Miles of Hingham. Governor and Mrs. Long left for Washington soon after the wedding.

Hon. John D. Long, the thirty-second governor of the Commonwealth of Massachusetts, under the Constitution, and whose wise, prudent administration reflected great credit upon himself, was born in Buckfield, Maine, October 27, 1838.

His father was a man of some prominence in the Pine Tree State, and in the year in which his more distinguished son first saw the light, he ran for Congress on the Whig ticket, and although receiving a plurality of the votes cast, he was defeated.

The son was a studious lad, more fond of his books than of play, and thought more of obtaining a solid education than of developing his muscles as an athlete. At the proper age he entered the academy at Hebron, the principal of which was at that time Mark H. Dunnell, subsequently a member of Congress from Minnesota.

At the age of fourteen young Long entered the Freshman class at Harvard College. He at once took high rank, stood fourth in his class for the course, and second at the end of the Senior year. He was the author of the class ode, sung on Commencement day.

After leaving college, Mr. Long was engaged as principal of the Westford Academy, an old institution incorporated in 1793. He remained at Westford two years, highly esteemed by his pupils and beloved of the whole people. As a teacher, he won marked success, and many of his contemporaries regret that he did not always remain in the profession. But he cherished another, if not a higher ambition. From Westford he passed to the Harvard Law School, and to the offices of Sidney Bartlett and Peleg W. Chandler, in Boston. In 1861 he was admitted to the bar, and then he opened an office in his native town, to practice his new profession.

16

He soon found, however, that Buckfield was not the place for him. People there were far too honest and peace-loving, and minded their own business too well to assist in building up a lawyer's reputation. After two years' stay, therefore, he removed to Boston, and entered the office of Stillman B. Allen, where he rapidly gained an extensive practice. The firm, which consisted of Mr. Allen, Mr. Long, Thomas Savage and Alfred Hemenway, had their offices on Court street, in an old building now on the site of the new Young's Hotel. Mr. Long remained in the firm until his election, in November, 1879, to the governorship of Massachusetts.

In 1870 he was married to Miss Mary W. Glover of Hingham, Mass., to which town he had previously removed his residence. During his executive administration he had the great misfortune to undergo bereavement by the loss of this most estimable lady, whose wise counsel often lent him encouragement in the perplexed days of his official life.

In 1875 Mr. Long was chosen to represent the Republicans of the second Plymouth district in the Legislature. He at once took a prominent position, and gained great popularity with his fellow members. In 1876 he was reelected to the House, and soon after he was chosen speaker. This position he filled with dignity, grace and with an ease surpassed by no speaker before him or since. He showed himself thoroughly versed in parliamentary practice, and his tact was indeed something remarkable. So great was his popularity that, in 1877, he had every vote which was cast for speaker, and in the following year every vote but six.

In the fall of 1877 the Republican State Convention assembled at Worcester, and it at once became apparent that many of the delegates were desirous to vote for Mr. Speaker Long for the highest office in the Commonwealth. At the convention he received, however, only 217 votes for candidate; and his name was then withdrawn.

At the convention of 1878 he again found numerous supporters, and received 266 votes for governor. He was then nominated for lieutenant-governor by a very large majority, and was elected. In the convention of 1879, Governor Thomas Talbot declining a re-nomination, Lieutenant-Governor Long received 669 votes to 505 votes for the Hon. Henry L. Pierce, and was nominated and elected, having 122,751 votes to 109,149 for General Benjamin F. Butler, 9,989 for John Quincy Adams, and 1,635 for the Rev. D. C. Eddy, D. D.

On the 15th of September, 1880, Governor Long was re-nominated by acclamation, and in November he was re-elected by a plurality of about 52,000 votes — the largest plurality given for any candidate for the governorship of Massachusetts since the presidential year of 1872. He continued to hold the office, by re-election, until January, 1883.

Several important acts were passed during the administration of Governor Long, and notably among these was an act fixing the penalties for drunkenness — an act providing that no person who has served in the United States army or navy, and has been honorably discharged from the service, if otherwise qualified to vote, shall be debarred from voting on account of his being a pauper, or, if a pauper, because of the non-payment of a poll tax — an act which obviated many of the evils of double taxation by providing that, when any person has an interest in taxable real estate as holders of a mortgage, given to secure the payment of a loan, the amount of which is fixed and stated, the amount of said person's interest as mortgagee shall be assessed as real estate in the city or town where the land lies, and the mortgagor shall be assessed only for the value of said real estate, less the mortgagee's interest in it.

The creditable manner in which Mr. Long conducted the affairs of the State induced his constituents to send him as their representative in Washington. He was elected a member of the

Forty-eighth Congress, and is now a member also of the Forty-ninth. His record thus far has been altogether honorable and characterized by a sturdy watchfulness of the interests intrusted to his care.

As a man of letters, Governor Long has achieved a reputation. Some years ago, he produced a scholarly translation, in blank verse, of Virgil's *Æneid,* which was published in 1879, in Boston. It has found many admirers among students of classical literature. Governor Long, amid busy professional and official duties, has also written several poems and essays which reflect credit upon his heart and brain. His inaugural addresses were masterpieces of literary art, and the same can be said of his speeches on the floor of Congress, all of them polished, forceful and to the point.

Mr. Long is a very fluent speaker, and without oratorical display, he always succeeds in winning the attention of his auditors. It is what he says, more than how he says it, that has won for him his great popularity on the platform. When, in February last, the Washington monument was dedicated, he it was that was chosen to read the magnificent oration of Robert C. Winthrop.

As a specimen of Mr. Long's happy way of expressing timely thoughts, the following passage, selected from an address which he delivered at Tremont Temple, Boston, on Memorial Day, 1881, deserves to be read:

"Scarce a town is there — from Boston, with its magnificent column crowned with the statue of America at the dedication of which even the conquered Southron came to pay honor, to the humblest stone in rural villages — in which these monuments do not rise summer and winter, in snow and sun, day and night, to tell how universal was the response of Massachusetts to the call of the patriots' duty, whether it rang above the city's din or broke the quiet of the farm. On city square and village green stand the graceful figures of student, clerk, mechanic, farmer, in that endeared and never-to-be-forgotten war-uniform of the soldier or the sailor, their stern young faces to the front, still on guard, watching the work they wrought in the flesh, and teaching in eloquent silence the lesson of the citizen's duty to the State. How our children will study these! How they will search and read their names! How quaint and antique to them will seem their arms and costume! How they will gather and store up in their minds the fine, insensibly filtering percolation of the sentiment of valor, of loyalty, of fight for right, of resistance against wrong, just as we inherited all this from the Revolutionary era, so that, when some crisis shall in the future come to them, as it came to us, they will spring to the rescue, as sprang our youth, in the beauty and chivalry of the consciousness of a noble descent."

II. BERTHA, b. 1862.

III. MARY W., b. 1864.

IV. HELEN, b. 1869.

98. **Mason W.**[6] **Pierce** (Mial[5], Mial[4], Mial[3], John[2], Michael[1]), b. Sept. 1, 1794; m. Oct. 1, 1815, Lucinda C. Davis, b. Mar. 23, 1791; d. Aug. 10, 1879. He d. Nov. 18, 1873. Res. Bristol, R. I.

CHILDREN.

198.   I. GEORGE C., b. July 14, 1816; m. Julianna Bliss.

     II. MARY C., b Feb. 21, 1818; m. Apr. 10, 1836, Francis E. Brown, b. May 18, 1813; d. June 20, 1883; res. Bristol, R. I. Ch. Mary F., b. Mar., 1837; m. Cory Williston; Fred'k P., b. Feb., 1843; d. Mar., 1843.

199.   III. MASON W., b. Feb. 13, 1820; m. Lydia M. Townsend.

     IV. NATHAN B., b. 1822; d. 1822.

200.   V. JAMES P., b. Sept. 16, 1823; m. Maria W. Disman and Eliza H. Hoar.

201.   VI. HENRY P., b. Feb. 12, 1826; m. Mary Pilling.

202.   VII. DAVID A., b. Mar. 5, 1828; m. Jane A. Pilling.

     VIII. LUCINDA B., b. 1830; d. 1832.

     IX. JESSE D., b. 1834; d. 1835.

     X. LAWRENCE B., b. 1836; d. 1841.

99. **Darius**[6] **Pierce** (Mial[5], Mial[4], Mial[3], John[2], Michael[1]), b. ——, m. Dec. 8, 1808, Mary Hapgood; m. 2nd, Dec. 1, 1811, Lucinda Walker. He d. 1837, Swansey, Mass.

CHILDREN.

     I. WALKER, b. ——; m. ——; res. Elizabethport, N. J.

100. **Isaac⁶ Pierce** (Asa⁵, Mial⁴, Mial³, John², Michael¹), b. Oct. 11, 1790; m. Sept. 15, 1822, Anna M. Chace, b. June 4, 1798. He d. Oct. 8, 1851. Res. Somerset, Mass.

CHILDREN.

203.   I. JOHN Q., b. June 22, 1823; m. Carrie C. Hasslegren.
   II. WILLIAM E., b. Aug. 27, 1824, unm.

101. **John H.⁶ Pierce** (Asa⁵, Mial⁴, Mial³, John², Michael¹), b. May 23, 1792; m. Sept. 21, 1815, Content Bowen, b. June 18, 1797; d. Mar. 2, 1880. He d. Oct. 9, 1829. Res. Freetown, Mass.

CHILDREN.

  I. EUNICE B., b. Apr. 15, 1816; d. Aug. 27, 1830.
  II. NANCY, b. Sept. 12, 1817; d. Oct. 10, 1817.
  III. HANNAH, b. Sept. 29, 1819; m. July 27, 1834, Job Collins.
  IV. JOHN H., b. June 9, 1821; d. June 9, 1822.
204.   V. JOHN H., b. Feb. 23, 1823; m. Ruth A. Buffington.
  VI. JAMES T., b. Oct., 1824; d. Sept., 1825.
  VII. CONTENT, b. June 9, 1827.
  VIII. SUSAN S., b. Nov. 23, 1828; m. Dec. 21, 1846, David P. Purington, b. Aug. 13, 1824; res. Fall River, Mass. Ch., Eunice B., b. Sept. 11, 1847; d. Dec. 26, 1873; Harriett T., b. Apr. 22, 1857; d. Dec. 5, 1874.

102. **Asa⁶ Pierce** (Asa⁵, Mial⁴, Mial³, John², Michael¹), b. Sept. 16, 1787; m. Sept. 29, 1814, Theolotia Perrin, b. Sept. 8, 1790; d. July 6, 1867. He d. Sept. 16, 1868. Res. Somerset, Mass.

CHILDREN.

  I. MARY A., b. Sept. 7, 1815; m. June 12, 1839, James T. Champlin, b. June 9, 1811; d. Mar. 15, 1882; res. 727 Congress street, Portland, Me. Ch., James Pierce, b. June 9, 1840, in Portland; m. Miss Helen Frances Perry of Portland, Nov. 2, 1864;

P. O. address, 292 Spring street, Portland, Me.; Augustus, b. in Waterville, Me., Mar. 9, 1842; unm.; P. O. address, 727 Congress street, Portland, Me.; Caroline, b. in Waterville, Me., Jan. 4, 1845; m. Rev. Henry S. Burrage, D. D., May 19, 1873; d. Nov. 24, 1875; Francis Armstrong, b. in Waterville, Me., Sept. 13, 1849; m. Leila F. Perry of Camden, Me.; P. O. address, Waterville, Me.

205.   II. WILLIAM G., b. Dec. 19, 1825; m. Almira F. Metcalf.

206.   III. GEORGE A., b. Aug. 12, 1828; m. Henrietta K. Angell.

103. **John[6] Pierce** (John[5], John[4], John[3], John[2], Michael[1]), b. Mar. 27, 1790; m. Oct. 2, 1815, Alice Pitts. Res. Dighton, Mass.

CHILDREN.

I. JOHN, b. Apr. 13, 1817; drowned Sept. 25, 1828.

II. PHILLIP, b. Oct. 17, 1820; d. May 24, 1821.

III. ALICE M., b. June 13, 1822; m. Jeremiah Edson; res. Dighton, Mass.

104. **Anthony[6] Pierce** (John[5], John[4], John[3], John[2], Michael[1]), b. July 16, 1795; m. Feb. 3, 1822, Oliver Lee of Swansey, Mass., b. 1804; d. May 6, 1872; m. 2nd, Deborah (Pierce) Brightman, b. ——; she d. Apr. 2, 1884. Res. Dighton, Mass.

CHILDREN.

207.   I. ANTHONY, b. Aug. 20, 1825; m. Hannah F. Briggs.

208.   II. GEORGE E., b. Apr., 1838; m. Mary J. Reed.

209.   III. SIMEON A., b. Apr. 8, 1835; m. Melissa A. Reed.

IV. OLIVE, b. ——; m. Lloyd B. Chace; res. Swansey, Mass.

V. MARY E., b. ——; m. John A. Sayles; res. Somerset, Mass.

VI. SUSAN M., b. ——; m. Silas D. Briggs; res. Dighton, Mass.

105. **Gamaliel⁶ Pierce** (John⁵, John⁴, John³, John², Michael¹),
b. Dec. 15, 1799; m. Dec. 5, 1822, Persis Baker, b. July 19, 1804;
d. Mar. 25, 1886. He d. Aug. 11, 1878. Res. Rehoboth and
Dighton, Mass.

CHILDREN.

I. NANCY G., b. Sept. 4, 1825; m. May 30, 1849,
George E. Gooding, b. Sept. 19, 1826; res. s.
p., North Dighton, Mass.

II. REBECCA, b. Oct. 19, 1827; m. May 16, 1847, Caleb B. Bowen, b. Dec. 22, 1820; res. Dighton,
Mass. Ch., Henry F., b. Dec. 30, 1847; Otis P.,
b. Dec. 20, 1851; d. Aug. 18, 1853; Mary O.,
b. June 2, 1855; m. May 6, 1875, James F. Briggs;
David I., b. May 29, 1857; m. July 4, 1877, Rebecca T. Briggs; all res. in Dighton, Mass.

III. SARAH, b. Feb. 19, 1830; m. May 17, 1847, Adoniram J. Smith, b. Jan. 5, 1824; d. Mar. 19, 1852;
res. Dighton, Mass. Ch., William W., b. Feb.
25, 1848; d. Aug. 16, 1851; Sarah W., b. July 23,
1853; d. Jan. 24, 1868; m. 2nd, Edwin B. Smith,
b. Apr. 14, 1828. Ch., Adoniram J., b. Mar. 3,
1867; Clara M., b. Jan. 24, 1869; d. July 22,
1869; res. Dighton, Mass.

IV. RUTH A., b. Apr. 13, 1831; m. Sept. 8, 1851, Otis
P. Bowen, b. Mar. 3, 1827; res. Rehoboth, Mass.
Ch., Nancy P., b. Mar. 3, 1852; m. Charles A.
Bowen, Mar. 3, 1871; res. Pawtucket, R. I.;
Leroy E., b. Mar. 1, 1854; m. Carrie O. Luther,
Oct. 19, 1887; res. Pawtucket, R. I.; Herbert,
b. Sept. 25, 1857; res. Rehoboth, Mass.; Nathan,
b. Nov. 26, 1860; m. Clara Pierce, June 8, 1887;
res. Rehoboth, Mass.; Henry O., b. June 16,
1862; m. Harriet Earle, Sept. 6, 1888; res. Rehoboth, Mass.

V. LAVINA, b. July 4, 1834; m. July 15, 1855, Hiram S.
Crowell, b. May 9, 1833. Ch., Ella M., b. July 13,

1856 ; m. May 29, 1877, Charles H. Talbot ; res. Pittsfield, Mass. ; Hiram L., b. Jan. 7, 1859; d. Jan. 18, 1865 ; Carrie L., b. Jan. 5, 1870 ; Hiram A., b. May 15, 1878 ; d. Jan. 5, 1879 ; res. Dighton, Mass.

106. **Bethuel⁶ Pierce** (Bethuel⁵, Elisha⁴, John³, John², Michael¹), b. Aug. 6, 1784 ; m. Elizabeth Goff. He d. 1810. Was lost at sea coming from Turk's Island with a cargo of salt, in a gale of wind. The vessel and all on board lost. Res. Freetown, Mass.

CHILDREN.

I. JOHN, b. Dec. 27, 1806 ; m. Dec. 24, 1835, Eliza Rex, b. 1803 ; d. Aug. 20, 1836, s. p.; res. 30 South Union street, Pawtucket, R. I.
II. Also two daughters, both married but did not have any children.

107. **Nathan⁶ Pierce** (Bethuel⁵, Elisha⁴, John³, John², Michael¹), b. Nov. 20, 1794; m. Aug. 5, 1832, Mary A. Chase, b. May 12, 1799; d. Feb. 18, 1881. He d. May 27, 1868. Res. Freetown, Mass.

CHILDREN.

210.   I. NATHAN ANDREW, b. Mar. 19, 1833; m. Olive E. French.
211.   II. ALEXANDER, b. Jan. 17, 1835; m. Annie A. Lawrence.
        III. ALFRED, b. Feb. 8, 1837; m. Oct. 20, 1884, Mary M. Barrows, b. Apr. 1, 1840; res. Berkley, Mass., s. p.
        IV. MARY E., b. Oct. 14, 1840; d. Feb. 6, 1852.
        V. ANN M., b. Feb. 2, 1843; m. Oct. 16, 1884, Phineas D. Fletcher, b. Sept. 28, 1841; res. Freetown, Mass. Ch., Mary M., b. Sept. 3, 1885. Phineas was in the war of the Rebellion, having enlisted in the 7th Mass. Vols. He served for three years,

17

endured great hardships, was in numerous battles, but returned home in safety. He was the son of Francis P. Fletcher.

108. **George**[6] **Pierce** (Bethuel[5], Elisha[4], John[3], John[2], Michael[1]), b. Dec. 24, 1792; m. Lucinda Chace, b. 1793; d. 1820; m. 2nd, Melinda Chace, b. Nov. 19, 1801; d. Mar. 15, 1823; m. 3d, Apr. 4, 1824, Betsey M. Hathaway, b. Dec. 2, 1802; d. Nov. 27, 1878. He d. May 17, 1879. Res. Berkley, Mass.

CHILDREN.

I. LUCINDA, b. Jan. 1, 1817; m. —— Harris. She d. July 21, 1864; one dau., Sarah E., m. —— Hathaway ; res. South Dighton.

II. HARRIETT, b. Mar. 15, 1822; m. —— Marble; res. Somerset, Mass.

III. GEORGE G., b. Aug. 21, 1825; res. Fall River.

212. IV. ICHABOD M., b. Feb. 14, 1827; m. Susan B. Rowley.

V. NANCY H., b. Mar. 7, 1828; m. —— Ripley; res. 110 Davol street, Fall River, Mass.

VI. ELIZABETH C., b. Jan. 15, 1830; m. May 20, 1849, James Maguire, b. July 31, 1828. She d. May 30, 1884; res. Berkley, Mass. Ch., Edward A., b. Thursday, Feb. 28, 1850, and m. June 27, 1873, to Annie A. Phillips; James E., b. Saturday, May 1, 1852; d. Oct. 11, 1864; Benjamin F. P., b. Wednesday, Feb. 27, 1856, and d. Oct. 16, 1864; Betsey E. S., b. July 11, 1860, and m. July 31, 1880, to Willard H. Hathaway; Frances E., b. Aug. 28, 1864; Eva S., b. Jan. 21, 1873.

VII. ABBIE A. H., b. Oct. 31, 1831; m. Feb. 13, 1861, Wm. Caswell, b. Aug. 20, 1820. Ch., George W., b. Dec. 22, 1863; Benjamin B., b. Feb. 12, 1866; Arthur G., b. June 27, 1870; res. Berkley, Mass.

VIII. BENJAMIN F., b. Jan. 25, 1834; d. July 13, 1854.

IX. SYBIL P., b. Dec. 27, 1841; m. July 19, 1865, Benjamin F. Luther, b. Jan. 22, 1842; res. Fairhaven, Mass. Ch., Sybil M., b. Jan. 8, 1868; George B., b. Oct. 5, 1870; Beulah A., b. Sept. 14, 1873; Anna J., b. Mar. 27, 1876; d. Sept. 13, 1881; Caleb R., b. June 30, 1878; d. Aug. 6, 1883.

X. SARAH D., b. Sept. 11, 1846; m. Apr. 4, 1867, John H. Grinnell, b. June 29, 1821; res. Berkley, Mass. Ch., John W., b. Sept. 22, 1869; Lyman B., b. May 2, 1872; Herbert C., b. July 22, 1874; Frank O., b. May 14, 1876; Hattie P., b. Oct. 25, 1878; Fred L., b. March 11, 1883.

109. **John⁶ Pierce** (Bethuel⁵, Elisha⁴, John³, John², Michael¹), b. July 9, 1798; m. 1820, Lydia Clark, b. Jan. 20, 1802; d. Mar. 20, 1858. He d. Nov. 7, 1856. Res. Berkley, Mass.

CHILDREN.

213.   I. ELNATHAN, b. June 14, 1822; m. Lucy H. Maxin.

    II. LYDIA, b. Mar. 29, 1824; m. Dec. 25, 1846, Thomas B. Paull, b. June 4, 1823; d. June 6, 1882. She d. Sept. 20, 1885; res. North Raynham, Mass. Ch., Anna F., b. Mar. 6, 1847; d. July 17, 1847; Seth W., b. Oct. 25, 1848; d. May 10, 1884; Ida F., b. Mar. 30, 1851; m. Edmund F. Wilbur; res. North Raynham, Mass.; Abby A., b. Mar. 26, 1853; d. June 13, 1872.

214.   III. JOHN, b. May 1, 1826; m. Sarah Hathaway.

    IV. ELIZA, b. June 9, 1829; m. Nov. 25, 1847, Elias W. Strange, b. Oct. 27, 1826; res. Taunton. Ch., Edwin F., b. Feb. 26, 1849; m. Phœbe M. Eldridge; res. Taunton; Ellen M., b. Dec. 11, 1852; m. Frederic C. Fuller; res. Taunton; Ettie G., b. Jan. 13, 1863; m. Frederic V. Fuller; res. Taunton.

V. JULIA, b. Mar. 13, 1831; m. May 23, 1852, Charles
   A. Jones, b. Apr. 18, 1831; res. 154 Sixth street,
   Providence, R. I.   Ch., Edward A., b. Nov. 26,
   1855; d. July 15, 1856; Ella May, b. May 21,
   1858; m. ―― Howland; res. Providence, R. I.
   Henry E., b. ――; d. 1862; Eddy E., b. Feb.
   29, 1864; d. Aug. 7, 1864.

110. **Subbinus**[6] **Pierce** (Elisha[5], Elisha[4], John[3], John[2], Michael[1]), b. Jan. 12, 1772; m. Mar. 24, 1797, Elsie Ballou, b. June
12, 1778; d. Apr. 25, 1864. He d. July 20, 1843. Res. Suffield, Ct.

CHILDREN.

       I. MARY, b. Aug. 12, 1798; d. 1870, Longmeadow,
         Mass.
215.   II. SABRA, b. Mar. 1, 1800; m. ―― Thayer; res.
         Woonsocket, R. I.
216.   III. OTIS, b. Nov. 14, 1801; m. Mary Bement.
217.   IV. SUBBINUS, b. Aug. 18, 1804; m. Deborah Alvord.
      V. ELISHA, b. Apr. 7, 1806; m. Hannah Sherman.
    VI. HARVEY, b. Sept. 12, 1809; drowned Dec., 1835.
   VII. ELSIE, b. May 16, 1812; d. Oct. 20, 1830. *
  VIII. MARANTHA, b. Mar. 2, 1815; m. ―― Pomeroy;
         res. Agawam, Mass. Their son William was the
         first one that enlisted for the war in the town of
         Suffield, Ct., for three months. He was given a
         nice revolver, but when he was taken prisoner in
         Louisiana, had time to hide it under a log. He
         was exchanged, but I think he had re-enlisted for
         three years, after that, for the war, but was shot
         while on picket duty. His brother Rollin was
         with him.
    IX. GEORGE, b. July 24, 1817; d. 1823.

111. **Eliphalet**[6] **Pierce** (Elisha[5], Elisha[4], John[3], John[2], Michael[1]), b. June 3, 1782; m. ――, Anise Mitchell, b. ――. He
was one of the first settlers in Springfield, Ill.

112. **Rev. Isaac**[6] **Pierce** (Daniel[5], Clothier[4], Clothier[3], John[2], Michael[1]), b. Nov. 14, 1776; m. Feb. 19, 1794, Elizabeth Taylor, b. Nov. 19, 1776; d. Sept. 7, 1826; m. 2nd, Feb., 1827, Mrs. Anne Pierce, the widow of Cromwell Pierce. He d. Feb. 23, 1860. Res. Deposit, N. Y.

Rev. Isaac Pierce was born in Vermont, Feb. 15, 1776. With his parents he removed to Hartford, N. Y., in 1788. There he was educated at the " Deestrect Skules." He was converted at an early age, and being an excellent extemporaneous speaker often spoke in the church meetings. He was persuaded to enter the ministry, and for many years was a very successful preacher in New York State.

CHILDREN.

I. LEVI, b. May 1, 1796; d. Sept. 27, 1797.

II. POLLY, b. July 29, 1797; m. Abel Ingraham; a dau., Levina, m. —— Thornton; res. Deposit, N. Y.

218. III. AMASA, b. Feb. 4, 1800; m. Alma Baldwin.

219. IV. DANIEL, b. May 10, 1802; m. Polly Day and Wealthy Wheelock.

V. ELIZA, b. April 22, 1804, m. Nov. 1, 1819, Jacob Ingraham, b. May 11, 1792; d. May 23, 1867; res. Mellette, Dak. She is a pensioner of the war of 1812. Ch., Sarah A., b. Jan. 8, 1821; m. Oct. 2, 1842, John McLein, and d. May 8, 1855; Elizabeth T., b. Dec. 30, 1823; m. Dec. 4, 1842, Daniel A. Strong; res. Mellette, Dak.; Lydia N., b. Mar. 4, 1825; d. Nov. 14, 1843; Jacob C., b. Mar. 31, 1827; m. Nov. 25, 1852, Lucy M. Franklin; res. Leodie, Neb.; Polly M., b. Apr. 22, 1830; m. Mar. 14, 1850, Wm. Studley, and d. Apr. 8, 1863; Isaac P., b. Aug. 1, 1833; m. July 20, 1856, Sarah A. Haven; res. Henry, Dak.; Mial F., b. May 25, 1836; m. Dec. 27, 1859, Miranda M. Bancroft; res. Beotia, Dak.; Lovey A., b. Oct. 15, 1840; d. Nov. 7, 1843; David A., b. Jan. 28, 1841; d. Aug. 9, 1854; George W., b. Dec. 10,

1843 ; d. Oct. 12, 1848; Newton A., b. Sept. 5, 1848 ; d. Nov. 2, 1848.

VI. PHEBE, b. Jan. 7, 1806 ; m. Thomas Patchin.

VII. PATIENCE D., b. Feb. 15, 1809; m. July 10, 1825, Abraham M. Palmer, b. Dec. 4, 1807 ; d. May 25, 1874; res. Glenwood, Utah. Ch., Isaac, b. Apr. 25, 1826; d. Apr. 30, 1826 ; Luther M., b. July 5, 1827 ; res. Juab, Utah ; John Q., b. Jan. 11, 1829 ; d. 1840; Elizabeth, b. May 13, 1831; d. Sept., 1843; Ann E., b. Aug. 27, 1833 ; Susan C., b. Oct. 15, 1835 ; d. Oct. 5, 1853 ; Abraham P., b. Feb. 19, 1838 ; d. May, 1846; James A., b. Dec. 25, 1841; d. Apr., 1843; Patience D., b. Nov. 11, 1844; d. Sept., 1851 ; William M., b. Dec. 10, 1846; res. Glenwood, Utah; Hyram S., b. Feb. 9, 1849 ; res. Aurora, Utah.

220. VIII. ISAAC W., b. July 3, 1811 ; m. Phebe Baldwin and Dily Carpenter.

221. IX. DAVID, b. Mar. 7, 1813 ; m. Dency Pierce.

222. X. MIAL R., b. May 25, 1815 ; m. Provider Rexford and Elizabeth Colburn.

XI. RUTH L., b. Feb. 11, 1818 ; m. Apr. 29, 1838, Monroe Crozier, b. Apr. 15, 1819; d. Nov. 10, 1859; m. 2nd, Aug. 14, 1861, John Harrington, b. Jan. 9, 1828 ; res. Glenwood, Utah. Ch., Joseph C., b. Mar. 13, 1839; d. Mar. 16, 1839; Willard L., b. Jan. 29, 1841; shot in war, d. May 26, 1824; Patience C., b. Mar. 1, 1844 ; Nancy C., b. Mar. 1, 1844; Sarah E., b. Mar. 8, 1846 ; John P., b. Aug. 28, 1849 ; m. Alice Jennings; res. Mecosta, Mich.

223. XII. JOHN T., b. Feb. 11, 1818 ; m. Anna Cole.

XIII. ALMIRA, b. Feb. 3, 1821; m. Nelson Bromley; res. Arcola, Dade Co., Mo.

113. **Daniel[6] Pierce** (Daniel[5], Clothier[4], Clothier[3], John[2], Michael[1]), b. Jan. 17, 1793; m. Feb. 10, 1816, Levina Clark, b. Apr.

2, 1797; d. Aug. 30, 1882. He d. May 4, 1868. Res. Kingsboro, N. Y.

    I. SILAS L., b. Apr. 13, 1817; d. Mar. 3, 1826.

    II. MIAL C., b. Oct. 1, 1818; res. Mt. Sterling, Ill.

224.   III. JOHN B., b. Oct. 16, 1820; m. Rebecca B. Clark.

    IV. SAMUEL W., b. Sept. 16, 1822; m. Cemantha Pierce.

    V. DANIEL H., b. Sept. 12, 1825; d. Mar. 2, 1826.

    VI. DANIEL H., b. June 16, 1828; d. Sept. 5, 1852.

    VII. PARTHENIA L., b. June 2, 1830; m. Nov., 1854, Anthony Tiedeman ; res. Manston, Wis. He was b. Aug. 20, 1820. Ch., Levina A., b. Oct. 30, 1855; d. Mar. 26, 1883; Florence C., b. Nov. 29, 1856 ; m. William Couch; res. St. Edward, Neb.; David D., b. Dec. 25, 1858; m. Minnie Lambert; res. 103 S. 14th street, Omaha, Neb.; Elmer J., b. Aug. 10, 1861 ; Frank A., b. June 5, 1865; d. Aug. 29, 1866; Adelmer C., b. Aug. 13, 1867; ClaraP., b. May 16, 1870; d. Sept. 25, 1883; William I., b. June 28, 1873.

    VIII. SILAS L., b. Dec. 10, 1832 ; d. Nov. 2, 1849.

    IX. ZERIAH B., b. May 6, 1833; res. Dodge Center, Minn.

    X. GEORGE I., b. May 1, 1840; res. Nordland, Dakota.

114. **Clothier**[6] **Pierce** (Clothier[5], Clothier[4], Clothier[3], John[2], Michael[1]), b. Sept. 4, 1784; m. July 22, 1822, Bethia C. Cleaveland, b. May 9, 1802; d. May 24, 1882, at Boston, Mass. He d. Dec. 12, 1875, at Dartmouth, Mass. Res. North Dartmouth, Mass.

    I. CHLOE, b. Dec. 8, 1823; m. Sept. 3, 1847, John W. Pierce (see 220¼); res New Bedford, Mass.

    II. HANNAH E. H., b. Jan. 16, 1837; m. Feb. 28, 1859, William Thomas Faunce; res. 473 Columbus avenue, Boston, Mass. He was b. Aug. 27, 1837.

Ch., William T., b. Mar. 7, 1860; m. Sept. 4, 1879; Edward P., b. Mar. 9, 1864; add. 41 Court street, Boston, Mass.

III. CLOTHIER, b. Feb. 18, 1825; d. unm. June 19, 1880.

225. IV. JOHN C., b. Nov. 11, 1826; m. Annie A. S. Pierce.

V. WILLIAM C., b. 1830; d. 1830.

VI. MARY B., b. Mar. 27, 1833; m. Sept. 25, 1855, Alden B. Howland, b. Jan. 27, 1831; d. Apr. 4, 1859. She d. Oct. 3, 1859. Ch., Alden B., b. June 14, 1859; m. Dec. 15, 1880, Phebe C. Sherman, b. June 7, 1861; res. Des Moines, Iowa. Ch., Bertha E., b. Oct. 10, 1881 ; Mary A., b. June 4, 1885.

115. **Thomas Q.**[6] **Pierce** (Barnabas C.[5], Daniel[4], Samuel[3], John[2], Michael[1]), b. Dec. 26, 1820; m. May 15, 1844, Fidelia Watrous, b. June 12, 1829; d. Aug. 29, 1854. Res. s. p., Bloomfield, O.

116. **Dr. Columbus D.**[6] **Pierce** (Barnabas C.[5], Daniel[4], Samuel[3], John[2], Michael[1]), b. Nov. 1, 1839; m. Nov. 1, 1867, Hortense Price, b. Feb. 7, 1846. He was in the late Rebellion, in an Ohio regiment, and was an orderly. Res. Bloomfield, O.

CHILDREN.

I. FRANK L., b. Apr. 22, 1870.
II. FLORENCE M., b. May 22, 1875.
III. BERTHA W., b. Mar. 16, 1872.

117. **Dr. Daniel H.**[6] **Pierce** (Barnabas C.[5], Daniel[4], Samuel[3], John[2], Michael[1]), b. Aug. 1, 1837; m. Jan. 7, 1870, Mariah Hartman, b. Nov. 22, 1855. Res. Clabourne, Ohio.

Dr. D. H. Pierce was born in the county of Knox, State of Ohio, in the year 1837; son of Barnabas C. Pierce; was raised on the farm until about the age of eighteen. Having a desire for an education, commenced attending school, having obtained his education among the Quakers. Commenced the study of medicine, and has been engaged in that pursuit nearly all the time, except a short time when the Murphy movement first came to the front. Wishing to benefit humanity and raise the fallen, left his pursuit and went to delivering public addresses on the subject of temperance, and was instrumental in securing many to sign the pledge. Was married to Mariah Hartman in the year 1870. Four children have been born to them, three of whom still survive.

CHILDREN.

I. JESSIE F., b. Feb. 3, 1871.
II. CLINTON C., b. Aug. 27, 1873; d. May 14, 1877.
III. SHERIDAN W., b. Apr. 11, 1878.
IV. ETHEL L., b. June 15, 1884.

118. **Edward H.**[6] **Pierce** (Abizer[5], Daniel[4], Samuel[3], John[2], Michael[1]), b. Apr. 13, 1803 ; m. Mar. 12, 1828, Betsey Field. Res. Dundee, N. Y.

CHILDREN.

I. GEORGIA P., b. Apr. 18, 1837 ; m. May 18, 1859, Gilbert F. Bailey, b. Oct. 12, 1833 ; res. Croton Falls, N. Y. Ch., Sumner P., b. June 14, 1860 ; Clement C., b. Nov. 1, 1863; Edith A., b. Feb. 15, 1873.

120. **Isaac B.**[6] **Pierce** (William[5], Daniel[4], Samuel[3], John[2], Michael[1]), b. Apr. 29, 1816 ; m. Jan. 3, 1844, Mary J. Hazleton. b. Feb. 4, 1820. Res. Mahopac Falls, N. Y.

CHILDREN.

226.   I. JOHN J., b. May 29, 1846 ; m. Fannie Moore.
II. WILLIAM B., b. Nov. 25, 1847 ; m. June 18. 1872, Mary E. Pinkney, s. p.
III. HENRIETTA A., b. Jan. 6, 1853 ; m. May 30, 1874, Charles Moore. Ch., Edith, b. Mar. 19, 1875 ; Frederick, b. Nov. 26, 1878 ; Arthur, b. Mar. 7, 1885.

18

III. Joseph F., b. Mar. 17, 1855 ; m. Dec. 3, 1885, Mary
    C. Barrett.
IV. Hannah H., b. Nov. 30, 1856; unm.
V. Cordelia R., b. Sept. 30, 1858 ; unm.
VI. Bessie, b. Oct. 4, 1863 ; unm.

121. **John**[6] **Pierce** (Azrikim[5], Samuel[4], Azrikim[3], Ephraim[2],
Michael[1]), b. July 31, 1756 ; m. Mary Gilmore, b. 1761; d. Dec.,
1844. He d. Aug., 1829. Res. Franklin, Mass.

John Pierce served eight years in the Revolutionary War ; was orderly for General Washington, and enlisted next day after the
battle of Lexington. Shouldered his musket and walked from
Franklin, Mass., to Boston. Was in the battles of Bunker Hill,
Eutaw Spring, Camden, Brandy Wine, Cowpens, siege of York
Town and others. He was with Washington at Trenton. After
he came home he attended church one Sunday to hear Dr. Em-
mons, who preached in Franklin. In his prayer the minister
prayed for the mother country, he prayed that they would lay
down their arms, taken up for the mother country. The old soldier was very much excited at what was said ; he met the minister
at the church door, and said, "you damned old Tory, if you had
served eight years in the army, as I have, and suffered as I did, you
would not have made such a prayer as that."

John Pierce was a shoemaker ; the Doctor sent his shoes to be
mended, but he said he would not mend the old Tory's shoes, and
threw them out of the shop. The Doctor came to see him after a
while, and they became quite friendly, although Mr. Pierce always
felt a little riled up if politics were mentioned.

While a soldier he did not have any shoes or stockings some
of the time, and his feet bleeding and done up in rags. He was
at Valley Forge that cold winter. He carried dispatches between
Gens. Green and Washington.

Children.

227.   I. Israel, b. May 8, 1795 ; m. Eliza A. Richardson
       and Almira Nickerson.

II. NANCY, b. July 28, 1798 ; m. Spooner Alden, and
d. 1870; res. Hampden, Me. Ch., Augustus,
Washington, Adeline, Elizabeth, Silas.

228. III. JOHN, b. Sept. 12, 1790; m. Julia A. Brownell,
Nancy M. Clark and Caroline F. Grant.

IV. JOSEPH, b. May 18, 1792. He served in the war of
1812 on board a privateer ; was taken prisoner
and confined in Dartmoor Prison, England, for a
year ; d. unm., 1820.

229. V. WASHINGTON, b. Oct. 19, 1810 ; m. Nancy G. Hancock.

122. **Squier⁶ Pierce** (Azrikim⁵, Samuel⁴, Azrikim³, Ephraim²,
Michael¹), b. Aug. 27, 1758; m. Oct. 3, 1779, Freelove Wood, b.
1756; d. Feb. 13, 1833 ; m. 2nd, Betsey Goff. He d. Oct. 24,
1840. Res. Rehoboth, Mass.

From an old record the following is copied, viz.: Israel Pearce
of Providence, R. I., "Taylor," &c—and in consideration of Ten
Pounds, and sixteen Shillings, currant money well and truly paid
unto me, by my Brother Squier Pearce of Rehoboth Mass. &c a
Minor, son of Arikam Pearce, late of Rehoboth &c. this bargain
being with the full and free consent of the said Squier "Gurdien"
Joseph Pearce 2ᵈ The whole of the lands, fell to my share in the
Division of my Honᵈ Father Arikam Pearceˢ Estate in Rehoboth
&c. Dated Aug 18, 1777 In the second year of the States of
America, Delared Independent of Great Britain &c &c

CHILDREN.

I. ROBE, b. Sept. 11, 1780 ; m. Capt. Nathaniel Wheaton; res. South Rehoboth, Mass.

230. II. ISRAEL, b. June 2, 1783; m. Hannah Cole.

III. NANCY, b. Nov. 29, 1785 ; m. Feb. 1, 1807, Nathaniel Davis ; res. New Bedford, Mass. Ch., Lorenzo D.

231. IV. SQUIER, b. Jan. 22, 1788 ; m. Elizabeth Hicks.

232. V. SAMUEL, b. Aug. 12, 1790; m. Jane Case.

VI. FREELOVE, b. Nov. 9, 1792 ; m. Nov. 23, 1817,
James Croswell and Israel Nichols ; res. So. Rehoboth ; one son, Andrew Nichols, res. there.

VII. MARY, b. Feb. 8, 1796; m. Nov. 8, 1840, Israel
Nichols; d. s. p.

VIII. SARAH, b. Jan. 30, 1799 ; m. Jan. 15, 1821, Samuel
D. Aylsworth ; res. East Greenwich, R. I. ; one
son, Lyman, res. there.

123. **Joseph[6] Pierce** (Azrikim[5], Samuel[4], Azrikim[3], Ephraim[2],
Michael[1]), b. Dec. 15, 1752 ; m. Mar. 23, 1755, Freelove Wood,
b. 1755; d. June 20, 1827. He d. Apr., 1831. Res. Rehoboth,
Mass.

CHILDREN.

I. SARAH, b. May 19, 1778 ; m. Avery Mason of Chester, Mass.; they had four daughters.

233.   II. NATHAN, b. Feb. 7, 1781 ; m. Hannah Hall.

III. RHODE, b. Sept. 15, 1783 ; m. Nov. 12, 1801, Joseph
Lewis, b. Mar. 26, 1782 ; d. Feb. 18, 1865 ; res.
Dighton, Mass. Ch., Jonathan, b. Nov. 15, 1802;
m. Oct., 1824; d. Mar. 7, 1871 ; Mary, b. Aug.
3, 1805; d. Nov. 28, 1834 ; Louisa, b. Apr. 14,
1807; d. Oct. 3, 1831 ; Hiram, b. July 21, 1809;
m. Dec., 1833 ; d. Aug. 10, 1875 ; Angeline, b.
Dec. 26, 1813 ; m. Oct. 12, 1840, F. P. Case ; res.
Dighton, Mass.

IV. FREELOVE, b. Oct. 31, 1785; m. Jan. 7, 1810, Arial
B. Horton ; res. South Rehoboth. Ch., Hiram.

V. NANCY, b. June 15, 1787 ; m. July 9, 1815, Gideon
Horton ; res. South Rehoboth. Ch., Gideon, Jr.

234.   VI. JOSEPH, b. Aug. 3, 1790 ; m. Arminia Mason.

235.   VII. AZRIKIM, b. Dec. 29, 1792 ; m. Abigail Harlow.

236. VIII. DANIEL, b. Nov. 20, 1795 ; m. Susannah R. Pierce.

124. **Abraham[6] Pierce** (Azrikim[5], Samuel[4], Azrikim[3],
Ephraim[2], Michael[1]), b. Feb. 18, 1770, in Rehoboth, Mass.; m.

Jan. 16, 1794, Lavinia Stoddard, b. June 26, 1768 ; d. Feb., 1802; m. 2nd, Dec. 19, 1802, Eliza Wood, b. Mar. 7, 1776 ; d. Feb. 11, 1829. He d. Aug. 15, 1860. Res. Geneva and Cooperstown, N. Y. He was in the war of 1812.

Lavinia was born in Lenox, Mass., June 26, 1768, and was united in marriage in that town to Abraham Peirce of Otsego, N. Y. She was the daughter of Anthony and Phebe (Reade) Stoddard of Lanesboro, Mass., and a descendant of Anthony Stoddard who emigrated from England and came to Boston in 1639; a freeman, 1640 ; representative, 1650–59–60, and for twenty successive years, from 1665 to 1684.

CHILDREN.

    I. STODDARD, b. Oct. 13, 1795. Was in the war of 1812, and was killed in battle Nov. 9, 1813.

    II. LAVINIA, b. Dec. 16, 1797; m. June 29, 1820, Jonas Foster of Hebron, N. Y.

    III. SARAH A., b. Apr. 29, 1804; d. Mar. 9, 1816.

237.   IV. ISRAEL, b. June 2, 1805; m. Louise Durham.

238.   V. DENNIS W., b. Oct. 27, 1806; m. Julia A. Secord and Sarah S. Wood.

    VI. ELEANOR H., b. Dec. 29, 1807; m. —— Heath, and d. May 4, 1881.

239.   VII. ABRAHAM, b. June 22, 1809; m. Charlotte Laws.

    VIII. JAMES H., b. Aug. 14, 1810.

240.   IX. ALANSON, b. Dec. 28, 1811; m. Sybil S. Smith.

    X. ELIZA E., b. June 26, 1814; d. May 30, 1883.

    XI. LUCY C., b. July 3, 1816; m. May 25, 1837, Hosea Mead, b. May 15, 1813; d. Aug. 11, 1847. She d. Jan. 10, 1866. Ch., Carrie F., b. July 17, 1839; m. Harmon D. Bissell; res. Galesburg, Ill. He was Q. M. and lieutenant in 83d Ill. Vols., and was killed at Fort Donaldson, Tenn., Feb. 2, 1863. John H., b. May 20, 1841; d. Nov. 18, 1852; Jane A., b. Nov. 6, 1842; d. May 8, 1843; Ellen A., b. Mar. 29, 1845 ; d. Sept. 4, 1845.

126. **Dr. Benjamin⁶ Pierce** (Azrikim⁵, Benjamin⁴, Azrikim³, Ephraim², Michael¹), b. ——; m. June 26, 1791, Sarah Carpenter, b. ——; d. ——. He d. 1824. Res. Warwick and Coventry, R. I., and Otego, N. Y.

CHILDREN.

   I. CALEB, b. Oct. 6, 1791.
241. II. WILLIAM L., b. ——; m. ——.
   III. HANNAH, b. ——.

127. **Jared⁶ Pierce** (Azrikim⁵, Benjamin⁴, Azrikim⁴, Ephraim², Michael¹), b. 1765; m. in Lawrence, Otsego Co., N. Y., Elsie Groton, b. ——; d. 1811.
Jared was born near Newport, R. I., where he learned the trade of tanning and currying. When a young man he emigrated to Otsego, N. Y., and settled. He d. 1830, in Albion, Orleans Co., N. Y. Res. Warwick, R. I., and Albion, N. Y.

CHILDREN.

   I. WARNER, b. ——; m. and res. Valparaiso, Ind.
   II. MERCY, b. —— ; m. —— Brown; res. Buffalo, d. s. p.
   III. LUCY, b. 1802 ; m. Horace Mack; res. Bath, Ohio,
      and d. in 1878, leaving many children.
242. IV. JARED, b. ——; m. Ruth Stone and Elizabeth Farns-
      worth.
243. V. ORA, b. —— ; m. Sylvia Rowley.
244. VI. JEFFERSON, b. Feb. 15, 1809 ; m. Lousa Green and
      Cynthia A. Sherman.

127a. **Samuel⁶ Pierce** (Joshua⁵, Isaac⁴, Azrikim³, Ephraim², Michael¹), b. abt. 1725; m. Vashti Cole, b. 1727, dau. of Lt. John Cole, who settled in Eastham in 1667; m. 2nd, Mercy Ryder. He d. ——. Res. Welfleet, Mass.

CHILDREN.

244-1. I. NATHANIEL, b. Jan. 29, 1751; m. Lydia Newcomb.
   II. ABIGAIL, b. ——; m. Oct. 28, 1773, in Welfleet,
      Mass., Solomon Higgins.

III. Zephaniah, b. ——.

244-2. IV. Samuel, b. Nov. 13, 1763; m. Naomi Lewis and Grace (Newcomb) Young.

244-3. V. John, b. ——; m. Phebe Newcomb.

244-4. VI. David, b. Aug. 31, 1769; m. Sally Atwood.

244-5. VII. Solomon, b. ——; m. Keziah Doan.

244-6. VIII. Joshua, b. Jan., 1772; m. Rachel Hatch and Sally Snow.

IX. Molly, b. ——; m. William Robinson.

X. Lucy, b. ——; m. Tatophilus Howes.

XI. Elizabeth, b. ——; m. Oliver Bowley.

127b. **Joshua⁶ Pierce** (Joshua⁵, Isaac⁴, Azrikim³, Ephraim², Michael¹), b. abt. 1740; m. Thankful ——; m. 2nd, Hepzibah ——. Res. Eastham, Mass.

CHILDREN.

244-7. I. Thomas, b. June 24, 1766; m. Elizabeth Ryder.

244-8. II. William, b. Oct. 15, 1768; m. Sally ——.

III. Joshua, b. Oct. 3, 1758; d. ——.

IV. Jane, b. Sept. 15, 1771; d. ——.

V. Phebe, b. Oct. 1, 1774.

127¹. **Joseph⁶ Pierce** (Joseph⁵, Isaac⁴, Azrikim³, Ephraim², Michael¹), b. Nov. 10, 1759; m. Aug. 7, 1787, Joanna Young, b. May 14, 1765; d. Dec. 15, 1841. He d. Mar., 1808. Res. Wellfleet, Mass.

She m. 2nd, Capt. Lemuel Newcomb, Nov. 10, 1814, who d. in 1841. He was born in Eastham June 11, 1756, and d. Apr. 22, 1821. He was a hero of the Revolutionary war. He entered the service in Winslow Lewis' company Jan. 11, 1776, at Cambridge, and served without absence until discharged. June, 1777, served also in company of Capt. Elijah Vose, regiment of Col. Graton. Was in the battle of Lake Champlain when Gen. Arnold was defeated. Was in the State militia service before and after the foregoing. He was pensioner under the act of 1818. Was representative to the General Court of Massachusetts 1801-4-6. In early life Mr. Newcomb was a mariner, subsequently a commander. Of the estate of Joseph Peirce of Welfleet administration was granted Mar. 17, 1808, to Joanna Pierce, his widow. Inventory indicates that he was a farmer and a blacksmith, and mentions one Isaac Pierce as owner of an adjoining wood lot. The settlement of the estate shows one-third was given to the widow, Joanna, one-third to Joshua T. Pierce, and one-third to Joseph Pierce. Joanna was appointed guardian of Joseph, a minor.

CHILDREN.

244-9.   I. JOSHUA Y., b. Mar. 25, 1789; m. Eunice Young.
       II. JOSEPH, b. Feb. 15, 1796; d. June 19, 1815.

127[2]. **Isaac[6] Pierce** (Joseph[5], Isaac[4], Azrikim[3], Ephraim[2], Michael[1]), b. May 13, 1754; m. Dec. 10, 1778, Drusilla Cole; d. Jan. 20, 1819. Res. Welfleet, Mass.

CHILDREN.

       I. SUSANNA, b. Jan. 9, 1780; d. Nov. 21, 1793.
      II. ISAAC, b. Oct. 23, 1791; d. Mar. 20, 1799.

128.   **Nathan[6] Pierce** (Nathaniel[5], Joseph[4], Azrikim[3], Ephraim[2], Michael[1]), b. 1756; m. Rhoda Giles, b. 1786; d. Feb. 3, 1858. He d. Feb. 25, 1861. Res. Rehoboth, Mass.

CHILDREN.

       I. NATHAN G., b. Feb. 9, 1800 ; m. Marie Shaw ; res. Rehoboth, Mass.
      II. ELIZA, b. Oct. 9, 1801 ; m. Warner Adams and Nathaniel Pierce ; res. Rehoboth.
     III. FANNY, b. Jan. 7, 1805 ; m. William Follett; res. Rehoboth.
245.   IV. REUBEN G., b. Sept. 10, 1806; m. Nancy Luther and Elsa Miller.
      V. NANCY G., b. Aug. 30, 1808; m. Aug. 22, 1844, Daniel B. Barney ; res. Rehoboth.

246. VI. JOSEPH S., b. Feb. 6, 1814; m. Lydia T. Mason and Sybil Horton.
247. VII. CHILDS, b. Oct. 16, 1820; m. Cynthia Millard Pierce.
VIII. EMELINE, b. ——; m. Asaph Chaffee.

129. **Jonathan⁶ Pierce** (Nathaniel⁵, Joseph⁴, Azrikim³, Ephraim², Michael¹), b. ——; m. Rebecca Gile, b. ——; d. ——; m. 2nd, Feb. 27, 1814, Betsey Bowen, b. ——. Res. Somerset and Rehoboth, Mass.

CHILDREN.

I. REBECCA G., b. Sept. 11, 1802.

130. **Aaron⁶ Pierce** (Nathaniel⁵, Joseph⁴, Azrikim³, Ephraim², Michael¹), b. Sept. 20, 1765 ; m. Nov. 14, 1793, Elipha Bliss, b. July 11, 1766, in Rehoboth; dau. of Capt. Samuel Bliss; m. 2nd, Jan. 23, 1800, Nancy Rounds, b. 1782; d. Apr. 11, 1860. He d. 1831. Res. Rehoboth, Mass.

CHILDREN.

I. NANCY, b. ——; d. young.
248. II. AARON, b. Sept. 11, 1810 ; m. Emily Brown and Frances E. Bailey.
249. III. BARNARD W., b. Sept. 11, 1810; m. Martha H. Smith and Mrs. Esther Arnold.
250. IV. JONATHAN W., b. 1800 ; m. Mariam A. Ray.
V. ELIPHA B., b. 1802 ; m. Sept. 10, 1838, Stephen C. Gavitt, b. South Kingston, R. I., 1801. She d. Sept. 22, 1864; res. Baltimore, Md. Ch., Elipha A., b. 1848; m. Dec. 22, 1865, Nathan Hall Vars, b. 1841; m. 2nd, Edwin Heron ; Stephen P., b. Sept. 1, 1839; m. Aug. 1, 1861, Mrs. Abbie A. Wilbur, b. 1846 ; d. Aug. 21, 1886 ; res. Westerly, R. I. Ch., Abbie J., b. Sept. 2, 1862; Alvira C., b. Feb. 2, 1864; Stephen F., b. Aug. 18, 1866 ; Mary E., b. Oct. 15, 1867; d. June 10, 1881; Elipha A., b. May 14, 1869 ; d. Sept. 10, 1888 ; Laura C., b. Dec. 14, 1870; d. Jan. 1, 1881; Charles P., b. May 18, 1873; d. Feb. 2, 1888.

19

VI. LOUISE, b. May 27, 1807; m. Oct. 24, 1833, Loren
    Brewster, b. Nov. 13, 1803; d. Aug. 14, 1870. Ch.,
    Laura A., b. Nov. 8, 1836 ; m. Reuben M. Ches-
    bro; Louisa E., b. June 17, 1838; m. Louis
    Robinson; Maria H., b. Feb. 20, 1840 ; m. Hor-
    ace Gallup ; res. Willimantic, Ct.
VII. ESTHER M., b. Jan. 2, 1806; m. Nov. 27, 1828, Ca-
    leb Miller, b. Nov. 20, 1805; d. Sept. 26, 1876.
    She d. Sept. 18, 1885; res. Rehoboth, Mass. Ch.,
    Caleb N., b. Dec. 31, 1829; m. Oct. 10, 1866,
    Jennie B. Smith; res. Oak Harbor, W. T. Ch.,
    Sarah A., b. Oct. 21, 1867 ; m. Chas. Hancock ;
    res. Stanwood, W. T. *Charles H.*, b. Apr. 18,
    1831 ; m. Oct. 10, 1865, Susan M. Tucker; res.
    Stanwood, W. T. Ch., Alma M., b. June 29,
    1866; d. Jan. 26, 1877 ; Joseph M., b. Apr. 6,
    1869 ; Frederic C., b. Dec. 25, 1871 ; Daisy D.,
    b. Mar. 18, 1878; Newton G., b. Feb. 12, 1884; res.
    Oak Harbor. *Alfred M.*, b. Mar. 19, 1833 ; m.
    Dec. 30, 1868, Jane Clemen, d. May 10, 1884;
    res. North Yakama, W. T. Ch., Francis M., b.
    June 19, 1872 ; Andrew B., b. Feb. 8, 1877 ; Flor-
    ence R., b. Feb. 11, 1880 ; Amos N., b. Aug. 13,
    1882. *Esther R.*, b. May 1, 1835 ; m. Feb. 15
    1853; Warren W. Palmer. Ch., Josephine A., b.
    Jan. 29, 1854 ; m. Dec. 25, 1884, Abner G. Brown;
    res. Oak Harbor, W. T. ; William W., b. Feb. 15,
    1859 ; m. Jan. 1, 1883, Cora Stors. *Nancy A.*,
    b. Mar. 18, 1838 ; m. Nov. 5, 1860, Thos. P.
    Ovenell. Ch., Thomas N., b. Aug. 25, 1861; res.
    Avon, W. T. ; Ella R., b. Dec. 20, 1862 ; m.
    Aug. 27, 1885, Chas. E. Larison ; res. Stanwood,
    W. T. *Andrew J.*, b. Feb. 4, 1840 ; d. Aug. 18,
    1888. *Francis P.*, b. Feb. 14, 1843 ; m. Aug. 9,
    1886, Inga Fokkland ; res. Oak Harbor, W. T.
251. VIII. NATHANIEL C. R., b. June 12, 1815 ; m. Eliza Rey-
    nolds and Sarah Elizabeth Reynolds.
IX. CALEB, b. 1818 ; m. Susan Pierce.
252. X. JAMES C., b. Feb. 29, 1820 ; m. Lucinda B. Bliss.

131. **Nathaniel[6] Pierce** (Nathaniel[5], Joseph[4], Azrikim[3],
Ephraim[2], Michael[1]), b. Nov. 30, 1766; m. Nov. 25, 1787, Rachel

Moulton, b. Dec. 16, 1763; d. June 5, 1831. He d. Sept. 14, 1839. Res. Rehoboth, Mass.

CHILDREN.

253. I. STEPHEN M., b. Sept. 18, 1789; m. Huldah Wheeler and Emeline Perry.

II. HANNAH, b. Sept. 5, 1791; d. 1794.

III. RACHEL, b. June 8, 1792; m. Dec. 12, 1813, Col. Solomon Wheeler, b. May 3, 1788; d. Nov. 13, 1854. She d. Apr. 4, 1841; res. Batavia, N. Y. Ch., Harriet, b. July 13, 1819; d. Oct. 26, 1838; George, b. Nov. 4, 1815; d. ———; Leonard, b. Jan. 22, 1818; d. Mar. 4, 1861; Henry, b. Oct. 8, 1819; d. Aug. 24, 1884; Charlotte, b. Aug. 5, 1821; d. Aug. 17, 1823; Simeon, b. Sept. 1, 1823; d. Oct. 9, 1882; Rachel M., b. Sept. 27, 1825; d. Aug. 30, 1826; Rachel, b. Mar. 10, 1827; d. ———; Huldah M., b. Nov. 20, 1828; Christopher C., b. Dec. 23, 1831; d. ———; Charlotte R., b. Feb. 26, 1833; d. June 15, 1861.

IV. HANNAH, b. Feb. 14, 1794; m. Loring Tisdale.

V. NATHANIEL, b. July 9, 1796; m. Nov. 30, 1819, and d. Dec., 1844.

VI. ROYAL, b. Mar. 18, 1798; d. Dec. 8, 1819.

VII. ASAHEL, b. Mar. 26, 1800; d. ———.

VIII. GEORGE, b. Dec. 4, 1801; d. Jan. 28, 1831.

IX. SARAH, b. Oct. 9, 1803; d. ———.

132. **Backus⁶ Pierce** (Stephen⁵, Joseph⁴, Azrikim³, Ephraim², Michael¹), b. Mar. 13, 1768; m. Jan., 1807, Lucy Goodenough, b. June 22, 1787; d. June 22, 1827. He d. Sept. 23, 1855. Res. East Calais, Vt.

CHILDREN.

254. I. IRA E., b. Aug. 12, 1822; m. Deborah F. Potter.

II. CALISTA, b. Aug. 30, 1811; m. Apr. 3, 1836, Charles B. Marsh, b. May 23, 1810; d. July 3, 1885. She

d. Mar. 7, 1852. Res. Montpelier, Vt. Ch.,
Delia A., b. Oct.13, 1836; m. to Aaron Bancroft,
Nov. 26, 1873; res. Montpelier, Vt.; Lucy E.
b. Jan. 20, 1839; m. to Marcus C. Keniston, Jan.
25, 1866; P. O., East Calais, Vt.; William H. H.,
b. Mar. 4, 1841; d. at Alexandria, Va., July 7,
1864, of wounds received at battle of Wilderness;
Frank E., b. June 4, 1842; m. to Clara J. Ainsworth, Feb. 13, 1869; P. O., East Calais, Vt.;
Elmina B., b. Nov. 8, 1844; m. to Warren E. B.
Bliss, Jan. 25, 1866; P. O., East Calais.

   III. IRENE G., b. Apr. 29, 1818; m. Freedom Eaton. She
       d. Apr. 29, 1854. Ch., Ann, m. a carpenter;
       res. Minneapolis, Minn., and Julius, res. Lyndon,
       Vt.

133. **Asahel[6] Pierce** (Stephen[5], Joseph[4], Azrikim[3], Ephraim[2],
Michael[1]), b. Apr. 7, 1771; m. June 12, 1798, Clarissa Peck, b.
Oct. 16, 1774; d. Nov. 12, 1856. He d. Apr. 19, 1858. Res.
Calais, Vt.

CHILDREN.

255.   I. STEPHEN, b. Mar. 27, 1806; m. Polly Ide.
      II. CLARISSA H., b. Dec. 28, 1816; m. Oct.11, 1842,
         Ira S. Dwinell, b. Jan. 21, 1816; res. East Calais,
         Vt. Ch., Byron L., b. Oct. 2, 1850, an M. D.;
         res. Taunton, Mass.
     III. ALFRED E., b. Dec. 20, 1803; d. Apr. 30, 1811.
256.   IV. ALONZO, b. Feb. 3, 1799; m. Thirza Dwinell.
      V. MILLARD E., b. July 9, 1812; d. July 12, 1812.

134. **Noah[6] Pierce** (Stephen[5], Joseph[4], Azrikim[3], Ephraim[2],
Michael[1]), b. Jan. 26, 1773; m. 1802, Ruth Gerry, b. July 26,
1780; d. Mar. 2, 1846. He d. Dec. 29, 1846. Res. Rehoboth,
Mass., and Calais, Vt.

CHILDREN.

257.   I. ASAHEL, b. June 30, 1812; m. Persis B. Abbott.
258.   II. ZEPHANIAH G., b. Dec. 16, 1822; m. Eliza S. Leonard.

III. HORATIO, b. May 30, 1800; d. young.

IV. MARY, b. Sept. 20, 1802; m. May 7, 1828, Asa Preston, b. Apr. 18, 1803; res. Lowell, Mass. Ch., Mary Ann Preston, b. Jan. 9, 1829; m. A. P. Miller; res. 57 Liberty street, Lowell, Mass.; William Ireson Preston, b. Feb. 9, 1831; m. Alice L. Sowter; res. Paxton, Mass.; Harriet Caroline Preston, b. Dec. 18, 1832; m. H. P. Hasey, Jan. 7, 1854; res. 128 Smith street, Lowell, Mass.

259. V. HORATIO, b. Oct. 12, 1807; m. Julia Merritt.

VI. HARRIETT, b. Nov. 8, 1805; m. Ziba Putnam.

VII. NOAH, b. Nov. 1, 1809; m. Amanda Hill; res. Doon, Lynn Co., Iowa.

VIII. ROBA, b. Mar. 23, 1816; m. M. L. White; res. Plattsmouth, Neb.

260. IX. ZALMON, b. June 30, 1818; m. Polly Goodenough.

X. EMELINE, b. Aug. 8, 1820; res. Plattsmouth, Neb.

135. **Calvin**[6] **Pierce** (Stephen[5], Joseph[4], Azrikim[3], Ephraim[2], Michael[1]), b. Dec. 2, 1780; Constant Bulroomb, b. 1765; d. Sept. 30, 1837. He d. Sept. 15, 1829. Res. Rehoboth, Mass.

CHILDREN.

261. I. CALVIN, b. ——; m. Nancy Taft.

136. **Noah**[6] **Pierce** (Noah[5], Joseph[4], Azrikim[3], Ephraim[2], Michael[1]), b. Feb. 26, 1776; m. Apr. 4, 1801, Betsey Desabaze, b. 1778; d. Dec. 10, 1806. He d. 1805.

Noah Pierce, Jr., was born in Rehoboth, Mass., in 1776. In 1800 he was a resident in Bristol, R. I., in the employ of William Bradford. In 1801 or 1802, he was married to a Miss Betsey Desabaze, a young girl, French by birth, living with Mrs. Sylvester Childs of Warren, R. I., a niece of Benjamin Cranston, then living in Warren, and a native of Martinique. He died a few years later, leaving his wife with four little children. She must have died within the year, as near as can be learned, and soon after two of the children died.   Lewis D. B., being the eldest of the two surviving, was taken from Warren to Rehoboth, to his grand-father Pierce's, where he remained for a short time, and then was placed with Mr. Anderson Marton of Barrington, where he grew up.   His home was Warren, R. I., until the last year of his life.   Res. Rehoboth, Mass., and Bristol, R. I.

CHILDREN.

I. MARIA, b. Jan. 10, 1802 ; d. young.

262.   II. LEWIS D. B., b. June 13, 1803; m. Sarah A. Algier.

III. EZEKIEL R., b. Oct. 23, 1804; d. young.

IV. NOAH, b. Dec. 6, 1805 ; m. Nov. 4, 1832, Elizabeth M. Pierce, b. May 28, 1811. He d. Jan. 24, 1869; res. Rehoboth, Mass.   (See another place for children.)

137. **Appollus⁶ Pierce** (Noah⁵, Joseph⁴, Azrikim³, Ephraim², Michael¹), b. Apr. 6, 1779; m. 1800, Hannah Brown, b. Oct. 29, 1784; d. Jan. 8, 1834. He d. Jan. 21, 1831. Res. North Providence, R. I.

CHILDREN.

I. LUCINDA, b. May 29, 1801 ; m. Aug. 1, 1824, Henry Earle, b. June 8, 1801; d. Oct. 12, 1858; res. 32 Orange street, Worcester, Mass. Ch., Henry, b. Sept. 20, 1825 ; Anthony, b. Nov. 11, 1838; Clarke, b. Jan. 1, 1840; Mary A., b. Jan. 10, 1848.

II. WILLIAM G., b. Apr. 13, 1803 ; d. May 15, 1837.

III. PATIENCE, b. June 12, 1805 ; d. 1841.

IV. LAVINA W., b. Sept. 8, 1807; d. Mar. 8, 1870.

V. MARY A., b. July 30, 1820; d. Feb., 1854.

263.   VI. ANTHONY, b. Sept. 10, 1814; m. Mary W. Snow.

VII. ELIZABETH, b. May 6, 1816; d. Apr. 2, 1833.

VIII. ALBERT, b. May 19, 1818; d. Sept. 14, 1819.

IX. ANGELINE, b. Mar. 9, 1821 ; d. Jan. 23, 1834.

X. ALBERT, b. Nov. 13, 1822 ; d. Jan. 25, 1824.

138. **Perez**[6] **Pierce** (Noah[5], Joseph[4], Azrikim[3], Ephraim[2], Michael[1]), b. June 14, 1789 ; m. ———. He d. Aug. 22, 1843.

CHILDREN.

 I. SARAH, b. ———; m. ——— Converse.
 II. FRANK, b. ———; res. California.

139. **Joseph H.**[6] **Pierce** (Joseph[5], Joseph[4], Azrikim[3], Ephraim[2], Michael[1]), b. Dec. 29, 1813; m. Oct., 1834, Rachel P. Jones, b. Dec. 29, 1810; d. Aug. 21, 1861. Res. South Rehoboth, Mass.

CHILDREN.

 I. OTIS H., b. Feb. 28, 1835; d. Feb. 25, 1863.
 II. CAROLINE M., b. Oct. 3, 1838; m. July 4, 1854,
  Orren N. Goff ; res. South Rehoboth, Mass.

140. **Wheeler**[6] **Pierce** (Wheeler[5], Mial[4], Ephraim[3], Ephraim[2], Michael[1]), b. ———; m. Mar. 31, 1760, Mrs. Elizabeth Bosworth, dau. of Ephraim Martin, b. abt. 1720; m. Ichabod Bosworth, and after his death m. Wheeler Pierce. Res. Rehoboth, Mass.

CHILDREN.

264. I. PHILLIP, b. 1762; m. Ann Manchester.

141. **Capt. Nathan**[6] **Pierce** (Nathan[5], Mial[4], Ephraim[3], Ephraim[2], Michael[1]), b. Jan. 22, 1745; m. Jan. 10, 1765, Sarah Davis. He d. 1776, and she m. 2nd, a Nathan Herndeen. Res. Lanesborough, Mass.

Capt. Nathan Pierce, the son of Rev. Nathan, was born in Rehoboth, Mass., in 1745. He was a farmer, but having learned the trade of silversmith, carried that on in connection with his farm. He was united in marriage in Rehoboth. Jan. 15, 1776, he enlisted in a regiment of Green Mountain Boys under command of Col. Seth Warner. They were transferred soon after with horses and sleighs to Newport.

Feb. 13, 1776. His company had left St. Johns for Montreal, as certified by the commissary, David Henry.

Feb. 19, 1776. His company was ordered to leave Montreal and proceed with "all possible expedition" to the camp before Quebec and then join the army under command of General Arnold. The order embraced Capts. Hinman and Pierce.

Apr. 9, 1776. He writes from camp before Quebec to James Barker, of Lanesborough, of their arrival Feb. 28. All his men except two were sick with small-pox, he had partially recovered from it.

May 4, 1776. Muster-roll records. Camp before Quebec, Capt. Nathan Pierce sick in quarters. No mention of him later, as soldier.

He died on the Island of Three Sisters, near Quebec, May 19, 1776. His widow, Sarah (Davis) Pierce, was married about 1782, to Nathan Herndeen and moved to New York, settling in Farrington, she died and was buried in the Friends' Burying-ground.

Deed from Jonathan Brooks of Lanesborough, to Nathan Pierce of Rehoboth, was recorded in Great Barrington, July 4, 1776, in Book No. 12, page 136, by Mark Hopkins, Register.

Another, given Aug. 16, 1776, by John Tibbets (or Jonathan), of Lanesborough, to Sarah Peirce, widow, and Sarah Peirce and Nathan Peirce and Lydia Peirce and Cromwell Peirce, all infants.

This deed was recorded also at Great Barrington, dated Sept. 15, 1785, Book No. 22, page 49. Moses Hopkins, Register.

Another given by Hicock Hubbell to Nathan Peirce, both of Lanesborough, Dec. 15, 1789, was recorded at Cheshire, Nov. 12, 1794, Book No. 3, page 429. James Barker, Register.

CHILDREN.

 I. SARAH, b. ——; m. John McLowth. She died and was buried in York, Mich., leaving two children, Cromwell and Daraxa.

265. II. NATHAN, b. 1770; m. Polly McLowth.

 III. LYDIA, b. ——; m. Benjamin Wheeler. Her only dau. m. William Davis; res. York, Mich.

 IV. CROMWELL, b. —— ; d. young.

142. **Benjamin**[6] **Pierce** (Nathan[5], Mial[4], Ephraim[3], Ephraim[2], Michael[1]), b. Jan. 29, 1747; m. Jan. 21, 1771, Content Luther, b. 1752; d. July 24, 1786; m. 2nd, Fanny ——, b. 1756; d. Aug. 5, 1836. He d. in South Carolina, 1796. Res. Rehoboth and Swansey, Mass., and Bristol, R. I.

CHILDREN.

266.   I. EARL D., b. May 15, 1780; m. Lydia Wheaton.
    II. CHAMPLIN, b. Jan. 15, 1773; lost at sea.
    III. LURAMA, b. Jan. 1, 1775; m. Jan. 17, 1796, James Bucklin; res. Rehoboth, Mass.
    IV. ELIZABETH, b. Mar. 19, 1777; m. Dec. 18, 1794, Philip Rounds; res. Rehoboth, Mass.
    V. FANNY, b. ——; m. Samuel Taylor.
    VI. FREELOVE, b. 1793; m. Samuel Phillips and John McIntyre. She d. May 18, 1872.
    VII. CONTENT, b. ——; m. Joseph Burt.

143. **Pardon**[6] **Pierce** (Nathan[5], Mial[4], Ephraim[3], Ephraim[2], Michael[1]), b. Oct. 23, 1749; m. ——, b. 1749; d. Mar. 24, 1783; m. 2nd, Elizabeth ——. He d. Aug. 5, 1796. Res. Rehoboth and Swansey, Mass.

CHILDREN.

    I. JOSEPH, b. 1768; drowned in Carolina, Dec. 25, 1784.
    II. EZRA, b. ——.
267.   III. PARDON, b. Aug. 12, 1773; m. Freelove Horton.
    IV. FREELOVE, b. ——; m. Feb. 10, 1793, in Rehoboth, Aaron Fuller.
267½.   V. DELANY, b. ——; m. Daniel Sanders. Ch., Benjamin, b.——; res. Poland, N. Y.
    VI. SALLY, b. —— ; m. Aug. 22, 1793, Reuben Barney; res. Rehoboth and Swansey.

144. **Martin**[6] **Pierce** (Nathan[5], Mial[4], Ephraim[3], Ephraim[2], Michael[1]), b. Feb. 15, 1752; m. Aug. 13, 1775, Keziah Wheeler,

20

b. 1758; d. Oct. 6, 1847. He d. 1844. He was the proprietor of a hotel in Boston, the best in the city, in 1810–14, but afterward returned to Rehoboth, where he died. Res. Boston and Swansey, Mass.

CHILDREN.

268.   I. JEREMIAH W., b. —— ; m. Sarah Shove.
　　　　 II. SUBMIT, b. May 10, 1778.
269.   III. MARTIN, b. —— ; m. Sarah Read.

145. **Peleg[6] Pierce** (Nathan[5], Mial[4], Ephraim[3], Ephraim[2], Michael[1]), b. Nov. 15, 1756; m. Dec. 3, 1778, Joanna Viall, b. ——; d. ——; m. 2nd, Mar., 1782, Hannah Martin, b. Jan. 16, 1765; d. Aug. 28, 1783; m. 3rd (his cousin), Abby Martin, b. May 17, 1764; d. Oct. 19, 1791; m. 4th, Nov. 28, 1792, Phebe Salisbury, b. 1754; d. Jan. 29, 1795; m. 5th, May 12, 1796, Mehitable Pierce (his cousin), b. 1776; d. Feb. 10, 1810 ; m. 6th, Sept. 26, 1810, Martha Cornell, b. 1772; d. Feb. 24, 1823; m. 7th, Mrs. Hammond. He d. Dec. 8, 1828. Res. Rehoboth, Mass.

CHILDREN.

270.   I. NATHAN, b. Nov. 24, 1784; m. Phebe Horton.
　　　　 II. CHLOE, b. Apr. 21, 1786; m. in Rehoboth, Dec. 20, 1807, Samuel Wheeler. She d. Jan. 27, 1859.
271.   III. ASA, b. Nov. 12, 1789; m. Sally Bryant.
　　　　 IV. BOWERS, b. Jan. 28, 1797; d. Feb., 1810.
272.   V. TISDALE, b. Mar. 4, 1798; m. Dorinda Bowen.
　　　　 VI. JULIA A., b. Nov. 8, 1799; m. July 4, 1819, Nathan Kingsley. She d. Feb. 27, 1873 ; res. Rehoboth, Mass.
273.   VII. GARDNER, b. Aug. 21, 1801; m. Sarah Wood and Elvira A. Grace.
　　　　 VIII. DELILA, b. Oct. 7, 1803; d. May 5, 1848.
　　　　 IX. NELSON, b. Jan. 9, 1806. He d. Mar. 29, 1872.
　　　　 X. STILLMAN, b. Mar. 16, 1809; m. Dorinda ——; d. Sept. 22, 1857. He d. Feb. 10, 1883.

XI. ARDELIA, b. Oct. 8, 1807; m. Oct. 4, 1829, George
W. Ingalls. She d. May 24, 1870; res. Rehoboth,
Mass.

XII. PELEG, b. Feb. 6, 1813. Had a son Henry.

XIII. VENONA, b. Apr. 7, 1816; res. unm. with Mrs.
Henry W. Thurber, North Swansey, Mass.

274. XIV. DEXTER, b. July 24, 1818; m. Amanda Sheldon.

XV. STEPHEN C., b. Nov. 11, 1820; d. unm. Dec. 6, 1872.

146. **Rev. Preserved**[6] **Pierce** (Nathan[5], Mial[4], Ephraim[3],
Ephraim[2], Michael[1]), b. July 28, 1758; m. May 15, 1784, Sarah
Lewis, b. 1765; d. Oct. 4, 1823; m. 2nd, May 10, 1824, in Dighton,
Nancy Cushing. He d. June 29, 1828. Res. Rehoboth and
Swansey, Mass.

CHILDREN.

275. I. LEWIS, b. Mar. 11, 1794; m. Phebe Wood.

II. LYDIA, b. Feb. 22, 1802; m. May 20, 1821, James
Wheaton, b. Feb. 20, 1797; d. Sept. 3, 1868; res.
Hill street, New Bedford, Mass. Ch., Almira P.,
b. Oct. 30, 1822; m. K. A. Kempton and Nicholas
Davis; she d. Jan. 18, 1872; James, Jr., b. Oct.
4, 1825; d. at Rio Janeiro, Apr. 6, 1851; Sarah
L., b. May 14, 1828; d. Sept. 6, 1830; Charles E.,
b. Jan. 27, 1833; m. Susanna Tripp; res. Provi-
dence, R. I.; Horatio C., b. June 29, 1835; m.
Mary E. Prescott; Ellen F., b. May 19, 1839; d.
Oct. 31, 1842; Emma A., b. Apr. 18, 1841.

276. III. PRESERVED, b. Aug. 1, 1785; m. Betsey Davis.

IV. SALLIE, b. Jan. 17, 1774.

V. LILLUS, b. July, 1787; m. June 26, 1808, Olney
Mason; d. June 14, 1852.

VI. CANDUS, b. Mar. 3, 1789; m. Feb. 27, 1821, Daniel
Fish. She d. May 10, 1870.

VII. PATIENCE, b. Mar. 30, 1792; m. Mar. 11, 1810,
Samuel Baker, b. Apr. 12, 1787; d. Apr. 16, 1872;
res. Rehoboth, Mass. Ch., Ira S., b. July 20,

1812; m. ——; res. South Rehoboth, Mass.;
Nancy, b. Mar. 15, 1814; m. Dec. 23, 1832, Samuel Nichols of Riverside, R. I.; Nelson O., b.
June 19, 1816; m. July 3, 1836; res. Pleasant
street, Providence, R. I.; Emeline, b. July 15,
1819; m. Apr. 14, 1842, Horace Le Baron Horton; res. Riverside, R. I.; Otis A., b. Nov. 5, 1821;
d. Oct. 26, 1833; Dr. George P., b. Jan. 27, 1826;
m. Aug. 9, 1859; res. Broad street, Providence,
R. I.; Electa A., b. Mar. 9, 1834; m. Mar. 8,
1860, Edwin L. Howland; both d. s. p.

277. VIII. MARTIN b. Feb. 21, 1796; m. Betsey Chase.

IX. POLLY, b. Nov. 22, 1799; m. Sept. 24, 1818, David
Wheaton; had one son, Charles; res. Bristol Cen-
tre, Ontario county, N. Y.

278. X. OTIS H., b. July 8, 1804; m. Joanna Lewis.

147. **Isaac**[6] **Pierce** (Nathan[5], Mial[4], Ephraim[3], Ephraim[2], Michael[1]), b. Sept. 22, 1763; m. Oct. 7, 1782, Anna Fitch, dau. of
Capt. Amos Fitch of Swansey, b. Mar. 1, 1763; d. Nov. 15, 1809,
and is buried in the Pierce burying ground in Rehoboth; m. 2nd,
Nov. 1, 1810, by Elder Preserved Pierce, Polly Bowen, b. Aug.
21, 1789; d. Mar. 10, 1838; m. 3rd, Elizabeth Carpenter. He d.
Nov. 26, 1849. Res. Rehoboth, Mass.

Isaac Pierce, the son of Rev. Nathan, was born in Rehoboth,
Mass., in 1763; always resided in that town, and within four miles
of the place where he was born. He was in the Revolutionary
army for a short time, when he was sixteen years of age, when the
British were at Newport. After his marriage he resided for a time
with his grandfather, Mial Pierce, at the end of two years he returned to his father's farm, where he passed the remainder of his
days. He was industrious and economical, a large family was
reared, and he always paid one hundred cents on the dollar.
When he was a boy there was not a vehicle in Rehoboth, every-
body rode horseback, there were a few ox-carts, heavy, clumsy
affairs, built after the pattern of the English. He has often been

to church with an ox wagon with seats placed in it. He was a man of good sound sense and judgment. When eighteen years of age he joined his father's church, but at the age of twenty-five he was excommunicated from that society because he went to hear, for a second time, a Universalist preacher.

CHILDREN.

I. HANNAH, b. Sept. 18, 1783; m. Feb. 26, 1804, William Peck; res. Rehoboth, Mass. Ch., Hannah P., b. Jan. 22, 1818; m. Philip Mowry; res. Woonsocket, R. I.; Noah L., b. Nov. 20, 1816; m. Polly Brown; res. Woonsocket; Matilda, m. James Martin; Mary, m. David Houghton; Martha, m. Obadiah Ross; res. Thompson, Conn.; Josephus and William; res. Northbridge, Mass.; Helen, m. —— Jencks; res. 15 Brunswick Flats, corner Chicago avenue and Cass street, Chicago; Hannah d. June 28, 1840; William d. 1820.

279. II. HIRAM W., b. Feb. 19, 1804; m. Cornelia Ryder.

280. III. LYMAN, b. Jan. 1, 1813; m. Freelove Horton.

IV. NANCY, b. Apr. 15, 1786; m. Mar. 3, 1805, Cyrus Peck, b. 1784; d. 1807; m. 2nd, 1809, Samuel B. Chaffee, b. 1757; d. 1836. She d. Dec. 9, 1874. Ch., Mary A., m. Reuben Emerson; Nancy, m. William Morse; res. Ellenville, N. Y.; Samuel Chaffee, m. Rebecca T. Peirce, and d. July, 1874; Cyrus, m. A. Melvina Miller, and d. Dec. 9, 1883; William, m. Sarah Miller, and d. May 4, 1888; Hannah B., m. Lewis Pierce, res. Pawtucket, R. I., and d. Mar. 2, 1850; Addie, res. Pawtucket, with ex-Gov. Davis' family; Susan, m. William West, and d. Nov., 1844.

281. V. ISAAC, b. Dec. 21, 1789; m. Penelope Horton.

VI. MAHALA, b. Apr. 29, 1792; m. May 19, 1811, David Bowen; m. 2nd, Mar. 28, 1820, Isaac Mason, b. Nov. 15, 1772; d. Sept. 29, 1826; m. 3rd, Jan. 13,

1833, George Stone, b. July 22, 1778. She d. Jan.
6, 1869; res. Smithfield and Coventry, R. I. Ch.,
Mahalea P., b. Aug. 12, 1822; d. Aug. 24, 1824;
Hiram P., b. June 8, 1825; res. Watertown, Mass.;
Annie M., b. Nov. 17, 1826; m. Charles M.
Andrews; d. Dec. 1, 1886; Emily P., b. Nov. 16,
1835; m. Joel Vaughn; d. Oct. 5, 1861.

282. VII. ANGIA, b. June 1, 1794; m. Mary Mason and Elizabeth Crowley.

283. VIII. LEVI, b. June 8, 1797; m. Betsey Wheeler.

IX. MARY A., b. May 29, 1799; d. Nov. 7, 1809.

284.   X. WATERMAN, b. Dec. 24, 1801 ; m. Betsey Baker.

XI. BETSEY, b. Feb. 3, 1807; m. —— Jacobs; d. Aug.
28, 1846. Ch., Delia, m. John Bond; res. Brook-
line, Mass.; Emma, m. —— Green; res. Worcester,
Mass.

XII. POLLY, b. Mar. 21, 1816; m. Paschal Newman. She
d. Feb. 26, 1876.

285. XIII. JEREMIAH B., b. Aug. 20, 1820; m. Sarah P. Horton.

XIV. DELANA, b. July 13, 1823; m. Dec. 29, 1844, Philip
A. Monroe, b. Nov. 27, 1821; res. East Providence, R. I. Ch., Sophronia Jane, b. Jan. 5, 1847;
m. Nov. 21, 1866; d. Apr. 29, 1869; Lyman Francis, b. June 14, 1848; m. Dec. 25, 1873; post-office
address, L. F. Munroe, Public street, Providence,
R. I.; Delana Genœ, b. Jan. 9, 1850; d. Mar. 20,
1856; Lena Augusta, b. Dec. 30, 1850; d. Aug. 28,
1851; Philip Allen, Jr., b. June 26, 1852 ; m. Nov.
2, 1877; res. No. 14 Cranston street, Providence,
R. I.; Josephine, b. Apr. 9, 1854; d. Nov. 30,
1854; Oliver Buchanan, b. May 22, 1856; m. Dec.
11, 1883; add. Journal office, Providence, R. I.;
Addison Pierce, b. Jan. 2, 1862; m. Dec. 22, 1885;
res. No. 116 Carpenter street, Providence, R. I. ;
Nellie Frances, b. May 4, 1868 ; res. East Providence, R. I.

XV. LAURA A., b. May 18, 1825; m. June 27, 1847,
Lemuel T. Gammons, b. Dec. 9, 1828; res. West-
port, Mass. Ch., Lyman T., b. Mar. 10, 1848;
d. Aug. 17, 1848; Sophronia A., b. July 28, 1849;
m. Benjamin P. King, d. Dec. 28, 1870; Lemuel P.,
b. May 7, 1852; m. Cornelia A. Hedge; Matthias
I., b. Nov. 21, 1853; m. Emma F. Whalon; John
W., b. Mar. 10, 1855; m. Flora H. Brightman;
Lewis W., b. Apr. 28, 1867; d. Nov. 17, 1869; Laura
F., b. May 21, 1860; m. William A. Simmons.

XVI. SEPHRONA, b. Aug. 12, 1827; m. William Martin;
res. corner Providence and Linden streets, Providence, R. I. Ch., Horace, James, res. Providence; Matilda.

XVII. CYRUS, b. June 9, 1788; d. Mar., 1789.

XVIII. HOLOFANES, b. Feb. 26, 1815; d. Apr. 7, 1815.

148. **David**[6] **Pierce** (Nathan[5], Mial[4], Ephraim[3], Ephraim[2], Michael[1]), b. Apr. 11, 1739; m. Mary ——. Res. Rehoboth, Mass.

CHILDREN.

286.   I. SAMUEL, b. Apr. 22, 1761; m. Hannah Bowen.

149. **Jobe**[6] **Pierce** (Jobe[5], Mial[4], Ephraim[3], Ephraim[2], Mi-
chael[1]), b. Aug. 7, 1753; m. Dec. 29, 1776, Hannah Bullock, b.
Sept. 18, 1755; d. May 30, 1850. He d. Aug. 30, 1818. Res.
Rehoboth, Mass.

CHILDREN.

287.   I. MICAH, b. Feb. 29, 1780; m. Hannah Pierce.
288.   II. JOHN M., b. Mar. 23, 1778; m. Elizabeth Monhouse,
           Elizabeth Hicok, and Mrs. Elizabeth Reed.
289.   III. BENONA, b. Oct. 21, 1781; m. Elizabeth Davis.
        IV. WILLIAM, b. Oct. 18, 1785; res. Hamburg, N. Y.
           He had two children and both are dead.
        V. SILAS, b. Nov. 9, 1783; d. Jan. 8, 1786.
290.   VI. GILBERT, b. Nov. 20, 1789; m. Lydia Davis.

VII. ABIGAIL, b. Aug. 19, 1792; m. Anson Wight. Ch.,
Anson, Bradford. She d. Oct. 16, 1882, at Cox-
sackie, N. Y.

291. VIII. SILAS, b. Sept. 9, 1787; m. ——.

150. **Samuel**[6] **Pierce** (Jobe[5], Mial[4], Ephraim[3], Ephraim[2], Michael[1]), b. abt. 1752; m. Phebe ——. After his death, Feb. 23,
1782, she m. David Bullock. He d. bef. 1781. Res. Dartmouth,
Mass.

CHILDREN.

292. I. SAMUEL, b. Jan. 23, 1774; m. Miriam Williams and
Prudence Crapo.
II. MERCY, b. 1775; m. Sept. 2, 1790, Capt. Philip
Allen, b. Mar. 4, 1762; d. Aug. 28, 1829. He
was a farmer, a Democrat and a Baptist. Res.
Dartmouth, Mass. She d. Feb. 21, 1857. Ch.,
Philip, d. Sept. 23, 1850; Shubel, d. Nov. 20,
1835; Thankful, m. Abel Ashley; d. Mar. 2,
1884. Two of her daughters, Mrs. Richard Wil-
son and Mrs. Oliver G. Brownell, res. in New
Bedford, Mass.; Thomas M., b. Dec. 22, 1792; d.
June 12, 1838; Samuel, d. 1850.
III. PHEBE, b.——; m. Dec. 19, 1784, Comfort Bullock
of Rehoboth, Mass.
IV. SYBIL, d. young.

151. **Sylvester**[6] **Pierce** (Caleb[5], Mial[4], Ephraim[3], Ephraim[2],
Michael[1]), b. 1749; m. Sept. 20, 1770, Patience Wheeler, b. ——;
He d. 1829. Res. Durham, N. Y.

CHILDREN.

I. HANNAH, b. July 22, 1782; m. Micah Pierce.
II. MARTHA, b. ——; m. —— and —— Lamphier.
III. HULDAH, b. ——; m. —— Wood.
IV. PATTY, b. ——; m. —— Eighmey.
V. MERCY, b. ——; m. —— Cleveland.
VI. FANNY, b. ——; m. —— White.

VII. EDWARD, b. ——. Had Rebecca, Eleanor, Martha, Emily, and Ann, who m. George D. Cunningham.

VIII. RUSSELL, b. ——. Had sons, Horace, d. s. p.; Hiram, he had a son George, in Albany, N. Y.; and Allen R.

293.   IX. SYLVESTER, b. 1792; m. Margaret Kneaskern.
294.   X. CROMWELL, b. ——; m. ——.

152. **Caleb[6] Pierce** (Caleb[5], Mial[4], Ephraim[3], Ephraim[2], Michael[1]), b. 1753; m. Mercy Wheelèr, b. 1750; d. 1826. Caleb was in the Revolutionary war, enlisting when he was but seventeen. He d. 1836. Res. Black Rock, Schoharie county, N. Y., and Dumpfries, Canada.

CHILDREN.

295.   I. JESSE, b. abt. 1788; m. Jennie Clough.
        II. ROWLAND, b. ——.
296.   III. LEVI, b. 1776; m. Amy Benedict.
297.   IV. WHEELER, b.——; m. ——.
        V. MIAL, b. ——.

154. **Shubal[6] Pierce** (Joshua[5], Mial[4], Ephraim[3], Ephraim[2], Michael[1]), b. 1758; m. Nov. 1, 1778, Abigail Mason; d. æ. 82. Shubal Pierce was born in Swansey, Mass., in 1758. During the Revolutionary war he took an active part, and was one of the historical minute men of that day. He moved to Hampton, N. Y., with his wife and six children, where he ever after resided. Though not particularly successful in business, he was well enough off in the world's goods to provide sufficiently. He d. June 9, 1833. Res. Swansey, Mass., Connecticut, and Hampton, N. Y.

CHILDREN.

298.   I. AMOS, b. ——; m. Betsey Brooks.
299.   II. MASON, b. Dec. 11, 1780; m. Ann Archibald.
        III. HANNAH, b. 1785; m. at Hampton, N. Y., Robert Archibald. Ch., Samuel; res. Caldwell, N. Y.
    21

He d. 1855; she d. 1821. Ch., Mary E. Archibald, b. July 24, 1849; res. Lake George, Warren Co., N. Y.; Lottie Archibald Eddy, b. Apr. 28, 1851; m. June 20, 1874; res. 1413 Second avenue, South Minneapolis, Minn.; Clara Archibald Wilcox, b. Jan. 5, 1853; m. Oct. 10, 1872; res. 3517 Dearborn street, Chicago, Ill.; Thomas Archibald, b. Mar. 24, 1856; res. Lake George, N. Y.; Samuel R. Archibald, res. Lake George, N. Y.; Robert Emmett Archibald, b. Oct. 19, 1862; res. Lake George, N. Y.; Katie Archibald, b. Dec. 31, 1867; d. June 22, 1870.

IV. PRUDENCE, b. Mar. 13, 1790; m. Oct. 1, 1812, John Gunnison, b. July 29, 1788; d. Feb. 22, 1864; res. Troy, N. Y. Ch., Caroline, b. Sept. 23, 1813; d. Apr. 17, 1819; James, b. Aug. 8, 1816; m. Nov. 29, 1842; res. Troy, N. Y.; William, b. July 16, 1818; m. Oct. 1, 1850; d. July 21, 1883. William Gunnison achieved great success. He was the largest manufacturer of collars in Troy, N. Y. Deceased was a man of unblemished integrity and eminently successful. The son, William, carries on the business at present in that city. Caroline, b. May 26, 1821; d. Sept. 1, 1822; John, b. Jan. 7, 1824; d. Oct. 15, 1827; Charlotte, b. Oct. 27, 1825; m. June 26, 1872, —— Case; res. Egypt, N. Y.; Mary, b. June 22, 1828; d. Dec. 20, 1882; George W., b. Oct. 11, 1831; d. Feb. 16, 1875.

V. ABIGAIL, b. —— ; m. —— Conkey.

300. VI. SHUBELL, b. Mar. 9, 1784; m. Lovina Bunnell.

VII. LYDIA, b. in Providence, R. I., Nov. 28, 1795; m. Harry Nichols; b. 1796, in Sandgate, Vt.; d. Jan. 26, 1865. She d. Jan. 28, 1868; res. Troy, N. Y. Children: Jane, m. Andrew Sherwin, both deceased; James H., m. Mary Jane Gardner; res.

2182 Fifth ave., Troy; Chancey, m. and died;
Elizabeth, m. Benjamin Sherwin and Holden Gay;
Charles, d. in the war; Martha, m. George Win-
nie; res. Sixth ave., Troy. Her father was a
carpenter by trade and died respected by all who
knew him.

VIII. CLARA, b. Oct. 18, 1795; m. Samuel Hoskins. She
d. Mar. 9, 1886. Ch., Laura L. A., b. Feb. 22,
1815; m. Dec. 31, 1829, —— Fuller; res. Wrentham, Mass.; Caroline L., b. Oct. 28, 1820; m.
Apr. 26, 1838, —— Jones; res. Pilgrim block,
Staniford street, Providence, R. I.

IX. JESSIE, b. ——.

X. MARTHA, b. Apr. 8, 1804; was always blind from
her youth; d. unm. June 18, 1860.

155. **Capt. Israel⁶ Pierce** (Joshua⁵, Mial⁴, Ephraim³, Ephraim²,
Michael¹), b. ——; m. Mar. 9, 1780, Hannah Pierce, b. ——; d.
—— ; res. Rehoboth, Mass., and removed to Pennsylvania.

CHILDREN.

301.   I. ISRAEL, b. ——; m. Polly Walker.
    II. JARVIS, b. ——.
    III. JOSEPH, b. ——.
    IV. ANNIE, b. ——.
    V. DAU., b. ——; m. Capt. Burt.

156. **Henry⁶ Pierce** (Joshua⁵, Mial⁴, Ephraim³, Ephraim², Michael¹), b. 1750; m. June 8, 1777, Lydia Mason, b. 1755; d. Aug.
21, 1839. He d. Feb. 12, 1829. Res. Rehoboth and Swansey,
Mass.

CHILDREN.

    I. LYDIA, b. 1781; m. Jan. 29, 1798, James Horton;
after his death, he being lost at sea, she m. Joseph
Pierce. (See.)

302.   II. JABEZ M., b. 1794; m. Mary Kelton and ——.

303. III. ESEK, b. 1786; m. Czarina Brown and Betsey Bushee.
   IV. HENRY, b. 1785; d. unm. Aug. 23, 1828.
   V. ROBIE, b. ——; m. Lt. Joseph Baker.
   VI. ABIGAIL, b. Jan. 16, 1780; d. unm. Feb. 20, 1869.
   VII. SALLY, b. ——; m. Aug. 18, 1818, Otis Horton of Rehoboth.
   VIII. SUSAN, b. ——; m. May 10, 1829, Nathaniel Baker of Rehoboth.

157. **Barnard**[6] **Pierce** (Joshua[5], Mial[4], Ephraim[3], Ephraim[2], Michael[1]), b. Feb. 4, 1764; m. Jan. 14, 1786, Mary Rounds, dau. of Chace Rounds, and sister of Mrs. Aaron Pierce, b. Nov. 12, 1767; d. Nov. 16, 1849. He d. May 5, 1842. Res. Rehoboth, Mass.

CHILDREN.

304. I. NATHANIEL R., b. Jan. 1, 1792; m. Mary West and Eliza Adams.
305. II. JEREMIAH, b. Aug. 29, 1786; m. Candace Wheeler.
306. III. CHARLES M., b. Aug. 9, 1799; m. Mary P. Maxfield.
   IV. MARY, b. Dec. 15, 1788; d. Mar. 12, 1791.
   VI. HANNAH M., b. Nov. 19, 1794; m. Nov. 20, 1811, Ephraim Goff; res. Rehoboth, Mass. She d. July 12, 1844. Ch., Alva, b. 1821; m. Oliver C. Allen; res. Division street, Providence, R. I.; Sabina T., b. 1813; m. Lorenzo D. Bullock; Ephraim, b. 1814; d. 1833; Hannah M., b. 1816; m. George A. Day; res. Providence; Luther W., b. 1819; res. Providence; Fanny F., b. 1823; m. Joseph E. Morse; Mary A., b. 1826; m. George D. Oatley; Anna, b. 1829; d. 1831; Ann B., b. 1832; m. Wm. F. White; Ephraim, b. 1835; m. Mary E. Dexter; res. Pawtucket.
307. VI. BARNARD, b. Mar. 15, 1797; m. Hannah Bliss.
308. VII. OTIS N., b. Feb. 3, 1803; m. Susan G. Cross.

309. VIII. CHASE R., b. May 12, 1805; m. Ruth T. Wilbur and
Louisa H. Hammond.
310. IX. BRADFORD S., b. Jan. 14, 1808; m. Hannah S. Cross.
X. MARY A., b. May 7, 1811; m. Nov. 3, 1831, Joseph
W. Pierce (see); res. New Bedford, Mass.; she d.
July 16, 1886.

158. **Joshua**[6] **Pierce, Jr.** (Joshua[5], Mial[4], Ephraim[3], Ephraim[2],
Michael[1]), b. ——; m. May 23, 1773, Susannah Rounds, b. 1753;
d. Dec. 9, 1850. He d. Nov. 25, 1804; was killed by falling
from his horse while attempting to let down the bars to a pasture.
Res. Rehoboth, Mass.

CHILDREN.

311. I. WILLIAM, b. 1773; m. Sarah Thresher.
II. ALFRED, d. young.
312. III. JOSHUA, b. Mar. 12, 1796; m. Betsey Wheaton.
313. IV. LEONARD, b. 1776; m. Jemima Rounds.
V. DIANA M., b. 1780; m. Paul Bowen; she d. Sept. 27,
1857; res. Bristol, R. I. Had a son James.
VI. RACHEL M., b. ——; m. July 29, 1810, Salathiel
Jones, Jr.; res. Warren, R. I. Had a son Charles
W., b. June 9, 1826; m. June 14, 1849, Louisa M.
Borden.
VII. HULDA, b. ——; d. unm.
VIII. BETSEY M., b. ——; m. June 3, 1804, Philip Mar-
tin ; res. Sandy Creek, N. Y.
IX. SUSANNAH, b. Oct. 31, 1799; m. Daniel Pierce (see).

159. **Obadiah**[6] **Pierce** (David[5], David[4], Ephraim[3], Ephraim[2],
Michael[1]), b. Feb. 12, 1762; m. Oct. 7, 1790, Susannah Luther,
b. June 26, 1772; d. May 21, 1843. He d. Dec. 28, 1836. Res.
Somerset, Mass.

CHILDREN.

314. I. DAVID, b. June 1, 1791 ; m. Louisa Chace.
II. ELIZABETH, b. Apr. 5, 1793; m. Alfred Harding; she
d. Dec. 24, 1880 ; son David; res. Mansfield, Mass.

III. PHEBE, b. July 22, 1795; m. Reuben Chase; she d.
Feb. 13, 1859; dau. Maria L. m. Clark Purington; res. Somerset, Mass.

IV. SUSANNAH, b. Aug. 17, 1797; m. Jeremiah Gardner;
she d. Feb. 19, 1851. Ch., Obadiah P., James L.;
res. Somerset, Mass., and Cranston, R. I.

V. OBADIAH, b. Jan. 14, 1800; d. Nov. 25, 1831.

315. VI. LUTHER, b. June 5, 1806; m. Lydia Gardner.

316. VII. JAMES L., b. May 3, 1808; m. Amanda Chase.

VIII. JULIAN, b. Aug. 26, 1810; d. Oct. 2, 1810.

IX. MASON, b. Aug. 31, 1811; d. Jan. 17, 1841.

317. X. DEXTER, b. Aug. 28, 1814; m. Hannah Hathaway.

XI. MARY, b. Dec. 11, 1816; m. Sept. 17, 1838, Wm. F.
Hathaway, b. Mar. 12, 1814; d. June 26, 1877.
Ch., Wm. F., b. Mar. 31, 1839; res. Somerset, Mass.

XII. LUTHER, b. Mar. 6, 1802; d. July 10, 1806.

XIII. ALMIRA, b. June 30, 1804; d. Sept. 5, 1838.

160. **David**[6] **Pierce** (David[5], David[4], Ephraim[3], Ephraim[2],
Michael[1]), b. Feb. 14, 1766; m. in Swansey, Aug. 23, 1792, Lydia
G. Gibbs, b. Aug. 7, 1774; d. Feb. 25, 1852. He d. Mar. 19, 1847.
Res. Somerset, Mass.

David, son of David and Elizabeth, was born in Somerset, Mass.,
Feb. 14, 1766. He worked at farming summers, and during the
winter worked at coopering. Aug. 23, 1792, he married Lydia
Gibbs of Swansey, Mass. In his old age he sold his farm, and re-
moved to New Bedford, Mass., where his children are living.
He had thirteen children.

CHILDREN.

318. I. ISAAC, b. Feb. 25, 1814; m. Deborah Purrington and
Elizabeth A. Adams.

II. MARY, b. Mar. 12, 1793; m. Apr. 24, 1811, Turner
Chace, b. Apr. 2, 1786; d. Jan. 19, 1845. She
d. Dec. 9, 1881; res. East Providence, R. I. Ch.,
Mary P., b. Jan. 1, 1820; m. Dec. 29, 1839, ——

Perkins; res. East Providence, R. I., P. O. box, 146; Mary A., b. July 5, 1812; d. Oct. 2, 1813; Louisa A., b. Feb. 1, 1814; m. Sept. 22, 1834; d. Aug. 6, 1868; Abigail, b. Dec. 3, 1816; m. Jan. 27, 1836, Capt. T. C. Gibbs; res. 24 Arnold street, Providence, R. I.; William T., b. Sept. 29, 1818; d. young.

319. III. CLOTHIER, b. Apr. 15, 1794; m. Comfort Chase.

IV. EUNICE, b. Aug. 18, 1796; m. Jan. 11, 1815, Samuel Purrington, b. Nov. 17, 1791; d. July 2, 1858. She d. Nov. 11, 1865; res. Pottersville, Mass. Ch., Clark, b. Nov. 23, 1815; m. Bethany Chace and Maria Chace; Samuel S., b. Dec. 15, 1817; m. Eliza A. Monroe; he d. July 4, 1875; David P., b. Aug. 13, 1826; m. Dec. 21, 1846; Reuben H., b. Nov. 28, 1827; m. Mary A. Mason; he d. Dec. 6, 1886; Eunice P., b. Nov. 3, 1830; m. Benjamin Wood.

320. V. JOHN, b. Jan. 11, 1798; m. Louisa Levin.

321. VI. DAVID, b. Oct. 3, 1799; m. Hope Remington and Maria Fuller.

VII. ABIGAIL, b. Sept. 27, 1801; d. May 16, 1802.

VIII. REUBEN, b. Sept. 20, 1803; d. Dec. 29, 1804.

IX. LYDIA, b. Sept. 7, 1805; m. Barney D. Chace of Swansey, and Capt. Benjamin Gibbs of Somerset, and d. s. p., Nov. 30, 1877.

X. NANCY, b. Sept. 5, 1807; m. 1826, Daniel Briggs. She d. Nov. 17, 1840; res. Bristol, R. I. Ch., William, b. Oct. 31, 1827; res. Bristol, R. I.

XI. CANDACE, b. Mar. 4, 1809; m. May 17, 1827, Capt. Daniel Brown, b. Dec. 14, 1804; d. Dec. 17, 1880; res. Fall River, Mass. Ch., Elizabeth C., b. Oct. 16, 1828; m. Mar. 8, 1844, Robert P. Reynard; Candace J., b. Feb. 12, 1831; m. Aug. 5, 1851, Albert F. Bellows; Daniel W., b. Nov. 23, 1833; d. Aug. 21, 1834; David F., b. Nov. 23, 1835; m. Carrie E. Haffards, June 20, 1859; Daniel R., b.

July 16, 1837; m. Oct. 17, 1866, Fannie M.
Howard; Charles T. Brown, b. Dec. 15, 1844; d.
Nov. 12, 1850; Ida P., b. May 19, 1847; m. Nov.
11, 1868, Griffith M. Haffards.

322. XII. LLOYD N., b. Mar. 5, 1811; m. Emeline Sanford and
Dighton Terry.

323. XIII. SEABURY, b. Mar. 30, 1812; m. Phebe Remington.

161. **John**[6] **Pierce** (Jonathan[5], David[4], Ephraim[3], Ephraim[2],
Michael[1]), b. 1768; m. Anna * Chase, b. ——; d. 1827. He d.
in Fall River, in 1855. Res. Somerset, Mass.

CHILDREN.

324. I. ASA, b. June 6, 1795; m. Lydia Chase.

II. JOHN, b. Dec. 7, 1805; res. Providence.

325. III. DAVID, b. Aug. 11, 1792; m. Sarah Butts and
Louise Chace.

IV. STEPHEN, b. Feb. 28, 1799; went West, n. f. k.

326. V. HIRAM, b. Mar. 24, 1808; m. Mary C. Gibbs and
Mary Slade.

161½. **John**[6] **Pierce** (Comfort[5], John[4], John[3], Ephraim[2], Michael[1]), b. May 16, 1762; m. Jan. 5, 1783, Betsey Bowen. Res.
Rehoboth, Mass.

CHILDREN.

I. BETSEY, b. Dec. 3, 1783.

II. JOHN, b. Dec. 30, 1785.

III. BETHIAH, b. Apr. 5, 1788.

IV. DANIEL, b. May 9, 1792.

161¾. **Comfort**[6] **Pierce** (Comfort[5], John[4], John[3], Ephraim[2], Michael[1]), b. ——; m. ——. Res. Rehoboth.

CHILDREN.

I. ABEL F., b., 1800; m. Abigail M. Bown.

---

* Town records say Lydia.

162. **Henry⁷ Pierce** (Benjamin⁶, Benjamin⁵, Benjamin⁴, Benjamin³, Benjamin², Michael¹), b. Dec. 20, 1806; m. 1830, Rebecca Tompkins, d. 1836; 2nd, Mary Fraser, b. ——; d. ——. He d. Feb. 3, 1880. Res. Lowell, Ind.

Henry Pierce was born in Chesterfield, Mass., on the 29th of December, 1806, and died in Crawfordsville, Ind., February 3, 1880. He was a son of Benjamin and Deborah Pierce. Benjamin, his father, was a son of another Benjamin, and he a son of still another Benjamin, and he of another Benjamin, who was son of Capt. Michael Peirce, who was killed in Phillip's war, March 26, 1676, at Pawtucket fight in Rehoboth. Henry moved with his father's family to the State of New York in 1818, and settled in Constantia, Oswego county, where he remained until he came of age. He then went to Canada, and spent several years as contractor in the construction of the Rideau and St. Lawrence canals, and also engaged in the lumber business on the Ottawa and the Modawaska rivers. He went to Virginia in 1836, where he had a contract on the James River and Kanawha canal. In 1838 he came to Indiana, and had a contract on the White Water canal. He afterward went into the hotel business, and continued that until he finally retired from business. He married Rebecca Tompkins about 1830, and their children were Henry Lyman, Seymour L., and Harvey T. She died in 1836, and in 1841 he married Mary Frasier, and their children were, Robert B. F., John D., Mary Jennie, Sarah Louisa, Charles Emerson, Frank C. and Edwin.

CHILDREN.

327.   I. JOHN D., b. Apr. 3, 1845 ; m. Mary B. Grant.
328.   II. SEYMOUR L., b. Jan. 18, 1832 ; m. Mary J. Ayers.
     III. HARVEY T., b. ——.
329.   IV. ROBERT B. F., b. Feb. 17, 1843 ; m. Harriet Blair and Mrs. Alice M. Van Valkenburg.
     V. CHARLES E., b. Aug. 21, 1856 ; res. Winfield, Kansas.
     VI. FRANK C., b. Mar. 3, 1860; res. Winfield, Kansas.
    VII. MARY JENNIE, b. Mar. 23, 1847; m. Jan. 1, 1874, John Fraser, b. Oct. 29, 1835; res. Winfield, Kan-

22

sas. Ch., James H. P., b. Feb. 2, 1875; Robert
A. P., b. Aug. 22, 1876; Hattie L., b. Sept. 26,
1877; Mary E., b. June 7, 1878; d. Aug. 15, 1880.
VIII. HENRY L., b. ——.
IX. SARAH L., b. ——.
X. EDWIN, b. ——.

163. **Benjamin⁷ Pierce** (Benjamin⁶, Benjamin⁵, Benjamin⁴, Benjamin³, Benjamin², Michael¹), b. May 26, 1812; m. June 28, 1843, Lusinai Jenkins, b. Sept. 12, 1822; d. Oct. 19, 1886. Res. Centreville, Ind.

Benjamin lived at home with his parents until he was twenty-one, when he went to Canada, and spent some three years, part of the time in the lumber business on the Modawaska river, and the balance of the time on the St. Lawrence river canaling near Cornwall. Later he went to Virginia and undertook some contracts on the James River and Kanawha canal, and when they were completed he went to Indiana and took some contracts on the White Water canal, and on their completion bought a farm and has lived a farmer's life since at Centreville, Ind.

CHILDREN.

I. BENJAMIN, } b. July 7, 1844; d. infants.
II. JOHN,
III. DAVID, b. Aug. 6, 1845; d. Oct. 19, 1845.
IV. JOHN B., b. Nov. 7, 1846; m. Sept. 21, 1870, Phebe Helms, b. Aug. 15, 1852. Ch., Rollo J., b. Sept. 4, 1872; res. Centreville, Ind.
V. ISAAC H., b. June 28, 1849; m. May 16, 1878, Mary J. Helms, b. Nov. 7, 1854; res. s. p., Centreville, Ind.
VI. NANCY M., b. Nov. 20, 1851; d. Dec. 10, 1863.
VII. ELLA S., b. Feb. 4, 1854; unm.
VIII. PHILLIP H., b. Nov. 25, 1856; m. July 27, 1881, Martha J. Daily, b. Dec. 29, 1853; d. May 22, 1884; m. 2nd, July 7, 1886, Lillian A. Baldwin, b. Nov. 24, 1862; res. Wamego, Kansas.

IX. JANE E., b. June 1, 1859; d. Dec. 18, 1863.

X. CHARLES D., b. Aug. 6, 1862; d. Feb. 3, 1878.

164. **John J.**[7] **Pierce** (Benjamin[6], Benjamin[5], Benjamin[4], Benjamin[3], Benjamin[2], Michael[1]), b. Apr. 14, 1801; m. Fanny Harwood. He d. Oct. 8, 1870. Res.

CHILDREN.

I. HARWOOD, b. ——.

II. HENRY M., b. ——; formerly res. Elk Point, Dakota.

III. MARIA, b. ——.

IV. MARY, b. ——.

V. BENJAMIN, b. ——.

VI. JULIA C., b. ——; m. Robert Bulmer; res. Ross Forrester's Falls, Ontario, P. Q.

331. VII. JOHN J., b. ——; m. ——.

VIII. EMILY.

IX. HARVEY A., res. St. Louis, Mo., and two of his sons, and four grandsons d. in the Union army.

165. **Harvey**[7] **Pierce** (Benjamin[6], Benjamin[5], Benjamin[4], Benjamin[3], Benjamin[2], Michael[1]), b. Sept. 26, 1804; m. Sept. 12, 1844, Sarah Dickinson, b. Feb. 10, 1818; d. Aug. 23, 1866. He d. Oct. 4, 1857. Res. Oxford, Miss.

CHILDREN.

I. EDWARD D., b. Aug. 13, 1850.

Edward was born in Mississippi in 1850, and has always resided in that State. An Oxford paper thus refers to the gentleman in 1886:

"We are pleased to announce the admission of our young and highly esteemed fellow-citizen, Mr. Edward D. Peirce, to the Bar as an 'attorney at law,' full-fledged. Mr. Peirce was examined on Saturday, the 11th, in Judge Featherstone's court at Water Valley, and the examining committee, appointed by the court, reported very favorably,

indeed, upon the examination. The many congratulations and hand-shakings extended Mr.
Peirce upon the occasion were warm and heartfelt, as the majority of the Bar there were old ac-
quaintants and friends to Mr. Peirce. We predict
success for Mr. Peirce. He is a man of known
integrity and worth, and of more than average
ability. We learn he will continue his present
connection with the firm of Sullivan & Whitfield,
and will continue reading the University course to
its completion, with the praiseworthy view of mas-
tering his profession thoroughly." He has since
graduated, and is now practicing his profession
with considerable success.

II. MARY D., b. Feb. 7, 1846; m. Feb. 4, 1865, Leoni-
das O. Lane, d. Sept. 16, 1865; m. 2nd, Nov. 7,
1866, Simeon D. Tucker; res. Geneva, Ohio.
Ch., Belle S., b. Aug. 29, 1867; A. Rubie, b. Feb.
20, 1875; Susie A., b. May 14, 1877.

III. JAMES H., b. July 11, 1848; m. Oct. 31, 1867, Artilla
Beauchamp. He d. Dec. 22, 1879, at Grenada,
Miss. James H. Peirce's eldest son, Edward B.
Peirce, is private secretary to chairman of faculty,
University of Mississippi. P. O., Oxford, Miss.

IV. SARAH J., b. June 6, 1856; d. Feb. 20, 1858.

166. **Dr. Paul[7] Pierce** (Libbeus[6], Jonathan[5], Benjamin[4], Benja-
min[3], Benjamin[2], Michael[1]), b. Apr. 24, 1801; m. Mar. 19, 1826.
He d. Feb. 28, 1854. Res. Harpersfield, Ohio, and Fairpoint,
Minn. Dr. Paul was born in Sudbury, Vt., and died in Fayette,
Wis. He was a physician and farmer, member of the Baptist
church, and respected by all who knew him. The doctor was a
Whig, but would never run for office, though often requested to
allow his name to be used.

CHILDREN.

I. URETTA V., b. Dec. 19, 1827; m. Dec. 6, 1847,
Elisha Russell, b. May 8, 1824; d. Mar. 12, 1884;

res. Fairpoint, Minn. Ch., George P., b. Apr.
30, 1853; Jay F., Dec. 14, 1857; Emma, b. May
3, 1866; Albert F., b. Mar. 12, 1871; Nord A., b.
Aug. 3, 1874.

II. MARY A., b. June 30, 1829; m. Feb. 9, 1855, Alonzo
W. Taft, b. May 21, 1831; res. Brookings, Dakota.
Ch., Mary D., b. Apr. 2, 1858; m. B. J. Kelsey,
Watertown, Dakota; Ida A., b. Apr. 14, 1860; d.
Aug. 14, 1863; Charles E., b. Feb. 8, 1862; res.
Aurora, Dakota.

III. CHARLES A., b. Nov. 4, 1833; m. July 4, 1865, Cynthia Anderson; res. Brookings, Dakota. She d.
Mar. 16, 1866.

332. IV. GEORGE W., b. Nov. 2, 1837; m. Delia L. Bartholomew.

V. FRANKLIN O., b. Aug. 1, 1829; d. at Nashville,
Tenn., Aug. 10, 1865.

VI. WILLIAM ERWIN, b. July 12, 1842; d. Frederick City,
Md., Mar. 10, 1862.

VII. FINLEY D., b. Sept. 5, 1843; res. Vinton, Iowa.

167. **William**[7] **Pierce** (Libbeus[6], Jonathan[5], Benjamin[4], Benjamin[3], Benjamin[2], Michael[1]), b. Jan. 29, 1799; m. Jan. 26, 1824,
Patty Fuller, b. Apr. 26, 1807; d. Feb. 2, 1840. He d. June 24,
1883. Res. Leicester Junction, Vt., and Potsdam, N. Y.

CHILDREN.

I. FULLER W., b. Nov. 11, 1824; res. Middlebury, Vt.

II. MARTHA V., b. Aug. 7, 1827; m. Sept. 6, 1851, E
M. Moores, b. Mar. 22, 1830; res. Lawrence,
Mass. Ch., Annie T., b. Mar. 4, 1864.

III. PARSANA B., b. July 28, 1831; m. June 1, 1864, W.
F. Farnham, b. May 5, 1832; res. s. p., Lawrence,
Mass.

IV. HARRIETT L., b. Mar. 2, 1834; m. John V. Doyle.
She d. Nov. 27, 1881; res. Woburn, Mass.

V. JULIA E., b. June 14, 1836; m. Sept. 28, 1857, E.
   M. Wallace, b. Oct. 8, 1816; res. Sudbury, Vt.
   Ch., Lulu M., b. Jan. 17, 1859; Fanny, b. Apr.
   2, 1861.

333.   VI. HIRAM M.* b. Dec. 21, 1841; m. Emma C. Hartt.

168. **Col. Hosea H.**[7] **Pierce** (Howard J.[6], Jonathan[5], Benjamin[4], Benjamin[3], Benjamin[2], Michael[1]), b. Rutland, Vt., Oct. 1, 1801; m. Nov. 12, 1825, Harriette Bernathy, b. Mar. 9, 1806; d. Mar. 22, 1832. He d. Oct. 6, 1876. Res. Canton, N. Y.

CHILDREN.

334.   I. SYLVESTER T., b. Mar. 1, 1826; m. Angie Scott.
335.   II. ALVIN C., b. May 23, 1829; m. Laura J. Arbor.
       III. ERSKINE P., b. May 7, 1831; a lawyer; res. Virginia
            City, Montana; is married and has four children.
336.   IV. DEMETRIUS Y., b. Feb. 13, 1833; m. Mary J. Powers.
337.   V. GILBERT L., b. June 23, 1835; m. Olive Van Klete.
       VI. ALVIRA H., b. Mar. 9, 1840; m. John Tyler Wells;
            has four children; res. Detroit, Mich.
338.   VII. HOSEA H., b. Dec. 3, 1837; m. Scelata Stewart.
       VIII. ANTOINETTE JANE, b. May 21, 1842; m. Oct. 2,
            1862, Watts S. Cooper, b. Aug. 22, 1839; res.
            Canton, N. Y. Ch., Howard B., b. Sept. 29, 1863.
       IX. MARTHA A., b. Oct. 3, 1846; m. Sept. 14, 1870,
            David L. Salls, b. Oct. 24, 1847; res. West Potsdam,
            N.Y. Ch., Maud L., b. Sept. 1, 1871; Mable P., b.
            Aug. 16, 1873; Lena A., b. Feb. 6, 1876; Pierce
            B., b. Mar. 19, 1878; David M., b. June 25, 1888.
       X. ALBERT R., b. Aug. 9, 1850; m. July 11, 1888, Bell
            Grant; res. West Potsdam, N. Y.

169. **Col. Onesimus O.**[7] **Pierce** (Howard J.[6], Jonathan[5], Benjamin[4], Benjamin[3], Benjamin[2], Michael[1]), b. Aug. 16, 1809; m. Jan. 3, 1839, Catherine Blue, b. Oct. 6, 1818.

---

* Nephew and adopted.

A Wayne county pioneer father, Hon. Onesimus O. Pierce, of Redford, died on Saturday, May 6, 1876, of erysipelas, after a very brief illness.

Mr. Pierce was born in the town of Potsdam, St. Lawrence county, New York, August 16, 1809. He received a liberal education, and in the early part of his life engaged in teaching school.

In the fall of 1833 he emigrated to Michigan, driving a span of horses and wagon, by way of Buffalo, round the southern shore of Lake Erie, through the then small towns of Cleveland, Sandusky and Toledo, to Detroit; thence to Redford, where he bought a piece of land and proceeded to make a home. He has resided in that township ever since, and by persevering industry and thrift, had acquired a handsome property.

On the 3d of January, 1839, he was married to Miss Catherine Blue, who survives him. They have had nine children, five of whom (four daughters and one son) are still living.

In early life he had a taste for military life. He was captain in the Toledo war, and has held every military rank in the militia, from corporal up to colonel. He still held his commissions as lieutenant-colonel and colonel which he received from Governor Steven Y. Mason.

In politics he was formerly a Democrat, but at the organization of the Republican party he became identified with it, and has ever since been a firm supporter of its principles. He has held some official position most of the time for the last forty years.

In the fall of 1872 he was elected by the Republicans of the third representative district, Wayne county, to the State Legislature, and was always at his post of duty, always attentive and careful to meet his responsibilities with honor to himself and with fidelity to those who had placed him in office. He was one of the delegates to the Wayne County Republican Convention which met at Detroit, April 29, and was by that body elected as one of the delegates to the State Convention, to meet at Grand Rapids the 10th inst.

At a recent meeting of the Wayne County Pioneer Society, he was elected as one of its vice-presidents.

During the past winter he had built a house and barn on National avenue, in Detroit, and was intending to move to the city this fall, but he has gone to the silent city of the dead and his spirit has returned to the God who gave it.

As a husband and father, he was loving, genial and indulgent; as a neighbor, kind and obliging; as a citizen, loyal to the government, true to his party, and firm in the support of its principles. Though not a member of any church, he was a believer in the

Christian religion, and contributed liberally for the support of the
gospel in his community. He was also a staunch temperance man.
The funeral services were conducted by Rev. J. G. Morgan,
pastor of the M. E. Church, on Sabbath, May 7, 1876, at the Baptist Church in Redford, and were participated in by Rev. T.
Shaftoe and Rev. Mr. Bancroft, the former and present pastors of
the Baptist Church. A very large concourse of citizens followed
his remains to their last resting place. He was buried with honors
by the members of the Redford Grange, to which he belonged.
He d. May 6, 1876. Res. Redford and Bell Branch, Mich.

CHILDREN.

I. MALCOMB B., b. Nov. 3, 1839; d. Oct. 11, 1841.

II. CHARLES S., b. June 12, 1858; a lawyer; res. Oscoda,
Mich.

III. LUCIA L., b. Jan. 16, 1841; m. Oct. 5, 1876, Albert
E. Bigelow, b. June, 1840; d. July 21, 1878; res.
Detroit, Mich.

> Mrs. Lucia Bigelow, wife of Albert Bigelow,
> and daughter of the late O. O. Pierce, died at her
> home in Detroit, Sunday, July 21. In the death
> of Mrs. Bigelow, education has lost a zealous
> friend, one who for years was a teacher of the
> first class. The following lines to her memory
> were contributed by Mrs. Young.
>
>> Sweet patient spirit, there is rest for thee.
>> Rest with the Lord through all eternity.

IV. ORLANDO O., b. Feb. 9, 1843; d. May 2, 1870.

> The deceased was a student at the State Normal
> School, whence he had graduated with unusual
> honors. Having crossed the threshold of manhood,
> his health became shattered, and he repaired to
> the more genial climate of the south to find the
> strength he so much needed. After an absence
> of nearly two years, he returned without finding
> the relief he sought, and the very day after his re-
> turn to the bosom of his friends was his last on
> earth. " Living, he lived as mothers wish their
> sons to live; and dying, he died as fathers wish
> their sons to die." Upright and honest, affection-
> ate, generous-hearted, and always courteous, his

enemies were few; his friends, now mourners, many. Mr. Pierce was a young man of much promise, a graduate of the State Normal School, a successful teacher, an esteemed friend, a dutiful son, an affectionate brother. In his death we have the truth of the adage, "*Death loves a shining mark.*"

V. ELMEDA E., b. ·Aug. 17, 1847; m. Aug. 23, 1871, Myndert H. Hunt, b. Oct. 16, 1844; res. Bell Branch, Mich. Ch., Edith D., b. Dec. 10, 1873; Elmer M., b. Jan. 16, 1877.

VI. ISABELLA C., b. Aug. 5, 1849; d. Jan. 2, 1863.

VII. EMILY B., b. Mar. 11, 1851; d. Apr. 21, 1885.

VIII. EFFIE M., b. Dec. 25, 1855; m. June 28, 1874, Robert Lawn; res. East Saginaw, Mich. Ch., Lucia A., b. Nov. 21, 1875; O. Pierce, b. June 4, 1880; drowned in Saginaw river Aug. 23, 1888; Forest C., b. May 25, 1882.

170. **Dennis D.**[7] **Pierce** (Howard J.[6], Jonathan[5], Benjamin[4], Benjamin[3], Benjamin[2], Michael[1]), b. Aug. 7, 1811; m. 1839, Phila M. Gibbons, b. Sept. 17, 1817. He d. July 12, 1876. Res. Canton, N. Y.

Dennis D. Pierce, the sixth child of Howard J. and wife, was born August 7, 1811. Attended common school, and at St. Lawrence Academy, taught school, chopped and cleared land; married at twenty-eight years of age, Phila M. Gibbons, a former pupil; was a farmer in Canton, N. Y., until his death, July 12, 1876. He raised a family of four boys and five girls. By industry, thrift and economy, he accumulated property valued at $16,000. He was temperate and of good morals; a Republican from the beginning of the party; undenominational; gave his children the advantages of a liberal education.

CHILDREN.

I. CANDACE C., b. Aug. 25, 1842; d. Sept. 26, 1882.

339. II. GEORGE P., b. Mar. 8, 1846; m. Augusta B. Hoskin.

23

III. DWIGHT C., b. Dec. 4, 1848; d. Dec. 1, 1868.
IV. CICERO E., b. July 23, 1850; d. Jan., 1873.
V. EVA E., b. May 10, 1852; res. Canton, N. Y.
VI. JENNIE A., b. Nov. 28, 1858; m. Sept. 15, 1886, Fred.
H. Church, b. Dec. 18, 1861; res. New York. Ch.,
Clarence C., b. Aug. 6, 1888.
VII. DELTA A., b. ——; res. New York.
340. VIII. PERRY B., b. Mar. 9, 1840; m. Susan Walker.

171. **John J.**[7] **Pierce** (Howard J.[6], Jonathan[5], Benjamin[4],
Benjamin[3], Benjamin[2], Michael[1]), b. July 19, 1816; m. Catherine
Rogain, b. June 20, 1819; d. May 1, 1873. Res. Canton, N. Y.
He d. Oct. 24, 1882.

CHILDREN.

341. I. LEROY E., b. Aug. 13, 1843; m. Alice A. Andrews.
II. CORA L., b. Dec. 16, 1863; res. Canton, N. Y.
III. EMMOGENE, b. May 14, 1850; res. Detroit, Mich.
IV. CHANCEY L., b. May 14, 1848; drowned Dec. 16, 1864,
off coast of Florida in steamship "North Amer-
ica," while being transferred from New Orleans to
New York as an invalid soldier.
V. MARY F., b. June 21, 1846; m. Apr. 26, 1870, Wil-
liam D. Perry, b. Sept. 12, 1848; d. Oct. 25,
1873; m. 2nd, June 15, 1881, Luther P. Wait, b.
Apr. 15, 1841 (see). Ch., Kate M., b. Apr. 9,
1871; res. Beech, Wayne Co., Mich.

172. **Hiram H.**[7] **Pierce** (Howard J.[6], Jonathan[5], Benjamin[4],
Benjamin[3], Benjamin[2], Michael[1]), b. July 5, 1818; m. June 7, 1843,
Prudence Sackett, b. Sept. 8, 1828; d. Aug. 28, 1865; m. 2nd,
Apr. 22, 1866, Eliza Fisher, b. Mar. 9, 1835. Res. Bell Branch,
Mich.

CHILDREN.

342. I. THOMAS H., b. Aug. 15, 1844; m. Emma Vaness.
II. CATHERINE, b. Jan. 19, 1846; m. Nov. 10, 1865,
Elmer W. Houk. She d. Feb. 13, 1887.

III. LUCINA E., b. July 29, 1847; d. Dec. 29, 1848.
343.   IV. GEORGE M., b. Apr. 12, 1848; m. Agnes D. Harris.
344.   V. JOHN B., b. June 17, 1851; m. Nellie Troup.
VI. JAMES F., b. Jan. 21, 1857; d. Dec. 1, 1857.
VII. DEMETRIUS D., b. Oct. 3, 1858; d. June 3, 1883.
VIII. FRANK H., b. Dec. 28, 1864; res. Bell Branch.
IX. CHARLES C., b. Oct. 18, 1867; d. Mar. 15, 1869.
X. PRUDA B., b. Aug. 5, 1869; res. Bell Branch.
XI. LOTTIE E., b. Nov. 13, 1871; res. Bell Branch.
XII. TINEY, b. July 14, 1873; d. July 17, 1873.

173. **Artemas A.**[7] **Pierce** (Howard J.[6], Jonathan[5], Benjamin[4], Benjamin[3], Benjamin[2], Michael[1]), b. Mar. 18, 1805; m. 1835, Celinda Carter, b. Mar. 31, 1815; d. May 16, 1866. He d.——. Res. Bell Branch, Mich.

CHILDREN.

345.   I. ANSEL B., b. Dec. 5, 1835; m. Lottie E. Watch.
II. SARAH B., b. Feb. 23, 1838.
III. SAVIAH C., b. Aug. 18, 1840.
IV. MARIAN C., b. Apr. 5, 1843.
V. SILENCE A., b. Aug. 14, 1845.
VI. CHARLES A., b. Nov. 21, 1847.
VII. JULIA, b. Dec. 25, 1852.
VIII. WILLIAM H., b. July 9, 1855.

174. **George A.**[7] **Pierce** (Waldo[6], Haywood[5], Benjamin[4], Benjamin[3], Benjamin[2], Michael[1]), b. Mar. 4, 1812; m. Sept. 16, 1848, Louisa T. Pike, b. Apr. 6, 1824. He d. June 11, 1873. Res. Frankfort, Me.

George A. Peirce, Esq., died at his residence, in Frankfort, Friday forenoon at eleven o'clock, at the age of sixty-one years. A few weeks ago he had two or three attacks of heart disease, which were followed by paralysis. Mr. Peirce was the senior partner of the firm of Peirce & Rowe, proprietors of Mount Waldo Granite Quarry. For some fifteen or twenty years past he has devoted himself unremittingly to his extensive business, and this

excessive application without rest or relaxation undoubtedly prepared the way for the disease of which he died.

Mr. Peirce was the son of Waldo Peirce of Frankfort, who was
well known to many of the older business men of this city, and
was brother of the late Waldo T. and Hayward Peirce who resided
here, and of Mrs. Stetson, wife of Hon. Charles Stetson. Mr.
Peirce lived a pure and unexceptional life. He was a man of
large business ability, and of untiring industry. His indomitable
energy united with that of his partner, Hon. J. T. Rowe, opened
and developed the largest granite quarry in the United States. In
his work he rendered a most important service to his native town.

Mr. Peirce was of an exceedingly kind and obliging heart. He
was universally esteemed by his townsmen and neighbors. He
was always prompt in his aid of every good work and enterprise.
His loss will be greatly felt in the community in which he lived,
and he will be sincerely mourned by a large circle of friends and
relatives. He leaves a wife and seven children. — *The Democrat*,
Bangor, June 19, 1873.

CHILDREN.

346.   I. GEORGE A., b. Feb. 16, 1851; m. Emma Patten.
347.   II. JOHN, b. Sept. 28, 1852; m. Mary H. Ward.
      III. KATHERINE, b. Dec. 21, 1854.
      IV. HAYWARD, b. Jan. 3, 1859; res. Frankfort, Me.
      V. ALBERT, b. Sept. 18, 1858; res. Frankfort, Me.
      VI. SARAH L., b. Mar. 28, 1860; res. Frankfort, Me.
      VII. LINCOLN, b. Dec. 21, 1866; res. Frankfort, Me.

175. **Waldo T.**[7] **Pierce** (Waldo[6], Haywood[5], Benjamin[4], Benjamin[3], Benjamin[2], Michael[1]), b. Sept. 16, 1804; m. Sept. 24, 1828,
Hannah Jane Hills, b. June 9, 1805 in Newbury, Mass.; d. Sept.
24, 1863, at Gorham, Me. He d. Apr. 24, 1858. Res. Frankfort,
Me.

Death of a well-known merchant.— We regret to announce the
decease of Waldo T. Peirce, Esq., of this city, whose long and
painful illness was terminated by death on Saturday morning,
about five o'clock. His disease has been one of the head, baffling

the skill of the best physicians, and subjecting him to much suffering for the past two years, which he has borne, however, with
fortitude and resignation.

Mr. Peirce,'although still in the prime of life, was one of the
oldest of our Bangor merchants, having commenced business in
this city more than thirty years ago, in company with his brother,
the late Hayward Peirce; he has during all that time transacted an
extensive and profitable business which grew with the growth of
the city, from the days when her merchants were few and her
population but a tithe of its present number. As a business man
he was an honor to his profession, and as a citizen highly respected.
His age was fifty-four years. A member of the Maine House of
Representatives in 1853 and 1854.

CHILDREN.

I. WALDO T., b. Nov. 17, 1831; res. Boston, Mass., at
   Commonwealth Hotel.

II. ADA H., b. Aug. 20, 1834; m. Oct. 22, 1857, Hon.
    Joseph Williamson, b. Oct. 5, 1828. She d. Mar.
    19, 1872; res. Belfast, Me. Ch., Ada C., b. Sept.
    14, 1858; res. Belmont, Mass.; Frances, b. Oct. 6,
    1860; res. Bangor, Me.; Joseph, b. Feb. 14, 1869;
    res. Augusta, Me.

    Hon. Joseph Williamson was the son of Joseph
    Williamson, Esq. He entered immediately upon
    legal study, and was admitted to the bar in 1852,
    and engaged in the practice of his profession in
    his native town, where he still resides. Besides
    the calls of his profession he has given himself
    much to historical investigations, especially relat-
    ing to the earlier history of that portion of Maine,
    in which he has shown peculiar aptitude for such
    inquiries, the fruits of his labors having done credit
    to himself, his city, and the State. In whatever
    relates to the earlier history of Maine he is re-
    garded a prominent authority. He published in
    1852, " The Maine Register and State Reference
    Book," in 1870, " An Address at the Centennial
    Celebration of the Settlement of Belfast," " His-

tory of the City of Belfast to 1875," octavo, 956 pages. He has also been a frequent contributor to the collections of the Maine Historical Society, and other historical publications. He has been for several years on the standing and publishing committees of the Maine Historical Society, and is an associate of the historical societies of Vermont, Buffalo, Wisconsin, and the Royal Society of London. Mr. Williamson was for seven years judge of the police court of his city.

III. LUTHER H., b. June 4, 1837; m. June 20, 1866, Helen C. Rees, b. Dec. 5, 1842; res. s. p., 1904 Surf street, Chicago, Ill.; a real estate broker.

IV. JUNE, b. July 9, 1840; m. June 20, 1867, Charles W. Roberts; res. Bangor, Me. He was b. Oct. 22, 1828. Ch., Charlotte R., b. July 2, 1871; Jenny P., b. Sept. 27, 1874.

V. FLORENCE McG., b. May 24, 1844; m. June 1, 1871, James M. Mott. Ch., Florence, b. Sept. 28, 1873; d. Jan. 20, 1882; June P., b. Oct. 18, 1875; res. 1624 Belmont avenue, Chicago, Ill.

348. VI. MELLEN C., b. Oct. 2, 1847; m. Anna C. Hoyford.

176. Hon. Charles H.[7] Pierce (Waldo[6], Haywood[5], Benjamin[4], Benjamin[3], Benjamin[2], Michael[1]), b. Apr. 1, 1810; m. Aug. 1, 1839, Ellen W. Kelly, b. Dec. 2, 1809; d. Dec. 14, 1882.

Hon. Charles Henry Peirce was born in Frankfort now Winterport, Maine. He died at Arlington Heights, Mass., October 23, 1888. Deceased was a son of the late Waldo Peirce, long a prominent citizen of that town. Graduating at Bowdoin College in 1834, he studied law in Cambridge Law School, was admitted to the Boston bar, and opened an office in that part of Frankfort which is now Winterport, where he continued to practice until a few years since. In 1837, he married Miss Ellen Kelly, daughter of Judge Kelly of Concord, N. H., who was a brother-in-law of Daniel Webster. During the administration of Presidents Taylor and Fillmore, Mr. Peirce was deputy collector of customs in the Bangor district. Under President Lincoln, he held a position in the Internal Revenue. Upon the death of his wife, in 1883, he removed to Massachusetts, where his two surviving children reside. He was a man of kind and affectionate disposition and of unblemished character.

Res. Needham and Arlington Heights, Mass. He d. Oct. 23, 1888.

CHILDREN.

    I. CHARLES H., JR., b. Aug. 4, 1840; d. Apr. 10, 1849.
    II. FRED'K W., b. Dec. 6, 1847; d. Apr. 14, 1849.
349.   III. WEBSTER KELLY, b. Dec. 1, 1842; m. Etta F. Lincoln.
    IV. ELLA R., b. May 18, 1850; res. Arlington Heights, Mass.

177. **Silas F.**[7] **Pierce** (Waldo[6], Haywood[5], Benjamin[4], Benjamin[3], Benjamin[2], Michael[1]), b. Dec. 18, 1825; m. May, 1859, Frances L. Griffin, b. 1830; d. 1877. Res. 68 Worcester street, Boston, Mass.

CHILDREN.

    I. HARMON, b. Oct., 1860; d. May, 1879.
    II. ELIZA, b. 1862; d. 1863.
    III. CARROLL E., b. Feb., 1867; unm.
    IV. FANNY C., b. Dec., 1868; unm.
    V. PHILIP W., b. June, 1871; unm.

178. **Elijah F.**[7] **Pierce** (Elijah[6], Haywood[5], Benjamin[4], Benjamin[3], Benjamin[2], Michael[1]), b. July 1, 1827; m. June 12, 1859, Sarah A. Perry, b. Jan. 20, 1834. Res. Egypt, Mass.

CHILDREN.

    I. ANNIE F., b. Nov. 7, 1859.

179. **Gilman G.**[7] **Pierce** (Artemas[6], Ezra[5], Benjamin[4], Ebenezer[3], Ebenezer[2], Michael[1]), b. May 4, 1817; m. Apr. 2, 1843, Elizabeth Woodworth, b, ——. Res. Melbourne, Australia.

CHILDREN.

I. ISABELLA, b. ——; m. Dec., 1868, Frank B. Clapp.
Ch., Mary E., Adda C., Ellen J., Harold, Isabell,
Frank, Leroy; res. Melbourne, Australia.

180. **William⁷ Pierce** (Artemas⁶, Ezra⁵, Benjamin⁴, Ebenezer³,
Ebenezer², Michael¹), b. Nov. 26, 1819; m. Nov. 25, 1843, Malinda
Abbott, b. June 20, 1820; d. Aug. 17, 1874; m. 2nd, 187 , Mary
V. Hesleton, b. Apr. 1, 1844. Res. Chester, Vt.

CHILDREN.

I. SARAH M., b. Aug. 25, 1844; m. Dec. 19, 1866;
William P. Dodge, b. July 8, 1841. Ch., Geo. D.,
b. Dec. 5, 1870; d. Feb. 4, 1872; res. Chester, Vt.
II. REBECCA E., b. Aug. 17, 1847; m. June 2, 1868,
Paul H. Pitkin, b. Oct. 30, 1841. Ch., Sarah E.,
b. Nov. 20, 1870; Cora M., b. Dec. 14, 1873; Paul
H., b. Mar. 19, 1886; res. Springfield, Mass.
III. GILBERT L., b. May 26, 1877.
IV. ALICE E., b. Mar. 19, 1882.

181. **Merrill⁷ Pierce** (Ezra⁶, Nehemiah⁵, Benjamin⁴, Ebenezer³,
Ebenezer², Michael¹), b. Feb. 18, 1830; m. Mar. 21, 1854, Amanda
Robbins, b. Mason, N. H., Sept. 28, 1835. Res. Putney, Vt.

CHILDREN.

I. LILLA J., b. June 2, 1855; m. July 3, 1877, David
Frost.
II. ARTHUR M., b. Apr. 6, 1857; d. June 7, 1871.
350. III. FRANK R., b. July 21, 1858; m. Ruby Yeaton.
351. IV. FRED. N., b. Aug. 24, 1860; m. Sarah Pierce.
352. V. EZRA F., b. Apr. 2, 1863; m. Ada Fuller.

182. **Josiah⁷ Pierce** (Sem.⁶, Nehemiah⁵, Benjamin⁴, Ebenezer³,
Ebenezer², Michael¹), b. Feb. 6, 1818; m. Feb. 8, 1843, Adeline
Whitman, b, Sept. 6, 1820. Res. Londonderry, Vt.

CHILDREN.

I. EVA, b. Oct. 14, 1844; d. May 3, 1845.
II. ALMA, b. Mar. 13, 1848; d. Sept. 23, 1849.
III. EMMA, b. Aug. 31, 1849; d. Nov. 5, 1851.
IV. JOSIAH, b. Dec. 27, 1855; d. Jan. 17, 1856.
V. HATTIE, b. May 2, 1857; res. 36 Linnean street, Cambridge, Mass.
VI. GENEVIEVE, b. Dec. 28, 1859; d. Nov. 23, 1861.

183. **Sem.**[7] **Pierce** (Sem.[6], Nehemiah[5], Benjamin[4], Ebenezer[3], Ebenezer[2], Michael[1]), b. Dec. 21, 1825; m. Eliza Howard. Res. South Londonderry, Vt.

CHILDREN.

353. I. FRANK O., b. Feb. 24, 1854; m. Ruth E. Cone.
II. MARY A., b. May 27, 1858.
III. W. HARRY, b. Mar., 1871.

184. **William W.**[7] **Pierce** (Sem.[6], Nehemiah[5], Benjamin[4], Ebenezer[3], Ebenezer[2], Michael[1]), b. Mar. 14, 1836; m. Lizzie A. Stone. Res. South Londonderry, Vt.

CHILDREN.

I. PHYLETTA M., b. Nov., 1868.
II. JOSIAH Q., b. Mar., 1870.
III. BERTHA A., b. Oct. 3, 1883.

185. **Rev. Nehemiah**[7] **Pierce** (Sem.[6], Nehemiah[5], Benjamin[4], Ebenezer[3], Ebenezer[2], Michael[1]), b. Nov. 5, 1837; m. Nov. 5, 1857, Jane A. Shumway, d. Nov. 9, 1867; m. 2nd, Dec. 22, 1868, Marcia A. Eddy. He d. Mar. 25, 1873. Res. Springfield, Ill.

Rev. Nehemiah Pierce, pastor of the First Baptist Church of Springfield, Ill., died of consumption at his residence in that city, March 25, 1873. He was the son of Rev. Sem. Pierce, a Baptist clergyman, who for twenty-five years preached the gospel at Londonderry, Vt. Deceased was born in Londonderry, Novem-

24

ber 5, 1837; was converted and baptized in the twenty-first year
of his age, and although previously married, entered at once upon
a course of study for the ministry. After innumerable hardships
and great self-denial, he graduated from the Vermont University
at Burlington in 1865. During his course of study he supplied,
for three years, the Baptist church at Westford, Vt., receiving for
his labors a very meager compensation, and by the severity of his
labors, as his journal clearly shows, sowing the seeds of that disease that so prematurely carried him to the grave. He was ordained in Bellows Falls, Vt., April 25, 1866. After a pastorate of
two years at this point, he labored two years as pastor of the
church at Coldwater, Mich. In November, 1870, he began his
labors with the First Baptist Church in Springfield, Ill. His pastorate at that point was eminently successful, although his labors
were performed amid great discouragements, arising from the dis-
tracted and disturbed condition of the church at the beginning of
the work, as well as the great physical suffering and nervous pros-
tration consequent upon the progress of the disease which ended
his life. During the year 1872, the church reluctantly, yet cheerfully gave him a leave of absence for a trip to Europe, in the vain
desire that permanent improvement in health might result. He
was absent four months, and returned to die in his own family.
His residence in Illinois, though brief, endeared him to the
churches of his denomination in this State. By the wisdom of
his plans, the earnestness of his labors, the catholicity of his spirit,
the kindness of his heart, the unaffected simplicity of his faith in
Christ, the consistent and unimpeachable integrity and purity of
his moral character, as well as by his earnest piety and cultivated
intellect he had so endeared himself to his brethren in the ministry,
that they have great sorrow at his early departure.

CHILDREN.

I. EUGENIA K., b. May 7, 1860; d. Dec. 1, 1866.
II. MARY HOIT, b. Sept. 5, 1862; m. Dr. E. A. Sawyer,
   of Gardner, Mass. She d. Dec. 7, 1883.
III. LAWRENCE B., b. May 30, 1865; d. Aug. 4, 1866.
IV. BERTHA E., b. Apr. 1, 1871; res. Olean, N. Y.

186. **Dr. Stephen Byron**[7] **Pierce** (Alson[6], Benjamin[5], Benjamin[4], Ebenezer[3], Ebenezer[2], Michael[1]), b. Apr. 15, 1839; m. May 9, 1870, Sophia E. Stilson, b. Sept. 23, 1846.

Dr. Byron Pierce was born at Cooper's Plains, Steuben county, N. Y., April 15, 1839, on his father's farm, and at suitable age worked on the farm during the summer and attended school winters till eighteen years old, when he began the study of medicine with Dr. Floyd Morse of Painted Post, N. Y. He attended two courses of lectures in the medical department of the University of Michigan at Ann Arbor, and one course at Buffalo Medical College, where he graduated in the spring of 1860. On his return at that time, he began the practice of medicine in his native town. In June, 1862, he entered the service as assistant surgeon, and was assigned to Batteries H and L of the First Regiment, Ohio Artillery, with whom he remained for about six months in the campaign from second battle of Bull Run to battle of Fredericksburgh, when business and care of infirm parents caused his return home.

Resumed the practice of his profession, also carried on the farm and manufactured lumber for about ten years. In the spring of 1870 he married Miss Sophia E. Stilson of Franklin, Delaware county, N. Y. In the fall of 1875, he engaged in mercantile business in Cooper's Plains, is still interested in same, and carrying on the farm on the "old place" first purchased by his father in 1815. Res. Cooper's Plains, N. Y.

CHILDREN.

I. LUCIA S., b. Oct. 11, 1871.
II. HELEN E., b. Mar. 29, 1873; d. June 18, 1886.
III. BENJAMIN S., b. Mar. 14, 1874.
IV. FRANK F., b. Mar. 11, 1876.
V. ALFRED C., b. Mar. 22, 1878; d. May 30, 1879.

187. **Albert R.**[7] **Pierce** (Nathan[6], Benjamin[5], Benjamin[4], Ebenezer[3], Ebenezer[2], Michael[1]), b. Feb. 16, 1837; m. June 17, 1875, Eliza S. Phelps, dau. of Hon. James Phelps of Townsend, Vt. She was b. June 1, 1851. He removed from Vermont in

1884 to Suffield, Conn., his present residence. He is a farmer and a fruit grower. Enlisted in the early part of '61, in Company C, Third Regiment Minnesota Volunteer Infantry, serving until discharged at close of war. Received a bad wound in leg at battle of Fitzhugh's Woods, Ark., April 1, 1864, which disabled him for a time. The wound continuing to trouble him, he was detailed first as clerk in Sanitary Commission, and later as acting commissary in Refugees' camp near Little Rock. Res. Suffield, Conn.

CHILDREN.

    I. JAMES P., b. June 2, 1876.
    II. WILLIS N., b. Oct. 16, 1879.
    III. LILLIAN, b. Jan. 13, 1881.
    IV. CHARLES A., b. May 11, 1883.

188. Prof. James E.[7] Pierce (Nathan[6], Benjamin[5], Benjamin[4], Ebenezer[3], Ebenezer[2], Michael[1]), b. Aug. 12, 1839; m. July 11, 1866, Frances Hall, dau. of Prof. Edwin Hall of Auburn, N. Y.

The following is part of an article taken from the Auburn, N. Y., *Journal*, of July 20, 1870:

Prof. Pierce was the son of Dea. Nathan Pierce of West Townshend, Vt., and was born August 12, 1839. He was prepared for college at Burr Seminary, Manchester, Vt., and at Kimball Union Academy, Meriden, N. H. He entered Middlebury College in 1857, and graduated with the Latin Salutatory in 1861. He immediately commenced preparation for the Christian ministry in Auburn Theological Seminary, and after an interruption of one year, spent as tutor at Middlebury College, he graduated in 1865. While a tutor he preached in West Cornwall, Vt., and afterward in the city of Portland, Me., with great acceptance. After graduation at Auburn he supplied the First Church at Norwalk, Conn., but before the opening of the Fall term, he was, in consequence of his rare ability and excellence as a scholar, elected upon a new foundation, donated by Mr. Christopher Robert, adjunct professor of the Hebrew Language and Literature, and in 1867, a full professor. During his first year as instructor in the seminary, he supplied for some time, writing new sermons, the Park Church, Syracuse, giving high satisfaction and witnessing much religious interest under his labors. He was subsequently ordained an Evangelist by the Presbytery of Cayuga. He was permitted to preach the gospel for six years and to instruct future preachers for five years.

Prof. Pierce had an admirable mind. He was not only a man of fine talents and fine culture; he was a man of genius.

His habits of study were of the very best, from his boyhood, and very much the same through the whole course. He wrote short hand and used the pen freely. He was steady and persistent in his studies and acquisitions, beyond most, even the best scholars.

As a professor his success was from the first remarkable. He had diligently studied Arabic and Sanscrit, and investigated geography, antiquities, etc., etc., which would illustrate his own department. He seemed certain, had he lived, to have attained high eminence among professors in Biblical science. The genius, character and work of Prof. Pierce, his admirable sermons deserve a memorial volume which we hope may be given to the world. The resting-place of the young and gifted professor will hereafter be a new object of interest in our beautiful and fast occupied Fort Hill Cemetery.

He d. July 15, 1870. Res. Auburn, N. Y.

CHILDREN.

I. EDWIN H., b. Dec. 25, 1868.

189. **Jerome W.**[7] **Pierce** (Simeon[6], Benjamin[5], Benjamin[4], Ebenezer[3], Ebenezer[2], Michael[1]), b. Nov. 29, 1836; m. July 19, 1864, Eugenie L. Stark of Morgan, Ohio, b. Feb. 14, 1840; d. Mar. 27, 1866; m. 2nd, Oct. 29, 1867, at Berlin, Ohio, Anna E. Brooks, b. May 19, 1837. He prepared for college at Oberlin, Ohio; graduated from Antioch College, Yellow Springs, Ohio, June, 1859, the year of the death of the president, Horace Mann. Had charge of a college in Mississippi till the breaking out of the war. Studied law with H. E. Stoughton, at Bellows Falls, Vt.; admitted to the bar in 1862; been in practice since at Springfield, Vt.; candidate of the Democratic party for Congress in 1872, and for Lieutenant-Governor in 1878; appointed postmaster at Springfield in 1885. Res. Springfield, Vt.

CHILDREN.

I. FRANK B., b. Aug. 25, 1868.

II. JEAN I., b. May 15, 1872; d. Sept. 15, 1876.

III. JESSIE B., b. May 27, 1878.
IV. CLARA A., b. July 13, 1881.

190. **Warren**[7] **Pierce** (Ebenezer[6], Ebenezer[5], Ebenezer[4], Ebenezer[3], Benjamin[2], Michael[1]), b. ——; m. ——, Sarah Williams.
Res. Cedar Falls, Iowa, and Pomona, Cal.

CHILDREN.
I. CHARLES, b. ——.

191. **Hiram**[7] **Pierce** (Adolphus[6], Ebenezer[5], Ebenezer[4], Ebenezer[3], Benjamin[2], Michael[1]), b. Feb. 22, 1815; m. June 13, 1839, Mary M. Messenger, b. Feb. 26, 1819.

Hiram Pierce was the only child of Adolphus and Mehitabel Pierce, and was born in Windham, Windham county, Vt., February 22, 1815. His parents removed to the State of New York when he was about three years old, and settled in the township of Newark, Tioga county. In the spring of 1831, he removed with his parents to Ohio, and settled on a new farm in the township of Windham, Portage county. He helped clear up the farm, attending school and teaching winters. He read law with Judge D. R. Tilden of Cleveland, and was admitted to practice in 1840. He, however, did not follow the profession, but chose the mercantile business, which at this date, December, 1888, he still follows.

June 13, 1839, he was united in marriage with Mary M. Messenger, also of Windham. Their children were a son and a daughter, Warren, born July 25, 1842, and Marion, born January 11, 1851.

In 1851, Mr. Pierce removed with his family to Garrettsville, where he still resides. He held the office of justice of the peace both in Windham and Garrettsville. He was also elected mayor of Garrettsville, but refused to serve. For sixteen years he was assistant postmaster in the Garrettsville office.

Res. Windham, Vt., and Garrettsville, Ohio.

CHILDREN.
354.   I. WARREN, b. July 25, 1842; m. Helen M. Webb.
       II. MARION, b. Jan. 11, 1851.

192. **Ezekiel[7] Pierce** (Solon[6], Ezekiel[5], Ezekiel[4], Thomas[3], Benjamin[2], Michael[1]), b. June 19, 1809 ; m. Feb. 5, 1832, Phebe Thornton, b. Apr. 22, 1815. He was a farmer, railroad contractor, merchant, Universalist and Republican. He d. Feb., 1889. Res. Yorkshire Center, N. Y.

CHILDREN.

I. PHEBE E., b. Jan. 2, 1833; m. Nov. 20, 1850, John H. Bond. She d. July 8, 1853.

II. ANDREW J., b. Dec. 18, 1834; d. May 20, 1835.

III. E. ANNETTE, b. July 21, 1837; d. June 19, 1860.

IV. MINERVA D., b. Aug. 15, 1840 ; m. J. S. Murphy ; res. Yorkshire Center, N. Y.

V. LYDIA O., b. Apr. 10, 1842; m. twice, and d. Nov. 27, 1865.

VI. SOLON E., b. Apr. 26, 1844 ; d. Feb. 11, 1846.

355. VII. ROLLIN G., b. Dec. 9, 1847 ; m. Lucy E. Sherman.

VIII. RICHARD T., b. Oct. 3, 1850; d. May 8, 1859.

IX. GEORGE E., b. Dec. 18, 1853 ; m. Feb. 20, 1884, Lizzie Hill; res. Yorkshire Center, N. Y.

193. **William B.[7] Pierce** (Solon[6], Ezekiel[5], Ezekiel[4], Thomas[3], Benjamin[2], Michael[1]), b. May 23, 1816; m. May 23, 1843, Clarissa J. Doty, b. Feb. 5, 1816; d. June 15, 1851; m. 2nd, Aug. 1, 1852, Jane M. Butterfield. Res. Kingsland, Eaton Co., Mich.

CHILDREN.

356. I. CHARLES J., b. Dec. 7, 1845 ; m. Mary A. Tutt and Minnie M. Elliott.

357. II. ELVAH S., b. Aug. 11, 1848 ; m. Lucretia J. More.

III. WILLIAM, b. May 16, 1850; d. 1851.

IV. FRANK E., b. Sept. 25, 1853.

V. CLARISSA J., b. July 16, 1855; d. 1855.

VI. ALBERT J., b. Apr. 1, 1857 ; d. 1858.

VII. SOLON J., b. June 17, 1858; d. 1873.

VIII. HATTIE L., b. Aug. 7, 1862; m. Dec. 28, 1877, William F. Berger. She d. 1886. Ch., Leo D., b. Feb. 2, 1879.

IX. ROSELLE, b. Oct. 14, 1864; d. 1864.

X. HORACE E., b. Feb. 14, 1866; d. 1866.

194. **Elvah F.**[7] **Pierce** (Solon[6], Ezekiel[5], Ezekiel[4], Thomas[3], Benjamin[2], Michael[1]), b. Aug. 21, 1818; m. Dec. 29, 1836, Merana N. Nye, b. Sept. 23, 1816. He d. at Centreville, Mich., May 10, 1887.

Died, at his residence in Centreville, Mich., Tuesday evening, May 10, 1887, Elvah F. Pierce, after an illness of five months, aged sixty-nine years.

Mr. Peirce was born August 21, 1818, in Penfield, Monroe county, N. Y. In 1836, he was married, and resided in that State until 1853, when he came to Michigan. He was the father of three children, all living. In 1861, he enlisted in the Eleventh Michigan Infantry, and was assigned to the commissary department, where he remained a year and a half, but was obliged to return home on account of ill health. In 1870, he was elected sheriff of St. Joseph county, which office he held with credit. After his term of official duties in this capacity he remained a citizen of Centreville, and under Garfield's administration was appointed postmaster at Centreville, which office he held four years. He had also been under-sheriff several years, and justice of the peace. He had gradually been failing in health for some time, until the light of life was totally extinguished. He was an honored member of the Three Rivers Commandery of Knights Templar, and a member of the Mt. Hermon Lodge, F. and A. M., of this place, and also a member of David Oaks Post, G. A. R. He was one of the leading members of the Baptist church, and united with that denomination as far back as 1838, when a resident of New York. Mr. Peirce was a man of very positive nature; he was always a ready champion for all things moral in humanity in general. The temperance cause never had a better friend or a more earnest worker, he was ever willing to lend a helping hand for its promotion, ever willing to counsel, mildly, reformations in men, and always assisted in lifting them up, rather than pulling them down, when he saw earnestness in their endeavors. Mr. Peirce, like all men, no doubt had his faults, but his good qualities far overshadowed them and placed him on the plane of manhood superior to the average of men. His funeral occurred at the Reformed church, Thursday afternoon, under the supervision of Mt. Hermon Lodge, F. and A. M., and an escort of the Three Rivers Commandery of Knights Templar. Rev. Cochrane, pastor of the Baptist church, officiated.

CHILDREN.

I. ARDELLA S., b. Dec. 6, 1837; m. Nov. 12, 1860, —— Barkman; res. Three Rivers, Mich.

358. II. WILLIAM H., b. Oct. 22, 1840; m. Carrie M. Brown.

359. III. CYRUS E., b. Oct. 15, 1845; m. Sarah E. Honeywell.

195. **Alonzo B.**[7] **Pierce** (Ira[6], Thomas[5], Seth B.[4], Thomas[3], Benjamin[2], Michael[1]), b. May 10, 1838; m. Mar. 2, 1859, Phebe Vaughn, b. Feb. 5, 1841; d. Dec. 9, 1875; m. 2nd, May 5, 1878, Louisa Gamble, b. Sept. 7, 1849. Res. Pleasant Prairie, Wis.

CHILDREN.

I. IRA E., b. Nov. 4, 1865.

II. MILTON A., b. Jan. 7, 1868.

III. CHARLES A., b. Jan. 8, 1875; d. July 14, 1876.

196. **Hon. Henry B.**[7] **Pierce** (Martin B.[6], Nathaniel[5], Seth B.[4], Thomas[3], Benjamin[2], Michael[1]), b. Aug. 6, 1841; m. Oct. 19, 1861, C. Elvira Carew, b. Sept. 26, 1839; d. s. p., Apr. 9, 1862; m. 2nd, Dec. 31, 1865, Augusta Arnold, b. Sept. 6, 1841; d. Feb. 10, 1882; m. 3d, Apr. 25, 1883, Fanny B. Pease, b. Oct. 19, 1843. Res. Abington, Mass.

Hon. Henry Bailey Pierce of Abington, was born in Duxbury, Mass., August 6, 1841, a descendant in the seventh generation from Captain Michael Peirce of Scituate. He was educated in the

25

public schools of his town, and in the Mercantile Academy of Boston. He enlisted October 14, 1861, as a private in Twenty-third Regiment Massachusetts Infantry Volunteers; received a warrant as commissary sergeant in 1862; was commissioned as first lieutenant in 1863; was appointed regimental quartermaster, January 3, 1864; was commissioned as captain September 20, 1864, served on the staff of General Edward Harland as assistant commissary of subsistence during the last campaign of the war, and was mustered out of the service July 10, 1865. He shortly after engaged in the insurance business. In 1870 he was appointed Assistant Adjutant-General of the Department of Massachusetts, Grand Army of the Republic, and was reappointed each year until 1876. In 1875, he was elected secretary of the Commonwealth, and is now serving his thirteenth year in that office, having been renominated each year by acclamation. He is the president of the Abington Mutual Fire Insurance Company; a trustee of the Abington Savings Bank; a trustee of the Public Library; one of the Park commissioners, and has held various other positions of trust and of responsibility.

CHILDREN.

I. EUGENE E., b. Apr. 16, 1868.
II. ANNE G., b. May 31, 1877.

197. **Frank H.**[7] **Pierce** (Henry T.[6], John[5], Seth B.[4], Thomas[3], Benjamin[2], Michael[1]), b. Oct. 25, 1850; m. Mar. 30, 1875, Mary Stocker, b. May 21, 1848. Res. 1416 Chestnut street, Philadelphia, Pa.

CHILDREN.

I. HENRY T., b. Apr. 19, 1876.
II. MARY S., b. Mar. 8, 1878.
III. WILLIAM E., b. Oct. 1, 1879; d. Nov. 19, 1884.
IV. JOSEPH D., b. Jan. 28, 1883.

198. **George C.**[7] **Pierce** (Mason W.[6], Mial[5], Mial[4], Mial[3], John[2], Michael[1]), b. July 14, 1816; m. Aug. 30, 1835, Juliana Bliss, b. Jan. 8, 1815. He d. Oct. 13, 1881. Res. Bristol, R. I.

CHILDREN.

360.   I. JAMES P., b. July 7, 1845; m. Maria Roward.
     II. GEORGE M., b. July 13, 1836. He d. Sept. 16, 1868, leaving Ireta M., who m. Elijah Burton; res. Warwick Bay Side, R. I.
   III. HENRY C., b. Feb. 28, 1838; res. Mattapan, Mass.
361.   IV. EZRA B., b. July 28, 1841; m. Sarah E. Potter.
     V. CORNELIUS C., b. Sept. 21, 1839; res. Boston, Mass.
   VI. EDWARD F., b. Mar. 28, 1843; res. 14 Carlton street, Dorchester, Mass.
  VII. EUGENE H., b. Mar. 7, 1847; res. Providence, R. I.
 VIII. LYDIA M., b. Jan. 22, 1852; d. Feb., 1852.

199. **Mason W.**[7] **Pierce** (Mason W.[6], Mial[5], Mial[4], Mial[3], John[2], Michael[1]), b. Feb. 13, 1820; m. June 19, 1842, Lydia M. Townsend, b. Oct. 18, 1819. He d. Nov. 18, 1873. Res. 3 Sprague street, Providence, R. I.

CHILDREN.

   I. RAYMOND F., b. Nov. 24, 1845; m. Nov. 24, 1867, Ellen A. Perry; res. 3 Sprague street, Providence, R. I.

200. **James P.**[7] **Pierce** (Mason W.[6], Mial[5], Mial[4], Mial[3], John[2], Michael[1]), b. Sept. 16, 1823; m. June 13, 1843, Maria W. Disman, b. ——; d. ——; m. 2nd, Eliza H. Hoar, b. ——. He d. Sept. 4, 1869. Res. Bristol, R. I.

CHILDREN.

   I. MARION W., b. Feb. 19, 1844; m. Dec. 13, 1864, Samuel J. Townsend, b. Apr. 7, 1844. Ch., Samuel J., b. July 2, 1876; res. Wareham, Mass.

201. **Henry P.**[7] **Pierce** (Mason W.[6], Mial[5], Mial[4], Mial[3], John[2], Michael[1]), b. Feb. 12, 1826; m. May 19, 1848, Mary Pilling, b. Dec. 25, 1828. Res. Bristol, R. I.

CHILDREN.

362.   I. CHARLES T. H., b. Apr. 4, 1849; m. Elizabeth E. Martin.

II. MARY P., b. Nov. 10, 1852; m. May 21, 1875, Edward M. Hartley, b. Jan., 1854, s. p.; res. corner Walnut and Durfee streets, Fall River, Mass.

III. FLORENCE A., b. Sept. 10, 1860; m. Aug. 10, 1879, James H. Fish, b. Mar. 23, 1858; res. Baylis, Pike Co., Ill. Ch., Herbert E., b. Apr. 24, 1881; Florence E., b. June 21, 1883; Henry M., b. Jan. 23, 1885; Benjamin H., b. Apr. 23, 1886.

202. **David A.**[7] **Pierce** (Mason W.[6], Mial[5], Mial[4], Mial[3], John[2], Michael[1]), b. Mar. 5, 1828; m. June 8, 1846, Jane A. Pilling, b. Mar. 1, 1830. Res. Bristol, R. I.

CHILDREN.

I. JOHN A., b. Mar. 22, 1847; d. Apr. 27, 1849.

II. FRED'K W., b. Mar. 17, 1850; m. June 9, 1879, Ella H. Albro, b. Aug. 7, 1858, s. p.; res. Bristol, R. I.

III. WALTER H., b. Aug. 12, 1853; d. Jan. 31, 1864.

IV. LUCINDA M., b. Dec. 16, 1854; m. June 22, 1886, James A. Reid, b. Jan. 5. 1848; res. Providence, R. I.

203. **John Q.**[7] **Pierce** (Isaac[6], Asa[5], Mial[4], Mial[3], John[2], Michael[1]), b. June 22, 1823; m. Aug. 20, 1863, Carrie C. Hasslegreen, b. Feb. 9, 1834. Res. 115 High street, Providence, R. I.

CHILDREN.

I. ANNIE M., b. May 30, 1864.

II. JOHN I., b. Feb. 25, 1866; res. 29 Benevolent street, Providence, R. I.

204. **John H.**[7] **Pierce** (John H.[6], Asa[5], Mial[4], Mial[3], John[2], Michael[1]), b. Feb. 23, 1823; m. Aug. 6, 1851, Ruth A. Buffington, b. Jan. 24, 1830. Res. Lawrence, Mass.

CHILDREN.

I. ELLA C., b. Aug. 11, 1852; m. May 28, 1872, Jeremiah Sullivan ; res. Lawrence, Mass.

205. **William G.**[7] **Pierce** (Asa[6], Asa[5], Mial[4], Mial[3], John[2], Michael[1]), b. Dec. 19, 1825; m. June 11, 1857, Almira F. Metcalf, b. Sept. 22, 1835. He d. Dec. 25, 1875. Res. 115 High street, Providence, R. I.

CHILDREN.

I. ARTHUR W., b. Aug. 5, 1860; res. 803 Congress street, Portland, Me.

206. **George A.**[7] **Pierce** (Asa[6], Asa[5], Mial[4], Mial[3], John[2], Michael[1]), b. Aug. 12, 1828; m. Feb. 19, 1859, Henrietta K. Angell, b. Dec. 24, 1837. Res. 214 Broad street, Providence, R. I.

CHILDREN.

I. ESTHER H., b. Nov. 11, 1860.
II. HENRY A., b. Mar. 25, 1863; d. Sept. 6, 1867.

207. **Anthony**[7] **Pierce** (Anthony[6], John[5], John[4], John[3], John[2], Michael[1]), b. Aug. 20, 1825; m. Dec. 6, 1847, Hannah F. Briggs, b. Dec. 6, 1823. Res. 1038 Acushnet avenue, New Bedford, Mass.

CHILDREN.

I. HANNAH A., b. Aug. 17, 1849; d. Aug. 9, 1851.
II. EUDORA J., b. Dec. 16, 1850; d. Aug. 15, 1851.
III. CLARA, b. Sept. 5, 1859; res. at 1038 Acushnet avenue, New Bedford, Mass.

208. **George E.**[7] **Pierce** (Anthony[6], John[5], John[4], John[3], John[2], Michael[1]), b. Apr., 1838; m. Nov. 24, 1859, Mary J. Reed, b. Jan. 14, 184—. Res. Dighton, Mass.

CHILDREN.

I. CHARLES W., b. June 28, 1861 ; m. Hattie Reynolds; res. Westport, Mass. Ch., Charles A., Orrin F., and a daughter.

209. **Simeon A.**[7] **Pierce** (Anthony[6], John[5], John[4], John[3], John[2], Michael[1]), b. Apr. 8, 1835; m. Sept. 4, 1860, Melissa A. Reed, b. Aug. 20, 1843. Res. Taunton, Mass.

CHILDREN.

   I. BION C., b. Nov. 23, 1864; res. Taunton, Mass.
   II. MARY E., b. Feb. 16, 1870; res. Taunton, Mass.
   III. HEBER A., b. Aug. 28, 1871; res. Taunton, Mass.

210. **Andrew N.**[7] **Pierce** (Nathan[6], Bethuel[5], Elisha[4], John[3], John[2], Michael[1]), b. Mar. 19, 1833; m. Dec. 25, 1857, Olive E. French, b. Dec. 26, 1838. He d. Jan. 9, 1876. Res. Berkley, Mass.

CHILDREN.

   I. IDA M., b. Oct. 11, 1858; m. Mar. 18, 1879, C. A. Reed; res. 28 Newberry street, West Somerville, Mass.
   II. EVERETT C., b. July 26, 1860; res. 19 Maple street, Taunton, Mass.
   III. FLORA A., b. Aug. 17, 1866; m. July 1, 1886, Wm. Whittier; res. 19 Maple street, Taunton, Mass.

211. **Alexander**[7] **Pierce** (Nathan[6], Bethuel[5], Elisha[4], John[3], John[2], Michael[1]), b. Jan. 17, 1835; m. May 29, 1864, Annie A. Lawrence, b. Dec. 15, 1842. Res. Weir village, Taunton, Mass.

CHILDREN.

   I. FRANK L., b. June 14, 1865; d. Sept. 1, 1866.
   II. CLARA A., b. Mar. 13, 1867.
   III. FRANK A., b. Nov. 13, 1868.
   IV. GEORGE E., b. Jan. 22, 1871.
   V. HARRY L., b. June 27, 1875.
   VI. MADELINE, b. July 12, 1877; d. Nov. 17, 1884.
   VII. MARY A., b. July 5, 1879; d. Nov. 17, 1884.

212. **Ichabod M.**[7] **Pierce** (George[6], Bethuel[5], Elisha[4], John[3], John[2], Michael[1]), b. Feb. 14, 1827; m. Feb. 14, 1851, Susan B. Rowley, b. Apr. 22, 1835. Res. 319 River street, Fall River, Mass.

CHILDREN.

I. MARY A., b. Sept. 4, 1854.
II. ABBIE S., b. Aug. 24, 1856.
III. SAMUEL P., b. Sept. 9, 1858. He is a conductor on Rock Island railroad; his home is in Trenton, Mo.
IV. CHARLES H., b. Dec. 10, 1860.
V. CORA B., b. June 29, 1866.

213. **Elnathan**[7] **Pierce** (John[6], Bethuel[5], Elisha[4], John[3], John[2], Michael[1]), b. June 14, 1822; m. Nov. 20, 1840, Lucy H. Maxim, b. Oct. 22, 1818; d. June 8, 1885. Res. Plymouth, Mass.

CHILDREN.

I. NANCY, b. Aug. 26, 1841; d. Nov., 1841.
II. REBECCA A., b. Aug. 26, 1842.
III. ELNATHAN, b. Sept. 9, 1844.
IV. JOHN, b. June 18, 1846; d. Sept., 1846.
V. MARY J., b. July 26, 1847; d. Aug., 1849.
VI. CHARLES A., b. July 26, 1848.
VII. JULIA A., b. Sept. 1, 1851.
VIII. ELIZA, b. Sept. 10, 1855.

214. **John**[7] **Pierce** (John[6], Bethuel[5], Elisha[4], John[3], John[2], Michael[1]), b. May 1, 1826; m. Nov. 30, 1848, Sarah Hathaway, b. Mar. 30, 1833. Res. 6 Green street, Fall River, Mass.

CHILDREN.

I. FANNIE B., b. Mar. 7, 1852; m. Aug. 27, 1866, —— Pratt; res. 6 Green street, Fall River, Mass.
II. GEORGE B., b. Jan. 16, 1854; m. Jan. 21, 1874; res. 104 Division street, Fall River, Mass.

III. JOHN F., b. Aug. 18, 1856; m. Nov. 10, 1880; res.
Little Compton, R. I.

IV. ALPHONSO E., b. June 10, 1859; m. June 10, 1880;
res. 13 Lynn street, Fall River, Mass.

V. RHODA H., b. Mar. 4, 1861; m. Mar. 27, 1879, ——
Ward; res. Somerville, Mass.

215. **Otis**[7] **Pierce** (Sabbinus[6], Elisha[5], Elisha[4], John[3], John[2],
Michael[1]), b. Nov. 14, 1801; m. Feb. 28, 1827, Mary Bement, b.
Feb. 18, 1803; d. May 20, 1871. He d. Feb. 10, 1864. Res.
Suffield, Conn.

CHILDREN.

363.   I. HENRY O., b. Mar. 18, 1830; m. Mary A. Thompson.

II. FRANCIS A., b. Sept. 10, 1832; d. Apr. 17, 1839.

III. GEORGE J., b. Jan. 7, 1835; d. Nov. 5, 1864, in a
rebel prison.

IV. SABRA A., b. June 9, 1838; m. Jan. 10, 1854, L. A.
Wood.

V. ELBRIDGE H., b. May 23, 1841.

VI. MARY S., b. July 20, 1843.

VII. ELMER J., b. Oct. 9, 1846.

216. **Sabbinus**[7] **Pierce** (Sabbinus[6], Elisha[5], Elisha[4], John[3],
John[2], Michael[1]), b. Aug. 18, 1804; m. Nov. 11, 1838, Deborah
Alvord, b. Sept. 8, 1817; d. Dec. 11, 1861. He d. Oct. 29, 1864.
Res. Manchester, Ohio.

CHILDREN.

I. ROBERT R. R., b. Oct. 23, 1840; d. Sept. 17, 1869. He
enlisted at Galveston, Ind., Company H, Seventy-
third Indiana. Discharged July 1, 1865.

II. MARIA A., ⎫ b. June 23, 1843; m. Aug. 10, 1865.
III. MARY E., ⎭ b. June 23, 1843; d. June 11, 1848.

IV. CHARLES, b. June 25, 1845; d. Feb. 10, 1864.

V. Martha, b. Oct. 15, 1847; m. June 24, 1867. She
    d. Aug. 31, 1869.
VI. Sarah, b. Feb. 22, 1850; m. Dec. 28, 1868.
VII. William, b. Apr. 15, 1852.
VIII. Celina, b. Aug. 13, 1854.

217. **Elisha**[7] **Pierce** (Sabbinus[6], Elisha[5], Elisha[4], John[3], John[2],
Michael[1]), b. Apr. 7, 1806; m. Apr. 30, 1832, Hannah Sherman,
b. May 16, 1811. He d. Sept. 23, 1864. Res. 258 Pine street,
Springfield, Mass.

Children.

  I. Maria E., b. July 31, 1833.
364. II. William C., b. June 25, 1835; m. Mary Reid.
365. III. Albert E., b. July 26, 1837; m. Etta J. Stevens.
  IV. J. Elizabeth, b. Feb. 29, 1844; m. Oct. 23, 1862,
    James S. Queen, b. Oct. 24, 1838. Ch., Sarah S.,
    b. Aug. 7, 1863; De Witt, b. Apr. 10, 1867;
    Louis C., b. Apr. 2, 1876.

218. **Amasa**[7] **Pierce** (Isaac[6], Daniel[5], Clothier[4], Clothier[3],
John[2], Michael[1]), b. Feb. 4, 1800; m. ——. He d. Mar. 11, 1844.
Res. Ogdensburgh, St. Lawrence county, New York.

Children.

  I. Truman, res. Ogdensburgh, N. Y.

219. **Daniel**[7] **Pierce** (Isaac[6], Daniel[5], Clothier[4], Clothier[3],
John[2], Michael[1]), b. May 10, 1802; m. 1825, Polly Day, b. Sept. 4,
1812; d. Feb. 2, 1841; m. 2nd, 1842, Wealthy Wheelock, b. Nov.
9, 1810; d. Sept. 7, 1882. He d. Aug. 28, 1882. Res. Geneva
Lake, Wis.

Children.

  I. Sarah B., b. Mar. 20, 1845; m. Dec. 16, 1862,
    Fred. Doney, b. May 11, 1823; res. Waupon, Wis.
26

Ch., Harry, b. Dec. 25, 1863; res. Faribault,
Minn.; Ed. D., b. Aug. 25, 1865; Nellie, b. Apr.
20, 1868; Fred., b. Oct. 13, 1870; d. Dec. 23, 1870.

II. HANNAH, b. Mar. 27, 1826; m. William Studley;
d. July 23, 1846.

III. CEMANTHA, b. May 3, 1828; m. Oct. 30, 1851, Sam-
uel W. Pierce, b. Dec. 16, 1822; res. Albion, Neb.
Ch., Judson A., b. Oct. 14, 1853; m. Harriett E.
Gardner; Frank J., b. Sept. 23, 1855; Jarrett A.,
b. Jan. 11, 1858; d. Oct. 10, 1877; Almon N., b.
Nov. 3, 1859; m. Addie L. Walters; Elvia A., b.
Sept. 22, 1861; res. Lincoln, Neb.; Ira J., b. Sept.
1, 1864.

365-1. IV. NATHAN D., b. Sept. 23, 1837; m. Oraville V.
Kingsbury.

365-2. V. ALFRED H., b. Jan. 27, 1841; m. Mary ——.

VI. NELLIE, b. July 23, 1848; m. Rev. R. B. Wolseley;
res. Deland, Fla.

220. Isaac W.[7] Pierce (Isaac[6], Daniel[5], Clothier[4], Clothier[3],
John[2], Michael[1]), b. Feb. 3, 1811; m. July 27, 1828, Phebe Baldwin, b. Mar. 2, 1810; d. Jan. 6, 1865. He d. Dec. 28, 1841; the
widow then m. Mar. 13, 1842, Daily Carpenter, b. Sept. 7, 1797;
d. 1877. They had four children. Isaac resided in New York
State, Jacksonville, Ill. and Desert City, Utah.

CHILDREN.

366. I. ISAAC W., b. Aug. 22, 1839; m. Hanna Carlson and
Elna Carlson.

II. AMASA, b. Dec. 22, 1829; d. July 11, 1847.

III. GEORGE H., b. June 27, 1832; m. Jan. 21, 1853, Lucinda Elworth; Apr. 6, 1859, Sarah Skinner; res.
Levan, Utah.

IV. NATHAN. b. Feb. 2, 1834; m. Apr. 4, 1857, Emma
Hart; res. Loa, Pinta county, Utah.

V. LUCY R., b. June 27, 1837; d. Sept. 13, 1838.

221. **David⁷ Pierce** (Isaac⁶, Daniel⁵, Clothier⁴, Clothier³, John², Michael¹), b. Mar. 7, 1813; m. Mar. 30, 1832, Dency Pierce, b. Aug. 29, 1815; d. May 14, 1880. Res. Macomb, St. Lawrence county, N. Y.

CHILDREN.

I. CHARLES A., b. Apr. 5, 1845; killed at the battle of Chancellorsville, May 4, 1863.
II. AVALINE M., b. Feb. 17, 1833.
III. PALINA, b. Apr. 27, 1837.
IV. JANE, b. June 24, 1841.
V. EVERETT D., b. Sept. 1, 1847.
VI. MIAL H., b. Sept. 27, 1842.

222. **Rev. Mial R.⁷ Pierce** (Isaac⁶, Daniel⁵, Clothier⁴, Clothier³, John², Michael¹), b. May 25, 1815; m. Dec. 6. 1836 at Black Lake, N. Y., Provider Roxford, b. Apr. 22, 1814; d. Nov. 25, 1858; m. 2nd, Oct. 25, 1859 at Waddington, N. Y., Elizabeth Colburn, b. Mar. 7, 1836. Res.Coulton and Burke, N. Y.

Rev. Mial R. Pierce was born in Oswegatchie (on the Black lake), N. Y., May 25, 1815, and died in Burke, N. Y., August 15, 1887. Rev. Pierce was converted in his nineteenth year, and joined the Methodist Episcopal Church. Soon after his conversion he had a call to preach the gospel, but was not willing to turn his back on the prospects of worldly success and become a humble, itinerant Methodist preacher. He resisted the call of the Spirit until through business transactions he found himself bereft of all his worldly effects. Overwhelmed with disappointment, he promised obedience to God. In 1841, he was licensed to exhort by John Lowrey, preacher in charge of the Oswegatchie circuit, Lewis Whitcomb, presiding elder. He was given a local preacher's license in 1843, signed by Nathaniel Salsbury, presiding elder of the Hammond district, Black River Conference. The following year, a vacancy occurring on the circuit where he resided, at the unanimous request of the quarterly conference he was appointed junior preacher. For four years he preached under the direction of the presiding elder. In 1848, he joined the Black River Conference, and was ordained a deacon by Bishop Janes. Six years later he was ordained an elder by Bishop Morris. He served the following charges with great acceptability: Fowler and Fine,

Natural Bridge, Lisbon, Morristown, Hermon, Waddington and Norfolk. He was at the latter place when the war of the rebellion commenced. His soul was filled with patriotic ardor. He induced many to enlist in the service of their country. When the Ninety-second Regiment, New York State Volunteer, was raised, he was offered and accepted the chaplaincy. During the war he came home, and raised a company of the Sixth New York Heavy Artillery and returned as its captain. On his health failing he was compelled to return home, and assumed the relation of a local preacher. In 1871, he found his health so far restored that he was again able to enter the itinerant ranks and served the following charges under the presiding elder: Bangor, Nicholville, Russell, Lisbon, Burke and Colton. In the spring of 1885, he was unable to take work, and was compelled to bid a final adieu to all pastoral labor. He retired to his home in Burke, Franklin county, N. Y., where he continued to reside until his death. During his residence there, he was able the greater part of the time to attend the service of the sanctuary. A week before his death he was in the church, and at the close of the sermon asked permission of the pastor to address the people. He spoke a few words with great earnestness and feeling, closing with the stanza:

> " Happy if with my latest breath,
> I may but grasp His name,
> Preach Him to all, and cry in death,
> Behold, behold the Lamb! "

Rev. Pierce, was one of God's chosen instruments to lead men to the Cross. His early ministry was blessed with multiplied revivals of great power. Hundreds of souls were led to God through his influence. He was a natural orator, and when under the power of the Spirit spoke with great efficiency. His judgment was good, and administration of the affairs of the church harmonious and successful. In the home he was kind, affectionate and gentle, affable and a lover of society.

He was twice married. First, December 6, 1836; to Miss Provider Roxford. The fruit of this marriage was six children, two of whom survive, Mr. Seymour Pierce of Norfolk, N. Y., and the Rev. David F. Pierce of Ilion, N. Y. After twenty-two years of married life and fourteen in the itinerancy, his faithful wife exchanged the toil and strife of earth for the rest of heaven, on November 25, 1858. He was again married to Miss Elizabeth Colburn, October 25, 1859, a woman of intelligence and Christian worth, who contributed her full share toward the efficiency and happiness of an itinerant's home. Of this marriage there were born three children, two of whom with their mother live to mourn the loss of an affectionate and indulgent father and husband.

CHILDREN.

I. SEYMOUR B., b. July 25, 1838; m. Apr. 25, 1866;
    res. Norfolk, N. Y.

367.   II. JAMES F., b. Feb. 22, 1840; m. Myrid Rundell.

368. III. DAVID F., b. Apr. 26, 1846; m. Mary Jardin and
    Addie Phillips.

IV. MARY A., b. Sept. 9, 1842; m. Sept. 15, 1868, Arte-
    mas Johnston. She d. Oct., 1868; res. Burke,
    N. Y.

V. ARTEMUS G., b. July 25, 1850; d. Aug. 22, 1851.

VI. GEORGE K., b. Apr. 9, 1862; d. Aug. 23, 1863.

VII. EMMA L., b. Oct. 25, 1863; m. Dec. 19, 1883, Albert
    Finney, b. Apr., 1857, s. p.; res. Burke, N. Y.

VIII. MINNIE A., b. July 24, 1865; m. May 25, 1884,
    George A. Smith; res. Burke, N. Y. He was b.
    Jan. 10, 1863. Ch., Clifford Pierce, b. May 7,
    1886.

223. **John T.[7] Pierce** (Isaac[6], Daniel[5], Clothier[4], Clothier[3],
John[2], Michael[1]), b. Feb. 11, 1818; m. Mar. 10, 1835, Anna Cole,
b. July 30, 1819. Res. Plainfield, Washington Co., Wis.

CHILDREN.

369.   I. CHESTER M., b. Sept. 27, 1847; m. Henrietta Alvord.

370.   II. GEORGE W., b. Apr. 28, 1837; m. Elizabeth Hark-
    ner.

III. RUTH A., b. June 23, 1839; m. June 1, 1856, Rich-
    ard Snyder, b. Feb. 28, 1831; res. Plainfield, Wis.
    Ch., Emmery M., b. May 29, 1860; James H., b.
    Jan. 19, 1862.

IV. PHEBE B., b. Sept. 17, 1841; m. Mar. 8, 1863, James
    Edmister, b. Feb. 27, 1840; res. Chippeway Falls,
    Wis. Ch., Amasa J., b. Jan. 29, 1865; Alvin W.,
    b. June 9, 1867; Annie A., b. Aug. 15, 1871.

V. MARTHA A., b. Oct. 12, 1843; d. Dec. 16, 1858.

371.   VI. LEWIS H., b. July 27, 1845; m. Helen Owen.

224. John B.[7] Pierce (Daniel[6], Daniel[5], Clothier[4], Clothier[3], John[2], Michael[1]), b. Oct. 16, 1820; m. July 4, 1852, Rebecca B. Clark, b. Sept. 22, 1821. Res. Concord, Minn.

CHILDREN.

 I. CLARA P., b. July 26, 1853; m. Nov. 28, 1872, Albro E. Beckwith, b. Jan. 2, 1850; res. Dodge Center, Minn. Ch., Florence E., b. Jan. 13, 1874; Myra E. b. June 22, 1876; Laura B., b. Sept. 26, 1881 ; Leslie, b. May 3, 1884.

 II. HARRIETT A., b. Apr. 13, 1857; d. Oct. 24, 1857.

 III. JOHN H., b. June 1, 1859.

 IV. ABBY V., b. July 11, 1862; m. Nov. 15, 1882, Leonard L. Weiss, b. Nov. 15, 1857; res. Concord, Minn. Ch., John J., b. Mar. 3, 1883; Mary E., b. Apr. 21, 1885.

225. Capt. John C.[7] Pierce (Clothier[6], Clothier[5], Clothier[4], Clothier[3], John[2], Michael[1]), b. Nov. 11, 1826; m. May 12, 1859, Amie A. S. Pierce, b. Sept. 2, 1829.

Capt. John C. Pierce, formerly of New Bedford, Mass., died Friday, October 7, 1887, at Cincinnati, Ohio. He was born in Hixville, Dartmouth, and went to sea in early life. His last voyage was a number of years ago in the Amie Ann. When he returned he gave up the sea, and bought the Ninety-Nine Cent Store on Purchase street, New Bedford. He conducted this for about a year, and then went to Cincinnati, where he established the same business. There he was very successful, and built up a large trade, with branch stores at Louisville and Columbus. Within a short time, however, the two latter had been sold.

Capt. Pierce had been in failing health some time.

He was a pleasant man, who made and kept many friends.

His death was at his country home in Loveland, O., but he was known as a resident of Cincinnati, as his business was there, and when able was in it daily. He d. Oct. 7, 1887. Res. Cincinnati, Ohio.

CHILDREN.

I. WILLIAM C., b. Sept. 5, 1868; res. No. 110 West 5th St., Cincinnati, Ohio.

226. **John J.**[7] **Pierce** (Isaac B.[6], William[5], Daniel[4], Samuel[3], John[2], Michael[1]), b. May 29, 1846; m. Oct. 12, 1870, Fanny Moore. Res. Mahopac Falls, N. Y.

CHILDREN.

I. LOUISA, b. Oct. 22, 1874.
II. MINNIE, } b. Nov. 15, 1878.
III. MABLE, }

227. **Israel**[7] **Pierce** (John[6], Azrikim[5], Samuel[4], Azrikim[3], Ephraim[2], Michael[1]), b. May 8, 1795 ; m. Sept. 6, 1822, Eliza A. Richardson, b. Dec. 10, 1803; d. Mar. 11, 1827; m. 2nd, May 6, 1829, Almira Nickerson, b. Feb. 10, 1808. He d. June 16, 1862. Res. Franklin, Mass.

CHILDREN.

372.   I. JAMES G., b. July, 1823; m. Mrs. Sarah Harvey.
      II. MARY E., b. Dec. 14, 1826; m. Dec. 29, 1845, Lowell Gilmore, b. June 7, 1821; res. Binghamton, N. Y. Ch., Ferdinand A., b. Sept. 18, 1846 ; d. July 16, 1866 ; Emma M., b. Aug. 3, 1848; m. B. S. Curran; Grace A., b. July 11, 1851; m. Jacob M. Hewood; Louisa C., b. Nov. 25, 1860; d. Aug. 6, 1861.
373. III. JOSEPH K., b. May 1, 1832; m. Margaret Phipps.
374.   IV. ALFRED J., b. Nov. 23, 1833 ; m. Susan A. Fuller and Anna Paine.
375.   V. FERDINAND I., b. Sept. 18, 1840; m. Anna Scott and Annie ——.
      VI. SUSAN A., b. Aug. 13, 1843; m. Feb. 11, 1866, Joshua G. Follett, b. Nov. 12, 1840; res. Saundersville, Mass. Ch., Lena E., b. Jan. 30, 1868; Mary A., b. Dec. 2, 1870; Helen L., b. Nov. 17, 1884.

228. **John**[7] **Pierce** (John[6], Azrikim[5], Samuel[4], Azrikim[3], Ephraim[2], Michael[1]), b. Sept. 12, 1790; m. Nov. 18, 1819, Julia A. Brownell; d. Mar. 22, 1831, s. p.; m. 2nd, May 9, 1832, Mary M. Clark; d. Mar., 1836, s. p.; m. 3rd, Oct. 5, 1836, Caroline F. Grant, b. Feb. 27, 1808; d. Apr. 20, 1881. He d. May 25, 1876. Res. Franklin, Mass.

CHILDREN.

376.   I. JOHN E., b. Aug. 24, 1840; m. Hope T. Pierce.

229. **Washington**[7] **Pierce** (John[6], Azrikim[5], Samuel[4], Azrikim[3], Ephraim[2], Michael[1]), b. Oct. 19, 1810; m. May 16, 1835, Nancy G. Hancock, b. June 14, 1814; d. Sept. 9, 1862. Res. Franklin, Mass.

CHILDREN.

    I. GEORGE W., b. Nov. 13, 1836; wid. res. Farmington, Me.

377.   II. CHARLES S., b. Mar. 23, 1839; m. Betsey M. Mason.

    III. AILSON D., b. July 15, 1842; d. Sept. 17, 1844.

    IV. EDSON M., b. July 17, 1845; d. Aug. 17, 1845.

    V. ADALINE N., b. Dec. 11, 1846; m. Hiram Briggs; res. Franklin, Mass.

    VI. MARY J., b. Oct. 29, 1848; m. Henry A. Gillmore; res. Sheldonville, Mass.

    VII. MIRANDA H., b. Mar. 28, 1852; m. Albert Worden; res. Sheldonville, Mass.

    VIII. ELLEN E., b. Apr. 24, 1855; d. Aug. 8, 1885.

230. **Israel**[7] **Pierce** (Squier[6], Azrikim[5], Samuel[4], Azrikim[3], Ephraim[2], Michael[1]), b. June 2, 1783; m. Hannah Cole, b. ——. Res. Rehoboth, Mass., and East Barnard, Vt.

CHILDREN.

    I. ISRAEL, b. June 30, 1805; m. Mary Moulton.

    II. OTIS N., b. Sept. 12, 1806; m. Oct. 22, 1826, Zepporah Small; res. Rehoboth, Mass.

III. ISAIAH, b. Oct. 21, 1808.
IV. IRA, b. Feb. 16, 1811.
V. ISAAC, b. Aug. 24, 1814 ; res. East Barnard, Vt.
VI. JACOB C., b. June 5, 1817.
VII. BERIAH, b. Sept. 11, 1819 ; res. East Barnard, Vt.
VIII. SARAH, b. Nov. 26, 1823.

231. **Squier**[7] **Pierce** (Squier[6], Azrikim[5], Samuel[4], Azrikim[3], Ephraim[2], Michael[1]), b. Jan. 22, 1788 ; m. Mar. 11, 1810, Elizabeth Hicks, b. Apr. 6, 1788; d. Oct. 6, 1872, He d. Mar. 2, 1846. Res. Rehoboth, Mass.

Squier Peirce, Jr., was born at South Rehoboth, Mass., January 22, 1788. He lived at home, worked on the farm, sometimes worked out, and all his earnings were given to his father (for his father had a family of eight children, five of them were girls) until he was twenty years of age. Then he told his father he wanted to learn a trade. He went with his brother Israel and worked at carpentering. He was married in 1810, then about twenty-two years of age. He removed to Providence, 1817, and worked at carpentering. About 1820 he went to the Providence bleachery, and soon became the boss mechanic. Staid there until 1843; then went to Providence Print Works as a mechanic, until March 2, 1844. When adjusting some machinery, his clothing caught on a very small cog-wheel, that was revolving a shaft about one hundred and twenty revolutions a minute. Both feet were very much broken by striking against a wall. The small cog-wheel crushed in several of his ribs. He was immediately taken to his home ; died in a half hour. He had his senses until the last minute. He did not seem to have any pain. I suppose he must have been benumbed. He was very much liked by his associates, and had many friends, and was very much missed in the community. He was one of the original members of the Broad Street Christian Church. The primary meetings were held at his residence some time before the church was organized. He contributed about $2,000 toward the building of the church.

27

CHILDREN.

I. CYRUS, b. Apr. 18, 1811; m. Mary Green; he d. Apr. 17, 1858, s. p.

378. II. CHARLES H., b. Mar. 8, 1813; m. Mary R. M. Dawson.

379. III. DEXTER H., b. Dec. 4, 1818; m. Corisanda M. Hunt.

IV. EDWIN H., b. Sept. 10, 1825; d. Sept. 1, 1835.

232. **Samuel⁷ Pierce** (Squier⁶, Azrikim⁵, Samuel⁴, Azrikim³, Ephraim², Michael¹), b. Aug. 12, 1790; m. June 23, 1814, Jane Case, b. July 13, 1791; d. Mar. 23, 1875. He d. Oct. 10, 1838. Res. South Rehoboth, Mass.

CHILDREN.

380. I. SAMUEL L., b. Apr. 13, 1828; m. Ann E. C. Horton.

II. MARY C., b. Mar. 22, 1820; m. Dec. 21, 1854, Esek H. Pierce (see); res. South Rehoboth, Mass.

III. JANE, b. Sept. 14, 1817; m. Nov. 28, 1847, Levi Bosworth, and d. Jan. 6, 1853.

IV. PRUDENCE, b. Aug. 29, 1815; m. Dec. 1, 1835, James M. Goff, and d. in Rehoboth, Mass., Mar. 25, 1843.

233. **Nathan⁷ Pierce** (Joseph⁶, Azrikim⁵, Samuel⁴, Azrikim³, Ephraim², Michael¹), b. Feb. 7, 1781; m. Hannah Hall, b. 1791; d. 1832. He d. Sept. 14, 1859. Res. Warsaw, N. Y.

CHILDREN.

I. MARY A., res. Geneva, Allen Co., Kansas.

381. II. ALONZO, b. July 27, 1812; m. Emeline Belknap.

III. JANE, b. July 3, 1814; m. Nov. 29, 1838, Daniel Judd, b. June 16, 1810; res. Warsaw, N. Y. Ch., Nancy, b. June 11, 1842; d. Aug. 22, 1869; Clark D., b. May 23, 1853.

IV. HANNAH, b. July 2, 1816; m. June 4, 1836, Jacob
    Shawn, b. June 18, 1841; res. Warsaw, N. Y. Ch.,
    Wallace W., b. Oct. 16, 1851; Mary E., b. Oct.
    10, 1838; Annie B., b. Nov. 1, 1850.

382. V. ALLEN, b. Dec. 4, 1825; m. Susan Whaley.
    VI. CLARISSA, b. 1822; m. June 16, 1840, Beman Wil-
        cox, b. 1819, s. p.; res. Warsaw, N. Y.

234. **Joseph⁷ Pierce** (Joseph⁶, Azrikim⁵, Samuel⁴, Azrikim³,
Ephraim², Michael¹), b. Aug. 3, 1790; m. Nov. 3, 1811, Arminia
Mason, b. Aug. 1, 1796; d. Jan. 20, 1877. He d. Mar. 28, 1880.
Res. Dighton, Mass.

CHILDREN.

383.   I. DEXTER T., b. July 30, 1833; m. Emma F.
           Bryant.
       II. BELINDA, b. Nov. 10, 1814; m. Mar. 3, 1839, Daniel
           S. Chace, b. Mar. 3, 1814; res. Dighton, Mass.
           Ch., Charles S., b. Jan. 10, 1840; m. Jan. 20, 1861;
           res. ——; d. ——.
      III. NANCY M., b. July 14, 1825; m. July 3, 1845, Amos
           Lee,* b. Dec. 8, 1824; res. 44 Vernon street,
           Providence, R. I. Ch., Oscar F., b. May 25,
           1851; res. 93 Merser street, Providence; Arme-
           nia M., b. Sept. 15, 1852; m. Mr. Baker; res. 18
           Pleasant street, Providence; Walter A., b. Aug. 7,
           1854; res. 44 Vernon street, Providence; Edgar
           L., b. Apr. 8, 1856; d. Nov. 3, 1857.

235. **Azrikim⁷ Pierce** (Joseph⁶, Azrikim⁵, Samuel⁴, Azrikim³,
Ephraim², Michael¹), b. Dec. 29, 1792; m. Abigail Harlow, b. Mar.
26, 1795; d. Mar. 26, 1853. He d. Oct. 6, 1829. Res. South
Rehoboth, Mass.

---
* Swansey Town Records say, July 24, 1844.

CHILDREN.

I.   NATHAN W., b. Mar. 4, 1820; m. Mar., 1842, Elizabeth Earl. He d. Nov. 29, 1877, in South Rehoboth, Mass.

384. II. ISAAC N., b. Oct. 26, 1816; m. Mary Earl.

III. SARAH H., b. Oct. 10, 1827; m. Oct. 17, 1851, Sam-
  uel Havens. He d. Sept. 16, 1868; res. Valley
  Falls, R. I. Ch., Alonzo R., b. Sept. 6, 1852;
  Sarah E., b. Apr. 21, 1854; d. July 28, 1854;
  Emma F., b. Jan. 7, 1855; m. John Alger; Edwin
  E., b. Aug. 20, 1857; d. July 9, 1859; Ira H., b.
  Jan. 31, 1860; Sarah A., b. Feb. 28, 1864; Elton
  E., b. Oct. 14, 1867.

IV. ABBY A., b. Aug., 1824; d. Sept. 25, 1839.

385. V. ANDREW T., b. Mar. 26, 1827; m. Eliza A. Marble
  and Mary E. Seeklisea.

386. VI. WILLIAM L., b. 1837; m. Sarah E. Wright.

236. **Daniel**[7] **Pierce** (Joseph[6], Azrikim[5], Samuel[4], Azrikim[3],
Ephraim[2], Michael[1]), b. Nov. 20, 1795; m. Nov. 28, 1819, Susan-
nah R. Pierce (see), b. Oct. 31, 1799. He d. Nov. 4, 1861. Res.
Rehoboth, Mass.

Daniel Pierce was born in Rehoboth, Mass., in 1795. He was
the youngest son of Joseph Pierce, and remained at home with his
father on the farm until near the close of the War of 1812, when he
was drafted into service. For a time after his return from the
war he taught in one of the district schools. After his marriage
with Susan Pierce in 1819, he opened a store, such as the country
trade demanded, and combined with this business that of an undertaker. As undertaker, his services were in demand, not only
in Rehoboth, but also in the towns of Dighton, Swansey, Seekonk
and Barrington. He was still active in business at the time of his
death, November 4, 1861. During his life he held several town
offices; was many years deacon of the Christian Baptist Church,
and was very benevolent toward all religious enterprises.

CHILDREN.

387. I. FREDERICK P., b. Dec. 26, 1820; m. Mary O. Bentley, Olevia Ovitt, and Mrs. M. W. Stewart.

II. CELIA ANN, b. Dec. 6, 1822; m. Otis Martin. She d. Jan. 6, 1851. Ch., Mary J., b. Apr. 28, 1850; m. —— Peck; res. South Rehoboth, Mass.

III. SUSANNAH, b. Jan. 6, 1825; m. Caleb Pierce. He was the son of Aaron, b. 1818 (see). Ch., Susan F., b. Nov. 1, 1846; Henry G., b. Nov. 12, 1848; m. Julia Spicer; Jannette M., b. Nov. 29, 1857; m. Samuel Horton; Harvey L., b. Aug. 1, 1852; res. South Rehoboth, Mass.

IV. DANIEL W., b. May 31, 1827; d. Dec. 23, 1832.

V. RUTH A., b. Nov. 23, 1833; m. Spencer Cronkhite; res. Warsaw, N. Y. Ch., Fred. P., b. July 21, 1867; Grace L., b. Dec. 19, 1869.

388. VI. LLOYD B., b. Nov. 19, 1835; m. Nancy J. Briggs.

VII. DEXTER D., b. Mar. 2, 1840; m. Ellen Bliven; res. s. p., 207 Transit street, Providence, R. I.

237. **Israel[7] Pierce** (Abraham[6], Azrikim[5], Samuel[4], Azrikim[3], Ephraim[2], Michael[1]), b. June 2, 1805; m. Sept. 12, 1843, Louisa Durham, b. Apr. 26, 1826. He d. May 30, 1885. Res. Chippawa, Ontario.

Israel Pierce emigrated to Canada, and settled in Chippawa, 1836. Married Louise Durham, September 12, 1843, and remained there ever since until his death, May 30, 1885.

CHILDREN.

389. I. J. HENRY, b. July 29, 1844; m. Louise Schvenacher.

II. GEORGE M., b. Nov. 24, 1846; res. San Louis Obispo, Cal.

III. CORNELIA, b. Sept. 30, 1848; res. Buffalo, N. Y.

IV. MARIA L., b. Sept. 12, 1850; d. Nov. 27, 1852.

V. MARY M., b. Mar. 22, 1853; res. Chicago, 1210 Wabash avenue.

VI. ELEANOR, ⎱ b. Mar. 3, 1855.
   FRANKLIN ⎰ b. Mar. 3, 1855; d. Mar. 5, 1855.
VII. CHARLES S., b. Feb. 11, 1857; res. Duluth, Minn.
VIII. DAPHINE, b. —— 4, 1859; d. May 22, 1886.
IX. JESSIE F., b. Mar. 15, 1861.
X. FRED F., b. June 6, 1863.
XI. ISRAEL, b. Nov. 23, 1865; res. Duluth, Minn.

238. **Dennis W.**[7] **Pierce** (Abraham[6], Azrikim[5], Samuel[4], Azrikim[3], Ephraim[2], Michael[1]), b. Oct. 27, 1806; m. June 17, 1833, Julia A. Seccord; d. Oct. 18, 1844; m. 2nd, Mar. 23, 1845, Sarah S. Wood, b. May 21, 1814. He d. Mar. 4, 1886. Res. Cooperstown, N. Y.

CHILDREN.

I. LUCY C., b. May 4, 1834; m. Jan. 1, 1850, Ganyard Wood; res. Bristol Springs, N. Y. Ch., Augusta M. Wood, b. July 11, 1851; d. Sept. 15, 1865; Albert Wood, b. Feb. 21, 1853; Frank M., b. Mar. 15, 1856 ; Veness, b. Apr. 25, 1858; Dennis P., b. July 26, 1859; Spencer B., b. Mar. 14, 1862; Melvin N., b. Sept. 13, 1864; Lana V. Wilcox, b. Feb. 8, 1869; res. P. O., Gulick, Ontario Co., N. Y.

390. II. JAMES A., b. Feb. 16, 1836 ; m. Mary A. Holcomb.

III. ELMIRA L., b. Nov. 30, 1845; m. Nov. 7, 1866, Frank L. Clark, b. Oct. 22, 1843. She d. Sept. 30, 1883; res. Naples, N. Y. Ch., Flora I., b. July 24, 1867; Arthur J., b. Sept. 14, 1868; Leon P., b. June 15, 1870; Maud E., b. June 25, 1875.

IV. AMELIA S., b. Aug. 30, 1848; m. June 26, 1881, Demster Brown, b. May 26, 1849; res. Bristol Springs, N. Y., s. p.

V. ELLEN M., b. Mar. 4, 1851; unm.; res. Bristol Springs, N. Y.

VI. ELIZA S., b. Apr. 11, 1853; m. Mar. 14, 1872, Frank
Miller, b. Dec. 29, 1847; res. Bristol Springs,
N. Y. Ch., Willis J., b. Dec. 8, 1875; Walter
S., b. Dec. 28, 1876.

239. **Abraham**[7] **Pierce** (Abraham[6], Azrikim[5], Samuel[4], Azrikim[3], Ephraim[2], Michael[1]), b. June 22, 1809; m. Charlotte Laws.
He d. Aug. 5, 1860. Res. St. Thomas, Ontario, and Faceton, Vt.

CHILDREN.

I. CARRIE L., b. Oct. 3, 1836; m. Sewell W. Whitcomb.
Ch., Charles M., b. May 15, 1862; Leila A., b.
Aug. 16, 1864; Cora L., b. Oct. 28, 1868; res.
in St. Thomas, Canada.
II. ABRAHAM, d. infant.

240. **Alonson**[7] **Pierce** (Abraham[6], Azrikim[5], Samuel[4], Azrikim[3], Ephraim[2], Michael[1]), b. Dec. 28, 1811; m. Sept. 13, 1840,
Sybil S. Smith, b. Oct. 3, 1816; d. Mar. 6, 1884. Res. Pompa-
noosuc, Winsor Co., Vt.

CHILDREN.

I. MYRON S., b. Jan. 1, 1852; m. Sept. 24, 1878, Julia
E. Bicknell, b. Sept. 24, 1858; res. s. p. Pompa-
noosuc, Vt.
II. GEORGE A., b. Sept., 1847; d. Nov. 19, 1847.
III. JAMES H., b. Dec. 16, 1850; d. July 12, 1851.
IV. CHARLES, b. Apr. 18, 1855; d. Dec. 16, 1855.
V. CLIFTON W., b. Oct. 18, 1865; d. Sept. 17, 1871.

241. **William L.**[7] **Pierce** (Benjamin[6], Azrikim[5], Benjamin[4],
Azrikim[3], Ephraim[2], Michael[1]), b. —— ; m. ——. Res. Ill.

CHILDREN.

I. DAU., b. —— ; m. Joseph L. Strang, the Mormon
prophet, his first and lawful wife. The encyclope-
dias and histories give chary mention of the

"Strangites" and of Joseph L. Strang, but none
of them furnish any thing like an adequate account
of the life and death of Mormonism on the islands
at the foot of Lake Michigan. The Strang phase
of Mormonism had its birth and came into prominence about the time of the Nauvoo settlement
in this State. Strang was a dissolute man; an
unscrupulous and ambitious one as well. He was
identified with the Young, Kimball, Smith, and
other factions which were powerful when the
church was in its infancy, and was jealous of the
strength which these men possessed through their
supposed association with Divine powers. This
led him also to receive a "revelation" from above
and set himself up as a leader under spiritual
guidance. His revelation was consistent with
Smith's in that it allowed a man more than one
wife; and not a few of the faithful enrolled themselves under the banner of the "Strangites."
When Nauvoo was destroyed Strang gathered his
people around him, refused to follow his former
companions westward, and started for the north.
The Beaver group of islands, consisting of Big
and Little Beaver, North and South Fox, Gull,
Garden, Hat, Hog and Squaw, located at the
mouth of the straits, were at this time, in 1846,
peopled by a shiftless lot of Indians and half-
breeds, who gained a precarious living by hunting,
fishing and wrecking. These quasi-settlers woke
up one morning to find their kingdom invaded
and the best part of Big Beaver pre-empted by
Mormons. The forces of Strang, about two hundred strong, had come in the night and "squatted."
Most of them settled on the northern side of the
island, on the shore of the bay, at the place
now known as St. James', and there they remained
for ten years. They built houses from the cedar
with which the islands abound, and traded for what
game and fish they needed. Fishermen and farmers began to come in, their numbers steadily grew,
and the settlement was in a fair way to rival the
one then springing up in Utah. Here Strang
was supreme — the great I am. He ruled his subjects with a rod of iron, and always to further his

own ends. He was a dissolute and unscrupulous man, who at bottom had no respect for morality or religion, and who increased his harem as fast as fancy dictated, although somewhat successful in managing to cloak his real character under religion and professed Divine sanction for his acts. But notwithstanding all his care, discontent took root after a few years, and a faction rose against him. The settlers in the vicinity secretly organized and armed themselves, and the night of July 11, 1856, made a descent upon the Big Beaver town. The Mormons were totally unprepared for such an attack. They awoke in the middle of the night to find their dry cedar houses burning like tinder over their heads, and the settlers driving every thing before them through the smoke and flying cinders. A slight attempt at resistance was made, but it was fruitless. Half the men in the Strangite party were killed and the town was burned down. Strang himself barely escaped with his life. In company with one of his wives he managed to reach another island, and in a day or two was taken off by a vessel and carried to the Wisconsin shore. Soon afterward he died near Milwaukee from the effects of wounds he had received in the mêlée. The captured Mormons were given choice of two things. They could take their turn at being "strung up," or could "get out." It is needless to say that they "got out," but whether they were absorbed by the farming communities of Wisconsin or Michigan, or made their way to Salt Lake City has never been known.

242. **Jared**[7] **Pierce** (Jared[6], Azrikim[5], Benjamin[4], Azrikim[3], Ephraim[2], Michael[1]), b.——, 1800; m. 1st,——, Ruth Stone, b.——; d. Mar. 14, 1826; m. 2nd, Apr. 10, 1828, Elizabeth Farnsworth, b. Nov. 22, 1802. He d. July 15, 1867. Res. Solon, N. Y., and Lacon, Ill.

28

CHILDREN.

I. FRANKLIN E., b. Jan. 10, 1834; res. Anita, Iowa.

II. NANCY L., b. May 10, 1829; m. —— Seymour; res. Necoma, Ill.

III. LUCY A., b. Mar. 25, 1831.

391. IV. JARED C., b. Mar. 14, 1826; m. Adelina Vaughn, Sarah M. Stewart, Mrs. Esther Powers.

V. OLIVE F.

VI. PLUMMER F., b. Apr. 7, 1838.

VII. STEPHEN M., b. Aug. 13, 1840; d. Oct. 7, 1845.

243. **Ora[7] Pierce** (Jared[6], Azrikim[5], Benjamin[4], Azrikim[3], Ephraim[2], Michael[1]), b. ——; m. in Manlius, N. Y., ——, 1828, Sylvia Rowley. Res. ——, Mich., and Angola, Ind. He d. 1869.

CHILDREN.

I. SUSAN, b. ——.

II. ORA, b. ——; res. Angola, Ind.

244. **Jefferson[7] Pierce** (Jared[6], Azrikim[5], Benjamin[4], Azrikim[3], Ephraim[2], Michael[1]), b. Feb. 15, 1809; m. Feb. 8, 1834, Laura Green, b. 1811; d. 18—; m. 2nd, Feb., 1863, Cynthia A. Sherman, b. 1818; d. May 18, 1884.

Jefferson Pierce was born in 1809, in Otsego, N. Y.; he married his first wife in Albion, N. Y., in 1834. They emigrated to the west and located at North Lansing, Mich., in the woods. A small log cabin was erected, and they were lulled to rest by the howling of the wolves which abounded in those early days. He followed farming, and that of carriage building. He is now, in 1889, eighty years of age, and resides in Gregory, Mich., with his daughter. He writes to the compiler as follows:

"I am living with my oldest daughter, Lucy Ann. For about one year past I have been growing young, and am able now to do light work some six to eight hours in a day, and for five years have not had a doctor nor had a poor appetite. Those homœopathic pills done it all. They eat all the diseased lining off of my stomach and bronchial tubes that had been gathering for twenty-five years. I now have a patent allowed me for a whiffletree spring-plate and spiral, working horizontal, of course, and thus revolutionizing the whole spring business. I have also discovered a new principle to be applied to all other plate-springs, which will give me another patent."

Res. Barre, N. Y., and North Lansing and Gregory, Mich.

CHILDREN.

I. BURTON D., b. May 24, 1835; d. July 12, 1856; unm.

II. LUCY A., b. June 2, 1837; m. Oct. 7, 1860, Jesse C. Dickinson, b. July 16, 1834; res. Gregory, Mich. Ch., Elmer D., b. at Howell, Livingston Co., Mich., Oct. 24, 1864; m. Nov. 14, 1883, at Plainfield, Livingston Co., Mich.; Lula J., b. at Plainfield, Jan. 28, 1874; both res. Gregory.

392. III. GUSTAVUS D., b. Dec. 28, 1840; m. Mattie A. Jenkins.

393. IV. FREEMAN A., b. Aug. 5, 1845; m. Henrietta L. Pruden.

V. HARRIET A., b. Dec. 2, 1847; m. Sept. 25, 1865, Luman T. Frink, b. Apr. 19, 1837; res. Stockton, Kansas. Ch., Nicholas B., b. July 7, 1866; Rutha L., b. Oct. 5, 1868; Caroline P., b. Sept. 15, 1870; Florence S., b. Sept. 6, 1872; Luther D., b. Aug. 19, 1876; d. Oct 13, 1879; Laura J., b. Dec. 31, 1878; Addie M., b. Nov. 19, 1881; Edith E., b. July 2, 1885.

VI. DE LOS., b. Sept. 14, 1848; d. ———.

VII. MYRON L., b. Aug. 14, 1852; res. unm. at Moberly, Mo.

244-1. **Nathaniel**[7] **Pierce** (Samuel[6], Joshua[5], Isaac[4], Azrikim[3], Ephraim[2], Michael[1]), b. June 29, 1751; m. Nov. 12, 1776, Lydia Newcomb, b. Mar. 25, 1758; d. June 14, 1842; dau. of Capt. Wil-

liam Newcomb of Eastham and wife Vashti (Cole) Pierce.   He
d. Aug. 6, 1841.

Nathaniel Pierce was born in Welfleet, Mass., in 1751, and with
many others was compelled to seek other employment than seamen during the Revolutionary war; he being a whaleman he served
a while in the army near Baltimore, so he used to tell his grandchildren.   He first came on the Penobscot river when it was
a perfect wilderness and bought of the Tarratine Sachem one
hundred acres for twenty dollars and a cow; constructed a rude
log house under a high bank close to the river.   Cleared and
planted ground with corn and potatoes, the soil returning very extraordinary crops.   After burning the mammoth growth of rock
maple and other trees.   The river at that time swarmed with the
finest fish, salmon and shad, which he often caught by the cart-
load, and fed not only his hogs, but land with them.   He soon
built a frame house, low posted and broad, a single huge chimney
in the center with immense fire-places; here he and his wife lived
frugally year after year.   Their wants were few in those days, a
very little money they had, in fact, they needed scarcely any, but
had plenty always to eat and to wear.   When the British came up
the river in 1814, their vessels were moored nearly opposite his
house, his family and all retreated back into the deep woods, but
he came every day to feed his swine, whose yard ran down to the
water.   Men from the tops of the ships fired at him at this time,
and he used to come back telling how the balls whistled.   A party
of them intoxicated came to the house one day, and in their absence run their cutlasses through every light of glass in one end
of the house.   Mr. Pierce reported them to the officer, who strung
the offenders up and applied the cat-of-nine-tails to their backs,
taking from their wages the price of the act.   This window always
after was boarded up, and his wife used to show it to her grandchildren.

Nathaniel was quite short of stature, full faced, florid complexion,
inclined to corpulency, piercing dark eyes, and an uncompromising Baptist; believing in the elect in its hardest sense.   Yet at
times there was a vein of humor that certain incidents would draw

out, one of which I give. His wife once was sitting making patchwork; he sat watching with one of his children beside them, when all at once he broke the silence with, " mother, do you know what your work reminds me of, it is this, Adam and Eve in the garden wearing fig leaves to cover their nakedness."

In their later years they resided with their son Samuel. Res. Welfleet, Mass., and South Orrington, Me.

CHILDREN.

393–1.   I. SAMUEL, b. Feb. 13, 1792; m. Dorcas Doone.

393–2. II. ISAAC, b. June 22, 1778; m. Rachel Fowler.

       III. POLLY, b. Dec. 4, 1780; m. Capt. Joshua Moody. They were married Sept. 6, 1804; res. Brewer Village, Me., and had a son Sirus.

393–3. IV. NATHANIEL, b. Jan. 26, 1783 ; m. Ruth Ryder and Mrs. Billington Smith.

       V. LYDIA, b. Oct. 22, 1786 ; m. Elisha Dale. They were united in marriage May 20, 1808. She d. 1821; res. Welfleet, Mass. Ch., Azuba, who m. —— Daniels.

393–4. VI. DAVID, b. Sept. 7, 1788; m. Polly Smith.

      VII. ABIGAIL, b. May 8, 1794; m. Nov. 9, 1815, James Smith. She d. Sept. 24, 1820. He was b. Oct., 1788; d. Nov. 15, 1883; res. Orrington, Me. Ch., James E., b. Aug. 11, 1816; d. Oct. 19, 1819; Abigail P., b. Nov. 28, 1818; m. John C. Nye, Aug. 22, 1837; res. 9 Morgan street, Salem, Mass.

244–2. **Samuel[7] Pierce** (Samuel[6], Joshua[5], Isaac[4], Azrikim[3], Ephraim[2], Michael[1]), b. Nov. 13, 1763 ; m. Mar. 7, 1787, Naomi Lewis; m. 2nd, Nov. 13, 1796, Grace (Newcomb) Young, b. Mar. 4, 1765 ; d. Oct. 7, 1833. She was the widow of Joshua Young, Jr., and dau. of Simeon Newcomb of Welfleet, who was born there Jan. 25, 1735. He d. July 22, 1816. Res. Welfleet, Mass.

CHILDREN.

I. SOLOMON L., b. Apr. 23, 1789; drowned, July 12, 1826 ; res. Welfleet, Mass.

II. ACHSAH, b. Nov. 27, 1791 ; m. Nov. 26, 1814, Samuel Kemp; res. Welfleet, Mass.

III. NAOMI L., b. Sept. 6, 1797.

IV. SAMUEL, b. Sept. 10, 1799 ; m. Mercy Pierce, b. Mar. 14, 1820; d. Oct. 3, 1829; res. Welfleet, Mass.

393–5. V. JOSHUA Y., b. July 3, 1802; m. Jennie Mason.

393–6. VI. THOMAS N., b. Sept. 11, 1804 ; m. Lucy Fuller and Emeline Field.

VII. BENJAMIN H., b. Oct. 25, 1806.

244–3. **John⁷ Pierce** (Samuel⁶, Joshua⁵, Isaac⁴, Azrikim³, Ephraim², Michael¹), b. abt. 1764; m. Nov. 3, 1785, Phebe Newcomb of Welfleet, b. abt. 1756; dau. of Lemuel and Phebe, d. June 26, 1825. He d. Apr. 21, 1808. Res. Welfleet, Mass.

CHILDREN.

I. LEMUEL N., b. Feb. 23, 1787; m. Tabitha Atwood.

II. SALLY, b. Oct. 13, 1790.

244–4. **David⁷ Pierce** (Samuel⁶, Joshua⁵, Isaac⁴, Azrikim³, Ephraim², Michael¹), b. Aug. 31, 1769; m. Mar. 15, 1794, Sally Atwood of Provincetown, b. Dec. 26, 1769; d. Apr. 18, 1850. Res. Welfleet, Mass.

CHILDREN.

393–8. I. SAMUEL, b. Sept. 3, 1795 ; m. Nancy Young.

II. SALLY, b. Sept. 9, 1797; m. Apr. 17, 1823, David Atwood. She d. Sept. 21, 1855.

III. POLLY, b. Dec. 15, 1799; m. Dec. 28, 1812, Hicks Smalley; m. 2nd, Robert S. Miller. She d. Aug. 11, 1879.

IV. HANNAH, b. Jan. 14, 1802; d. July 29, 1803.

393-9.   V. DAVID, b. Aug. 10, 1804; m. Ruth F. King.

    VI. HANNAH, b. May 31, 1808; m. Mar. 29, 1833, William Cleverly, b. Aug. 18, 1797; res. Welfleet, Mass. Ch., Sarah A. Atwood, b. Sept. 7, 1837; P. O. box 30, Welfleet, Mass.; Clarissa A. Cole, b. Sept. 9, 1839; res. 141 Chester avenue, Chelsea, Mass.; Winefred L. Kemp, b. Sept. 9, 1841; res. 35 Alaska street, Roxbury station, Boston, Mass.; Jane A. Baker, b. July 8, 1845; res. Newark, N. J.; Robert F. Cleverly, b. Jan. 20, 1848; address, care of Atwood & Bacon, Norfolk, Va.; Mary H. Talbot, b. Apr. 11, 1850; res. Chelsea, Mass.

244-5. **Solomon[7] Pierce** (Samuel[6], Joshua[5], Isaac[4], Azrikim[3], Ephraim[2], Michael[1]), b. ——; m. Apr. 18, 1799, Hezekiah Doane, d. Sept. 8, 1841. Res. Welfleet, Mass.

CHILDREN.

    I. JAMES, b. Sept. 15, 1799; d. July 11, 1836; res. Welfleet, Mass.

393-10.   II. ZEPHENIAH, b. July 24, 1801; m. Sally Lauman.

    III. HOPE, b. Oct. 19, 1802; m. Nov. 23, 1834, John McDonald; res. Dorchester, Mass.

    IV. ELIZABETH, b. Dec. 8, 1803.

    V. JOHN, b. Oct. 28, 1805; m. Annie ——.

    VI. SOLOMON, b. Dec. 22, 1807; d. at sea.

    VII. SABRA, b. July 1, 1810; m. May 4, 1830, Nehemiah Cole; m. 2nd, May 19, 1871, Seth N. Covell. She d. July 17, 1874. Ch., Daniel Cole; res. Welfleet, Mass.

244-6. **Joshua[7] Pierce** (Samuel[6], Joshua[5], Isaac[4], Azrikim[3], Ephraim[2], Michael[1]), b. June, 1772; m. Jan. 9, 1800, Rachel Hatch, b. 1778; d. Mar. 28, 1842; m. 2nd, July 4, 1843, Sally Snow. He d. May, 1854. Res. Welfleet, Mass.

CHILDREN.

393-11. I. OLIVER B., b. June 6, 1818; m. Mary A. Chipman.

II. JOSHUA, b. Aug. 29, 1801; n. f. k.

III. HARVEY, b. Nov. 15, 1803; d. Oct. 23, 1819.

IV. ELISHA, b. Nov. 14, 1805; lost at sea, Mar. 30, 1823.

V. ISAAC, b. Aug. 26, 1808; d. 1827.

VI. ATKINS, b. Oct. 31, 1812; m. Nov. 26, 1835, Martha S. Burton; he m. 2nd, —— Ross; res. 19 Everett street, Bunker Hill district, Boston, Mass.

VII. RACHEL, b. Sept. 16, 1815; m. Jan. 8 1832, Joseph S. Cole; res. Welfleet, Mass.

244-7. **Thomas[7] Pierce** (Joshua[6], Joshua[5], Isaac[4], Azrikim[3], Ephraim[2], Michael[1]), b. June 24, 1766; m. Dec. 4, 1787, Elizabeth Ryder. Res. Welfleet, Mass.

CHILDREN.

393-12. I. REUBEN, b. 1804; m. Ruth Rich.

393-13. II. NATHANIEL, b. Sept. 14, 1791; m. Martha Rich.

III. THOMAS, b. Aug. 15, 1802; m. Joanna C. Young.

IV. HANNAH, b. Sept. 16, 1793; m. May 6, 1813, Martin Wareham.

V. ABIGAIL, b. ——; m. Alexander Lovett; res. Provincetown, Mass.

244-8. **William[7] Pierce** (Joshua[6], Joshua[5], Isaac[4], Azrikim[3], Ephraim[2], Michael[1]), b. Oct. 15, 1768; m. Sally ——. Res. Provincetown, Mass.

CHILDREN.

393-14. I. ISRAEL, b. ——; m. Deborah Rich.

II. JOHN, b. July 30, 1791.

244-9. **Joshua Y.[7] Pierce** (Joseph[6], Joseph[5], Isaac[4], Azrikim[3], Ephraim[2], Michael[1]), b. Mar. 25, 1789; m. Dec. 12, 1810, Eunice

Young, b. 1786, d. Nov. 4, 1870. He d. Dec. 3, 1869. Res. Welfleet, Mass.

CHILDREN.

393-15. I. JOSHUA Y., b. Apr. 20, 1818; m. Recca C. Burgess.
393-16. II. ISAAC, b. Sept. 10, 1811; m. Drusilla Snow.
393-17. III. JOSEPH, b. June 6, 1813; m. ——.
    IV. JOANNA, b. July 28, 1812; d. June 20, 1852.
    V. MARY A., b. Dec. 1, 1822; m. Dec. 15, 1844, Samuel Higgins, Jr., b. Apr. 17, 1817. She d. Jan. 1, 1850, leaving Cassius A., b. May 12, 1849; res. 290 Bowen street, South Boston, Mass.
    VI. EUNICE, b. Mar. 16, 1825; d. Oct. 16, 1826.

245. **Reuben G.**[7] **Pierce** (Nathan[6], Nathaniel[5], Joseph[4], Azrikim[3], Ephraim[2], Michael[1]), b. Sept. 10, 1806; m. Nancy Luther; m. 2nd, Elso B. Miller. Res. Rehoboth, Mass.

CHILDREN.

    I. MARGARET S., b. Mar. 7, 1832.
    II. NELSON G., b. Sept. 18, 1833.
    III. LUCY C., b. Aug. 27, 1835.

246. **Joseph S.**[7] **Pierce** (Nathan[6], Nathaniel[5], Joseph[4], Azrikim[3], Ephraim[2], Michael[1]), b. Feb. 6, 1814; m. June 6, 1841, Laura A. Lawton, b. 1823; d. Apr. 2, 1842, s. p.; m. 2nd, Oct. 29, 1843, Lydia T. Mason, b. 1825; d. Feb. 5, 1844, s. p.; m. 3rd, Dec. 3, 1845, Sybil Horton, b. Nov. 10, 1810. Res. Rehoboth. Mass.

CHILDREN.

394.   I. CHARLES E., b. May 26, 1851; m. John A. Blackmer.
    II. ASENATH E., b. Feb. 12, 1847; m. Jan. 21, 1867, William Goff, b. Nov. 19, 1840; res. Rehoboth, Mass. Ch., Dora May, b. May 25, 1879; Emma

29

F., b. Nov. 14, 1881; George A., b. Dec. 13, 1882; Howard E., b. Jan. 22, 1884; Clifford D., b. Aug. 5, 1885.

247. **Childs[7] Pierce** (Nathan[6], Nathaniel[5], Joseph[4], Azrikim[3], Ephraim[2], Michael[1]), b. Oct. 16, 1820; m. Mar. 21, 1841, Cynthia Miller Pierce (see vid.), b. Aug. 10, 1822. He d. Sept. 27, 1845, and she m. L. Collanore. Res. Warren, R. I.

CHILDREN.

395.   I. GEORGE C., b. Jan. 17, 1842; m. Sarah M. Torme.
II. JOHN H., b. Mar. 1, 1844; d. June 13, 1847.

248. **Aaron[7] Pierce** (Aaron[6], Nathaniel[5], Joseph[4], Azrikim[3], Ephraim[2], Michael[1]), b. Sept. 11, 1810; m. Mar. 10, 1845, Emily Brown, b. Feb. 20, 1827; d. July 6, 1854; m. 2nd, Apr. 16, 1855, Frances E. Bailey, b. Sept. 29, 1835. Res. Westerly, R. I.

CHILDREN.

I. CURTIS J., b. May 18, 1849; res. unm. at Westport, Mass. In early life he was a carpenter by trade, and worked in that capacity until 1874. Since that time he was engaged in pastoral and other church work in the Christian denomination in that town, having received a license to preach from the Broad street Christian Church in Westerly, R. I. In writing of his ancestors, he says: " I would, however, say that we are on an average with the best so far as morality and general education is concerned, as for finances, we are all in a fair, comfortable condition by hard work, which we consider a necessity and a luxury. None are wealthy, but remain quite well provided in the world's goods. All but one of grandfather's sons and nearly all of his grandsons are masons by trade, excepting my father, Aaron Pierce, who was a carpenter."
II. CARRIE B., b., Mar. 27, 1862; m. Charles H. Leonard, b. Apr. 9, 1883; res. Westerly, R. I.

249. **Barnard W.**[7] **Pierce** (Aaron[6], Nathaniel[5], Joseph[4], Azrikim[3], Ephraim[2], Michael[1]), b. Sept. 11, 1810; m. Oct. 29, 1835, Martha H. Smith, b. Sept. 27, 1816; d. Aug. 19, 1853; m. 2nd, Oct., 1855, Mrs. Esther Arnold, b. Aug., 1814. Res. Westerly, R. I.

CHILDREN.

 I. MARTHA B., b. Mar. 11, 1837.
 II. MARY E., b. Mar. 12, 1838.
 III. HARRIET S., b. May 26, 1840; m. Aug. 14, 1862, Edwin G. Shepardson, b. Apr. 5, 1842; m. 2nd, Aug. 20, 1873, Stephen Whitaker, b. May 11, 1835; res. Pawtucket, R. I. Ch., Jennie S., b. Oct. 18, 1864; Stracy P., b. Oct. 13, 1874; d. June 2, 1879; Emma R., b. Mar. 21, 1878; Bertha P., b. July 7, 1881.
396. IV. EDGAR B., b. Oct. 10, 1842; m. Eliza R. Smith and Mrs. Gertrude N. Smith.
 V. WILLIAM O., b. Mar. 8, 1846.
 VI. CHARLES A., b. Nov., 1856.
 VII. JESSE D., b. Oct., 1859; d. Aug. 19, 1880.

250. **Jonathan W.**[7] **Pierce** (Aaron[6], Nathaniel[5], Joseph[4], Azrikim[3], Ephraim[2], Michael[1]), b. 1800; m. 1824, Mariam Aldridge Ray, b. 1805. He d. ——. Res. Westerly, R. I.

CHILDREN.

 I. CHARLOTTE R., b. Oct. 21, 1824; d. young.
397. II. NELSON M., b. ——; m. Eliza Geers.
 III. MALANEY M., b. ——; m. William Sheldon; res. Rhode Island. Ch., Mary, b. 1852; d. 1870; Alvy, m. Miss Maine; res. Westerly, R. I., and d. 1880, leaving a son Melaney.
398. IV. RUFUS W., b. May 31, 1829; m. Sarah E. Kingsley.
 V. CHARLES L., b. ——; m. twice, s. p.; res. New London, Conn.

VI. EDWARD A., b. ——; m. twice, s. p.; res. New York
    city.
VII. LUCY A., b. Nov. 12, 1833; m. Jan. 4, 1852, Edmund
    Slocum, b. Cumberland, R. I., May 11, 1829;
    res. Hopkinton, R. I., and New London, Conn.
    Ch., Charlotte R., b. Oct. 17, 1852; m. Jan. 21,
    1875, Daniel C. Wetmore, b. May 31, 1855; res.
    New London, Conn.; Walter M., b. Nov. 30, 1864;
    m. Mar. 29, 1886; Lilian A. Rogers, b. Apr. 8,
    1863 ; res. New London, Conn.
399. VIII. HORACE L., b. Mar. 25, 1835; m. Harriett E. Horton.
    IX. WILLIAM H., b. ——; d. when a child.

251. **Nathaniel Chase Rounds**[7] **Pierce** (Aaron[6], Nathaniel[5],
Joseph[4], Azrikim[3], Ephraim[2], Michael[1]), b. June 12, 1815; m. Nov.
23, 1840, Eliza Reynolds, b. 1814; d. May, 1848 ; m. 2nd, Jan. 3,
1853, Sarah Elizabeth Reynolds, b. June 29, 1829, in Richmond,
R. I. He d. ——. Res. Richmond and Westerly, R. I.

CHILDREN.

I. GEORGIANA, b. May 13, 1845; m. Sept. 17, 1872,
    Frederick Cook, b. at Cumberland, R. I., June 29,
    1840. Ch., George F., b. Oct. 15, 1880; Nathan-
    iel P., b. July 26, 1884; Bertha W., b. June 15,
    1886; d. Aug. 15, 1886; res. Woonsocket, R. I. ·

252. **James C.**[7] **Pierce** (Aaron[6], Nathaniel[5], Joseph[4], Azrikim[3], Ephraim[2], Michael[1]), b. Feb. 29, 1820; m. July 6, 1845,
Lucinda B. Bliss, b. Aug. 18, 1824. Res. Taunton, Mass.

CHILDREN.

I. HERBERT N., b. Jan. 19, 1848; m. Sept. 30, 1885,
    Elizabeth A. Briggs, b. Nov. 16, 1850; res. s. p.,
    Taunton, Mass.
II. ABDIAL B., b. Nov. 16, 1849; d. Dec. 22, 1876.
    Killed by bridge on top of car at Chicago.

400.
   III. LEONARD A., b. Nov. 19, 1851; m. Alida P. Stetson.
   IV. JAMES, b. Mar. 31, 1855; d. Oct. 16, 1855.
   V. CHARLES H., b. Mar. 24, 1857; res. Taunton, Mass.
   VI. CORA, b. Aug. 11, 1858; d. Apr. 13, 1862.
   VII. CLARA E., b. Mar. 17, 1861.

253. **Stephen M.**[7] **Pierce** (Nathaniel[6], Nathaniel[5], Joseph[4], Azrikim[3], Ephraim[2], Michael[1]), b. Sept. 18, 1789; m. May 12, 1813, Hulda Wheeler, b. 1791; d. May 20, 1840; m. 2nd, Mar. 1, 1843, Emeline Perry. He d. 1872. Res. Rehoboth, Mass.

CHILDREN.

   I. MARY A., b. Feb. 21, 1814; m. Nov. 20, 1841, Shepard C. Stanley, b. Aug. 6, 1813; d. Dec. 7, 1883; res. Wilber, Neb. Ch., Shepard C., b. Sept. 30, 1845; d. Oct. 6, 1845; Charles S., b. Sept. 15, 1847; d. Oct. 8, 1848; Charles W., b. Oct. 2, 1849; m. Ida V. Barnes; res. Wilber, Neb.
   II. CAROLINE, b. Nov. 2, 1815; m. May 8, 1844, Ebenezer W. Allen, b. Feb. 6, 1824; res. Foxboro, Mass. Ch., George F., b. Sept. 4, 1847; res. Brockton, Mass.
   III. HULDA W., b. Feb. 12, 1817; res. Brockton, Mass.
   IV. LUCY M., b. Dec. 1, 1820; d. ———.
   V. RACHEL M., b. Oct. 27, 1823.
   VI. CHARLOTTE, b. June 20, 1826; m. Apr. 1, 1847, Albert Keith, b. Dec. 31, 1823. She d. May 29, 1874; res. Brockton, Mass. Ch., Marcia A., b. Oct. 18, 1848; d. Aug. 20, 1850; Alice M., b. Oct. 19, 1850; m. Alexander Welden; Herbert, b. Aug. 29, 1852; d. Aug. 25, 1859; Charlotte R. and Lillian M., b. Jan. 14, 1865.
   VII. EMELINE P., b. Mar. 25, 1844; d. Mar. 30, 1844.
   VIII. CORDELIA R., b. Feb. 28, 1846; d. Apr. 15, 1869.
   IX. STEPHEN H., b. Apr. 24, 1848; d. May 19, 1869.

254. **Ira E.**[7] **Pierce** (Backus[6], Stephen[5], Joseph[4], Azrikim[3], Ephraim[2], Michael[1]), b. Aug. 12, 1822; m. Nov. 1, 1849, Deborah F. Potter, b. Feb. 23, 1828. Res. Windom, Minn.

CHILDREN.

I. WILLIAM D., b. Jan. 6, 1851; d. Jan. 7, 1883.
II. CHARLES B., b. Sept. 14, 1852.
III. ABBEY F., b. June 17, 1856; d. Oct. 12, 1863.
IV. IRA E., b. Jan. 17, 1868.

255. **Stephen**[7] **Pierce** (Asahel[6], Stephen[5], Joseph[4], Azrikim[3], Ephraim[2], Michael[1]), b. Mar. 27, 1806; m. Feb. 22, 1829, Polly Ide, b. Nov. 12, 1808; d. May 4, 1885. He d. Nov. 10, 1856. Res. Calais, Vt.

CHILDREN.

I. FANNY J., b. June 14, 1835; m. Jan. 10, 1854, Willard Lilley, b. May 17, 1828. She d. Dec. 23, 1884; res. East Calais, Vt. Ch., Ella E., b. Oct. 7, 1854; m. Heman W. Bullock, b. May 1, 1871; res. East Calais, Vt.
401. II. ALONZO E., b. July 12, 1838; m. Nellie A. White.
402. III. ORION A., b. Aug. 28, 1840; m. Sophia H. Orcutt.
IV. AMELIA C., b. Sept. 22, 1844; m. Dec. 19, 1876, Benjamin P. White, b. July 11, 1835; res. East Calais, Vt. Ch., Mabel H., b. June 19, 1878.
V. LYMAN I., b. May 26, 1847; d. Aug. 10, 1865.

256. **Alonzo**[7] **Pierce** (Asahel[6], Stephen[5], Joseph[4], Azrikim[3], Ephraim[2], Michael[1]), b. Feb. 3, 1799; m. Oct. 4, 1821, Thirza Dwinell, b. June 19, 1803; d. Aug. 6, 1872. He d. July 25, 1879. Res. East Calais, Vt.

CHILDREN.

403. I. ALONZO D., b. Sept. 17, 1825; m. Dulcena Nelson.
II. LAVINIA, b. July 3, 1822; m. Mar. 28, 1848, Simeon

Webb. She d. s. p., at East Calais, Vt., Feb. 15, 1886.

III. EMENERANCY, b. Aug. 18, 1823; m. Nov. 22, 1842, Orson Putnam, b. Sept. 16, 1818; res. East Calais, Vt. Ch., Clara E., b. Oct. 17, 1850; m. Edwin Burnham; res. Albany, Ga.

IV. CYRENA, b. May 21, 1827; m. Mar., 1849, Ezekiel Pierce. She d. Sept. 19, 1874. He d. Oct. 11, 1870. Ch., Alice M., b. Feb. 4, 1852; m. Nov. 1, 1873, William E. Stoddard. She d. Dec. 29, 1875. Ch., Ralph, b. Jan. 7, 1875; d. Nov. 1, 1875; res. East Calais, Vt.

404. V. HENRY C., b. Dec. 7, 1829; m. Margaret Riley.

VI. MARTHA, b. Mar. 23, 1831; m. Dec. 19, 1856, Edwin Gilmore; res. Montpelier, Vt.

VII. LOZENO J., b. Nov. 7, 1833; m. May 15, 1858, Harriett Nelson; res. Montpelier, Vt.

257. **Asahel**[7] **Pierce** (Noah[6], Stephen[5], Joseph[4], Azrikim[3], Ephraim[2], Michael[1]), b. June 30, 1812; m. Oct. 18, 1835, Persis B. Abbott, b. Dec. 27, 1811. He d. Dec., 1887. Res. 721 Bowen avenue, Chicago, Ill.

The subject of this sketch, Asahel Pierce, a native of Calais, Vermont, was born on the 30th of June, 1812, the son of Noah Pierce and Ruth, *nee* Garey. His parents, natives of Rehoboth, Massachusetts, were married in 1802, and during the same year his father with three brothers removed to Calais, Vermont, where each purchased a large tract and continued in agricultural pursuits, becoming wealthy and influential men.

Asahel, the fifth child of his parents, passed his boyhood upon his father's farm, dividing his time between study in the district school and farm work. He had an excessive fondness for horses, and when old enough was given charge of them, while his brothers had the management of the ox-teams. Finding the narrow routine of farm life ill-suited to his tastes, he, at the age of eighteen, through an arrangement made by his father, apprenticed himself to Mr. Samuel Upham of Montpelier, to learn the blacksmith's trade, and faithfully devoted himself to his work and studies. After completing his apprenticeship, in 1833, he found employment at Barre, Vermont, in furnishing granite for the State-house, and later went to Stanstead, Lower Canada, where he was employed for a short time by Messrs. Armes & Brown, and afterward returned to Vermont.

Having decided to settle in the west, he left his home on the 15th of September, 1833, traveling by stage-coach, steamer and railroad from Saratoga to Schenectady (the cars being drawn by horses), canal, and the steamer *Great Western* on Lake Erie to Detroit, Mich.; thence by stage to Chicago, where he arrived on the 8th of October, finding it a village of three or four stores, six or eight houses, and a population of about two hundred white people besides those in the fort, and from fifteen hundred to two thousand Indians, who received their annual payment from the government. Pleased with the prospects which the place offered, he at once erected a shop, hauling the lumber from Plainfield, a distance of forty miles; and purchasing an old set of tools from Rev. William Lee, a Methodist, began business with a capital of $10 and a firm determination to succeed. His business prospered from the first, and he was soon obliged to enlarge his shop.

He did the iron work for the first stage line connecting Chicago and St. Louis, an enterprise which was undertaken by Dr. John T. Temple & Co., January 1, 1834.

In the ensuing spring he commenced the manufacture of the old-fashioned "*Bull-plow*," with wooden mould-board, which he believed to have been the first plow made in the State of Illinois north of Springfield. Finding that it could not be used in the prairie sod, he next made an improvement, by substituting a two-inch band-iron, with a space between for the wooden mould-board. The improvement of the new country, and the demands of the farmers, necessitated a plow that would polish in the stubble-field. To meet this demand, Mr. Pierce was constantly making improvements, and by testing the cast and wrought iron mould-board with steel share, discovered that although his plow received a high polish, the mould-board would rust in damp weather, while the steel share retained its polish. Fortunate in finding a few cast-steel plates, he succeeded in producing the first self-polishing steel plow ever made in Illinois.

A few years later, Mr. Gifford of Elgin, Mr. Jones of Naperville, and Messrs. Deer & Andrews, and others began using steel. Having thus met the demand of the farming community for a concave polishing plow, he still continued his improvements, and by reducing the angle gave an oval or convex turn to the mould-board and producing a plow that was run with less draft, and which proved the best stubble-plow that had ever been introduced.

The same form afterward adopted by Mr. Pierce in his Chicago " Clipper plow," has been retained by Messrs. Furst & Bradley, Jones, Deer and all other plow manufacturers in the west. Such was the wide-spread reputation which the plow received, both for its utility and durability, that at times the demand was far greater than could be supplied. Taking a load of plows out of his usual stock to the State fair held at Plainfield, Illinois, Mr. Pierce, after a very close competition and trial, was awarded six premiums on his different kinds of plows, and a gold medal. He also invented a breaking plow with round rods to turn the sod. Of two of these, turning a furrow forty inches wide, and taken to Big Foot prairie by Judges Douglas and Maxwell, the first propelled by twelve yoke of oxen, turned a furrow six miles long and without having a hand put to it.

Mr. Pierce had also been engaged in the manufacture of wagons and other agricultural implements; but in 1854 decided to divide his business, turned over that portion connected with the manu-facture of plows to his brother-in-law, Mr. David Bradley, now known as the Furst & Bradley Manufacturing Company.

In 1856, after twenty-three years of hard work, he retired from business, having worked it up from a small beginning until it had become the largest in its line in the north-west. Aside from his manufacturing interest Mr. Pierce has been largely interested in

30

real estate operations, and contributed much to the improvement and material prosperity of Chicago.

He has always shown a worthy public spiritedness, and has been honored by his fellow-citizens with many trusts. In 1835, he was one of the first trustees of the then village of Chicago, and two years later was elected alderman on the Democratic ticket, a position which he held for ten years.

In the spring of 1861, Mr. Pierce engaged in the wholesale clothing business, and three years later conducted an extensive trade with annual sales amounting to $800,000. His was the first American house to manufacture clothing in Chicago, a business he found very profitable, and which is now adopted by all the wholesale clothing houses in the city. He was a supporter of the Republican administration. In religion he was associated with the First Presbyterian Church. As a business man, he was noted for upright and fair dealings; while his personal and social qualities were of such a character as drew around him a large circle of acquaintances and many warm friends.

He was married in 1835 to Miss Persis Abbott of Barre, Vt., daughter of Abijah and Abigail Abbott from Holden, Mass. Of their nine children, three sons and three daughters are now living, and enjoy a high social standing.

The above sketch was written by a friend of Mr. Pierce prior to his death. The Chicago papers all contained long obituaries of the deceased at the time of his death. The *Times*, in referring to the funeral, says:

"The sweet breath of roses and lillies-of-the-valley perfumed the parlor of the house at 474 Bowen avenue, where was enacted the last scene of a life-drama whose beginning was three-quarters of a century ago, away back in the hills of old Vermont. When he came into the world his first speech was a wail. He has departed, and tears and sighs are left behind.

"He who lay there in his casket as if he slept was Asahel Pierce. Fifty-four years ago he came to the little hamlet of Chicago, then with a population of scarcely two hundred souls besides the garrison. He left it a thriving city four thousand times as great.

"All of this he saw and a great part of it he was. A strong, sturdy youth of twenty-one years, ruddy-cheeked and strong-armed as a blacksmith should be, he determined that Chicago was the place for him to swing the ringing hammer and shape the glowing iron, scattering showers of sparks from the anvil. He had to bring the lumber for his shop forty miles. But he worked ahead, and finding how difficult it was to rip up the tough prairie sod he set his keen New England wits to work. As a result, he was the first man to make a self-polishing steel plow. The farmers wanted just such a plow, and the brawny young blacksmith could not turn them out fast enough. In 1856, he retired from the manufacturing of agricultural implements and went into the real estate business for five years, after which he became interested in the wholesale clothing business, and in a short time his annual sales amounted to $1,000,000. In 1868 he returned to real estate, with his son Lucius as partner. He continued in that business until 1873. Since then he has been almost an invalid from chronic bronchitis, which finally overcame him Tuesday morning.

"Mr. Pierce not only helped his fellow-pioneers by assisting them to plow the virgin soil of the prairie, but he was foremost in establishing government and maintaining order.

"Two years after he came here and about the time he had found out what kind of a plow the prairie farmer wanted he was elected trustee of the village of Chicago. The village of Chicago! It seems as remote in history as New Amsterdam or the Continental Congress. But the man who lay in that coffin saw the palace follow the log cabin, and the outskirts of the town where he had his blacksmith shop is now the corner of Canal and Lake streets, the eastern edge of the great west side.

"In 1837 he became an alderman, and served until 1847. One of his colleagues was Judge Caton. He and the judge were the last of that council of the fathers. Now Judge Caton stands alone.

"Mr. Pierce left a widow seventy-five years old and two daughters, the Misses Aurora and Abbie Pierce, and three sons, Lucius S. Pierce, now in Redcliff, Col.; George H. Pierce, with Marshall Field, and William F. Pierce, with J. V. Farwell.

"Tender smilax and pure, sweet hyacinths twined around the portrait of Mrs. Hattie Howard, a beloved daughter who died four years ago. Beautiful cut flowers, a pillow with ' Rest' in purple immortelles upon it, a broken column of camelias, hyacinths, and roses, and a floral star comprised the offerings, which had been sent by the nearest friends in spite of the request that there be no flowers."

CHILDREN.

I. AURORA S., b. Sept. 11, 1836; unm.; res. Chicago.

II. ABBIE A., b. Apr. 12, 1839; unm.; res. Chicago.

III. Zephaniah G., b. Sept. 10, 1840; d. in infancy.

IV. Alburtis, b. Aug. 9, 1842; d. Sept. 24, 1847.

V. Lucius S., b. Nov. 16, 1844; unm.; res. Colorado.

VI. George H., b. Apr. 12, 1849; m. Feb. 12, 1884, Ella F. Bensley, b. Sept. 2, 1856; res. s. p., Chicago, Ill.

VII. Harriett R., b. Aug. 11, 1851; m. Dec. 13, 1881, Lansing B. Howard, d. Mar. 12, 1884; res. s. p., Chicago, Ill.

VIII. William F., b. Jan. 8, 1855; unm. Of the firm of J. V. Farwell & Co., Chicago, Ill.

IX. Persis, b. June 12, 1847; d. infant.

258. **Zephaniah G.**[7] **Pierce** (Noah[6], Stephen[5], Joseph[4], Azrikim[3], Ephraim[2], Michael[1]), b. Dec. 16, 1822; m. Apr. 22, 1845, Eliza S. Leonard, b. May 6, 1826. He d. May 27, 1880. Res. East Calais, Vt.

CHILDREN.

405.   I. Walter L., b. Oct. 20, 1855; m. Dianna F. Tubas.

259. **Horatio**[7] **Pierce** (Noah[6], Stephen[5], Joseph[4], Azrikim[3], Ephraim[2], Michael[1]), b. Oct. 12, 1807; m. Nov., 1827, Julia Merritt, b. Mar. 19, 1805; d. Feb. 7, 1848. He d. Aug., 1855. Res. Woodbury, Vt.

CHILDREN.

I. Merrill H., b. Sept. 30, 1828; m. Sept. 16, 1854. He d. May 17, 1876; res. Yuba City, Cal. Ch., Melvin P.

II. Maria J., b. Oct. 16, 1832; m. Sept. 1, 1858, Edwin Merritt, b. Aug. 14, 1834. She d. June 6, 1882; res. Mansfield, Vt. Ch., Edwin A., b. Aug. 15, 1870; Julia E., b. Jan. 1, 1860; m. —— Page; res. Mansfield, Vt.; Bertha M., b. Jan. 29, 1862; m. —— Pitkin.

406. III. Marcus, b. July 26, 1830; m. Eliza A. Ames.

IV. ANGELINE M., b. Nov. 17, 1834; m. Dec. 14, 1869, Edward J. Whipple, b. June 22, 1842; res. Ashland, Neb. Ch., Edward P., b. Dec. 26, 1870; Charles A., b. May 10, 1875; Florence A., b. Oct. 12, 1878; Mabel H., b. Dec. 20, 1879.

V. ALFRED E., b. Jan. 22, 1837; d. Apr. 19, 1870.

VI. NOAH, b. July 18, 1839.

VII. SARAH M., b. Sept. 14, 1841.

VIII. LUCIA, b. Dec. 25, 1844; m. Sept., 1876, John Cavanah; res. Visulia, Cal.

260. **Zalmon**[7] **Pierce** (Noah[6], Stephen[5], Joseph[4], Azrikim[3], Ephraim[2], Michael[1]), b. June 30, 1818; m. June 22, 1841, Polly Goodenough, b. Nov. 7, 1819. Res. East Calais, Vt.

CHILDREN.

I. LEWIS P., b. Jan. 12, 1845; m. Oct. 26, 1866, Amelia E. Pierce, b. Sept. 10, 1844. He d. s. p., Feb. 18, 1870; res. East Calais, Vt.

II. GEORGE O., b. Sept. 5, 1847; m. Nov. 29, 1877, Mrs. Clara J. Marsh, b. Sept. 1, 1852; res. East Calais, Vt.

III. PHILUSA M., b. Dec. 5, 1851; d. Nov. 13, 1864.

IV. HATTIE M., b. June 30, 1856; m. Nov. 26, 1879, Fred. Burnham, b. Jan. 1, 1855; res. East Calais, Vt. Ch., Dean, b. May 28, 1881; Lewis, b. Apr. 4, 1883.

261. **Calvin**[7] **Pierce** (Calvin[6], Stephen[5], Joseph[4], Azrikim[3], Ephraim[2], Michael[1]), b. ——; m. Nov. 25, 1828, Nancy Taft, b. Jan. 5, 1810; d. Feb. 19, 1875. He d. July 19, 1883. Res. Springfield, Mass.

CHILDREN.

I. CALVIN B., b. ——; d. æ. 2 years.

II. MARTHA A., b. ——; æ. 11 months.

III. ASAHEL T., b. June 31, 1832; m. Nov. 25, 1863, Sarah F. Stephens, b. Mar. 11, 1835, s. p.; res. Pawtucket, R. I.

IV. NANCY M., b. ———; m. Horatio H. Valentine, s. p.; res. 65 Grove street, Providence, R. I.

V. MARY E., b. ———; m. Nicholas N. Wood; res. Division street, North Attleboro, Mass.

VI. CLARA E., b. ———; m. John A. C. Wightman; res. Woonsocket, R. I.

262. **Lewis D. B.**[7] **Pierce** (Noah[6], Noah[5], Joseph[4], Azrikim[3], Ephraim[2], Michael[1]), b. July 13, 1803; m. Sept. 4, 1826, Sarah A. Alger, b. June 22, 1806. He d. Feb. 23, 1886. Res. Warren, R. I.

Mr. Lewis D. B. Pierce, one of our aged citizens, who has been spending the winter with relatives in Jamestown, N. Y., died on Tuesday, the 23d of February, 1886, and the remains are expected to arrive this evening, and will be deposited with those of his kindred in this town. Mr. Pierce had arrived at the advanced age of eighty-two years eight months and ten days; a large majority of which he had spent in Warren, where he was well and favorably known. He was a man of cheerful disposition, and an upright Christian character. In the prime of life he devoted himself to deeds of Christian charity, and was accustomed to visit the sick who needed his kind offices, interesting himself and others in their behalf. Many a poor family, who would otherwise have been overlooked, were brought to the notice of the benevolent who had means, and much distress relieved. Mr. Pierce giving his personal attention and of his means according to his ability. Many will bless his memory and shed tears of sorrow when they hear of his departure from earth. "Well done, good and faithful servant, enter thou into the joys of thy Lord." [From a Warren, R. I., paper.]

A Providence paper has the following notice of his funeral:

The remains of the late Lewis D. B. Pierce arrived in Warren. R. I., Thursday evening by rail, and the obsequies were held Friday morning in the Methodist Episcopal Church, of which society he had been a member since 1827, or nearly sixty years. Notwithstanding the severe storm which was raging at the hour of the services, a good many of the relatives and friends of the deceased attended them, though no opportunity was given for public notice after the arrival of the remains, which it was feared might be delayed. The services were conducted by the pastor, assisted by Rev. Sidney Dean, a former pastor of the deceased, who delivered an appreciative and impressive address, the speaker being well acquainted with the character and interesting peculiarities of Mr. Pierce. Rev. Mr. Nutting read the Scriptures and offered prayer. In accordance with what was understood to have been the taste of the deceased, the congregation, led by the organ, at which Miss McKenzie presided, united in singing the hymns, "Come unto Me when the shadows darkly gather," etc., and in closing, "From every stormy wind that blows," etc. The burial was in the South Cemetery, where the committal service in the ritual of the Methodist Episcopal Church was used.

CHILDREN.

I. JULIA A., b. Nov. 7, 1834; m. Oct. 4, 1852, Samuel C. Smith, b. Apr. 14, 1828; res. Jamestown, N. Y. Ch., Adelaide L., b. July 25, 1853; m. —— Simmons; Samuel C., b. Aug. 12, 1855; d. Aug. 16, 1856; Sarah M., b. Aug. 1, 1857; m.—— Partridge; Anetta G., b. May 9, 1859; m. K. W. Ingham; Brightman B., b. July 29, 1860; Clara E., b. Dec. 26, 1861; Samuel C., b. Nov. 13, 1863; res. Caldwell, Kansas; Charles F., b. May 29, 1866; Julia A., b. June 29, 1868; Louis D., b. Apr. 14, 1870.

II. ELIZABETH, b. May 19, 1827; d. May 22, 1827.

III. WILLIAM H., b. May 15, 1828; d. Sept. 3, 1832.

IV. LEWIS B., b. Mar. 7, 1830; res. Warren, R. I.

V. BETSEY B., b. Mar. 7, 1832; m. Mar. 18, 1858, Capt. George H. Kelley. She d. July, 1880; res. Warren and Newport, R. I. Ch., Harriett, m. —— Seabury; res. Springfield, Mass.

VI. MARIA F., b. June 1, 1837; m. May 17, 1868, Alexander A. Gifford, b. June 5, 1837. She d. Aug. 13, 1885; res. 40 Fourth street, Fall River, Mass. Ch., Mary F., b. Nov. 28, 1872; Chester, b. Feb. 21, 1871; d. Feb. 22, 1871.

407. VII. WILLIAM H., b. Feb. 2, 1840; m. Ruth P. Martin.
  VIII. GEORGE S., b. Jan. 6, 1842.

263. **Dea. Anthony[7] Pierce** (Appollus[6], Noah[5], Joseph[4], Azrikim[3], Ephraim[2], Michael[1]), b. Sept. 10, 1814; m. Sept. 2, 1835, Mary W. Snow, b. May 14, 1812. He d. Jan. 22, 1887. Res. 564 Eddy street, Providence, R. I.

The Providence *Journal* of January 27, 1887, has this:

The late Deacon Anthony Pearce, whose obsequies were held at the residence No. 54 Comstock avenue, yesterday afternoon, had been in the service of the Providence Machine Company as book-keeper since 1844, and that establishment was closed in the afternoon to give the employes opportunity to attend the funeral. Among the floral tributes was a magnificent piece in the form of a ledger lying open on a desk of flowers, on which, together with a proper inscription, rested Mr. Pearce's pen and holder. Rev. M. C. Cunningham of the Shawmut Avenue Messiah Church, Boston, conducted the service. Mr. Pearce was one of the oldest and staunchest supporters of the Adventist Church in this State.

The Messiah's *Herald* has this of Deacon Pierce:

Died, in Providence, R. I., January 22, 1887, of neuralgia of the heart and paralysis, Deacon Anthony Pearce, in the seventy-fourth year of his age.

Our brother was born April 10, 1814; and was "born again" in early life, so that for more than a half century he has been in active service in the Master's vineyard. As to earthly employment he was engaged awhile in his youthful days in driving a bread-wagon in Pawtucket; then he entered into the jewelry business, but was told he was too honest to succeed in that, and so he soon left it for a grocer's store. Ere long he was offered and accepted a situation as book-keeper in one of the banks in Providence; but in 1844 he entered the employ of the Providence Machine Company, as its book-keeper, which position he held until his death. His kindness, integrity and Christian character won for him the love, confidence and respect of two hundred employes. "If there is a Christian man on earth," they frequently said, "Anthony Pearce is one." He would not take a sheet of paper or letter stamp from the company without charging himself with it, I was told. The foreman of the shop said (as we were riding to the cemetery): "I could have had a hundred men in line to-day marching to the grave, had I said the word; but it is too cold for them to be exposed so long." But their respect for him was seen in a beautiful design of flowers (suggested by the agent, George J. Hazard), which stood at the head of his casket. It was in the form of a writing desk and on it was an open ledger. On the left-hand page of the book were the letters P. M. Co. (Providence Machine Company), and underneath were the figures 1844. On the opposite page, 1888, underneath the word *Finis*, and at the bottom of the page was the gold pen, long used by our brother, inserted in a cluster of flowers. Forty-four years of service in one establishment! But the active pen is now laid down, though its faithful record remains. The president of the company, Thomas J. Hill, ordered the shop closed on the afternoon of the funeral in honor of the deceased — a thing never done before. "The memory of the just is blessed."

Our lamented brother was among the number of those who listened to the lectures given by William Miller in Providence, on his first visit to that city in 1841. He then embraced the faith presented, respecting our Lord's premillennial advent, which he has maintained, loved, and sought to make known in every possible way to the end of his life. He has been liberal in sustaining the cause, not only locally but generally; and also in helping the ministers of the Gospel, as many can testify.

The obsequies were observed at his residence on Friday afternoon, the 27th ult. The large attendance on that very cold day was a clear evidence of the high esteem in which he was held. His faith and hope respecting the Saviour's personal premillennial and speedy advent, with kindred truths, were emphasized by the Scriptures read and remarks made. Three excellent hymns were sweetly sung by a quartet; the first, "We shall sleep, but not forever." "Abide with me," was the closing one. His bearers represented four denominations — Congregationalist, Baptist, Methodist and Adventist. May God sanctify this death to his family and friends, and also to the Church of God, which has met with a great loss in his removal from earth. "Help, Lord; for the godly man ceaseth; for the faithful fall from among the children of men."

CHILDREN.

   I. CARRIE V., b. Aug. 3, 1836; d. Mar. 30, 1885.

408. II. MARK A., b. Apr. 18, 1841; m. Mary E. Howland.

409. III. FRANKLIN, b. Mar. 5, 1849; m. Mary A. Smith.

  31

264. **Rev. Phillip⁷ Pierce** (Wheeler⁶ Wheeler⁵, Mial⁴, Ephraim³, Ephraim², Michael¹), b. 1762; m Dec. 15, 1782, Ann Manchester, b. 1763; d. Jan. 27, 1842. He d. Oct. 27, 1829. Res. Rehoboth, Mass.

CHILDREN.

410.   I. PHILLIP, b. Feb. 12, 1784; m. Chloe Horton.
     II. WILLIAM, b. ——.
    III. MANLEY, b. 1805; d. Apr. 14, 1856.
    IV. ANNA, b. ——; m. —— Mason.
     V. POLLY, b. ——.
    VI. LYDIA, b. ——.
   VII. BETSEY, b. Mar. 2, 1793; d. Oct. 20, 1878.
  VIII. HANNAH, b. 1799; d. July 12, 1870.
    IX. REBECCA, b. ——; m. Stephen Chase.

265. **Nathan⁷ Pierce** (Nathan⁶, Nathan⁵, Mial⁴, Ephraim³, Ephraim², Michael¹), b. in Lanesboro, Mass., 1770; m. in Cheshire, Mass., 1789, Polly McLowth, b. 1764; d. 1853. He d. 1814. Res. Cheshire, Mass., and Manchester, N. Y.

CHILDREN.

411.   I. EZRA, b. June 17, 1806; m. Eliza Gurley.
412.   II. NATHAN, b. Sept. 27, 1790; m. Amy Aldrich.
   III. DARIAS, b. ——; had a son, Nathan; res. in Chelsea, Mich.
   IV. POLLY A., b. ——.
    V. ANNA G., b. ——; has a daughter, Mrs. Cynthia Brouk, Shortsville, N. Y.
   VI. SARAH, b. ——.
  VII. BETSEY, b. ——.

266. **Earl D.⁷ Pierce** (Benjamin⁶, Nathan⁵, Mial⁴, Ephraim³, Ephraim², Michael¹), b. May 15, 1780; m. Lydia Wheaton, b. 1785; d. Apr. 13, 1876. He d. Dec. 30, 1839. Res. Providence, R. I.

CHILDREN.

413. I. EARL D., b. Sept. 23, 1818; m. Sarah B. Mauran.

II. MARY W., b. Jan. 3, 1809; m. Aug. 28, 1827, Samuel
Congdon, b. Nov. 28, 1803. She d. Dec. 12,
1864; res. Englewood, N. J. Ch., Mary Elizabeth,
b. May 3, 1828; d. July 12, 1854; Robert Whea-
ton, b. Feb. 3, 1831; d. Oct. 31, 1852; Anna
Pearce, b. Oct. 29, 1833; m. Peter Remsen Chad-
wick, Dec. 4, 1856; res. Cohoes, N. Y.; Walter, b.
June 1, 1837; d. Apr. 4, 1864; Matilda, b. May
10, 1839; d. June 7, 1839; Edward Douglass, b.
Jan. 21, 1843; res. Englewood, Bergen Co., N. J.;
Horace Lincoln, b. May 6, 1846; m. H. M. R.
Cooper, Oct. 15, 1867.

III. ANNA E., b. ——; m. Charles Congdon; res. New
Brighton, Staten Island, N. Y.

IV. MARTHA B., b. May 29, 1814; m. Oct. 23, 1833,
William H. Waterman, b. June 19, 1805; d. Dec.
16, 1880; res. Providence, R. I. Ch., Marcus, b.
Sept. 1, 1834; res. 616 Washington street, Boston,
Mass.; Olivia, b. Dec. 15, 1836; d. Mar. 12, 1839;
Richard, b. Jan. 29, 1839; res. 13 Angell street,
Providence, R. I.; Laura Pearce, b. Mar. 28, 1841;
d. Mar. 2, 1864; William C., b. Feb. 20, 1844;
res. 13 Angell street, Providence, R. I.; Alice, b.
Aug. 5, 1847; d. Mar. 12, 1873.

V. ABBY W., b. ——; m. George T. Chase.

VI. LAURA E., b. Mar. 5, 1821; m. July 29, 1846, Prof.
John L. Lincoln, b. Feb. 23, 1817. He is an
instructor in Brown's University, Providence, R.
I. Ch., William Ensign, b. Sept. 27, 1847; m.
Mary B. Porter, b. June 7, 1877, dau. of George
Porter of Pittsburgh, Pa.; res. Pittsburgh, Pa.;
Arthur, b. June 5, 1849; banker and broker 45
Exchange place, New York; firm, Thomas Tiles-
ton & Co.; Adeline, b. Mar. 12, 1850; d. Apr. 21,

1853; John Larkin, Jr., b. Feb. 9, 1854; address Deane Brothers & Lincoln, Chicago, Ill. ; Laura, b. Dec. 2, 1855; m. Feb. 12, 1876, Charles Sidney Waldo, son of Henry Sidney and Emma (Haven) Waldo; address, Jamaica Plains, Mass.; James Granger, b. June 30, 1859; address, Boston, Mass.; Hope, b. Dec. 22, 1863; d. July 12, 1864.

VII. WILLIAM W., b. ——; unm.

VIII. CAROLINE E., b. Nov. 26, 1827; m. Apr. 24, 1855, Alpheus C. Morse, b. June 3, 1818; res. Providence, R. I. Ch., Anne Goddard, b. in Providence, Jan. 17, 1856; Caroline, b. in Providence, Sept. 26, 1859; m. in Providence, May 6, 1886, to Robert Lane Keach, Providence, R. I.; Isabel, b. in Providence, Apr. 4, 1862.

267. **Pardon**[7] **Pierce** (Pardon[6], Nathan[5], Mial[4], Ephraim[3], Ephraim[2], Michael[1]), b. Aug. 12, 1773; m. in Rehoboth, Mass., Dec. 25, 1795, Freelove Horton, b. 1773; d. Apr., 1860. He d. Mar. 24, 1835. Res. Newport, N. Y.

CHILDREN.

414.   I. OTIS, b. Oct. 4, 1796 ; m. Polly Giles.

II. ELIZA, b. Oct. 11, 1800; m. Sept. 22, 1821, Hiram Barrett. He d. Mar. 26, 1835; res. ——. Ch., Eli P., b. ——; res. Hannibal, N. Y.; Henry, b. ——; res. Hannibal, N. Y.; Charles, b. ——; res. Hannibal, N. Y.

III. ROBY, b. Aug. 20, 1802; d. unm., Dec. 24, 1860.

IV. EZRA H., b. Mar. 12, 1805; d. May 27, 1806.

V. FREELOVE, b. Sept. 12, 1808 ; m. Mar. 7, 1832, William Kane; res. ——. She d. Sept. 15, 1850. Ch., William P., b. ——; res. Newport, N. Y.; Maria, b. —— ; m. Henry Parks; res. Trenton, Oneida Co., N. Y.

VI. SARAH F., b. Mar. 14, 1814; m. Mar. 16, 1830, William Dodd; res. ——. She d. s. p., June 16, 1883.

VII. MATILDA, b. Sept. 1, 1811; m. Mar. 30, 1831, Edward Eldridge; res. Port Leyden, Lewis Co., N. Y.

268. **Jeremiah W.**[7] **Pierce** (Martin[6], Nathan[5], Mial[4], Ephraim[3], Ephraim[2], Michael[1]), b. ——; m. 1824, Sarah Shove, b. July 9, 1801; d. May 5, 1839. He d. July 15, 1885. Res. Swansey, Mass.

CHILDREN.

415.   I. SAMUEL S., b. Aug. 27, 1833; m. Mary E. Boyce.

   II. JEREMIAH W., b. ——; d. young.

269. **Martin**[7] **Pierce** (Martin[6], Nathan[5], Mial[4], Ephraim[3], Ephraim[2], Michael[1]), b. ——; m. Jan. 29, 1798, Sarah Read. Res. Swansey, Mass.

CHILDREN.

416.   I. EZRA, b. ——; m. Joanna Horton.

270. **Nathan**[7] **Pierce** (Peleg[6], Nathan[5], Mial[4], Ephraim[3], Ephraim[2], Michael[1]), b. Nov. 24, 1787; m. May 26, 1805, Rhobe Horton, b. ——; d. Oct. 2, 1824. He d. Feb. 25, 1875. Res. Rehoboth, Mass.

CHILDREN.

   I. NANCY T., b. Apr. 8, 18—; m. June 27, 1847, Samuel O. West, b. ——; d. ——; m. 2nd, —— Merchant, b. ——; res. South Rehoboth, Mass. Ch., Sarah F., b. Apr. 17, 1848; Eveline, b. Nov. 20, 1849; John, b. Nov. 6, 1851; res. Warren, R. I.

271. **Asa**[7] **Pierce** (Peleg[6], Nathan[5], Mial[4], Ephraim[3], Ephraim[2], Michael[1]), b. Nov. 12, 1789; m. Oct. 31, 1811, Sally Bryant,[*] b.

---

[*] Swansey Town Records say Sally O'Brien.

May 19, 1794; d. Aug. 17, 1880. He d. Feb. 11, 1853. Res. Rehoboth, Mass.

CHILDREN.

I. MARIAH, b. Jan. 5, 1812; m. 1832, David C. Marble, b. June 7, 1811; d. June 11, 1877; res. Munday, Mich. Ch., Sally, Charles, Phebe.

417. II. ASA T., b. Aug. 18, 1814; m. Hannah Hopkins.

418. III. WILLIAM B., b. Jan. 1, 1819; m. Louise J. Conant.

IV. HENRY B., b. 1824; d. 1853.

V. SALLY, b. Nov. 5, 1828; m. Orson White. She d. Feb. 15, 1857. Ch., Gardner O.

VI. MARY, b. Feb. 9, 1832; m. Charles Durance. She d. Nov. 20, 1862. Ch., Adelia and Nancy.

272. **Tisdale[7] Pierce** (Peleg[6], Nathan[5], Mial[4], Ephraim[3], Ephraim[2], Michael[1]), b. Mar. 4, 1798; m. Sept. 20, 1821, Dorinda Bowen, b. 1803; d. Sept. 22, 1857. He d. Apr. 16, 1849. Res. Rehoboth, Mass.

CHILDREN.

I. CYNTHIA M., b. Aug. 10, 1822; m. Childs Pierce (see vid.).

II. TISDALE B., b. Sept. 15, 1826; d. Aug. 17, 1847.

III. HIRAM, b. Apr. 30, 1831; m. 1853.

IV. JULIA F., b. Apr. 20, 1833; m. June 11, 1853. She d. Oct. 13, 1862.

V. GEORGE L., b. Apr. 13, 1837; m. Apr. 7, 1855, Susan F. Hastings, b. Sept. 18, 1836; res. 131 Dexter street, Providence, R. I., s. p.

VI. JAMES, b. Dec. 15, 1841; res. Kansas.

VII. BENJAMIN, b. Dec. 15, 1841; res. Ohio.

273. **Gardner[7] Pierce** (Peleg[6], Nathan[5], Mial[4], Ephraim[3], Ephraim[2], Michael[1]), b. Aug. 21, 1801; m. July 9, 1826, Sarah Wood of Swansey, b. Sept. 27, 1806; divorced, and d. Mar. 3,

1861; m. 2nd, Oct. 5, 1851, Elvira A. Grace, b. Dec. 25, 1808. He d. Sept. 21, 1869. Res. Providence, R. I.

Gardner Pierce, son of Peleg and Mehitable Pierce, was born in the town of Rehoboth, Bristol county, in the State of Massachusetts, on the 21st day of August, 1801, and died in Providence, R. I., where he had resided since early manhood, September 21, 1869. Mr. Pierce learned the trade of a mason, but for the greater portion of his life was engaged in business as a dealer in groceries and provisions. He was twice married; in early life to Sarah Wood, by whom he had six children, and in October, 1851, to Elvira A. Grace. One son was the fruit of his second marriage.

The subject of this sketch was distinguished by an energetic and persevering character, and by his strict fidelity to all pecuniary engagements. In politics he was in early life a Jackson Democrat, and then a Republican from the birth of the latter party. Although not identified with any religious denomination he was a regular attendant upon public worship, preferring the Methodist Episcopal Church.

CHILDREN.

419.   I. EDWIN C., b. Jan. 11, 1853; m. Martha A. Collingham.

      II. CHARLES S., b. Sept. 7, 1827; m. Feb. 27, 1848.

      III. GARDNER F., b. Sept. 14, 1830; m. Oct. 26, 1851; d. in the army.

420.   IV. WILLIAM H., b. Dec. 11, 1832; m. Ellen M. Graves.

      V. POLLY H., b. June 11, 1835; d. in infancy.

      VI. MARY P., b. Aug. 26, 1837; m. Dec. 7, 1854, William P. Chace, b. Nov. 27, 1830; res. 38 Gardner street, Providence, R. I. Ch., Russell W., b. June 29, 1859; Nellie Z., b. Jan. 27, 1861; Howard L., b. May 19, 1862; Walter L., b. Sept. 31, 1872.

      VII. DELIGHT B. H., b. Feb. 15, 1840; m. June 24, 1875, —— Perry; res. Santa Cruz, Cal.

274. **Dexter**[7] **Pierce** (Peleg[6], Nathan[5], Mial[4], Ephraim[3], Ephraim[2], Michael[1]), b. July 24, 1818; m. Nov. 25, 1841, Amanda Sheldon, b. Sept. 21, 1820. He d. Nov. 19, 1883. Res. 47 Dudley street, Providence, R. I.

CHILDREN.

I. MARTHA C., b. May 25, 1845; m. May 4, 1876, Daniel W. Steere, b. Aug. 14, 1843; res. Providence, R. I., s. p.

II. EARL D., b. June 30, 1849; d. Oct. 5, 1873.

421.   III. WILLIAM C., b. Feb. 6, 1855; m. Lilla M. Bent.

422.   IV. WALTER C., b. Feb. 6, 1855; m. Mary C. Clark.

275. **Lewis**[7] **Pierce** (Preserved[6], Nathan[5], Mial[4], Ephraim[3], Ephraim[2], Michael[1]), b. Mar. 11, 1794; m. Jan. 8, 1815, Phebe Wood, b. May 7, 1797, d. Mar., 1864. Res. Swansey, Mass., and Pittstown, N. Y.

Lewis Pierce was born in Rehoboth, and resided there until after his marriage in 1815. He learned the trade of a stone-cutter, and assisted in constructing Fort Adams in Newport Harbor, R. I. He afterward removed to Pittstown, N. Y., where he died in 1840.

CHILDREN.

423.   I. ALFRED, b. May 7, 1817; m. Marietta P. Williams.

424.   II. BENJAMIN W., b. Apr. 9, 1819; m. Clarissa E. Carpenter and Mary A. Bragg.

III. LEANDER, d. young.

IV. FREDERICK, d. young.

276. **Capt. Preserved**[7] **Pierce** (Preserved[6], Nathan[5], Mial[4], Ephraim[3], Ephraim[2], Michael[1]), b. Aug. 1, 1785; m. Jan. 14, 1808, Betsey Davis, b. Mar. 8, 1784; d. Sept. 3, 1877. He d. Apr. 3, 1829. Res. Rehoboth, Mass.

CHILDREN.

425.   I. ELISHA D., b. Sept. 1, 1809 ; m. Lydia P. Potter.
426.   II. LEWIS, b. June 15, 1813; m. Hannah B. Chaffee,
      Lucy Merchant and Caroline Kent.
427.   III. ALLEN F., b. May 22, 1818; m. Lydia B. Brown.
428.   IV. GEORGE M., b. May 9, 1823 ; m. Mary A. Thurber.
      V. PRESERVED, b. ——; d. Dec. 29, 1811.
      VI. PRESERVED, b. June 15, 1813; d. June 30, 1813.
      VII. PRESERVED, b. ——; d. Mar. 14, 1821.
      VIII. BETSEY, b. —— ; d. May 17, 1828.

277. **Martin**[7] **Pierce** (Preserved[6], Nathan[5], Mial[4], Ephraim[3], Ephraim[2], Michael[1]), b. Feb. 21, 1796; m. May 12, 1822, Betsey Chase, b. Apr., 1801 ; d. Sept. 11, 1885. He d. Jan. 1, 1872. Res. New Bedford, Mass.

CHILDREN.

429.   I. OTIS, b. Mar. 12, 1827 ; m. Judith C. C. Devoll.

278. **Otis H.**[7] **Pierce** (Preserved[6], Nathan[5], Mial[4], Ephraim[3], Ephraim[2], Michael[1]), b. July 8, 1804; m. Dec. 14, 1828, Joanna Levin, b. —— ; d. June 22, 1885. He d. May 10, 1871. Res. Swansey, Mass.

CHILDREN.

430.   I. OTIS W., b. Apr. 1, 1831; m. Sarah C. Haskins.

279. **Hiram W.**[7] **Perce** (Isaac[6], Nathan[5], Mial[4], Ephraim[3], Ephraim[2], Michael[1]), b. Feb. 19, 1804; m. Dec. 28, 1826, Cornelia Ryder, b. Oct. 29, 1800 ; d. Feb. 10, 1888. He d. Jan. 30, 1883. Res. Rehoboth, Mass., Buffalo, N. Y., New York city, and Chicago, Ill.

Hiram Wheeler Perce, the sixth son of Isaac and Anna (Fitch) Pierce, was born in Rehoboth, Mass., February 19, 1804. When

32

about sixteen years of age he moved to Providence, R. I., to attend the schools there, residing with an older brother. At the completion of his schooling he turned his attention to a practical education in the line of architecture and building. This accomplished, at the age of twenty-one, having read an advertisement in a New York paper that an architect and builder was wanted in an interior town in South Carolina, he wrote to the parties and sent plans which were accepted. Securing ten practical workingmen he started upon a journey which in those days seemed as far away as any of the European countries. His friends endeavored to dissuade him, but he saw the shining star of success ahead, and in nine months had satisfactorily completed the undertaking. It had been his intention to permanently locate in the south when he left Providence, but his education had been of that character that slavery was very distasteful, and he was soon on his return to the north. He liked the stir and activity of New York city, and located there in 1825, and married Cornelia Ryder of Rhinebeck, N. Y., December 28, 1826. He remained in New York adding to an already large business, as many massive buildings for those days testified. To this business was added that of merchandise. In 1833 he removed to Buffalo, N. Y., and in 1858 to Chicago, Ill., where he died January 30, 1883. A man of most lovable character, commanding both in personal appearance and intelligence, he gained the esteem and friendship of all with whom he came in contact. " A noble man the noblest work of God."

The letter *a* was dropped from the original name *Pearce* of this family about 1830. This was done by mutual consent of some of the family, because so many of the different families of Pearce, Pierce and Peirce had the same given names or initials, and all residents of the same locality, the result being a confused identification. Hence the change.

CHILDREN.

I. FRANCES C., b. Apr. 12, 1828; m. June 29, 1848, Thaddeus P. Sears of Buffalo, N. Y., in Thompson, Conn., Rev. Charles Willetts officiating.

Hon. Thaddeus P. Sears, husband of Frances
C. Perce, lineal descendant of Robert Cushman
of the *Mayflower*, born at Hoosick Falls, N. Y.,
September 2, 1825, was educated at Princeton,
N. J., and until nineteen years old resided with
his parents at Albion, Orleans county, N. Y. In
the year 1844, he entered the Patchin Bank of
Buffalo. Afterward was cashier of Pratt Bank of
Buffalo. In 1849, he went to California, crossing
Mexico from Vera Cruz to San Blas, then taking
sail for San Francisco. In 1851, he was elected
a State senator from Calaveras county. He returned to Buffalo in November, 1852, removing
to Chicago in the spring of 1859. He removed
during the Rebellion to New Orleans, thence to
Natchez, Miss. On the reorganization of the
State at the close of the War, he was elected secretary of the Constitutional Convention. Was a
delegate to National Convention held in Chicago
in 1868 from Mississippi when General Grant was
nominated for President. He has resided in Chicago since 1871. Res. 548 Washington Boulevard,
Chicago, Ill. Ch., Percy, b. June 26, 1854; d.
Feb. 18, 1862; Frances Cornelia, b. July, 20, 1871;
d. Jan. 13, 1872; Mark H., b. Dec. 25, 1858;
studied medicine and graduated at the Chicago
Medical College in 1879. Removed to Leadville,
Col., in the spring of 1880. Has practiced his
profession there since, and was elected city physician in 1883; Robert Cushman, b. May 28, 1875;
attending the Brown School in Chicago.

431. II. LE GRAND W., b. June 19, 1836; m. Sarah M.
Wallace.

432. III. ELBERT, b. Aug. 21, 1831; m. Margaret A. Dickey.

280. **Hon. Lyman**[7] **Pierce** (Isaac[6], Nathan[5], Mial[4], Ephraim[3],
Ephraim[2], Michael[1]), b. Jan. 1, 1813; m. Feb. 25, 1834, Freelove
Horton, b. Feb. 10, 1810; d. June 22, 1874; m. 2nd, Nov. 30,
1875 —— ——. Res. Providence, R. I.

Lyman Pierce, the son of Isaac and grandson of Rev. Nathan
Pierce, was born in Rehoboth, Mass., January 1, 1813, on a rocky

farm in the eastern part of the town, upon which his father had resided for over sixty years. Lyman remained with his parents on the farm until he attained his majority, when he was married and opened a small store in the vicinity of his birthplace, and since that time, 1834, he has conducted business for himself. When he was nineteen years of age he was elected and received a military commission from Governor Lincoln of Massachusetts. In 1835, the military law was repealed, and his commission died in his hands. At the age of twenty-four he came within three votes of being elected a member of the Assembly in the old Bay State. After five years' experience in a general country store he moved to Providence in 1839, where he opened a flour and provision store. In that he continued for twenty-five years. In 1864, he embarked in the flour and grain business, in which he continued until 1870, when he retired upon the accumulations of years of industrious and indefatigable work. His schooling, when a boy, was very limited, as his services were needed on the farm. He was also of the opinion, as many another has been before and since, that an education was not necessary, but he often experienced the value of what he could not purchase with gold — an education. He had decided views on politics since he was twenty-two years of age, but was in no sense of the word a politician. One year he was elected to the Legislature, and on four other occasions, having been nominated for Governor, made quite a successful canvass, the last time being in 1870; he was twice nominated for mayor, and five times for alderman. On two occasions he has attended the National Conventions of the Democratic party which placed in nomination a President of the United States.

CHILDREN.

I. ADELINE F., b. Aug. 5, 1835; m. Sept. 12, 1855, James Tiffany; d. May 14, 1880. Ch., James F., res. Sydney, Australia; Hattie L., m. William A. Morgan; Lillie A.

II. SARAH J., b. Dec. 12, 1837; m. Nathaniel M. Burr; res. Seekonk, Mass.

III. FREELOVE A., b. Oct. 14, 1842; m. C. H. Williams; res. Providence, R. I.

IV. VIENNA B., b. Nov. 11, 1845; m. 1868, John M. Plummer. She is well known as a poetess and artist.

V. ISABELLA L., b. May 15, 1851; d. Dec. 25, 1864.

281. **Capt. Isaac[7] Pierce** (Isaac[6], Nathan[5], Mial[4], Ephraim[3], Ephraim[2], Michael[1]), b. Dec. 21, 1789; m. Jan. 1, 1809, Penelope Horton, b. June 2, 1791; d. Aug. 24, 1866. He d. Oct. 11, 1864. Res. Rehoboth, Mass., where he was the captain of the militia company, and later at Smithfield, R. I.

CHILDREN.

433. I. LEVI L., b. Sept. 2, 1829; m. Melissa A. Hopkins; res. Woonsocket, R. I.

434. II. EDWIN A., b. Feb. 18, 1832; m. Mariah Illingworth.

III. BELINDA P., b. Sept. 21, 1809; m. Feb. 24, 1828, Eugene T. Martin, b. Sept. 3, 1807. He went to California and is supposed to be dead. Ch., Lida A., b. Oct. 10, 1829; m. May 24, 1847, Olney Crock, b. ——; James T., b. Sept. 23, 1833; m. Oct. 25, 1852; Charles H., b. June 1, 1834; d. Sept. 11, 1844; res. Woonsocket, R. I.

IV. ANNA F., b. Jan. 31, 1812; m. Sept. 9, 1832, Silas Tanner, b. Feb. 16, 1808. Ch., Abbey A., d. in infancy; Hiram A., b. ——; Isaac S., b. ——; Abby J., b. June 1, 1842; m. Apr. 22, 1869; David Needham, b. Mar. 19, 1876; George E., b. ——; res. East Blackstone, Mass.

V. MAHALA B., b. Sept. 3, 1814; m. Dec. 25, 1833, Isaac Jacques. Ch., Sarah J., George H., Caroline, Emma, Hiram, Paulina, Henry, Mahala B., d. June 29, 1886. Three of the children are now living.

VI. CAROLINE, b. Nov. 10, 1816 ; m. July 4, 1836, Alfred
Allen. Ch., Alfred A., d. in infancy.

435. VII. WILLIAM F., b. Feb. 16, 1819; m. Paulina Brown.

VIII. ISAAC H., b. Mar. 6, 1821; m. Feb. 19, 1845, Abby
Lawrence. They had two children, but they are
now deceased. Res. California.

IX. SABRINA T., b. Apr. 1, 1823; d. Oct. 15, 1838.

X. HIRAM L., b. July 7, 1825 ; m. Sarah Murray; res.
Petaluma, California.

XI. JOSEPH H., b. Sept. 9, 1827; d. Sept. 10, 1827.

XII. SARAH E., b. July 30, 1834; m. Jan. 4, 1854, Henry
Babbitt ; he d. and she m. Mar., 1873, Isaac Pettis.
Ch., Ellen P., b. May 20, 1855; m. Oct. 28, 1875,
Charles Sherman; Fanny C., d. in infancy ; Henry
F., d. in infancy; Melissa A., b. June 11, 1867 ;
m. June 20, 1887, George L. Sheppardson; Frank
H., b. Aug. 5, 1869 ; res. North Attleboro, Mass.

XIII. GEORGE W., b. May 7, 1839 ; d. Sept., 1840.

282. **Angia**[7] **Pierce** (Isaac[6], Nathan[5], Mial[4], Ephraim[3],
Ephraim[2], Michael[1]), b. June 1, 1794; m. Dec. 21, 1815, Mary
Mason, b. Feb. 3, 1799 ; d. ——; m. 2nd, Elizabeth Crowley, b.
——; d. ——. He d. Oct. 2, 1854. Res. Providence, R. I.

CHILDREN.

436. I. EDWARD M., b. Jan. 21, 1822 ; m. Celia J. Anthony;
res. Fall River.

437. II. JAMES F., b. Aug. 26, 1826 ; m. Amelia L. White.

III. ANGIA F., b. Apr. 19, 1818; d. at sea.

IV. SAMANTHA B., b. Dec. 21, 1823; d. unm. 1843.

V. MARY A., b. June 24, 1816 ; m. Mar. 12, 1838, Micah
B. Allen, b. Jan. 23, 1811; d. Oct. 1, 1882; res.
Swansey, Mass. Ch., Josephine D., b. Apr. 21,
1840; m. Oren H. Crossman ; res. Brockton,
Mass.; Mary A. E., b. Oct. 22, 1841 ; m. Oscar
F. Heym; res. Providence, R. I.; Eunice P., b.

Feb. 8, 1843; m. James G. Church; William H.,
b. Mar. 24, 1851; m. Martha F. Clapp; res. Chelsea, Mass.; Micah B., b. Aug. 28, 1847; m. Nellie
Tarbox.

VI. KEZIAH, b. Feb. 25, 1820; m. 1858, John Myricks.
Ch., Ida S., d. unm., and Elizabeth, also dead.

438. VII. ANGIE W., b. Nov. 5, 1853; m. Mary E. Mott.

VIII. CATHERINE, b. Feb. 11, 1855; m. Aug., 1885, Frank
Murphy; res. Bristol, R. I.

283. **Levi**[7] **Pierce** (Isaac[6], Nathan[5], Mial[4], Ephraim[3], Ephraim[2],
Michael[1]), b. June 8, 1797; m. Mar. 9, 1818, Betsey S. Wheeler,
b. 1800; d. Feb. 23, 1881. He d. 1838. Res. Providence, R. I.,
and New York city.

Levi Pierce was born in Rehoboth, Mass., and brought up on
the farm of his father, Isaac. At the age of nineteen becoming
dissatisfied with the life of a farmer lad he started for the city of
Providence, R. I., much against the wishes of his father. He soon
mastered the mason trade, and in a short time became a contractor and builder, erecting the first factory near Providence. Later
he engaged in the livery business, but becoming dissatisfied with
his partner, he disposed of his share to his associate and embarked
in the manufacture of clothing. He owned two schooners which
he ladened with clothing and shipped south. Soon after he went
west taking with him his son Franklin F. During their absence
the family moved to Buffalo, N. Y., on a canal-boat. Soon after
the family settled in their new home news came to them in the
year 1838, that the father was dead. As Franklin never returned
it was supposed he too died. Mr. Pierce was a noble, fine-looking man; kind-hearted and generous; a kind father and fond of
his family, an excellent provider, and quite anxious his children
should have all the advantages possible.

CHILDREN.

439. I. CHARLES W., b. Jan. 12, 1833; m. Emma Haddock,
and Mrs. Anna Commons.

440.   II. LEVI L., b. Nov. 18, 1830; m. Ellen E. Wright.
        III. ELIZABETH S., b. Mar. 22, 1822; m. Dec. 16, 1840,
        in Buffalo, N. Y., to Cortland Philip Livingston
        Butler, b. Mar. 8, 1813; res. 287 Town street,
        Columbus, Ohio. Ch., Maria Livingston, b. in
        Buffalo, N. Y., 1842; d. 1842; Frances Livingston, b.
        in Zanesville, Ohio, 1843; d. 1843; Charles Henry,
        b. in Columbus, Ohio, Jan. 7, 1845; m. 1866,
        Belle Howard, dau. of Dr. Richard Howard, an
        eminent physician and surgeon of Columbus. He
        is engaged in the wholesale and retail furniture
        business; William Livingston, b. Mar. 22, 1848; d.
        May, 1851; Mary Elizabeth, b. June 17, 1851; m.
        Oct., 1869, Robert E. Sheldon, a member of the
        wholesale dry goods house of Miles, Bancroft &
        Sheldon; Harriett Livingston, b. Feb. 18, 1853;
        m. Nov., 1872, Levi Reinhart Doty, president of
        the Ohio Coal Exchange; Cortland P. L., Jr., b.
        July 16, 1857. He studied law at the New York
        Law School, is a graduate of Union College in
        Schenectady, and one of the promising young
        attorneys of Columbus; Theodore Earl, b. Oct.
        16, 1861. He was graduated from Marietta Col-
        lege in 1885, and is a gifted artist. For two years
        and a half he studied at the Art League in New
        York city. He is now (1889) in Paris, where he
        has been for two years. One of his paintings was
        admitted to the French Salon and commented
        on as most admirable, and for which he received
        honorable mention and a diploma. Mr. and Mrs.
        Butler were married in 1840, and moved west in
        1841, traveling in a stage coach, and were one
        week in reaching Columbus, Ohio, a thrifty
        town of less than one thousand inhabitants. They
        have lived there to see it grow to a large and pros-
        perous city of seventy-five thousand inhabitants.

Her husband, C. P. L. Butler, was in the confectionery and baking business for many years, then in the wholesale furniture house, and is now interested in the coal business and a banker. He was a member of the city council many years, and president of the Home Insurance Company, and was a helper in the building of three railroads. He is well known through that State as an upright, practical business man.

IV. FRANKLIN FITCH, b. Mar. 25, 1824; d. in the west, 1838(?).

441. V. EARL H., b. Mar. 14, 1827 ; m. Martha M. Marr.

442. VI. WARREN S., b. July 25, 1828; m. Eliza M. Sturdy.

VII. SARAH A., b. Sept. 30, 1833; m. Jan., 1851, James Oscar Robson, b. Jan., 1828; d. May 6, 1882; res. 162 Allen street, Buffalo, N. Y. Mr. James O. Robson carried on the jewelry and gunsmith business for thirty years on Main street in Buffalo, N. Y., honored and respected by all who knew him ; an upright man and an exemplary Christian. Ch., Lilly Dell, b. Apr., 1855; d. Oct., 1857; Cora Percy, b. Jan., 1858 ; m. Jan., 1880, Charles Sherman of Buffalo; d. s. p., Mar., 1880; Flora Elizabeth, b. Aug. 1860; d. Aug., 1878; Jennie Olivia, b. 1862 ; d. in infancy; Cortland James, b. 1865; d. Mar., 1884; Le Grand Oscar, b. Dec., 1875 ; living.

VIII. SOPHRONIA A., b. Apr. 30, 1820; m. 1837, Francis Budd. He lived only three months. She m. Oct. 17, 1839, Martin Rowley, b. Sept. 25, 1813; res. Chaffee, Erie Co., N. Y. Ch., Francis Budd, b. Sept. 22, 1842; m. Dec. 8, 1859; d. Feb. 20, 1860; George C., b. Dec. 14, 1843; d. Mar. 2, 1844; Elizabeth A., b. Aug. 5, 1845; m. Sept. 29, 1860, Menzo Wood; res. Sardinia Village, Erie Co., N. Y.; Almira I., b. July 6, 1847 ; d. Jan. 22, 1849 ;

33

Earl Perce, b. May 31, 1851; m. Jan. 23, 1874,
Nettie Vanocker; res. Lockport, N. Y.; Ida
Louisa, b. June 10, 1854; m. Feb. 19, 1873, Mar-
tin Ernst; res. Unionville, Lake Co., Ohio; Flora
Isabel, b. Apr. 28, 1859; Willie M., b. July 4, 1862.

IX. ALMIRA W., b. Mar. 30, 1819; m. in New York city
in 1837, Joseph Moore of Providence, R. I., b.
1813; d. 1878. She d. 1885. Ch., Almira, b.
1839; m. 1868, A. Olney, s. p.; res. Providence,
R. I. Four other children were born and died in
infancy. Frank F., b. 1847; m. 1874, Ida Chees-
man; had two children. He d. 1886; res. Sardinia,
N. Y. Mrs. Almira W. P. Moore (above) was a
beautiful and accomplished woman with marked
literary ability. She had a bright and cheerful
disposition, and took great pleasure in making
others happy, although a great sufferer herself for
many years.

284. **Rev. Waterman**[7] **Pierce** (Isaac[6], Nathan[5], Mial[4],
Ephraim[3], Ephraim[2], Michael[1]), b. Dec. 24, 1801; m. June 15,
1820, Betsey Baker, b. Mar. 8, 1801. Res. East Providence, R. I.

Rev. Waterman Pierce was born in Rehoboth, Mass., December
24, 1801. He was brought up on a farm, and his early education
was therefore necessarily curtailed. He was united in marriage
when but nineteen years of age, and was blessed with eleven children. They now (1888) have twenty-three grandchildren and
eight great grandchildren. Each one of his sons has been a
member of the Providence City Council, and the youngest is now
a member of the General Assembly of that State. For forty-two
years Rev. Waterman has been pastor of the Free Will Baptist
Church at Barneyville, North Swansey, Mass. He has baptized
hundreds of persons and united in marriage nearly as many. He
has been called upon to officiate at funerals in fourteen cities and
towns. His grandfather was a clergyman, and his grandson now
occupies his pulpit with him.

CHILDREN.

443.   I. GEORGE L., b. Sept. 9, 1837 ; m. Sarah E. Cory.
444.   II. BRADFORD B., b. Nov. 7, 1821; m. Martha K. Bowan and Susan Shelley.
    III. SARAH F., b. July 25, 1826; m. Sept. 11, 1853, Gilbert M. Horton; res. Rehoboth, Mass.
445.   IV. ELISHA W., b. Jan. 22, 1829; m. Elizabeth W. Barney.
    V. MARY E., b. Apr. 27 1831; d. Mar. 10, 1845.
    VI. MARIA B., b. Feb. 1, 1835; m. Oct. 2, 1859, Samuel S. Barney; res. Seekonk, Mass.
    VII. JULIA E., b. Nov. 16, 1839; m. Aug. 6, 1863, Dexter West; res. Seekonk, Mass.
    VIII. MERCY A., b. July 14, 1842 ; m. June 17, 1864, Burden Monroe; res. Swansey, Mass.
    IX. RICHMOND, b. July 2, 1847; d. Mar. 13, 1848.

285. **Jeremiah B.**[7] **Pierce** (Isaac[6], Nathan[5], Mial[4], Ephraim[3], Ephraim[2], Michael[1]), b. Aug. 20, 1820; m. Aug. 29, 1841, Sarah P. Horton, b. Aug. 30, 1823. He d. 1866. Res. Rehoboth, Mass.

CHILDREN.

446.   I. WARREN R., b. June 30, 1843; m. Annie E. Kenyon.
    II. IDA F., b. Dec. 5, 1847; m. Dec. 2, 1873, Carroll M. Foster; res. 1 Woods avenue, Providence, R. I. Ch., Mabel, b. May 18, 1875.

286. **Samuel**[7] **Pierce** (David[6], Nathan[5], Mial[4], Ephraim[3], Ephraim[2], Michael[1]), b. Apr. 22, 1761; m. Oct. 12, 1786, Hannah Bowen, b. Jan. 31, 1761; d. Jan. 16, 1822. He d. Feb. 1, 1840. Res. Rehoboth, Mass.

CHILDREN.

447.   I. BENJAMIN, b. Sept. 4, 1800; m. Rosanna Horton.
448.   II. JOSEPH, b. Feb. 15, 1798; m. Lydia Lawton.

449.   III. SAMUEL, b. July 12, 1787; m. Sarah Eddy and Sally Mason.
450.   IV. HOLDEN, b. June 22, 1789; m. Mary Sanford.
451.   V. JAMES, b. June 8, 1791; m. ——.
        VI. HANNAH, b. Nov. 5, 1793; m. John Phillips. She d. Sept. 14, 1831.
       VII. SARAH, b. Feb. 27, 1796; d. May 28, 1798.
      VIII. MARY A., b. Jan. 21, 1803; m. Ichabod Walling. She d. May 13, 1885.
        IX. BENJAMIN, b. Feb. 15, 1798; d. Feb. 18, 1798.

287. **Micah**[7] **Pierce** (Jobe[6], Jobe[5], Mial[4], Ephraim[3], Ephraim[2], Michael[1]), b. Feb. 29, 1780; m. Feb. 17, 1802, Hannah Pierce, b. July 22, 1782; d. Jan. 4, 1872. He d. Aug. 16, 1864. Res. Durham, N. Y.

CHILDREN.

452.   I. ROYAL, b. Jan. 19, 1803; m. Mary Clark.
        II. REUBEN, b. Feb. 12, 1804; m. Oct. 14, 1826, Eliza Wright. He d. Mar. 30, 1880, in Oakland, Cal., leaving one daughter.
453.   III. WILLIAM, b. Jan. 28, 1807; m. Gertrude N. Ames and Caroline M. Phelps.
454.   IV. STEPHEN V. R., b. Jan. 1, 1809; m. Amey Maria Lockwood.
         V. WILLARD, b. Aug. 18, 1810; d. Oct. 1, 1831.
        VI. SEMANTHE, b. Mar. 8, 1812; m. Nov. 24, 1830, Joel Bullock, b. May 31, 1806; d. July 9, 1885; res. Strawberry Point, Iowa. Ch., Addison, b. Aug. 27, 1833; killed in war, June, 1864; George, b.Aug. 22, 1835; d. Dec. 18, 1878; Amanda, b. Apr. 10, 1839; m. H. C. Crandall, Jan. 1, 1857; res. Shellrock, Iowa; Lyman, b. Feb. 2, 1847; d. Dec. 25, 1848; Mirah E., b. June 9, 1854; m. J. D. Inger, b. Nov. 19, 1869; res. Strawberry Point, Iowa.

VII. AMOS, b. Mar. 6, 1814; m. Sept. 18, 1844, Bethia
Pratt, b. Nov. 25, 1821; d. Mar. 10, 1885. He d.
s. p., 1888; res. Blaine, Ill.
455. VIII. LYMAN, b. Sept. 17, 1817; m. Catherine H. Nier.
IX. JEMIMA, b. Mar. 27, 1819; d. Oct. 22, 1831.
X. WESLEY, b. May 11, 1821; d. Dec. 30, 1873; res.
Poplar Grove, Ill.
XI. ALLEN D., b. Sept. 10, 1823; m. Aug. 15, 1844, s.
p., res. Pinos Altos, Grant Co., New Mexico.
XII. DIANA, b. Aug. 15, 1824; m. Feb. 23, 1846, Orrin
A. Wood, b. Aug. 15, 1822; res. Freehold, N. Y.
Ch., Courtney B., b. Dec. 17, 1853; m. Alice S.
Lake; res. Freehold, N. Y.

288. **John M.**[7] **Pierce** (Jobe[6], Jobe[5], Mial[4], Ephraim[3],
Ephraim[2], Michael[1]), b. Mar. 23, 1778; m. Hannah Morehouse;
m. 2nd, Dec. 24, 1816, Elizabeth Hickok, b. Sept. 27, 1786; d.
Aug. 20, 1823; m. 3d, Jan. 1, 1824, Mrs. Eliza Reed; d. Dec.,
1865. He d. May 19, 1846. Res. Taunton, Mass., and Norton
Hill, N. Y.

CHILDREN.

456. I. PHILIP M., b. May 31, 1818; m. Ann M. Bartlett.
II. PHEBE M., b. Nov., 1816; m. May 2, 1836, Loren
P. Cole; b. June 15, 1808; d. Dec. 20, 1884.
She d. Mar. 18, 1837; res. Windham, N. Y. Ch.,
Phebe A., b. Feb. 29, 1837; res. Conesville, N. Y.
457. III. CARLOS M., b. May 9, 1821; m. Catherine C. Bartlett.
IV. CAROLINE M., b. May 9, 1821; m. Apr. 15, 1840,
Ahaz Cole, b. Dec. 23, 1817; res. Windham, N. Y.
Ch., John M., b. Apr. 9, 1841; res. Windham,
N. Y.; Adelbert M., b. Mar. 12, 1842; res. Wind-
ham, N. Y.; Edward M., b. Oct. 26, 1844; res.
Windham, N. Y.; editor *Journal;* Edwin M.,
b. Oct. 26, 1844; d. Nov. 10, 1866; Simeran
M., b. Apr. 26, 1848; res. Hunter, N. Y.; Carrie

E., b. Mar. 4, 1856; m. —— Ormsbee; res. Stuy-
vesant, N. Y.; Emma D., b. May 18, 1860; m. ——
Houghtaling; res. Bath-on-the-Hudson, N. Y.

  V. ELIZABETH, b. Aug., 1823; d. s. p.

458. VI. MAXON, b. Mar. 5, 1800; m. Charity Nelson.

  VII. CHARLES W., b. Aug. 31, 1825; m. June 12, 1849,
Elizabeth Cheritre, b. Sept. 28, 1824; res. s. p.,
Oak Hill, N. Y.

289. **Benona**[7] **Pierce** (Jobe[6], Jobe[5], Mial[4], Ephraim[3], Ephraim[2],
Michael[1]), b. Oct. 21, 1781; m. Jan. 1, 1805, Elizabeth Davis, b.
May 9, 1789; d. Sept. 26, 1881. He d. June 26, 1855. Res.
North Blenheim and Gilboa, N. Y.

CHILDREN.

459. I. HIRAM, b. Jan. 22, 1806; m. Miriam Strong.

460. II. LEMUEL, b. Apr. 9, 1810; m. Lydia Ruliffson.

  III. LOVEL B., b. Jan. 26, 1814; d. Aug., 1846; res.
Big Foot Prairie, Ill., and Orleans Co., N. Y.

  IV. CARLTON K., b. Mar. 16, 1816; res. Binghamton,
N. Y.

461. V. ⎰ ELECTUS, b. Jan. 13, 1829; m. Clarissa Wood.

  VI. ⎱ ELECTA, b. Jan. 13, 1829; m. June 11, 1868,
Washington Graham, d. Apr. 4, 1873, s. p.; m.
2nd. Wm. M. Pase, Sept. 13, 1881; res. Lysle,
Minn.

  VII. HANNAH E., b. Feb. 12, 1808; m. Mar. 1, 1832,
Nelson K. Martin, b. May 1, 1794; m. 2nd, Dec.
31, 1873, Ira R. Martin; res. Aquetuck, N. Y.
Ch., Helen M., b. July 21, 1833; Oscar P., b.
Oct. 19, 1834; Mary M., b. Aug. 28, 1836; d.
Nov. 9, 1860; Harriett A., b. Oct. 19, 1837; d.
Dec. 23, 1839; Harriett A., b. Aug. 16, 1840;
Almira E., b. Apr. 5, 1842; d. July 25, 1863;
Emma E., b. Aug. 27, 1844.

  VIII. HARRIETT, b. June 6, 1820; m. Dec. 25, 1841, Jacob

Hubbell, b. Nov. 11, 1820; res. Seward, N. Y.
Ch., Richtmer H., b. Feb. 2, 1843; res. Jefferson,
N. Y.; Chas. B. H., b. Sept. 9, 1844; res. Jefferson, N. Y.; Hiram P. H., b. Nov. 29, 1847; res.
Harpersfield, N. Y.; Elizabeth H., b. Feb. 19,
1850; Sophia, b. Mar. 31, 1852; Fred E., b. Mar.
31, 1863; res. Mechanicville, N. Y.

IX. ROXELINE, b. Sept. 16, 1823; m. May 28, 1845,
Mathew St. John, b. Sept. 7, 1820; res. Otrantro
Station, Iowa. Ch., Andre M., b. May 6, 1846;
m. Helen D. Finch, Oct. 24, 1872; res. Otranto
Station, Iowa; Alice H., b. June 16, 1848; d. Dec.
20, 1850; Ella E., b. 1850; d. 1862; Wiley P.,
b. Nov. 7, 1858; m. Miss Minnie E. Hill, Dec.
24, 1883; res. Waltham, Minn.; Benonia P., b.
Dec. 7, 1866.

290. **Gilbert[7] Pierce** (Jobe[6], Jobe[5], Mial[4], Ephraim[3], Ephraim[2],
Michael[1]), b. Nov. 20, 1789; m. Dec. 25, 1810, Lydia Davis, b.
Aug. 30, 1791; d. Oct. 15, 1882. Res. Durham, N. Y.

CHILDREN.

462.   I. JOHN M., Oct. 11, 1811; m. Charlotte Sickel.

      II. LAURA, b. Aug. 23, 1813; m. Jan. 1, 1833, Jas.
Dunn. She d. Oct., 1870.

463.   III. ALBERT, b. Aug. 28, 1815; m. Oct., 1857, Loiza
Coller; d. 1874; res. Elwood, N. J.

      IV. SILAS G., b. Feb. 4, 1818; m. Huriel Green and
Mariah Aldridge.

      V. HENRY, b. July 20, 1820; m. Dec. 25, 1840, Sarah
Green; res. Cauyga(?), N. Y.

      VI. BUEL, b. Feb. 23, 1823; unm.

      VII. LOVINA, b. ——; d. 1848.

    VIII. LORINDA, b. ——; d. Oct., 1864.

      IX. ABBY.

291. **Silas**[7] **Pierce** (Jobe[6], Jobe[5], Mial[4], Ephraim[3], Ephraim[2], Michael[1]), b. Sept. 9, 1787; m.   . Res. Blenheim, N. Y.

CHILDREN.

I. GARRY; res. Kentucky.

II. GEORGE, b. ——; d. ——.

III. JOHN, b. ——; res. Patchen Hollow, Blenheim, Schoharie Co., N. Y.

IV. HARRIETT, b. ——; m. ——; res. Blenheim, N. Y.

V. MARY, b. ——; m. Rev. Robt. Kerr.

VI. ELIZA, b. ——; m. Richard Shaver; res. North Blenheim, N. Y.

292. **Samuel**[7] **Pierce** (Samuel[6], Jobe[5], Mial[4], Ephraim[3], Ephraim[2], Michael[1]), b. Jan. 23, 1774; m. at Grafton, N. H., Miriam Williams, b. May 22, 1777; d. Aug. 31, 1832; m. 2nd, Prudence Crapo of Taunton. He d. at Taunton, Mass., in 1870. Res. Grafton, N. H., and Taunton, Mass.

Samuel Pierce was born in Dartmouth, Mass., where he resided until his removal to Grafton, N. H., where he married his wife. Later he moved to Moira, N. Y., where he reared his family. He married a second wife in Taunton, Mass., Mrs. Crapo, and had four children born in that city.

CHILDREN.

I. OLIVER, b. ——; m. Jane Ford; res. Grafton, and had a dau., Sybil, who m. —— Smith.

II. EARL, b. ——; m. Lovina Peck; res. Moira, N. Y., and had an only son, Searl. who res. there.

464.   III. JESSE, b. 1812; m. Chloe B. Martin and Charlotte Harlow.

465.   IV. HIRAM, b. May 12, 1803; m. Hannah Marsh.

V. SAMUEL, b. ——; d. unm. at Dartmouth.

VI. GREENLEAF, b. ——; m. Mary Denio; res. North Star, Minn.

465-1. VII. PHILLIP, b. ——; m. Elizabeth F. Terry.

VIII. CYNTHIA, b. Sept. 25, 1793; m. Solomon Sayles, b. Apr. 6, 1798; d. Nov. 10, 1886; res. Moira, N. Y. Ch., Solomon Pinkney, b. June 2, 1820; Emeline, b. May 30, 1824; m. —— Follett; res. Lawrence, N. Y.; Elmira, b. Nov. 14, 1830; m. —— Keeler; res. Lawrence.

IX. MERCY, b. Mar. 14, 1808; m. May 31, 1829, Benjamin Goddard, b. July 22, 1804. She d. Feb. 16, 1887; res. Freeport, Ill. Ch., Miriam, b. Feb. 22, 1831; m. Jan. 14, 1861, David N. Peck, and 2nd, James E. Frisbie; res. Freeport; Alpheus P., b. Aug. 29, 1833; m. Sept. 13, 1866, Mercy Pierce; res. Freeport; Byron S., b. Apr. 15, 1846 ;m. Aug. 28, 1869, Mary ——; res. Freeport; Benjamin E., b. July 3, 1843; m. Nov. 18, 1865, Annie Leslie; res. Freeport; Franklin, b. Feb. 14, 1848; d. Feb. 3, 1857.

X. CHARLES, b. ——; m. Martha Crapo; res. Taunton, Mass.

XI. JAMES, b. ——; m. Hattie ——; res. Albany, N. Y.

XII. ABNER, b. ——.

XIII. PRUDENCE, b. ——; m. Charles Marsh; res. Belfast, Me.

293. **Sylvester[7] Pierce** (Sylvester[6], Caleb[5], Mial[4], Ephraim[3], Ephraim[2], Michael[1]), b. 1792; m. Margaret Kneaskern, b. ——; d. ——. He d. 1879. Res. Blaine, Ill.

CHILDREN.

466.   I. SETH W., b. ——; m. Mary Cheesborough.

II. AMOS S., b. ——; res. Belvidere, Ill.

III. WILLIAM H., b. ——; res. Garden Prairie, Ill.

IV. MARTHA, b. ——; m. —— Barker.

V. ARMITA, b. Dec. 7, 1816; m. Jan. 7, 1843, Joel N. Head, b. Sept. 5, 1816; res. Poplar Grove, Ill.

34

Ch., Marion L., b. Mar. 18, 1846; Charles S., b. June 2, 1847; Rovilla A., b. Aug. 30, 1848; Elnora, b. Oct. 24, 1854.

VI. MARY A., b. ——; m. Edward Lindsley; res. Poplar Grove, Ill.

VII. CAROLINE, b. ——; m. Peter Egnor; res. South Cairo, N. Y.

294. **Cromwell⁷ Pierce** (Sylvester⁶, Caleb⁵, Mial⁴, Ephraim³, Ephraim², Michael¹), b. ——. Res. Tioga Co., Pa.

CHILDREN.

I. SYLVESTER, b. ——.

II. JOHN, b. ——.

III. ABRAHAM, b. ——; res. Syracuse, N. Y.

295. **Jesse⁷ Pierce** (Caleb⁶, Caleb⁵, Mial⁴, Ephraim³, Ephraim², Michael¹), b. in Schoharie Co., N. Y.; m. 1810, Jennie Clough, b. 1790; d. 1824. He d. 1839. Res. Hamburg, N. Y.

CHILDREN.

467.　I. HARRY H., b. May 10, 1812; m. Elner Jane Rowland.

468.　II. SIMEON, b. Mar. 20, 1814; m. Amanda F. Pratt.

III. RUFUS, b. 1816; res. Muskegon, Mich.

IV. GINETTE, b. 1818; d. 1837 in Michigan City, Ind.

469.　V. DAVID C., b. Apr. 3, 1820; m. Sallie E. Lindsay.

VI. WILLIAM, b. 1824; d. 1830.

VII. JANE, b. ——; m. James Adams, b. ——; res. Hobart, Ind.

296. **Levi⁷ Pierce** (Caleb⁶, Caleb⁵, Mial⁴, Ephraim³, Ephraim², Michael¹), b. 1776; m. Amy Benedict, b. ——; d. ——. He d. ——. Res. Hamburg, N. Y.

CHILDREN.

I. SYLVIA, b. 1808; m. Thomas Burgess, s. p.; res. Richmond, Pa.

470. II. SENECA, b. Aug. 22, 1809; m. Lucy Pitcher.

III. HARRIETT, b. 1811.

IV. FANNY, b. 1813; m. —— Blakeslee; res. Spartansburg, Pa.

297. **Wheeler**[7] **Pierce** (Caleb[6], Caleb[5], Mial[4], Ephraim[3], Ephraim[2], Michael[1]), b. ——; m. ——. Res. Michigan, where he died.

CHILDREN.

I. LEVI, b. ——.

II. PROXY, b. ——.

III. MERCY, b. ——.

298. **Amos**[7] **Pierce** (Shuball[6], Joshua[5], Mial[4], Ephraim[3], Ephraim[2], Michael[1]), b. ——; m. Betsey Brooks. Res. Poultney, Vt., and Whitehall, N. Y.

CHILDREN.

471. I. AMOS M., b. Nov. 17, 1818; m. Harriett N. Frost.

II. CHARLOTTE, b. Oct. 5, 1816; m. Royal Hodges, b. Oct. 30, 1824; d. Oct. 17, 1873; m. Ahira Scovel; res. Vergennes, Vt. Ch., William H., b. Apr. 4, 1855; d. Dec. 5, 1860; Henrietta J., b. Sept. 5, 1857; m. Apr. 4, 1883, H. O. Carr; res. Bristol,Vt.

III. JANE, b. 1812; m. L. Grover. She d. 1871.

IV. SARAH, b. ——; m. —— Ordway. She d. ——. Ch., Augusta, b. ——; m. —— French; res. Ætna Mills, Cal.

V. WESLEY, b. ——; d. young.

299. **Mason**[7] **Pierce** (Shubal[6], Joshua[5], Mial[4], Ephraim[3], Ephraim[2], Michael[1]), b. Dec. 11, 1780; m. in Salem, N. Y., Anna

Archibald, b. Mar. 1, 1779; d. Apr. 11, 1829.   He d. in Windsor Mich., in 1857.

CHILDREN.

472.   I. HIRAM, b. Apr. 13, 1803; m. ——.

II. PRUDENCE, b. Nov. 24, 1805 ; m. Mar., 1828.   Had six children, and d. Aug. 23, 1854.   She was the first white woman to live in Eaton, Mich., going there in 1829.

III. LUCINA, b. Nov. 10, 1807; m. Hiram Hotchkiss. He was a well-to-do farmer, and they had four daughters.   The eldest married Dr. Buel G. Streeter of Geneva Falls, N. Y.; the second married Barritt Collins, a successful merchant; the third married S. A. Knapp; res. Lake Charles, La.; the fourth daughter married M. C. Stoddard of Poultney, Vt., a prominent manufacturer engaged in making dairy goods, of the firm of the New England Manufacturing Company.

IV. DIADANA S., b. Feb. 11, 1810; m. Feb. 24, 1830, Horace Hotchkiss, b. Apr. 20, 1811; d. Dec. 24, 1882; res. Lake Geneva, Wis.   Ch., James L., b. Sept. 15, 1831; m. Jan., 1854; a commercial traveler; res. Whitehall, N. Y.   He has three sons, Frank, a hardware merchant, and Charles, superintendent of the water-works at Whitehall, N.Y. and William, a prominent young attorney in Auburn, N. Y.; Lovina M., b. May 15, 1833; unm.; res. Lake Geneva, Wis.; Mason King, b. Feb. 22, 1836; m. Jan. 24, 1861; d. Sept. 30, 1884.

V. SOLOMON, b. Feb. 9, 1812; m. ——.

VI. ELIZABETH A., b. May 11, 1816; m. Cyrus Streeter; res. Potterville, Eaton Co., Mich.

300. **Shuball**[7] **Pierce** (Shuball[6], Joshua[5], Mial[4], Ephraim[3], Ephraim[2], Michael[1]), b. Mar. 9, 1784; m. at Hampton, N. Y.,

Lovina Bunnell, b. Apr. 15, 1785; d. Feb. 19, 1852. He d. July 25, 1852. Res. Sherman, N. Y.

CHILDREN.

I. HEZEKIAH M., b. Aug. 21, 1820; res. Hopkinton, Iowa.

II. HANNAH, b. Aug. 4, 1822; m. at Hemlock, N. Y., Luke Fish, b. Oct. 31, 1823; res. Mt. Vernon, Iowa. Ch., Edson Orlando, b. Apr. 22, 1848; res. Mt. Vernon; Charles Wesley, b. Dec. 3, 1849; d. June 15, 1852; Sarah Jane, b. Sept. 20, 1851; m. Mar. 7, 1871; Elwin M. Wood; address, Sykeston, Dakota; Carlos Mark, b. Apr. 7, 1854; d. May 10, 1882; Addison Luke, b. Sept. 6, 1856; d. July 11, 1878.

III. FILO F., b. Aug. 6, 1824; d. Feb. 21, 1832.

IV. HESTER ANN, b. Oct. 15, 1826; res. Minneapolis, Minn.

V. DENNIS, b. Sept. 20, 1829; res. Cora, Pa.

VI. PRUDENCE, b. July 11, 1831; res. Mt. Vernon, Iowa.

301. **Israel**[7] **Pierce** (Israel[6], Joshua[5], Mial[4], Ephraim[3], Ephraim[2], Michael[1]), b. ——; m. June 19, 1809, Polly Walker of Dighton, b. May 10, 1784. Res. Rehoboth, Mass.

CHILDREN.

I. WALKER, b. 1810.

II. ISRAEL, b. ——.

302. **Jabez M.**[7] **Pierce** (Henry[6], Joshua[5], Mial[4], Ephraim[3], Ephraim[2], Michael[1]), b. 1794; m. Jan. 1, 1818, Mary Kelton, b. 1799; d. Jan. 18, 1831; m. 2nd, 1835. He d. July 22, 1837. Res. Swansey, Mass.

Jabez Mason Pierce was born in Rehoboth, Bristol Co., Mass. His father was Henry Pierce of Rehoboth; his mother, Lydia

Mason of Providence, R. I. He married Mary Kelton, January 1, 1818, in Swansey, where he lived working at the cooper's trade till his death in 1837. His wife died in January, 1831. They had nine children; one died in infancy. In 1835, he married again, one child resulting from this union.

CHILDREN.

I. IRA, b. Dec. 15, 1828; res. Maine Prairie, Minn.

II. MARY K., b. Oct. 20, 1818; m. Mar. 16, 1840, Dr. Solomon F. Brown, b. Sept. 15, 1817; res. 1512 Twentieth avenue, North Minneapolis, Minn.

Solomon Fuller Brown was born in Douglas, Worcester county, Mass., September 11, 1817. He was brought up by his father as a mechanic, and followed the mason's trade for a number of years. He was allowed such educational advantages as the common schools afforded. He lived in the State working at his trade until 1852, when he went to California, remaining three years. While there he began the study of medicine, and at the same time acted as Spanish interpreter in the courts.

In 1855, he returned to his native State, and in 1857, moved to St. Cloud, Stearns county, Minn. The following year he pre-empted a farm in Maine Prairie township, Stearns county, where he resided until 1861. Then enlisted in the Fourth Minnesota Volunteer Infantry, Company D, as a private, but was promoted from time to time, and when discharged was first lieutenant, and in command of his company. He was engaged in seven battles receiving seven wounds at Vicksburg, Miss., on account of which he was discharged. After his discharge he practiced medicine one year in Memphis, Tenn., but returned to Maine Prairie in 1865, continuing the practice of his profession. He took a leading part in every public enterprise, and at all public meetings that he attended was invariably given the chair. He was elected justice of the peace, which office he held for six years, refusing to continue in office longer.

In 1885, he moved to Minneapolis to enter into the practice of medicine with his son, where he now resides. He was married to Mary K. Pierce March 16, 1840.

Ch., Freeman S., b. Nov. 25, 1840; d. Dec. 11, 1844; James S., b. Oct. 14, 1841; d. 1841; S. Francis, b. Sept. 11, 1856; Dr. and Prof. Chem. et Toxicol., Minnesota Homœopathic Medical College; res. Minneapolis.

    III. JABEZ, b. Jan. 4, 1820; unm.; res. Hornitos, Cal.

473. IV. JAMES M., b. July 12, 1821; m. Mrs. (Bancroft) Palmer.

    V. ALVAH, b. Feb. 24, 1823; d. July 18, 1842.

    VI. CHARLES M., b. Aug. 12, 1824; d. Sept. 30, 1842.

    VII. LYDIA M., b. Sept. 12, 1825; m. June 13, 1853, Abraham G. Hart, b. Sept. 23, 1831; res. Fall River, Mass.; member of the State Board of Lunacy and Charity. Ch., Marietta, b. Apr. 2, 1854; d. Aug. 13, 1854; Charles S., b. Nov. 1, 1855; m. Oct. 11, 1879; now clerk at Massachusetts Reformatory; P. O., Warnerville, Mass.; Albion A., b. Oct. 18, 1862; d. Sept. 29, 1863.

474. VIII. JOHN H., b. Oct. 2, 1827; m. Esther J. Ryder.

    IX. IRA, b. Sept. 20, 1826; d. young.

303. **Esek**[7] **Pierce** (Henry[6], Joshua[5], Mial[4], Ephraim[3], Ephraim[2], Michael[1]), b. 1786; m. Jan. 1, 1818, Czarina Brown, b. Aug. 1, 1795; d. Oct. 24, 1841; m. 2nd, Dec. 28, 1843, Betsey Bushee, b. Mar. 20, 1821; d. Dec. 24, 1882. He d. Aug. 4, 1870. Res. Rehoboth, Mass.

CHILDREN.

    I. AMANDA M., b. Dec. 21, 1818; m. Feb. 22, 1844, in Rehoboth, George L. Case; had two children; res. East Providence.

    II. ESEK H., b. June 25, 1830; m. Dec. 22, 1857, Mary C. Pierce, b. Nov. 22, 1820; res. s. p., Rehoboth, Mass.

304. **Nathaniel R.**[7] **Pierce** (Barnard[6], Joshua[5], Mial[4], Ephraim[3], Ephraim[2], Michael[1]), b. Jan. 1, 1792; m. Nov. 2, 1814, Mary West, b. Apr. 22, 1797; d. June 22, 1841; m. 2nd, Mar. 6, 1842, Eliza Adams, b. Oct. 9, 1801. He d. Jan. 14, 1860. Res. Dighton, Mass.

Nathaniel R. Pierce was born in Rehoboth, Bristol county, January 1, 1792. He was the son of Barnard and Mary Pierce, was the second of seven brothers. When quite young he exhibited a talent to till and cultivate the soil, displaying a fondness for raising cattle, horses, sheep, etc., choosing to remain with his parents and work on the farm, while the other brothers chose to learn trades.

In the year 1812, his oldest brother, Jeremiah, was drafted as a soldier to serve in the war, then existing between the United States and England, but his calling was such, that he employed his brother, Nathaniel, to take his place as a substitute. Accordingly, he equipped himself and reported for duty under the command of one Captain Baker, at the fort and barracks of the United States, at the head-quarters in Fair Haven in Bristol county, and served as a soldier till the close of the war, when he received an honorable discharge, and later on, a warrant entitling him to one hundred and sixty acres of the public land of the United States. After the close of the war he was appointed bass-drummer in the State militia. He served in this capacity until exempt from military duty, at the age of forty-five years. He was married to Mary West of Swansey, November 2, 1814, after which, with the assistance of friends, he purchased a farm of sixty acres. On the north it joined his father's farm; on the east it bordered the town line between Rehoboth and Dighton, and Rehoboth and Swansey. He went to house-keeping January 4, 1815, in a small house then standing on his newly-purchased farm. The house was sixteen feet square and contained one room 12 x 16 feet, closet, entry and attic. The door was locked by pulling in the latch-string. The attic was approached by a ladder through a trap-door in the upper floor; the cellar was also entered by a trap-door through the lower floor. The walls of the house were constructed of planks and shingles, minus of lath, plastering, paint or whitewash. Their furniture consisted of one fold-up bedstead and feather bed, one table, four chairs, cradle, wash-tub, two spinning-wheels, one weaver's loom and swift, one cobbler's bench and tools, water and milk pails, two meal tubs, etc. Their crockery-ware consisted of earthen milk pans, pewter platters, plates, mugs, etc.; fire-set, one pair of hand-iron dogs, crane hooks and trammels, shovel and tongs, tea kettle, frying pan and cake griddle ; also a few wooden bowls, etc. In more modern times this would have been considered house-keeping under difficulties. His farm and out-buildings, fences, stone walls, etc., gave evidence of his ability to manage a farm. His fields, orchards and garden showed signs of his handiwork. The horse, cattle, swine and poultry, also gave evidence of care and pride. His practice was to rise early, and never let the horizon get below the sun until his stock was fed and cows milked ; he claimed that one hour in the morning was worth more on a farm than two hours in the afternoon. He was conversant with the Scriptures and belonged to the Christian Church, and was a strict churchgoing man; social with all his neighbors, kind and affectionate to his family, was beloved by all who knew him. His library consisted mostly of the Old and New Testament, Cumming's Spelling book, Daboll's Arithmetic, Thomas' Almanac, etc. He read such newspapers as he could get, and was well informed in general matters of interest; a Democrat in politics. He was a good mathematician, industrous and temperate in his habits, worked his farm in fair weather ; in wet and stormy weather he employed his time on the cobbler's bench, repairing boots, shoes, harness, etc. ; liberal in his religious views, and practiced the Golden Rule, by doing unto others as he would that others should do unto him. April 20, 1815, his first child was born (a daughter), and was named Nancy W. Pierce; she died in 1841. In January, 1817, he moved for a few months across the town line into Dighton, while repairing and enlarging the house was in progress. During this period his second child (a son) was born, March 27, 1817, and was named Mason R. Pierce. After which he moved back to his home, which was then in a more comfortable and enlarged condition. November 18, 1818, a third child (a daughter) was born and was named Choice M. Pierce. June 27, 1823, a fourth child (a daughter) was born and named Lucindy D. Pierce. On October 27, 1826, a fifth child (a son) was born and named Otis M. Pierce ; he died November 12, aged three years and sixteen days. Lucindy D. Pierce, the fourth daughter, died March 3, 1839, aged fifteen years and eight months. In 1839, he built a new and comely house, convenient and adapted to a farmer with a large family. April 20, 1831, a sixth child was born and named Mary W. Pierce. Mary West, his wife; died June 22, 1841, in the forty-fourth year of her age. He was married to his second wife, Eliza Adams, March 6, 1842. Joseph L. Pierce, his first and only child by his second wife, was born February 6, 1843, and died September 25,

35

1843, aged seven months and nineteen days. He, Nathaniel R. Pierce, died January 11, 1860, in the sixty-ninth year of his age. He left a widow and three children living, and was free from debt, and his farm well stocked and in good working order. He was missed by all who knew him, and especially by his family, whom he taught many important maxims of life. He taught his children that to be respected, they must respect themselves. And that they would know the value of a dollar better, by trying to borrow one. His advice was not to spend money until they had it to spend, if they did, it would seem to them that they were working to pay for a dead horse. These and many other maxims left a profitable impression upon their minds, which will not be forgotten by them in this, their generation.

CHILDREN.

I. NANCY W., b. Apr. 25, 1815; m. Jan. 5, 1839, Gideon Horton. She d. Nov. 25, 1839. Ch., Nancy J.; res. San Francisco, Cal.

475. II. MASON R., b. Mar. 27, 1817; m. Betsey S. Hall and Mary R. Bagley.

III. CHOICE M., b. Nov. 18, 1818; m. May 25, 1841, Thomas P. Goff; res. 89 Cohannett street, Taunton, Mass. Ch., Annie Frances Blake, b. Oct. 28, 1842; m. Apr. 24, 1868; Sarahphine Agustia Arnold, b. June 27, 1845; m. Nov. 27, 1873; Emma Jane De Blois, b. Apr. 24, 1849; m. Nov. 26, 1874; Mary Emily Goff, b. Oct. 6, 1852; Thomas Arthur Goff, b. June 30, 1854; Willie Otis Goff, b. Sept. 7, 1858; d. Mar. 31, 1859.

IV. LUCINDA D., b. June 27, 1823; d. Mar. 3, 1839.

V. OTIS M., b. Oct. 27, 1826; d. Nov. 12, 1829.

VI. MARY W., b. Apr. 20, 1831; m. Jan. 3, 1846, George Grant, b. July 11, 1824; res. 50 Davis street, Providence, R. I. Ch., Cordelia A., b. Apr. 20, 1848; d. July 11, 1848; George H., b. Feb. 12, 1850; res. 50 Davis street, Providence, R. I.; Clara E., b. Apr. 12, 1852; m. William E. Whit-

ford; Lilly, b. Sept. 26, 1866; d. Sept. 27,
1866.

VII. JOSEPH L., b. Feb. 6, 1843; d. Sept. 25, 1843.

305. **Jeremiah**[7] **Pierce** (Barnard[6], Joshua[5], Mial[4], Ephraim[3],
Ephraim[2], Michael[1]), b. Aug. 29, 1786; m. Nov. 9, 1806, Candace
Wheeler, b. Sept. 30, 1789; d. Oct. 18, 1882. He d. Mar. 23,
1837. Res. Rehoboth, Mass.

CHILDREN.

476. I. ABRAHAM, b. Feb. 1, 1828; m. Harriett E. Freeman.

II. MARY W., b. Jan. 13, 1809; m. May 15, 1825, Gilbert Carpenter; res. Sioux Falls, Dakota.

III. JEREMIAH, b. June 23, 1811; m. Mar. 21, 1843, Hepsebath Mallette, b. Mar. 2, 1814; d. s. p., Mar. 10, 1882; m. 2nd, Oct. 26, 1882, Laura E. Godfrey, b. Mar. 10, 1822; s. p., res. East Norton, Mass.

IV. CHLOE M., b. Nov. 27, 1810; m. Apr. 14, 1834, Stephen Clarke, b. Aug. 18, 1806; d. Dec. 1, 1857; res. North Attleboro, Mass. Ch., Ann F., b. Nov. 26, 1835; James J. B., b. Dec. 9, 1837.

V. CANDACE, b. July 9, 1813; m. Sept. 29, 1833, Leprelate Capron, b. July 25, 1807; d. Feb. 2, 1883; res. East Attleboro, Mass. Ch., Ellen E., b. Apr. 25, 1835, in Rehoboth, Bristol Co., Mass.; m. Nov. 2, 1857, Charles H. Aldrich; res. Kingston, R. I.; Lydia A., b. June 25, ——; m. Isaac H. Bullard; Henry S., b. Feb. 26, 1840; P. O., Albany, N. Y.; Frank H. P., b. Aug. 16, 1842; P. O., Attleboro, Mass.

VI. CHARLOTTE, b. Nov. 5, 1818; m. Nov. 27, 1840, Horace Carpenter. She d. 1874. Ch., Horace F.; res. Page street, Providence, R. I.

VII. ALBERT, b. Dec. 30, 1821; m. Aug. 28, 1850, Ellen Farlon. Ch., George; res. Paterson, N. J.

VIII. ALFRED, b. Dec. 30, 1821; m. Dec. 6, 1865, Martha
      Williams; res. East Attleboro, Mass.

476½.   IX. GALEN, b. July 18, 1824; m. Phebe A. G. Barney.

    X. SARAH J., b. Apr. 29, 1830; m. Sept. 12, 1850, Ho-
      ratio Biggs, b. Sept. 22, 1819; d. Apr. 16, 1854;
      res. East Attleboro, Mass. Ch., Mary, b. Aug.
      11, 1853; res. 23 Bank street, Attleboro, Mass.

   XI. MARTHA, b. Sept. 15, 1832; m. Sept. 17, 1854, Hale
      S. Luther, b. Apr. 6, 1830; res. Rehoboth, Mass.
      Ch., s. p., Jennie (adopted), b. Oct. 28, 1864;
      m. Oct. 26, 1884, Edward J. Holmes; res. Reho-
      both.

306. **Charles M.**[7] **Pierce** (Barnard[6], Joshua[5], Mial[4], Ephraim[3],
Ephraim[2], Michael[1]), b. Aug. 9, 1799; m. Oct. 27, 1822, Mary P.
Maxfield, b. July 16, 1801; d. Apr. 16, 1863. He d. Aug. 9, 1880.
Res. 75 Elm street, New Bedford, Mass.

Charles M. Pierce was born August 9, 1799, in Rehoboth, Bristol county, Mass. He was the third son of Barnard and Mary
Rounds Pierce of Rehoboth. His father was a farmer and his
first industrial employment was in agriculture on his father's farm.
Not being satisfied with a farmer's life, his ambition led him to
leave his home at an early age, and learn the trade of a mason in
the adjoining, then town of Providence, R. I. At the age of
twenty-one he went to New Bedford, Mass., and continued the
same business. Shortly after he was united in marriage to Mary
P. Maxfield of New Bedford. In a few years he became a large
contractor and builder, and for half a century was identified with
the building operations of the city of his adoption. The private
and prominent public buildings of brick and stone which were
constructed under his supervision, identified him so closely with
the interests of the city, that the words of one of the " city fathers,"
that " Charles M. Pierce nearly built New Bedford," were fully
justified. He was foremost in the making and procuring a patent
on the cement sewerage and well pipes, the former for many years

being the only pipes used for drainage of the city. He was a man of sound, sterling character — his integrity was unquestioned. He was not prominent in politics, but always taking a decided stand, being true to the principle he advocated. A thorough Christian, filling many places of honor and trust in the church of which he was a member for more than half a century. At the ripe old age of four score years he passed from a life filled with usefulness, leaving the priceless legacy — " an unblemished Christian character."

CHILDREN.

477.   I. CHARLES M., b. July 26, 1823; m. Susan A. Durfee and Amanda E. Hill.

II. MARY, b. July 8, 1825; m. June 27, 1849, Robert Allan; res. Newport, R. I. Ch., Charles N. P., b. Apr. 1, 1850; d. June 13, 1869.

III. SUSAN P., b. July 29, 1827; m. June 27, 1849, John P. Nash; res. New Bedford, Mass. She d. Apr. 11, 1850.

IV. RUBY A., b. Dec. 12, 1829; unm.; res. 75 Elm street, New Bedford, Mass.

478.   V. WARREN G., b. Apr. 25, 1832; m. Mary M. Manchester.

VI. HARRIETT S., b. June 24, 1834; m. Oct. 18, 1860, Charles E. Hendrickson, b. Oct. 2, 1834; res. 75 Elm street, New Bedford, Mass. Ch., Nathan P., b. Oct. 7, 1861; Edward D., b. Sept. 24, 1863.

VII. AVERILL H., b. Jan. 6, 1838; d. Mar. 11, 1841.

VIII. EMILY F., b. Jan. 16, 1840; m. June 4, 1865, George W. Howland. She d. Aug. 28, 1884. He d. June 6, 1865; res. New Bedford, Mass.

307. **Barnard[7] Pierce** (Barnard[6], Joshua[5], Mial[4], Ephraim[3], Ephraim[2], Michael[1]), b. Mar. 15, 1797; m. Apr. 3, 1822, Hannah Bliss, b. Mar. 22, 1794; d. Oct. 14, 1837. He d. May 6, 1869. Res. Providence, R. I.

CHILDREN.

479.   I. ASA B., b. Dec. 30, 1826; m. Angenette Hardon.
480.   II. IRA C., b. Sept. 11, 1823; m. Susan H. Soule and
Catherine Burbank.
III. SUSAN H., b. 1834; m. 1883, Linzy J. Wells; res.
429 Ninth street, Brooklyn, N. Y.

308. **Otis N.**[7] **Pierce** (Barnard[6], Joshua[5], Mial[4], Ephraim[3],
Ephraim[2], Michael[1]), b. Feb. 3, 1803; m. Nov. 4, 1828, Susan G.
Cross, b. May 25, 1805; d. May 24, 1865. He d. June 23, 1856.
Res. New Bedford, Mass.

CHILDREN.

I. SARAH A., b. Aug. 14, 1831; m. Aug. 18, 1859, Eli-
jah H. Chisholm, b. Apr. 8, 1824; d. s. p., Dec.
26, 1874.
II. BENJAMIN F., b. Sept. 30, 1833; d. Feb. 23, 1863.
III. ELIZABETH H., b. Apr. 22, 1837; m. Feb. 20, 1867,
Jonathan Handy, b. Jan. 7, 1837. Ch., Frank
G., b. Oct. 24, 1867; d. Aug. 10, 1868; Susan O.,
b. Sept. 16, 1870; Bessie H., b. Oct. 13, 1875.
IV. OTIS N., b. Oct. 28, 1839; m. Nov. 23, 1870, Anna
Thornton, b. Jan. 30, 1846, s. p.; res. 98 Cottage
street, New Bedford, Mass.
V. ELLEN N., b. Feb. 26, 1842; m. Apr. 3, 1866, Timo-
thy D. Cook, Jr., b. Mar. 4, 1838; res. Troy, N.
Y. Ch., Eliza H., b. Aug. 3, 1867; Otis P., b.
Mar. 30, 1874.
481.   VI. ANDREW G., b. Aug. 9, 1829; m. Caroline L. Wil-
liams.

309. **Chace R.**[7] **Pierce** (Barnard[6], Joshua[5], Mial[4], Ephraim[3],
Ephraim[2], Michael[1]), b. May 12, 1805; m. Aug. 28, 1828, Ruth T.
Wilbur, b. Feb. 9, 1810; d. Mar. 5, 1857; m. 2nd, Apr. 25, 1858,
Louisa H. Hammond. He d. June 11, 1886. Res. Taunton,
Mass.

CHILDREN.

I. WARREN L., b. May 29, 1829 ; d. Oct., 1886.

II. WILLIAM F., b. Dec. 5, 1830 ; d. Jan. 8, 1864.

III. OTIS B., b. July 11, 1839.

IV. EVERETT G., b. Nov. 4, 1835.

V. EUGENE, b. Nov. 3, 1838; d. July 3, 1864.

VI. ANDREW W., b. May 17, 1841.

VII. RUTH C., b. Nov. 2, 1849; d. July 20, 1855.

VIII. MABEL C., b. Mar. 16, 1864.

310. **Bradford S.**[7] **Pierce** (Barnard[6], Joshua[5], Mial[4], Ephraim[3], Ephraim[2], Michael[1]), b. Jan. 14, 1808; m. Feb., 1831, Hannah Cross, b. Aug. 21, 1813 ; d. July 11, 1886. He d. Aug. 3, 1878. Res. New Bedford, Mass.

CHILDREN.

482.   I. ERSKINE H., b. Dec. 17, 1849; m. Henrietta M. Fisher.

II. ANN E. K., b. Jan. 5, 1832; m. Jan. 2, 1853, John C. Dexter. She d. 1858; res. New Bedford.

III. MARY C., b. Aug. 14, 1833; m. Nov. 18, 1851, William A. Gray. She d. Oct. 17, 1881; res. New Bedford.

IV. LUTHER C., b. Aug. 5, 1835 ; d. Aug. 6, 1835.

V. DEBORAH C., b. Aug. 30, 1837; m. Apr., 1858, Alfred P. Fletcher. She d. Aug. 29, 1870; res. New Bedford.

VI. GEORGIANA, b. Feb. 17, 1839; m. June 1, 1871, Charles F. Clark; res. New Bedford.

VII. HORATIO B., b. Mar. 23, 1841 ; d. Oct. 8, 1850.

VIII. LATHAM C., b. Mar. 15, 1843 ; unm.; res. 85 North Second street, New Bedford.

IX. ELANORA S., b. Sept. 9, 1845; m. Nov. 28, 1867, Andrew C. Pollard, b. June 6, 1838; res. New Bedford.

483.   X. Crawford S., b. Sept. 10, 1847; m. Elizabeth Delano.
       XI. Emma B., b. Apr. 17, 1853; d. Oct. 17, 1853.
     XII. Carrie E., b. June 15, 1854; d. Oct. 6, 1854.
   XIII. Hannah B., b. Mar. 16, 1857; m. Apr. 7, 1882, Walter R. Myrick; res. New Bedford.

311. **William⁷ Pierce** (Joshua⁶, Joshua⁵, Mial⁴, Ephraim³, Ephraim², Michael¹), b. 1773; m. Mar. 10, 1805, Sarah Thresher. He d. Oct. 24, 1839. Res. Bristol, R. I.

Children.

484.   I. Mason, b. in Bristol; m. Susan Lewis and Anna D. Paine.
485.   II. Alfred, b. in Bristol; m. Alvira Horton.
     III. William H., b. Sept. 27, 1828; m. Eliza Horton; res. Bristol, R. I., and d. May 8, 1885.
    IV. Huldah, b. in Barrington, R. I.; m. Dec. 4, 1831, William H. West; res. Bristol, R. I.
     V. Betsey, b. ——; m. Nov. 1, 1835, James E. Brown.
    VI. Rosanna, b. ——; m. Apr. 18, 1824, Mason Baker; res. Hortonville, Mass.

312. **Joshua⁷ Pierce** (Joshua⁶, Joshua⁵, Mial⁴, Ephraim³, Ephraim², Michael¹), b. Mar. 12, 1796; m. Nov. 7, 1824, Betsey Wheaton, b. Mar. 17, 1804. He d. Nov. 19, 1875. Res. Rehoboth, Mass.

Joshua Pierce was born in Rehoboth, Mass., in 1796, and always resided there, on the land cleared by his father. He was a silver buckle maker, and carried buckles in saddle-bags to Boston. He erected a mill, and at the age of seventeen engaged in the manufacture of clothes-pins, which were packed in saddle-bags and taken to Boston. In 1827 he engaged in the manufacture of plows.

CHILDREN.

486. I. FRANK H., b. May 29, 1848; m. Hannah J. Helton.

II. BETSEY, b. Aug. 31, 1825; d. May 15, 1827.

487. III. JOSHUA, b. Dec. 27, 1826; m. Mary A. Lamb and Mrs. Sarah (Booth) Joslyn.

IV. ELMIRA, b. June 24, 1828; m. Nov. 11, 1860, James Robinson, b. July 4, 1836. Ch., Mary B., b. May 11, 1861; res. Hortonville, Mass.

V. MARY, b. Feb. 15, 1830; m. Sept. 28, 1856, David S. Smith, b. Dec. 27, 1829; res. Dighton, Mass. Ch., David F., b. Oct. 10, 1857; Mary E., b. Apr. 17, 1868.

488. VI. WHEATON, b. June 1, 1832; m. Hannah M. Sollett.

489. VII. CHARLES M., b. Mar. 18, 1834; m. Almira Holley and Harriett Whipple.

VIII. ARDELIA, b. Oct. 7, 1835; m. Dec. 16, 1866, Henry Clark, b. Aug. 5, 1840; d. s. p., Sept. 20, 1883; res. Hortonville, Mass.

490. IX. DANIEL B., b. Mar. 24, 1834; m. Elsia A. Adams.

X. ROSINA B., b. July 7, 1840; m. Nov. 11, 1867, Benjamin F. Joslyn, b. Aug. 29, 1844; d. Mar. 30, 1875; res. Rehoboth, Mass. Ch., Robert M., b. July 5, 1872; Clinton J., b. Feb. 14, 1874; d. July 30, 1874.

491. XI. WILSON D., b. July 22, 1842; m. Alasada Horton.

XII. SARAH B., b. Aug. 28, 1844; d. Apr. 30, 1867.

XIII. ANDREW J., b. July 29, 1851; m. Mar. 1, 1882, Louisa A. Goff; res. Rehoboth, Mass.

313. **Leonard[7] Pierce** (Joshua[6], Joshua[5], Mial[4], Ephraim[3], Ephraim[2], Michael[1]), b. 1776; m. June 28, 1795, Jemima Rounds, d. Sept. 16, 1850. He d. July, 1812. Res. Rehoboth, Mass., and Ellisburgh, N. Y.

CHILDREN.

492. I. MARTIN R., b. May 3, 1807; m. Nancy Bartlett and Emily M. Graham.

36

II. DAU., m. —— Graham, son of Elisha D.; res. Italy, N. Y.

III. DAU., m. —— Norris, a son Martin; res. Grand Traverse, Mich.

IV. WELTHA, b. Sept. 6, 1804; m. Oct. 30, 1823, Prentiss Bebee, b. June 12, 1796; d. Dec. 27, 1849; res. Wahoo, Neb. Ch., Charles C., b. June 6, 1827; res. Chadran, Neb.; Mary I., b. July 11, 1828; res. Inman, Neb.; H. P., b. Feb. 22, 1831; res. Fremont, Neb.; Phebe A., b. Dec. 30, 1833; d. 1858; John, b. Nov. 5, 1839; res. Wayne, Neb.; Martin B., b. July 25, 1842; res. Hooper, Neb.; Charles P., b. May 4, 1845; res. Wahoo, Neb.

V. LEONARD, b. ——; m. Joanna Baker.

VI. POLLY, b. Feb. 12, 1810; m. Nov. 17, 1826, John Bartlett, b. Jan. 17, 1801; d. Nov. 3, 1869; res. West Bloomfield, Wis. Ch., William, b. July 10, 1855; res. West Bloomfield; Lester P., b. Oct. 15, 1827; d. Apr. 3, 1828; Benjamin P., b. June 24, 1829; Nancy L., b. Aug. 30, 1831; d. Dec. 18, 1839; John H., b. Dec. 27, 1834; d. Oct. 20, 1862; Alexander, b. Apr. 13, 1837; res. Oconomowoc, Wis.; Harriet E., b. June 23, 1839; Malisa L., b. Nov. 15, 1843; d. Apr. 15, 1866; Edgar P., b. Mar. 1, 1848; res. Alestr, Dakota; Hannah A., b. Apr. 5, 1842; d. June 24, 1881.

314. **David⁷ Pierce** (Obadiah⁶, David⁵, David⁴, Ephraim³, Ephraim², Michael¹), b. June 1, 1791; m. Sept. 18, 1822, Louisa Chace, b. Jan. 20, 1804; d. Dec. 13, 1854. He d. May 27, 1842. Res. Somerset, Mass.

CHILDREN.

I. LOUISA M., b. Jan. 26, 1824; d. ——.

II. DAVID P., b. Apr. 30, 1823; unm.

III. AMY, b. Mar. 2, 1827; d. ——.

IV. ROBY G., b. Mar. 12, 1829; m. Isaac Brownell; res. Pine street, Fall River, Mass.

V. ABBY, b. Mar. 31, 1831; d. Aug. 24, 1842.

VI. PHEBE, b. Mar. 15, 1835 ; d. ——.

493. VII. OBADIAH, b. Mar. 5, 1833; m. Betsey G. Stilwell.

VIII. MARY F., b. Dec. 7, 1837 ; d. Oct. 28, 1840.

315. **Luther**[7] **Pierce** (Obadiah[6], David[5], David[4], Ephraim[3], Ephraim[2], Michael[1]), b. June 5, 1806; m. Jan. 20, 1833, Lydia Gardner, b. June 26, 1812. He d. Mar. 23, 1879. Res. Warren, R. I.

CHILDREN.

I. LYDIA M., b. Nov. 4, 1835 ; res. Warren, R. I.

II. CHARLES E., b. Mar. 13, 1834; d. Mar. 26, 1836.

III. MARY E., b. Feb. 17, 1838; res. Warren, R. I.

IV. ANNIE E., b. Oct. 12, 1840 ; d. Dec. 25, 1877.

V. HELEN A., b. Jan. 22, 1843; d. Jan. 28, 1880.

VI. LUTHER, b. May 14, 1845; d. Feb. 21, 1871.

VII. EMMA L., b. Sept. 14, 1848; d. Mar. 3, 1873.

VIII. JOSEPH G., b. Oct. 6, 1855; d. Apr. 3, 1876.

316. **James L.**[7] **Pierce** (Obadiah[6], David[5], David[4], Ephraim[3], Ephraim[2], Michael[1]), b. May 3, 1808; m. Jan., 1835, Amanda Mason Chase, b. Jan. 5, 1816. He d. Mar. 29, 1853. Res. 82 Purchase street, New Bedford, Mass.

CHILDREN.

494. I. HURBERT S., b. Apr. 18, 1852 ; m. Annette Blanchard and Jennie Cory Howland.

II. JAMES M., b. June, 1840; m. June, 1887, Mattie Beardsley; res. New Bedford, Mass.

III. AMANDA M., b. Feb. 7, 1837; m. 1866, Capt. William J. Macy, b. Feb. 5, 1827. She d. Oct., 1884. Ch., James F., William C., Robert J., and Louis W.

IV. SUSAN L., b. Mar. 8, 1838; m. Oct. 17, 1860, William S. Mosher, b. Jan., 1834.

V. EMMA E., b. Nov. 30, 1848; unm.; res. New Bedford.

VI. JEANETTE, b. ——; d. May, 1850.

VII. M. JOSEPHINE, b. Dec. 2, 1842; m. June, 1866, Thomas Edwards. Ch., George T., Lillian T., Florence and Violet.

VIII. CLARA V., b. Dec. 23, 1845; m. Sept. 13, 1877, Edward H. Mason, b. Nov., 1840, s. p.

317. **Dexter**[7] **Pierce** (Obadiah[6], David[5], David[4], Ephraim[3], Ephraim[2], Michael[1]), b. Aug. 28, 1814; m. Jan. 8, 1837, Hannah Hathaway, b. Apr. 3, 1819. Res. 7 Pallas street, Providence, R. I.

CHILDREN.

I. ANNA R., b. June 2, 1838; m. Oct. 8, 1863, James P. Walker, b. Feb. 16, 1835; d. Mar. 5, 1877, s. p.; res. 7 Pallas street, Providence, R. I.

495.   II. JAMES M., b. Jan. 28, 1840; m. Catherine R. Warner.

III. MARY A., b. Jan. 23, 1842; d. Sept. 4, 1844.

IV. JOHN F., b. Jan. 18, 1844.

496.   V. DEXTER L., b. Apr. 7, 1846; m. Clara G. Henshaw.

VI. EMMOGENE, b. Nov. 15, 1850; m. Sept. 14, 1870, P. E. Weld; res. 334 East Sixty-ninth street, New York city. Ch., Jennie, d. July 14, 1874.

VII. CLARIBEL, b. Sept. 8, 1854; d. June 4, 1883.

318. **Isaac**[7] **Pierce** (David[6], David[5], David[4], Ephraim[3], Ephraim[2], Michael[1]), b. Feb. 25, 1814; m. Nov. 3, 1839, Deborah E. Purrington, b. Dec. 26, 1818; d. Jan. 27, 1849; m. 2nd, Jan. 17, 1853, Elizabeth A. Adams, b. Jan. 12, 1832. Res. Warren, R. I., and Dighton, Mass.

Isaac Pierce, son of David and Lydia, was born in Somerset, Mass., February 25, 1814, the youngest of thirteen children. He worked with his father on the farm until nineteen years old, when he went to New Bedford and learned the cooper's trade of his brother Clothier. After working at his trade two years he ship ped as cooper on the whale ship " Magnolia," Captain Cornelius Howland. He remained away four years, cruising in the Pacific ocean, and stopping at South America. After his return he worked a short time as journeyman in Fairhaven, Mass.; he then returned to New Bedford and went into business for himself.

November 3, 1839, he married Deborah E. Purrington of Somerset, Mass. January 27, 1849, his wife died, leaving three children: Isaac N., Natalia D., and Corrinne C. In December, 1849, Mr. Pierce left his business and went to California, working at mining three years. After returning home he married, January 17, 1853, Elizabeth A. Adams of Warren, R. I. He then took a position as foreman in a cooper's shop, New Bedford, where he remained four years. In the spring of 1856, he bought a farm in Dighton, Mass., where he lived until his house and buildings were destroyed by fire, December 4, 1885. After the fire Mr. Pierce with his family went to live in Gushee's homestead, where he still lives (June, 1887), about a mile from his farm. By his second marriage Mr. Pierce had five children.

CHILDREN.

497. I. ISAAC N., b. May 27, 1843; m. Harriett E. Barnes and Minnie L. Thomas.

    II. CORRINNE C., b. Dec. 18, 1846; m. Dec. 19, 1869, Dr. T. A. Haley, b. July 24, 1840, s. p.; res. Tuftonboro Centre, N. H.

498. III. CHARLES S., b. June 4, 1856; m. Irene G. Marble.

    IV. ARTHUR C., b. Nov. 15, 1858; res. Drownville, R. I.

    V. CLOTHIER, b. July 14, 1861; m. Sept. 14, 1887; res. Dighton, Mass.

    VI. LIZZIE C., b. Jan. 2, 1864; res. Dighton, Mass.

    VII. WINFIELD S., b. Oct., 6, 1867; d. Apr. 19, 1872.

319. **Clothier[7] Pierce** (David[6], David[5], David[4], Ephraim[3], Ephraim[2], Michael[1]), b. Apr. 15, 1794; m. Dec. 19, 1816, Com-

fort Chace, b. Feb. 13, 1791; d. Feb. 27, 1856. He d. Sept. 24, 1864, while on a visit to Somerset, Mass. Res. Swansey, Mass.

Clothier Pierce was born in Swansey. The first part of his life he was in the coopering business, later he was a merchant; toward the close of his life he bought a farm and managed it for a number of years. In religion, he was a Methodist. In politics, a staunch Republican. He married three other wives after the decease of his first wife, none of whom had any children; the last of his wives is now living in Somerset, Mass. He held several offices in the Methodist Episcopal Church during the largest part of his life, and was very much respected by all who knew him.

CHILDREN.

499. I. LORENZO, b. July 20, 1817; m. Mary R. Gifford.
501. II. JOHN W., b. Mar. 19, 1819; m. Corrinna C. Purrington and Chloe Pierce.
502. III. WILLIAM C., b. July 31, 1821; m. Julia A. Slocum.
        IV. JAMES H., b. 1823. He d. in 1840; was lost at sea by the capsizing of a whale boat.
        V. BARNEY D., b. 1827; d. 1832.
        VI. ANNIE A. S., b. Sept. 2, 1829; m. May, 1859, John C. Pierce of North Dartmouth, Mass.; res. Cincinnati, Ohio. He d. Oct. 7, 1887. (See.)
        VII. JOSEPH C., b. 1833; d. 1835.

320. **John**[7] **Pierce** (David[6], David[5], David[4], Ephraim[3], Ephraim[2], Michael[1]), b. Jan. 11, 1798; m. Jan. 24, 1836, Louisa Lewin. He d. Sept. 12, 1860; was drowned. Res. Somerset, Mass.

CHILDREN.

I. JOHN A., b. May 8, 1837. He was lost on board the United States frigate "Cumberland" in the naval engagement at Hampton Roads, March 8, 1862.

II. ALONZO, b. 1841; was drowned at sea May 9, 1865.

III. FREDERIC C., b. ——; res. Fall River, Mass.

321. **David⁷ Pierce** (David⁶, David⁵, David⁴, Ephraim³, Ephraim², Michael¹), b. Oct. 3, 1799; m. Aug. 26, 1824, Hope Remington, b. Mar. 19, 1802; d. July 21, 1842; m. 2nd, Maria Fuller, b. Aug. 10, 1811; d. Apr. 30, 1878. He d. Feb. 24, 1867. Res. Taunton, Mass.

CHILDREN.

503.   I. THOMAS R., b. Sept. 16, 1827; m. Lucy B. Fuller.

    II. DAVID, b. ——.

    III. LYDIA A., b. ——.

    IV. MARIA J., b. ——.

322. **Lloyd N.⁷ Pierce** (David⁶, David⁵, David⁴, Ephraim³, Ephraim², Michael¹), b. Mar. 5, 1811; m. May 11, 1838, Emeline Sanford, b. Sept. 21, 1816; d. Mar. 24, 1880; m. 2nd, Dighton Terry of Dartmouth, Mass. He d. June 6, 1885. Res. 81 Summer street, New Bedford, Mass.

CHILDREN.

    I. LLOYD D., b. Apr. 3, 1843; unm.; res. 122 Acushnet avenue, New Bedford, Mass.

    II. NANCIE C., b. Aug. 27, 1839; m. Sept. 14, 1859, —— Aiken.

504.   III. LAVELLO I., b. Dec. 14, 1850; m. Addie B. Sherman and Sarah A. Mahan.

323. **Seabury⁷ Pierce** (David⁶, David⁵, David⁴, Ephraim³, Ephraim², Michael¹), b. Mar. 30, 1812; m. Phebe Remington of Tiverton, R. I. He d. Mar. 30, 1873. Res. Barre, Vt.

CHILDREN.

    I. PHEBE J., b. Oct., 1837; d. July 14, 1840.

    II. ALICE G., b. ——.

III. PHEBE J., b. ——.

IV. SEABURY F., b. ——; d. at the Sandwich Islands.

V. ELLEN M., b. ——.

324. **Asa[7] Pierce** (John[6], Jonathan[5], David[4], Ephraim[3], Ephraim[2], Michael[1]), b. June 6, 1795; m. Nov. 22, 1820, Lydia Chase, b. July 28, 1795; d. Feb., 1864. He d. July, 1872. Res. New Bedford, Mass.

CHILDREN.

505.   I. BENJAMIN W., b. Aug. 13, 1821; m. Abbie A. W. Kempton.

506.   II. ASA C., b. Oct. 16, 1823; m. Elizabeth Church and Felecia H. Church.

    III. ANNA, b. Sept. 26, 1822; d. 1840.

507.   IV. CHARLES H., b. Oct. 23, 1835; m. Charlotte Hinckley Smith.

325. **David[7] Pierce** (John[6], Jonathan[5], David[4], Ephraim[3], Ephraim[2], Michael[1]), b. Aug. 11, 1792; m. Sept. 22, 1819, Sarah Butts, b. ——; d. ——; m. 2nd, Sept. 18, 1822, Louise Chase. Res. Swansey, Mass., and Colorado.

CHILDREN.

    I. WILLIAM C., b. Aug. 7, 1822.

    II. STEPHEN, b. June 22, 1820; went to California; n. f. k.; supposed to have died in New Mexico.

    III. SARAH B., b. June, 1822.

    IV. HORATIO, b. Apr., 1824.

    V. LYDIA, b. ——; res. Somerset, Mass.

326. **Hiram[7] Pierce** (John[6], Jonathan[5], David[4], Ephraim[3], Ephraim[2], Michael[1]), b. Mar. 24, 1808; m. Jan. 28, 1836, Mary C. Gibbs, b. ——; d. ——; m. 2nd, Sept. 30, 1840, Mary Slade, b. ——. He d. Mar., 1885. Res. Pottersville, Mass.

CHILDREN.

I. CHARLES W., b. ———.

327. **Rev. John D.**[8] **Pierce** (Henry[7], Benjamin[6], Benjamin[5], Benjamin[4], Benjamin[3], Benjamin[2], Michael[1]), b. Apr. 3, 1845; m. Feb. 13, 1868, Mary B. Grant, b. July 30, 1848. Res. Birmingham, Ala.

Rev. John D. Pierce, son of Henry and Mary Pierce, was born in Laurel, Franklin county, Ind., April 3, 1845. In September, 1861, in the sixteenth year of his age he volunteered in the service of his country, joining the Thirty-seventh Indiana Regiment of Infantry. He served three years and two months, and was honorably discharged. He began the study of medicine with W. F. Green, M. D., Shelbyville, Ind., February 1, 1866. He pursued a regular course, taking his first course of lectures at Rush Medical College, Chicago, and the last course at the Cincinnati College of Medicine and Surgery at Cincinnati, Ohio, where he graduated, February, 1870.

After practicing medicine for five years, he gave up his chosen profession to enter the ministry in the Methodist Episcopal Church, South-east Indiana Conference. He is now in his twelfth year in the ministry, and filling his second appointment to the First Methodist Episcopal Church, Birmingham, Alabama, with success.

CHILDREN.

I. JENNIE B., b. Dec. 29, 1868.

II. JAMES H., b. Aug., 1870; d. Sept., 1870.

III. MARY S., b. Sept., 1871; d. Sept., 1872.

IV. CHARLES L., b. Aug., 1873.

V. EDITH C., b. June 5, 1876.

VI. ROBERT G., b. July 6, 1880.

328. **Seymour L.**[8] **Pierce** (Henry[7], Benjamin[6], Benjamin[5], Benjamin[4], Benjamin[3], Benjamin[2], Michael[1]), b. Jan. 18, 1832; m. Jan. 1, 1868, Mary J. Ayers, b. July 9, 1844. Res. Shelbyville, Ind.

CHILDREN.

I. ALBERT L., b. Jan. 3, 1869; d. Jan. 7, 1871.
II. GEORGE H., b. Feb. 27, 1873.
III. HARRY S., b. Dec. 24, 1877; d. Mar. 7, 1880.

329. **Hon. Robert B. F.**[8] **Pierce** (Henry[7], Benjamin[6], Benjamin[5], Benjamin[4], Benjamin[3], Benjamin[2], Michael[1]), b. Feb. 17, 1843; m. Nov. 28, 1866, Hattie Blair, b. Aug. 29, 1842; d. Oct. 26, 1878; m. 2nd, Dec. 14, 1886, Mrs. Alice M. Van Valkenburg. Res. Crawfordsville and Indianapolis, Ind.

Robert B. F. Pierce, son of Henry and Mary F. Pierce, was born in Laurel, Franklin county, Ind., February, 1843. After attending the common schools where he lived for several years, he entered Wabash College at Crawfordsville, Indiana, in September, 1860, and took a regular collegiate course, graduating with honor in June, 1866. Read law for one year with Benjamin F. Love, at Shelbyville, Ind., and during that time served as city attorney under an appointment by the council. He located at Crawfordsville in 1866, and began the practice of the law. In 1868, 1870 and 1872, he was elected prosecuting attorney for the Eighth Judicial Circuit, composed of Boone, Clinton, Fountain and Montgomery counties. In 1880, he was elected to Congress as a Republican from the eighth district. In 1887, he removed to Indianapolis, where he now lives, and is engaged in the practice of the law, largely railroad business. He was married in 1866 to Miss Hattie Blair of Crawfordsville, by whom he had two children, now living: Lois J., aged nineteen, and Edwin B., aged fifteen. In December, 1887, he was again married to Mrs. Alice Van Valkenburg of Plymouth, Ind.

A Crawfordsville paper has this of Mr. Pierce's second marriage:

The parties to this great social event in northern Indiana are two of the best and most favorably known among the people of the State. In our own town, the bride has occupied a leading position, socially, religiously, and in the hearts of a host of admiring friends, who regret her prospective removal from their midst.

In various parts of the State also, large numbers of persons would testify that few ladies in private life have so many friends as " Mrs. Van Valkenburg-that-was." The Hon. Robert B. F. Pierce, while not personally known to many of our people, is not unknown by reputation, as one of the leading men of the State. He represented the eighth district in the forty-eighth Congress, and is at present a distinguished railroad attorney. The wedding took place in the presence of a few intimate friends. Quiet elegance characterized every thing connected ,with it. The bride wore a robin-egg-blue brocaded satin dress, imported, drapery point lace, and diamond ornaments; the groom wearing the conventional black. The happy pair took the limited express for New York city, whence they are to sail for the Bermudas, for a few weeks' sojourn.

CHILDREN.

I. Lois J., b. Aug. 18, 1868.

II. Edwin B., b. Feb. 5, 1873.

III. Frank H., b. Sept. 29, 1870; d. June, 1882.

330. **Abel F.**[7] **Pierce** (Comfort[6], Comfort[5], John[4], John[3], Ephraim[2], Michael[1]), b. 1800; m. Mar. 26, 1823, Abigail M. Bowen. He d. Nov. 22, 1881. Res. Rehoboth, Mass.

CHILDREN.

508.   I. Allen F., b. Sept. 3, 1824; m. Lydia ——.

509.   II. Chancey B., b. June 21, 1826; m. Ellen M. ——.

331. **John J.**[8] **Pierce** (John J.[7], Benjamin[6], Benjamin[5], Benjamin[4], Benjamin[3], Benjamin[2], Michael[1]), b. ——; m. ——. Res. Waltham, Pontiac Co., Canada.

CHILDREN.

510.   I. John H., b. Feb. 29, 1848; m. Marie E. R. de Belisle.

       II. Lewis, b. ——; d. ——.

   VII. Clarissa M., b. ——; m. —— Smith; res. Ionia, Dixon Co., Neb.

332. **Hon. George W.**[8] **Pierce** (Paul[7], Libbeus[6], Jonathan[5], Benjamin[4], Benjamin[3], Benjamin[2], Michael[1]), b. Nov. 2, 1837; m. June 5, 1862, Delia L. Bartholomew, b. Mar. 4, 1842. Res. Brookings and Castlewood, Dakota.

George W. Pierce is a prominent member of the Methodist Episcopal Church; has been a merchant for twenty-five years; also member of Dakota Legislature. There were three tickets in the field, but he was elected by an overwhelming majority as a Republican.

CHILDREN.

  I. HERBERT E., b. Oct. 15, 1862; d. Jan. 5, 1881.
 II. ETTIE B., b. Mar. 13, 1865.
III. ELENA C., b. Aug. 1, 1867.
 IV. ARTHUR R., b. Aug. 20, 1875.

333. **Hiram M.**[8] **Pierce** (William[7], Libbeus[6], Jonathan[5], Benjamin[4], Benjamin[3], Benjamin[2], Michael[1]), b. Dec. 21, 1841; m. Oct. 1, 1868, Emma C. Hartt, b. July 30, 1847. Res. Montpelier, Vt.

CHILDREN.

  I. JOSEPHINE M., b. May 26, 1873.
 II. LAWRENCE H., b. Oct. 1, 1877.

334. **Sylvester T.**[8] **Pierce** (Hosea H.[7], Howard J.[6], Jonathan[5], Benjamin[4], Benjamin[3], Benjamin[2], Michael[1]), b. Mar. 1, 1826; m. Aug. 1, 1861, Angie Scott, b. June 30, 1841. He d. in Dubuque, Iowa. Res. Anamosa, Iowa.

CHILDREN.

  I. HELLEN H., b. May 28, 1862; m. May 9, 1880, F. L. Coe ; res. Anamosa, Iowa.
 II. JAY L., b. Aug. 7, 1866; res. Anamosa, Iowa, and is engaged in the fancy grocery and fruit business.
III. FANNIE E., b. Apr. 10, 1870; res. Anamosa, Iowa.

335. **Alvin C.**[8] **Pierce** (Hosea H.[7], Howard J.[6], Jonathan[5], Benjamin[4], Benjamin[3], Benjamin[2], Michael[1]), b. May 23, 1829; m. July 4, 1863, Laura J. Arbor, b. Dec. 25, 1847. Res. Bell Branch, Mich.

CHILDREN.

I. IDA I., b. Oct. 12, 1864; m. June 29, 1887.
II. MINNIE J., b. Oct. 11, 1865.
III. NELLIE A., b. Jan. 29, 1869.

336. **Dr. Demetrius Y.**[8] **Pierce** (Hosea H.[7], Howard J.[6], Jonathan[5], Benjamin[4], Benjamin[3], Benjamin[2], Michael[1]), b. Feb. 13, 1833; m. Jan. 19, 1862, Mary J. Powers, b. Jan. 19, 1841. Res. Canton, N. Y.; P. O. box 84.

Dr. Demetrius Ypsilanti Pierce was born in Canton, N. Y., February 13, 1833. He was educated at the public schools of St. Lawrence county, and later studied medicine. For several years he resided in Bell Branch, Mich., where he practiced his profession. Later for twenty years he taught school. At present he is a farmer, residing in Canton, N. Y.

CHILDREN.

I. DOUGLASS O., b. Feb. 27, 1869.
II. GERTRUDE E., b. Apr. 29, 1871.

337. **Gilbert L.**[8] **Pierce** (Hosea H.[7], Howard J.[6], Jonathan[5], Benjamin[4], Benjamin[3], Benjamin[2], Michael[1]), b. June 23, 1835; m. Sept. 18, 1881, Olive Van Klete. Res. Detroit, Mich.

Gilbert L. Pierce was married the day that President Garfield died. His oldest child was born the day that Guiteau was hung.

CHILDREN.

I. ELMA, b. June 30, 1882.

338. **Dr. Hosea**[8] **Pierce** (Hosea H.[7], Howard J.[6], Jonathan[5], Benjamin[4], Benjamin[3], Benjamin[2], Michael[1]), b. Dec. 3, 1837; m.

May 1, 1862, Scelata Stewart, b. Apr. 13, 1838. Farmer, Universalist, " Black Republican." Res. South Potsdam, N. Y.

CHILDREN.

I. BENJAMIN H., b. Oct. 16, 1863.
II. HARRIETTE A., b. Sept. 27, 1864.
III. SUMNER S., b. Nov. 28, 1874.

339. **George P.**[8] **Pierce** (Dennis B.[7], Howard J.[6], Jonathan[5], Benjamin[4], Benjamin[3], Benjamin[2], Michael[1]), b. Mar. 8, 1846 ; m. May 19, 1887, Augusta B. Hoskin, b. June 4, 1864. Res. Yorktown, Dakota.

George P. Pierce, the second son of Dennis B. and wife, was born March 8, 1846; studied at St. Lawrence and Yale Universities; graduated at Columbia College; a teacher in common and high schools; is at present farming and stock raising in Yorktown, Dakota. Is married, and has one son, Servius Rex Pierce.

CHILDREN.

I. SERVIUS REX, b. June 5, 1888.

340. **Perry B.**[8] **Pierce** (Dennis D.[7], Howard J.[6], Ziba[5], Benjamin[4], Benjamin[3], Benjamin[2], Michael[1]), b. Nov. 9, 1840 ; m. Dec. 26, 1872, Susan Walker, b. Oct. 6, 1845. Res. Washington, D. C., 1119 Seventeenth street, N. W.

Perry B. Pierce graduated from Hobart College, and is now Commissioner of Patents, United States Patent Office.

CHILDREN.

I. TALBOT E., b. Aug. 10, 1874.
II. MARY W., b. Aug. 23, 1878.

341. **Leroy E.**[8] **Pierce** (John J.[7], Howard J.[6], Jonathan[5], Benjamin[4], Benjamin[3], Benjamin[2], Michael[1]), b. Aug. 13, 1843; m. Jan. 12, 1868, Alice A. Andrews, b. Sept. 17, 1846. Res. 378 Bagg street, Detroit, Mich.

CHILDREN.

I. EUNICE L., b. Mar. 27, 1873.
II. OLIVE A., b. July 5, 1881.
III. LEWIS J., b. Jan. 23, 1884.

342. **Thomas H.**[8] **Pierce** (Hiram H.[7], Howard J.[6], Jonathan[5], Benjamin[4], Benjamin[3], Benjamin[2], Michael[1]), b. Aug. 15, 1844; m. June 1, 1867, Emma Vaness. Res. Bell Branch, Mich.

CHILDREN.

I. ELMER H., b. Sept. 4, 1867.
II. ETHEL M., b. Nov. 22, 1869.

343. **George M.**[8] **Pierce** (Hiram H.[7], Howard J.[6], Jonathan[5], Benjamin[4], Benjamin[3], Benjamin[2], Michael[1]), b. Apr. 12, 1848; m. Mar. 4, 1870, Agnes D. Harris, b. Nov. 7, 1854. Res. De Witt, Clinton Co., Mich.

CHILDREN.

I. DEXTER G., b. June 7, 1871.
II. HATTIE D., b. May 24, 1874.
III. ADELBERT, b. Mar. 26, 1876.
IV. HIRAM H., b. ——.
V. LUCINA C., b. ——.
VI. ELGA E., b. ——.

344. **John B.**[8] **Pierce** (Hiram H.[7], Howard J.[6], Jonathan[5], Benjamin[4], Benjamin[3], Benjamin[2], Michael[1]), b. June 17, 1851; m. Mar. 1, 1880, Nellie Troup. Res. Dearborn, Wayne Co., Mich.

CHILDREN.

I. CHAUNCEY, b. Nov. 14, 1880.
II. EDITH, b. Aug. 12, 1882.

345. **Hon. Ansel B.**[8] **Pierce** (Artemas A.[7], Howard J.[6], Jonathan[5], Benjamin[4], Benjamin[3], Benjamin[2], Michael[1]), b. Dec. 5,

1835; m. Oct. 11, 1876, Lottie E. Watch, b. Feb. 9, 1847. Res. Bell Branch, Mich.

Hon. Ansel B. Pierce is one of those straightforward, intelligent farmers, whose toil-hardened hand it is a real pleasure to grasp. He has been a hard-working farmer all his life, and the fair competency he is now enjoying is the fruits of his own enterprise, and was built up by honest toil and frugal industry. Mr. Pierce was born at Canton, St. Lawrence county, N. Y. His parents were from New England States. He received his earlier education at the district school, and at the age of fifteen years he entered the St. Lawrence Academy, remaining there four years, and teaching three terms in the meantime. At the age of twenty-one he started out to hew for himself a way in the world. He came west and settled in the township of Redford, Wayne county, where he has resided ever since, teaching school during the winter and working on his farm in the summer season. So thoroughly is his abilities as an educationalist understood and appreciated in the neighborhood in which he lives that he has taught school, within three miles distant from his home, twenty-two winters in succession. Mr. Pierce has held the offices of supervisor, town clerk, school inspector, and justice of the peace, and the capable and intelligent manner in which he has conducted the affairs of each office has won for him golden words of praise from all. Mr. Pierce is nothing if not a painstaking man. He believes in the old maxim, that what is worth doing at all is worth doing well, and consequently in each sphere of life in which he has been engaged he has carried to the duties of the position the most earnest effort and careful and assiduous attention.

An agriculturalist himself, Mr. Pierce has always taken the deepest interest in all things likely to elevate the position of agriculture in the county. He is always willing to give of his time and means to further the farmer's interests. Mr. Pierce was one of the inceptors of the idea of holding a yearly fair in his township, and the manner in which he and a few other public-spirited men worked early and late, without compensation or hope of reward, to make the Redford Agricultural Society a success, has endeared him to the hearts of every farmer in the district. He has been president of the society since its organization. Mr. Pierce is not a politician, that is, not in the opprobrious sense generally implied to the term. He believes in honesty and uprightness, as much in public as in private life, and he has always given emphasis to these ideas in every office he has ever held. As a workingman himself, who has earned his living from his boyhood up by the sweat of his brow, he can appreciate the efforts made by the workingmen to elevate their position in society. In every such effort he wishes them God speed. As to Mr. Pierce's ability to represent the second district in an able manner there can be no doubt. He has been a close student of all the economic questions of the day, and has made a particular study of Michigan affairs. A man of Mr. Pierce's mental calibre, who is capable of serving the people well and faithfully in smaller matters, seldom abuses their confidence when called up higher. He was elected by 266 majority for two years.

CHILDREN.

I. ETHEL E., b. Feb. 9, 1878.

II. PRESTON B., b. Nov. 28, 1880.

346. **George A.**[8] **Pierce** (George A.[7], Waldo[6], Haywood[5], Benjamin[4], Benjamin[3], Benjamin[2], Michael[1]), b. Feb. 16, 1851; m. Dec. 3, 1878, Emma Patten. Res. Frankfort, Maine.

CHILDREN.

I. RUTH, b. Dec. 8, 1879.

II. CHRISTINE, b. July 28, 1882.

III. GEORGE A., b. Jan. 28, 1885.

IV. EARLE S., b. Sept., 1886.

347. **John**[8] **Pierce** (George A.[7], Waldo[6], Haywood[5], Benjamin[4], Benjamin[3], Benjamin[2], Michael[1]), b. Sept. 28, 1852; m. May 9, 1877, Mary H. Ward, b. Aug., 1853; d. June 11, 1885. Res. Frankfort, Maine.

CHILDREN.

I. JOHN R., b. Feb. 11, 1878.

II. LOUISE, b. July 7, 1881.

III. HELEN, b. Mar. 14, 1885.

348. **Mellen C.**[8] **Pierce** (Waldo T.[7], Waldo[6], Haywood[5], Benjamin[4], Benjamin[3], Benjamin[2], Michael[1]), b. Oct. 2, 1847; m. Dec. 25, 1882, Anna C. Hoyford. Res. Bangor, Maine.

38

CHILDREN.

I. HOYFORD, b. Sept. 10, 1883.
II. WALDO, b. Dec. 17, 1884.
III. MELLEN C., b. July 13, 1886.
IV. ADA S., b. Mar. 28, 1888.

349. **Rev. Webster Kelley**[8] **Pierce** (Charles H.[7], Waldo[6], Haywood[5], Benjamin[4], Benjamin[3], Benjamin[2], Michael[1]), b. Dec. 1, 1842; m. June 1, 1875, Etta F. Lincoln, dau. of Capt. F. D. Lincoln, b. July 2, 1853. Res. Brimfield, Mass.

Rev. Webster Kelley Peirce was born in Winterport, Waldo county, Maine, in 1842. He studied for the Christian ministry, and graduated at the Bangor Theological Seminary in 1871, and was installed pastor of the Congregational Church in Brimfield, Mass., April 30, 1874. Prior to this time he had preached or had charge of the Congregational churches at Eastport and Orland, Maine.

CHILDREN.

I. FRANCIS L., b. May 12, 1876.
II. CHARLES L., b. Apr. 11, 1881.

350. **Frank R.**[8] **Pierce** (Merrill[7], Ezra[6], Nehemiah[5], Benjamin[4], Ebenezer[3], Ebenezer[2], Michael[1]), b. July 21, 1858; m. Feb. 5, 1887, Ruby Yeaton, b. ——. Res. California.

CHILDREN.

I. ARTHUR M., b. Nov. 15, 1887.

351. **Fred. N.**[8] **Pierce** (Merrill[7], Ezra[6], Nehemiah[5], Benjamin[4], Ebenezer[3], Ebenezer[2], Michael[1]), b. Aug. 24, 1862; m. at Newfane, Vt., Dec. 27, 1886, Sarah Pierce, b. ——. Res. Putney, Vt.

CHILDREN.

I. ELLA L., b. June 19, 1888.

352. **Ezra F.**[8] **Pierce** (Merrill[7], Ezra[6], Nehemiah[5], Benjamin[4],

Ebenezer[3], Ebenezer[2], Michael[1]), b. Apr. 2, 1863; m. Dec. 23, 1886, Ada Fuller, b. ——. Res. ——.

353. **Frank O.**[8] **Pierce** (Sem[7], Sem[6], Nehemiah[5], Benjamin[4], Ebenezer[3], Ebenezer[2], Michael[1]), b. Feb. 24, 1854; m. Nov. 1, 1874, Ruth E. Cone, b. June 1, 1854. Res. Londonderry, Vt.

CHILDREN.

I. LYLE O., b. Apr. 23, 1877.
II. LOREN R., b. Dec. 26, 1878.

354. **Warren**[8] **Pierce** (Hiram[7], Adolphus[6], Ebenezer[5], Ebenezer[4], Ebenezer[3], Benjamin[2], Michael[1]), b. July 25, 1842; m. June 29, 1864, Helen M. Webb, b. Apr. 4, 1845. Res. Garrettsville, Ohio.

Warren Peirce, the only son of Hiram and Mary Peirce, was born in Windham, Portage county, Ohio, July 25, 1842. He lived on the farm where he was born until 1851, when with his father's family he removed to Garrettsville, in the same county, which place has since been his home.

His education, commenced in the district school in Windham, was continued in the village school for several years, and concluded by a few terms in the W. R. Eclectic Institute at Hiram, now Hiram College. When not in school he was engaged in his father's hardware store, afterward becoming a partner in the business. During his spare moments his attention was turned to the "art preservative," or to becoming a printer. After several years of amateur work he started a small monthly which bore the heading "Garrettsville Monthly *Review*." This was the first paper printed in the town. After continuing the *Review* sixteen months it was discontinued, and after a few months Mr. Pierce started a weekly paper, the Garrettsville *Journal*. After continuing its publication for six years and building up a large circulation and good job printing business, he sold his newspaper interest to his brother-in-law, Charles B. Webb, retaining the job department, which he is still carrying on. He also published a monthly called the *Home Bazar* for two or three years, until the circulation reached several thousand, when he disposed of that also.

At about twenty-one years of age he received the appointment of postmaster of Garrettsville, holding the office continuously for seventeen years. During this time, in addition to his printing business, Mr. Peirce was carrying on the book and stationery business, which he is also still engaged in. He has held numerous public and private offices, being at the present time a member of the council, and of the board of education.

It may be proper to add that Mr. Pierce is an enthusiastic beekeeper, having at present an apiary of about one hundred colonies.

June 29, 1864, he was united in marriage with Helen M. Webb of Freedom, Portage county.

CHILDREN.

I. EDITH M., b. Nov. 3, 1865; m. Apr. 19, 1885, Henry A. Atwood. Their children are: Helen V., born July 9, 1886; Walter P., born March 23, 1888.

II. MYRA F., b. Nov. 20, 1867.

III. NELLIE M., b. June 20, 1874.

IV. ELSIE V., b. Dec. 6, 1882.

355. **Rollin E.**[8] **Pierce** (Ezekiel[7], Solon[6], Ezekiel[5], Ezekiel[4], Thomas[3], Benjamin[2], Michael[1]), b. Dec. 9, 1847; m. Aug. 2, 1871, Lucy E. Sherman, b. May 4, 1849. Res. Sioux City, Iowa.

CHILDREN.

I. GRACE A., b. Jan. 31, 1874.

II. RAY E., b. Mar. 2, 1878.

III. GEORGE EMORY, b. May 15, 1881.

356. **Charles J.**[8] **Pierce** (William B.[7], Solon[6], Ezekiel[5], Ezekiel[4], Thomas[3], Benjamin[2], Michael[1]), b. Dec. 7, 1845; m. July 20,

1871, Mary A. Tutt, b. Jan. 29, 1850; d. Mar. 31, 1879; m. 2nd, Nov. 17, 1886, Minnie M. Elliott, b. Sept. 19, 1859. Res. 61 Henry street, Detroit, Mich.

CHILDREN.

I. WILLIAM J., b. Nov. 26, 1873; d. Jan. 2, 1875.
II. HARRY E., b. Jan. 10, 1876.
III. RICHARD M., b. June 30, 1888.

357. **Elvah S.**[8] **Pierce** (William B.[7], Solon[6], Ezekiel[5], Ezekiel[4], Thomas[3], Benjamin[2], Michael[1]), b. Aug. 11, 1848; m. Jan. 21, 1869, Lucretia J. More, b. Oct. 22, 1849 ; d. Aug. 19, 1883. Res. Eaton Rapids, Mich.

CHILDREN.

I. MINNIE C., b. Oct. 27, 1869.

358. **William H.**[8] **Pierce** (Elvah F.[7], Solon[6], Ezekiel[5], Ezekiel[4], Thomas[3], Benjamin[2], Michael[1]), b. Oct. 22, 1840; m. June 13, 1865, at Fulton, N. Y., Carrie M. Brown, b. Sept. 4, 1840; d. Feb. 20, 1884. Res. Centreville, Mich.

CHILDREN.

I. MAUD S., b. Nov. 5, 1866; d. June 30, 1867.
II. HARRY A., b. Aug. 19, 1869.

359. **Cyrus E.**[8] **Pierce** (Elvah F.[7], Solon[6], Ezekiel[5], Ezekiel[4], Thomas[3], Benjamin[2], Michael[1]), b. Oct. 15, 1845; m. June 6, 1869, Sarah E. Honeywell, b. Mar. 7, 1840. Res. Centreville, Mich., McPherson, Newton and Gove City, Kans.

CHILDREN.

I. ELLA MAY, b. June 13, 1870; d. Mar. 4, 1871.
II. LUELLA J., b. Oct. 30, 1871.
III. BLANCHE D., b. Mar. 4, 1873; d. Jan. 29, 1879.
IV. JENNIE S., b. Nov. 30, 1874; d. Aug. 8, 1875.

V. DELLA A., b. Nov. 28, 1878; d. Mar. 8, 1879.
VI. PEARL E., b. Dec. 15, 1881; d. July 4, 1882.
VII. LEWIS G., b. Apr. 2, 1883.

360. **James P.**[8] **Pierce** (George C.[7], Mason W.[6], Mial[5], Mial[4], Mial[3], John[2], Michael[1]), b. July 7, 1845; m. May 22, 1871, Maria Roward, b. Oct. 12, 1849. Res. Providence, R. I.

CHILDREN.

I. WALTER P., b. May 7, 1872.

361. **Ezra B.**[8] **Pierce** (George C.[7], Mason W.[6], Mial[5], Mial[4], Mial[3], John[2], Michael[1]), b. July 28, 1841; m. Oct. 24, 1864, Sarah E. Potter, b. Sept. 17, 1846. Res. Phœnix, R. I.

CHILDREN.

I. MINNIE A., b. Aug. 20, 1865; m. J. F. Whittemore; res. 426 Benefit street, Providence, R. I.
II. NETTIE M., b. Aug. 15, 1868.
III. ADIN B., b. Apr. 24, 1875.

362. **Charles L. H.**[8] **Pierce** (Henry P.[7], Mason W.[6], Mial[5], Mial[4], Mial[3], John[2], Michael[1]), b. Apr. 4, 1849; m. Dec. 8, 1872, Elizabeth C. Martin, b. Dec. 5, 1851. Res. Baylis, Pike Co., Ill.

CHILDREN.

I. JENNIE A., b. Oct. 8, 1873.
II. GRACE E., b. Nov. 10, 1875.
III. CHARLES F., b. Sept. 9, 1882.
IV. MARIE E., b. Mar. 14, 1884.
V. HERBERT P., b. Jan. 28, 1886.

363. **Henry O.**[8] **Pierce** (Otis[7], Subbinus[6], Elisha[5], Elisha[4], John[3], John[2], Michael[1]), b. Mar. 18, 1830; m. Sept. 18, 1856, Mary A. Thompson, b. Aug. 29, 1833. Res. Agawam, Mass.

CHILDREN.

I. IDA R., b. June 5, 1857; d. Sept. 7, 1858.
II. EVA M., b. Dec. 20, 1858; m. June 25, 1884, Lewis
C. Pomeroy, b. May 13, 1841; res. Agawam, Mass.
Ch., Clarence L., b. Nov. 7, 1885.
III. WALTER H., b. Dec. 23, 1860; m. Jan. 1, 1884.
IV. GEORGE W., b. July 12, 1864.
V. LEROY S., b. Nov. 22, 1867; d. Mar. 16, 1868.
VI. LILLIE A., b. Dec. 27, 1868; m. Jan. 1, 1886, George
Nelson; res. Agawam, Mass.
VII. BYRON J., b. Dec. 4, 1874.

364. **William C.**[8] **Pierce** (Elisha[7], Subbinus[6], Elisha[5], Elisha[4],
John[3], John[2], Michael[1]), b. June 25, 1835; m. June 30, 1862,
Mary Reid, b. Jan. 17, 1840. Res. ——.

CHILDREN.

I. ALBERT R., b. Feb. 4, 1863.
II. ROBERT H., b. Apr. 20, 1870.
III. WILLIAM E., b. July 8, 1872.

365. **Albert E.**[8] **Pierce** (Elisha[7], Subbinus[6], Elisha[5], Elisha[4],
John[3], John[2], Michael[1]), b. July 26, 1837; m. May 9, 1871, Etta
J. Stevens, b. May 11, 1853. Res. 710 Fulton street, Chicago, Ill.

CHILDREN.

I. HANNAH S., b. Mar. 25, 1872.
II. CARRIE M., b. Sept. 20, 1874.
III. FANNIE E., b. Sept., 1876.
IV. CORA B., b. Nov. 17, 1881.

365-1. **Nathan D.**[8] **Pierce** (Daniel[7], Isaac[6], Daniel[5], Clothier[4],
Clothier[3], John[2], Michael[1]), b. Sept. 23, 1837; m. July 18, 1863,
Oraville V. Kingsbury, b. Mar. 14, 1844. Res. Sterling, Neb.

CHILDREN.

I. MILLIE H., b. Aug. 3, 1868.
II. FRANKIE I., b. Aug. 9, 1872.
III. FREDDIE D., b. Dec. 21, 1878.

365-2. **Alfred H.**[8] **Pierce** (Daniel[7], Isaac[6], Daniel[5], Clothier[4], Clothier[3], John[2], Michael[1]), b. Jan. 24, 1841; m. Nov. 26, 1862, Mary ——. Res. Mecosta, Mich.

366. **Isaac W.**[8] **Pierce** (Isaac W.[7], Isaac[6], Daniel[5], Clothier[4], Clothier[3], John[2], Michael[1]), b. Aug. 22, 1839; m. May 4, 1863, Hannah Carlson, b. Jan. 29, 1839; d. Jan. 22, 1864; m. 2nd, Mar. 27, 1864, Elna Carlson, b. Mar. 26, 1842. Res. Glenwood, Sevier Co., Utah.

Isaac W. Pierce is an attorney for several law firms or unions; has been postmaster for ten years and finally resigned ; has been commissioned as justice of the peace and county prosecuting attorney, and held many offices of trust, but lately resigned from some of those honors, as it took too much of his time from business. He is one of the sect commonly called Mormons, and his father was among the first to embrace this doctrine or belief. It is "true that our religious views differ some from the balance of the Christian world, but the great difference is in our being misrepresented by evil and designing men. I am also a minister of the Gospel according to our faith." He went to Utah in the year 1852, and has resided there ever since.

CHILDREN.

511.   I. JOHN M., b. Sept. 19, 1862; m. Christina Hendrickson.
II. PHEBE E., b. Feb. 24, 1865; m. Peter K. Lemmon; res. Glenwood, Utah.
III. ISAAC W., b. Jan. 29, 1867.
IV. MIAL C., b. Sept. 17, 1869.
V. HANNAH A., b. Dec. 8, 1871.

VI. ANN E., b. Feb. 24, 1874.
VII. CORA A., b. Jan. 26, 1876.
VIII. MARY L., b. Jan. 20, 1879.
IX. EVA R., b. Dec. 21, 1881.

367. **James F.**[8] **Pierce** (Mial R[7], Isaac[6], Daniel[5], Clothier[4], Clothier[3], John[2], Michael[1]), b. Feb. 22, 1840; m. Feb., 1860, Myrid Rundell, b. ——. He d. Dec. 19, 1882.

CHILDREN.

I. CHARLES R., b. 1867; res. Milwaukee, Wis.; address, 35 Mitchell Building.
II. CLARA, b. ——; m. —— Moulding; res. Milwaukee, Wis.

368. **Rev. David F.**[8] **Pierce** (Mial R.[7] Isaac[6], Daniel[5], Clothier[4], Clothier[3], John[2], Michael[1]), b. Apr. 26, 1846; m. July 1, 1877, Mary Jardin, b. ——; d. ——; m. 2nd, Addie Phillips. Res. Ilion, N. Y.

CHILDREN.

I. OLIVE, b. May, 1887.

369. **Chester M.**[8] **Pierce** (John T.[7], Isaac[6], David[5], Clothier[4], Clothier[3], John[2], Michael[1]), b. Sept. 27, 1847; m. July 11, 1869, Henrietta Alvord, b. Jan. 15, 1850. Res. Plainfield, Wis.

CHILDREN.

I. WILLIAM A., b. Mar. 10, 1873.
II. LOUISA A., b. Feb. 6, 1876.
III. CLARENCE A., b. Mar. 5, 1881.

370. **George W.**[8] **Pierce** (John T.[7], Isaac[6], David[5], Clothier[4], Clothier[3], John[2], Michael[1]), b. Apr. 28, 1837; m. Mar. 16, 1862, Elizabeth Horkner, b. Jan. 17, 1844. Res. Plainfield, Wis.

39

CHILDREN.

I. ROSA M., b. Mar. 8, 1863.
II. GEORGE T., b. May 20, 1865; d. Sept. 19, 1867.
III. JOHN T., b. Sept. 21, 1868.
IV. WARD D., b. Sept. 11, 1870; d. Apr. 22, 1872.
V. GUY N., b. July 25, 1872.
VI. ALVIN E., b. Nov. 2, 1874.
VII. URUSULA J., b. Jan. 14, 1877.
VIII. EVA V., b. June 13, 1879.
IX. MARY R., b. Sept. 24, 1882.

371. **Lewis H.**[8] **Pierce** (John T.[7], Isaac[6], David[5], Clothier[4], Clothier[3], John[2], Michael[1]), b. July 27, 1845; m. Aug. 18, 1866, Helen Owen, b. Mar. 1, 1849. Res. Plainfield, Wis.

CHILDREN.

I. ALFRED N., b. June 12, 1867.
II. MINNIE A., b. Oct. 20, 1869.
III. CORNELIUS U., b. Apr. 8, 1872.
IV. SYBLE M., b. Sept. 7, 1874.
V. LEMUEL A., b. Feb. 25, 1877.
VI. GUY A., b. Feb. 28, 1879.
VII. MALCRUM S., b. Jan. 11, 1881.
VIII. ARTHUR, b. Dec. 21, 1883; d. June 17, 1884.

372. **James G.**[8] **Pierce** (Israel[7], John[6], Azrikim[5], Samuel[4], Azrikim[3], Ephraim[2], Michael[1]), b. July, 1823; m. ——, Mrs. Sarah Harvey. Res. 12 Norman street, Boston, Mass.

CHILDREN.

I. ALICE P., b. 1857.
II. GILMORE, b. 1867.

373. **Joseph K.**[8] **Pierce** (Israel[7], John[6], Azrikim[5], Samuel[4], Azrikim[3], Ephraim[2], Michael[1]), b. May 1, 1832; m. Nov. 20, 1858,

Margaret Phipps, b. Nov. 18, 1835; d. Oct. 12, 1864. Res. Holliston, Mass.

CHILDREN.

I. MARY A., b. Oct. 21, 1861.

374. **Alfred J.**[8] **Pierce** (Israel[7], John[6], Azrikim[5], Samuel[4], Azrikim[3], Ephraim[2], Michael[1]), b. Nov. 23, 1833; m. June 1, 1866, Susan A. Fuller; d. s. p.; m. 2nd, June 23, 1881, Anna F. Paine, s. p. Res. 48 Point street, Providence, R. I. He enlisted February 27, 1862; discharged at Hilton Head, S. C., March 17, 1865, Third Rhode Island, Battery M.

375. **Ferdinand I.**[8] **Pierce** (Israel[7], John[6], Azrikim[5], Samuel[4], Azrikim[3], Ephraim[2], Michael[1]), b. Sept. 18, 1840; m. Anna Scott, b. ——; d. ——; m. 2nd, Annie ——. Res. 31 Causeway street, Boston, Mass.

CHILDREN.

I. MARION R., b. Nov. 28, 1864.

II. LEON E., b. July 4, 1870.

376. **John E.**[8] **Pierce** (John[7], John[6], Azrikim[5], Samuel[4], Azrikim[3], Ephraim[2], Michael[1]), b. Aug. 24, 1840; m. Sept. 22, 1864, Hope T. Pierce. Res. Clinton, Mass.

CHILDREN.

I. EMMA G., b. Feb. 20, 1866.

II. FRANK D., b. Apr. 11, 1867.

III. MARTHA N., b. Feb. 20, 1876; d. June 25, 1878.

377. **Charles S.**[8] **Pierce** (Washington[7], John[6], Azrikim[5], Samuel[4], Azrikim[3], Ephraim[2], Michael[1]), b. Nov. 23, 1839; m. Sept. 25, 1861, Betsey Maria Mason, b. June 20, 1841. Res. North Attleboro, Mass.

CHILDREN.

I. ARTHUR B., b. Jan. 18, 1863.

II. BENJAMIN E., b. June 17, 1865.

III. Edson W., b. Nov. 27, 1868.
IV. Lewis M., b. July 15, 1871
V. Charles A., b. Oct. 15, 1873.
VI. Marion A., b. Feb. 9, 1876.

378. **Charles H.[8] Pierce** (Squier[7], Squier[6], Azrikim[5], Samuel[4], Azrikim[3], Ephraim[2], Michael[1]), b. Mar. 8, 1813; m. Sept. 9, 1832, Mary R. M. Dawson, b. June 8, 1814; d. Feb. 20, 1881; m. 2nd, 1882, ——. Res. 253 Pine street, Providence, R. I.

Charles H. Peirce was born at South Rehoboth, Mass., March 8, 1813; parents moved to Providence, R. I., April, 1817; commenced going to school quite young; when about ten years of age went to work in finishing department of a bleachery; went to school about six months of the year until about fourteen years of age, then worked steadily until seventeen years of age, but in the meantime went to evening schools in the winter seasons. His father being a mechanic, he wanted him to learn a carpenter's trade; went and worked about three years; then was married to a lady about one year younger than himself. In the start, mutually agreed to try to get a home of their own. They accomplished it in ten years and had it all paid for; did not work much at carpentering after marriage; but was employed at the same establishment as before he went to learn a trade. Then went to a print works in 1836; had charge of finishing department. In 1845, went to print works in Fall River, Mass., and soon after was clerk and paymaster until 1853; then the same owners wanted him to be paymaster at the large mill of theirs in Providence; was there about ten years; after that time was paymaster of another mill of theirs until 1873. Since that time, he has not done much, only to look after what little he had saved during all the time from the first start. He was in Fall River the most part of two years settling up a concern that had failed; that was just previous to 1881. He lost some by trying to help others; but has enough to carry him through by living prudently. In February, 1881, his wife wanted to go and call on a friend of theirs about four miles from the city; on their return their horse became frightened by a dog; the horse shied and backed, but did not run; his wife became excited and jumped from the carriage; he supposed she could not be much injured, for the carriage was quite low. It was some time before he could prevail upon her to enter the carriage again. Then she seemed very much distressed, and found it difficult to breathe. He hurried home, and soon had a doctor, who lived in the house with them. The doctor seemed to relieve her some, so she became quiet. He went to put his horse in the stable in the yard; before he had the horse unharnessed, they called and said she was dying; before he got into the house she was gone. They lived together happily for forty-eight years. This was a very sorrowful and sad time for him.

CHILDREN.

    I. THOMAS D., b. Aug. 30, 1834; d. July 22, 1837.

    II. MARY E. D., b. Feb. 7, 1837; m. Sept. 3, 1861, William A. Cushman; d. s. p., June 20, 1862.

512.   III. CHARLES E. D., b. June 4, 1841; m. Eliza L. Metcalf.

379. **Dexter H.**[8] **Pierce** (Squier[7], Squier[6], Azrikim[5], Samuel[4], Azrikim[3], Ephraim[2], Michael[1]), b. Dec. 4, 1818; m. Oct. 13, 1840, Corisander M. Hunt, b. Sept. 12, 1822. He d. Sept. 17, 1853. Res. Providence, R. I.

CHILDREN.

    I. ELIZABETH, b. 1841; m. May 1, 1859, Andrew J Dexter; m. 2nd, Nov. 2, 1872, Jacob L. Myers, b. Feb. 24, 1830; res. Corner Corey street, Providence, R. I. Ch., Mary L., b. June, 1863; d. Nov., 1863.

    II. CORA, b. Nov. 2, 1848; m. Nov. 22, 1863, George M. Sawin, b. 1845; m. 2nd, June 13, 1878, Newton A. Wing, b. Mar. 13, 1853; res. 349 West Twenty-ninth street, New York city. Ch., George E., b. July 28, 1870.

380. **Samuel L.**[8] **Pierce** (Samuel[7], Squier[6], Azrikim[5], Samuel[4], Azrikim[3], Ephraim[2], Michael[1]), b. Apr. 13, 1828; m. Aug.

10, 1851, Ann E. C. Horton; b. Mar. 26, 1832. Res. South Rehoboth, Mass.

CHILDREN.

I. NELLIE L., b. Nov. 16, 1866.

381. **Alonzo**[8] **Pierce** (Nathan[7], Joseph[6], Azrikim[5], Samuel[4], Azrikim[3], Ephraim[2], Michael[1]), b. July 27, 1812; m. Mar. 4, 1835, Emeline Belknap, b. May 3, 1815; d. June 20, 1867. Res. Warsaw, N. Y.

Alonzo Pierce, son of Nathan Pierce, was born July 27, 1812, at Warsaw, N. Y. On arriving at manhood he engaged at teaching school for a while; afterward he selected the occupation of a farmer in his native township. In 1870, he sold his farm and removed to the village of Warsaw, where he now resides. While his life has been an uneventful one, he has always occupied the position of a good and valuable citizen, and has long been considered by his friends and neighbors as a consistent, Christian man. His children now alive are Beriah N. Pierce of Indianapolis, Ind., and Melford A. Pierce of Corning, Iowa.

CHILDREN.

513. I. BERIAH N., b. Nov. 18, 1835 ; m. Kate M. Cormac.
      II. MELFORD J., b. Sept. 17, 1840; d. Apr. 17, 1841.
514. III. MELFORD A., b. Sept. 17, 1842; m. Hattie Dwight.

382. **Allan**[8] **Pierce** (Nathan[7], Joseph[6], Azrikim[5], Samuel[4], Azrikim[3], Ephraim[2], Michael[1]), b. Dec. 4, 1825; m. Mar. 10, 1855, Sarah Whaley, b. May 14, 1836. He d. Sept. 4, 1869. Res. Warsaw, N. Y.

CHILDREN.

515. I. FRED. H., b. July 8, 1858; m. Ada N. Stearns.
516. II. ELMER E., b. Oct. 6, 1861; m. Florence Bacon.
      III. CELIA E., b. Aug. 14, 1856 ; d. Sept. 11, 1859.

383. **Dexter T.**[8] **Pierce** (Joseph[7], Joseph[6], Azrikim[5], Samuel[4], Azrikim[3], Ephraim[2], Michael[1]), b. July 30, 1833; m. Dec. 14, 1876, Emma F. Bryant, b. Sept. 27, 1852. Res. Dighton, Mass.

CHILDREN.

I. HOWARD D., b. Jan. 5, 1880.

II. EDITH V., b. Sept. 5, 1884.

384. **Isaac N.**[8] **Pierce** (Azrikim[7], Joseph[6], Azrikim[5], Samuel[4], Azrikim[3], Ephraim[2], Michael[1]), b. Oct. 26, 1818; m. Mar., 1837, Mary Earl, b. ——. He d. July 24, 1852. Res. Rehoboth, Mass.

CHILDREN.

I. ISAAC M.; res. Taunton, Mass.

385. **Andrew T.**[8] **Pierce** (Azrikim[7], Joseph[6], Azrikim[5], Samuel[4], Azrikim[3], Ephraim[2], Michael[1]), b. Mar. 26, 1827; m. Dec. 11, 1842, Eliza A. Marble, b. Aug. 10, 1824; d. Sept. 3, 1851; m. 2nd, Mar. 20, 1852, Mary E. Seeklisea, b. June 15, 1832. Res. Hortonville, Mass.

CHILDREN.

517.   I. ANDREW J., b. Feb. 1, 1844; m. Elizabeth S. Winman.

518.   II. NATHAN F., b. July 12, 1846; m. Hattie E. Whitmarsh.

III. GEORGE P., b. Nov. 6, 1848; m. Nov. 24, 1873, Cora B. Hines, b. Feb. 7, 1855; d. s. p.; m. 2nd, Jan. 31, 1883, Mary J. Boardman, b. Nov. 20, 1858, s. p.; res. Lonsdale, R. I.

519.   IV. WILLIAM H., b. Apr. 7, 1858; m. Martha S. Douglass.

520.   V. SILAS A., b. Jan. 27, 1860; m. Sarah F. Baker.

386. **William L.**[8] **Pierce** (Azrikim[7], Joseph[6], Azrikim[5], Samuel[4], Azrikim[3], Ephraim[2], Michael[1]), b. 1837; m. Apr. 11, 1861, Sarah E. Wright, b. ——. He d. Aug. 11, 1885.

CHILDREN.

I. JOHN W., b. Oct. 10, 1862; res. Hortonville, Mass.
II. CHARLES L., b. July 12, 1867.

387. **Frederick P.**[8] **Pierce** (Daniel[7], Joseph[6], Azrikim[5], Samuel[4], Azrikim[3], Ephraim[2], Michael[1]), b. Dec. 20, 1820; m. July 2, 1843, Mary O. Bentley, b. Dec. 11, 1819; d. June 7, 1851; m. 2nd, July 4, 1852, Olivia Ovitt, b. Apr. 21, 1818; d. Apr. 15, 1876; m. 3rd, May 14, 1877, Mrs. M. W. Stewart, b. Feb. 8, 1830. Res. 310 Wickenden street, Providence, R. I.

Frederick P. Pierce, oldest son of Daniel, was born in Rehoboth, December 20, 1820. He remained at home until eighteen years of age, when he went to Providence, R. I., to learn the business of a carriage manufacturer. For the past thirty-five years, was senior partner of the firm of F. P. Pierce & Co. His present partner is his youngest brother, Dexter D. Pierce. No other carriage manufacturers in the State do a business larger than is done by this firm. He has been three times married: first, to Mary Bentley, in July, 1843; second, to Olivia Ovitt, in July, 1852; third, to Mrs. Mary W. Stewart, in May, 1877, with whom he is now living. He has four children living. He has been for many years a member of the Methodist Episcopal Church, in which for thirty years he has held the office either of steward or trustee, sometimes both. In politics he is a Prohibitionist, fighting the rum saloon.

CHILDREN.

     I. EMMA E., b. Aug. 29, 1845 ; d. Sept. 7, 1861.
521.   II. WILLIAM F., b. May 25, 1848; m. Eliza J. Brown.
    III. MARY P., b. Nov. 7, 1850; m. May 26, 1870, Arthur
       M. Baker, b. May 11, 1848; res. Providence, R.
       I. Ch., Walter M., b. Oct. 24, 1876.
522. IV. CHARLES L., b. Apr. 28, 1853; m. Nellie R. Newcomb.
     V. MARTHA O., b. Jan. 12, 1859; m. Nov. 26, 1879,
       Browning B. Nickerson, b. June 21, 1857. Ch.,
       Elmer D., b. Nov. 8, 1884; res. Providence, R. I.

388. **Lloyd B.**[8] **Pierce** (Daniel[7], Joseph[6], Azrikim[5], Samuel[4], Azrikim[3], Ephraim[2], Michael[1]), b. Nov. 19, 1835; m. May 23, 1859, Mary J. Briggs, b. June 4, 1840. Res. Rehoboth, Mass.

CHILDREN.

I. ARTHUR W., b. Feb. 6, 1861.
II. NELLIE M., b. Oct. 15, 1863; m. Oct. 16, 1884, Herbert L. Horton; res. South Rehoboth, Mass.
III. BYRON C., b. Mar. 2, 1866.
IV. DE FORREST D., b. Apr. 6, 1870.
V. EDGAR, b. Aug. 8, 1874.
VI. ERASTUS, b. Nov. 28, 1876; d. Feb. 19, 1877.
VII. ERBEN, b. June 25, 1878; d. Aug. 15, 1878.
VIII. ERNEST, b. June 25, 1878; d. Aug. 25, 1878.
IX. TWINS, b. Sept. 17, 1879; both d. young.
X. JOSEPHINE E., b. Dec. 27, 1882; d. Sept. 10, 1883.

389. **J. Henry**[8] **Pierce** (Israel[7], Abraham[6], Azrikim[5], Samuel[4], Azrikim[3], Ephraim[2], Michael[1]), b. July 29, 1844; m. Sept. 12, 1867, Louisa Schoenacher, b. June 14, 1850. Res. Chippewa, Ont.

He is in the hardware business in Chippewa, and is the successor of his father. He is highly respected by his fellow citizens.

CHILDREN.

I. WILLIAM H., b. June 22, 1868.
II. LOUISA S., b. Apr. 29, 1870.
III. LOUIS T., b. June 27, 1872.
IV. CORNELIA C., b. June 23, 1874.
V. CHARLES E., b. Aug. 2, 1879.
VI. JESSE A., b. July 10, 1882.
VII. PEARL A., b. June 8, 1885.

390. **James A.**[8] **Pierce** (Dennis W.[7], Abraham[6], Azrikim[5], Samuel[4], Azrikim[3], Ephraim[2], Michael[1]), b. Feb. 16, 1836; m. Nov. 24, 1857, Mary A. Holcomb, b. Apr. 27, 1836. Res. South Bristol, N. Y.

40

CHILDREN.

I. EMMA, b. Dec. 30, 1858; d. July 2, 1861.
II. C. AUSTIN, b. July 3, 1863.
III. JULIA A., b. July 20, 1866.

391. **Jared C.**[8] **Pierce** (Jared[7], Jared[6], Azrikim[5], Benjamin[4] Azrikim[3], Ephraim[2], Michael[1]), b. Nov. 14, 1826; m. Mar. 9, 1848, Adaline Vaughn, b. Nov., 1830; d. Feb. 17, 1855; m. 2nd, Oct. 26, 1856, Sarah M. Stewart, b. ——; d. Mar. 17, 1864; m. 3rd, Dec. 25, 1870, Mrs. Esther Powers. Res. Lacon, Ill.

CHILDREN.

I. GEORGE L., b. 1850; res. Asherville, Mitchell Co., Kans.
II. ADALINE M., b. Sept. 4, 1856; m. Edwin Haddon of Henry, Ill.
III. ELLA E., b. Feb. 17, 1860.
IV. LUCY, b. May, 1862; m. William Mier.

392. **Gustavus D.**[8] **Pierce** (Jefferson[7], Jared[6], Azrikim[5], Benjamin[4], Azrikim[3], Ephraim[2], Michael[1]), b. Dec. 28, 1840; m. Nov. 7, 1872, Mattie A. Jenkins, b. 1849. Res. Hastings and Benkleman, Neb.

Gustavus D. Pierce was born in Michigan. He took a full academical course of study, and afterward graduated at the Ann Arbor Law School, in April, 1871. He served in the army during the war, three years and seven months; was not wounded; was in the Ninth Army Corps, Army of the Potomac, and in most of its principal battles; first Bull Run, and at Appomattox. He enlisted as a private, and mustered out at the close of the war, first lieutenant. He came west in the spring of 1872, located at Hastings, Neb., and practiced law there about ten years. He was city attorney two terms. He located in Benkleman, Neb., in the spring of 1886, and is now county attorney.

CHILDREN.

I. BURTON, b. Feb. 28, 1873.
II. JENNIE L., b. May, 1878.
III. CLIFFORD, b. June, 1882.

393. **Freeman A.**[8] **Pierce** (Jefferson[7], Jared[6], Azrikim[5], Benjamin[4], Azrikim[3], Ephraim[2], Michael[1]), b. Aug. 5, 1845; m. Sept. 23, 1866, Henrietta L. Pruden, b. June 25, 1848. Res. 209 Cedar street, North Lansing, Mich.

CHILDREN.

I. MINERVA, b. Jan. 7, 1868.
II. OLIVE, b. Sept. 16, 1869.
III. FRANK A., b. June 3, 1871; d. June 7, 1872.
IV. LOUIE, b. Dec. 5, 1872.
V. IRA B., b. Mar. 3, 1878.
VI. ERNEST B., b. Jan. 7, 1881.
VII. J. ROY, b. May 7, 1886.
VIII. BESSIE L., b. Apr. 28, 1888.

393-1. **Samuel**[8] **Pierce** (Nathaniel[7], Samuel[6], Joshua[5], Isaac[4], Azrikim[3], Ephraim[2], Michael[1]), b. Feb. 13, 1792; m. Nov. 8, 1815, Dorcas Doane, b. Jan. 1, 1798; d. Apr. 28, 1881. He d. Mar. 28, 1876. Res. South Orrington, Me.

CHILDREN.

523.   I. ASHMAN, b. Mar. 13, 1816; m. Elizabeth Mansfield.
II. MARY A., b. May 3, 1818; m. Oct. 13, 1844, Eben H. Gibbs, b. Jan. 27, 1817; d. June 21, 1877; res. Bangor, Me. Ch., Asham P., b. Aug. 3, 1845; d. Apr. 17, 1846; Louise P., b. Mar. 8, 1847; m. Warren Nickerson; res. Orrington, Me.; Ella A., b. Dec. 24, 1848; m. James O. Parsons; Hortense, b. Feb. 27, 1851; d. Aug. 17, 1854; John P., b. Mar. 12, 1853; Rosena E., b. Mar. 15, 1855.

III. SALLY N. F., b. Aug. 15, 1822; d. Apr. 25, 1823.
IV. SAMUEL W., b. Nov. 27, 1823; d. July 17, 1843.
524. V. JOHN W., b. Oct. 16, 1825; m. Lucinda Forbes.
VI. DORCAS R., b. Mar. 14, 1828; d. Apr. 19, 1855.
VII. SARAH W., b. Nov. 10, 1831; d. Oct. 15, 1856.
VIII. CORRILLOR N., b. Nov. 11, 1834; m. Dec. 24, 1857
William Y. Dillingham, b. Nov. 23, 1832. Ch.,
Lizzie K., b. Dec. 5, 1859; Fuller A. P., b. Feb.
23, 1861; res. South Orrington, Me.
IX. CALEB F., b. June 21, 1837; d. Mar. 17, 1861.

393-2. **Capt. Isaac**[8] **Pierce** (Nathaniel[7], Samuel[6], Joshua[5], Isaac[4], Azrikim[3], Ephraim[2], Michael[1]), b. June 22, 1778; m. May 31, 1800, Rachel Fowler. He d. Sept., 1863. Res. Bangor, Me. Captain Isaac Pierce was born in Orrington in 1778. He followed the sea for a few years. He was captain in the militia, and was severely wounded in the battle of Hampden in September, 1814. The bullet flattened against the bone to the size and shape of a coin. This piece of lead is now in existence. He was very tall and straight; black haired. A very exemplary man indeed, and a successful farmer.

CHILDREN.

525. I. NATHANIEL, b. Jan. 30, 1802; m. Dorcas Godfrey,
Calista Sheppard and Mary H. Young.
526. II. SIMEON, b. Oct. 22, 1803; m. Sarah D. Dean.
III. DORCAS, b. Nov. 13, 1805; m. Dec. 25, 1828, Alan-
son Rackliff.
IV. LYDIA, b. ——; d. young.
V. DORINDA, b. ——; m. Oct. 22, 1829, Sewall Abbott.
VI. SYRENA, b. ——; m. Oct. 20, 1829, John G. Smith.
VII. ISAAC, b. ——; m. June 12, 1836, Mary Dean; m.
2nd, July 16, 1840, Abigail Dean.
VIII. ELIJAH S., b. ——; m. Dec. 15, 1840, Rachel Brown;
res. Hermon, Me.
IX. ELIZA K., b. ——; m. Ephraim K. Dean.

X. ABIGAIL F., b. ——; m. June 20, 1829, John Lakin.

XI. JOSEPH D., b. ——; d. young.

XII. ALANSON H., b. ——; d. young.

393–3. **Nathaniel**[8] **Pierce** (Nathaniel[7], Samuel[6], Joshua[5], Isaac[4], Azrikim[3], Ephraim[2], Michael[1]), b. Jan. 26, 1783; m. June 3, 1806, Ruth Ryder, b. Sept., 1784; d. Sept., 1826; m. 2nd, Mrs. Billington Smith, b. 1794; d. Aug. 13, 1880. He d. Dec. 27, 1870. Res. South Orrington, Me.

Nathaniel Pierce went to sea in his earlier days, but soon returned to Orrington, Me., and settled on lands of his father, built a large, square house; married Ruth Ryder of Chatham, Cape Cod, dau. of Harding Ryder. Issue, David, Harding, Charles, George, Allen, Nathaniel, Lucinda, Rosella. Married the second time the widow Smith. Issue, Jane and Rebecca R.; the latter being a fine scholar and poetess. He lived a steady, sober life, industrious and frugal, and accumulated a good property; a respected citizen, positive as a Democrat, clear-headed, of a highly nervous temperament. He was in the battle of Hampden, and I believe was not the last to run. With axe in hand he cleared his acres, rearing and supporting a large family; never in debt, always enough to wear and eat. Many a time on his knee has he told of bears he used to capture, the deer he shot, in his earlier years, of the hardships he encountered and successfully came off conqueror, as he was a man of iron with sharp, keen eye. "I see him now, though eighty-six years old, as straight as a young tree, with ruddy cheeks and snow-white hair, always a boy to the last."

CHILDREN.

527.   I. ALLEN B., b. Apr., 1, 1821; m. Charlotte Osgood.

528.   II. GEORGE F., b. June 6, 1820; m. Lucy A. Eldridge.

529.   III. HARDING R., b. Feb. 7, 1807; m. Abbie R. Smith.

530.   IV. DAVID, b. Sept. 13, 1808; m. Mary Crockett.

      V. LUCINDA, b. Apr. 19, 1811 ; m. May 29, 1841, David E. Flanders, b. June 4, 1815. She d. Feb. 12, 1884; res. East Hampden, Me. Ch., Herbert G.

P., b. ——; m. Livonia S. Swan; res. East Hampden, Me.; Albert A. P., b. Nov. 15, 1846; m. Augusta B. Ferguson.

Lucinda Pierce was a woman of medium height well-rounded figure, a clear complexion, large, intelligent black eyes, and hair straight, and black as the raven's wing, of very superior intellect and quick discernment; possessing extreme will power and tenacity. Early in life she lost her mother, when the care of a large family devolved upon her and her only sister. In her youth she joined the Methodist Church, and through a long life she shone as a zealous Christian, an upright woman, pure in life and its duties, and by her life set an example worthy to imitate; living in the hopes of a glorious immortality. Peace to her name, as she sleeps in the tomb, the marble above her bearing her last request. *Gone but not lost.* She married David E. Flanders, who was born in Alton, N. H., of good, old revolutionary stock, whose grandsire served under Washington, and who participated at the battle of White Plains, and whose father was a first cousin to Daniel Webster. Issue: Herbert George Pierce Flanders and Albert Allen Pierce Flanders.

VI. CHARLES M., b. July 12, 1814; m. Mary Atwell; res. East Hampden, Me. Ch., Kate and Rose.

Charles M. Pierce was a man of medium height, black curling hair, and very handsome. He, too, followed the sea, and through much energy soon arrived to be master of fine vessels; he went on foreign voyages, and bringing at one time Irish emigrants to this country. A skillful navigator, and who succeeded well in his profession. He married Mary Atwell of Orono, Me., and had two daughters, Kate and Rose.

VII. ROSILLA, b. May 13, 1817; m. Captain Elias Boynton, b. 1815; d. Jan. 13, 1881; res. Bangor, Me. Ch., Emma R., b. Nov. 24, 1843; m. Captain George Cummings; Alice C., b. Feb. 4, 1857; Cecelia.

531. VIII. NATHANIEL H., b. Sept. 30, 1822; m. Sarah Bartlett.

IX. JANE, b. ——; m. Capt. George Atwood, s. p.

X. OLIVE, b. ——; m. Melville Trask; res. California.

XI. REBECCA, b. ——; unm.

393–4. **Capt. David**[8] **Pierce** (Nathaniel[7], Samuel[6], Joshua[5], Isaac[4], Azrikim[3], Ephraim[2], Michael[1]), b. Sept. 7, 1788; m. 1817, Polly Smith, b. May 30, 1795; d. Sept. 14, 1878. He d. Apr. 30, 1866. Res. South Orrington, Me.

Captain David Pierce was born in Orrington, Me., in 1788. He early took to the sea, and for many years run a packet between Bangor, Me., and Boston. This was before a steamer was seen on those waters. He amassed a fortune in that way, and was considered a shrewd, keen, business man, and he had the confidence of all. The captain stood six feet, and was as straight as an arrow. His word was as good as his bond, and he was respected by all who knew him. He died at Orrington.

CHILDREN.

532. I. DAVID W., b. Jan. 29, 1817; m. Deborah B. Snow.

533. II. HORACE W., b. July 11, 1828; m. Elizabeth J. Bartlett.

III. MARY A., b. Sept. 8, 1827; m. Nov. 15, 1844, Jabez H. Snow, b. June 1, 1818; d. Feb., 1877, lost at sea; res. Bucksport, Me. Ch., Albert H., b. Sept. 23, 1845; lost at sea, Feb., 1873; Mary L., b. Nov. 29, 1847; Walter, b. Mar. 7, 1856; res. St. Paul, Minn.; Horace E., b. May 5, 1860; Kittie McE., b. Nov. 30, 1866; d. Nov. 11, 1883.

IV. WILLIAM M., b. ——; d. Nov. 3, 1843.

534. V. REUBEN S., b. Oct. 10, 1821; m. Mercy T. Eldridge.
VI. EDWIN R., b. Apr. 12, 1831; d. Oct. 18, 1854.

393-5. **Joshua Y.**[8] **Pierce** (Samuel[7], Samuel[6], Joshua[5], Isaac[4], Azrikim[3], Ephraim[2], Michael[1]), b. July 3, 1802; m. Apr. 30, 1828, Jemima Mason. Res. Welfleet, Mass.

CHILDREN.

I. SALLY M., b. Aug. 4, 1829.
II. EPHRAIM G., b. Nov. 6, 1830; m. Elizabeth ——.
III. SAMUEL M., b. Aug. 7, 1828.
IV. BENJAMIN W., b. Nov. 19, 1836.
V. JOSHUA, b. July 23, 1840.

393-6. **Thomas N.**[8] **Pierce** (Samuel[7], Samuel[6], Joshua[5], Isaac[4], Azrikim[3], Ephraim[2], Michael[1]), b. Sept. 11, 1804; m. July 1, 1828; Lucy Fuller, b. 1806; d. Apr. 23, 1839; m. 2nd, June 2, 1846, Emeline Field. He d. Mar. 20, 1876. Res. Walpole,Mass.

CHILDREN.

I. BENJAMIN H., b. Mar. 6, 1829; m. Mar. 1, 1849, Anna M. Nevin. He d. Apr. 8, 1886, in Brooklyn, N. Y.
535. II. THOMAS G., b. Sept. 12, 1832 ; m. Mary A. Fales.
III. WILLIAM H., b. May 5, 1839; m. July 25, 1864, Sarah Grover.
IV. CHARLES A., b. ——.   VI. ANNIE N., b. ——.
V. ABBIE F., b. ——.   VII. MARY L., b. ——.

393-8. **Samuel**[8] **Pierce** (David[7], Samuel[6], Joshua[5], Isaac[4], Azrikim[3], Ephraim[2], Michael[1]), b. Sept. 3, 1795; m. Oct. 19, 1820, Nancy Young, b. Aug. 31, 1794; d. Sept. 21, 1872. He d. Mar. 3, 1841. Res. Welfleet, Mass.

CHILDREN.

536. I. ELISHA, b. Jan. 18, 1826; m. Mary S. Gallup.

II. JAMES S., b. Oct. 7, 1828; d. unm., Sept. 25, 1853, in Portsmouth, N. H.

III. ANNA Y., b. July 3, 1841; m. June 10, 1860, James J. Doane; res. Provincetown, Mass.

IV. DAVID Y., b. Oct. 23, 1823; m. Nov. 24, 1847, Hannah P. Ryder; m. 2nd, Jan. 11, 1866, Matilda A. Kemp; res. Welfleet, Mass.

V. SAMUEL W., b. Apr. 28, 1831; m. Oct. 14, 1850, Elizabeth W. Jacobs; res. Boylston station, Boston, Mass.

VI. WASHINGTON F., b. Mar. 19, 1835; m. Feb. 7, 1858, Mary A. Daniels; res. Welfleet, Mass.

393–9. **David**[8] **Pierce, Jr.** (David[7], Samuel[6], Joshua[5], Isaac[4], Azrikim[3], Ephraim[2], Michael[1]), b. Aug. 10, 1804; m. Aug. 21, 1825, Ruth F. King. He d. May 15, 1870. Res. Welfleet, Mass.

CHILDREN.

I. BETSEY A., b. Nov. 23, 1825; m. May 5, 1844, Samuel Roberts; m. 2nd, July 22, 1878, William C. Atwood; res. Welfleet, Mass.

II. RUTH P., b. Sept. 11, 1828; m. Nov. 15, 1846, Stillman Brown, Jr.; res. Swampscott, Mass.

III. SARAH C., b. Oct. 23, 1830; m. Nov. 26, 1848, John Barnes; res. Swampscott, Mass.

IV. ELKANA H., b. June 1, 1833; d. Sept. 8, 1833.

V. CLARISSA A., b. Sept. 9, 1834; m. July 1, 1855, Freeman Myrick; res. Welfleet, Mass.

VI. DAVID H., b. Mar. 1, 1837; m. May 30, 1861, Mary A. Myrick; res. Welfleet, Mass.

VII. ANN M., b. June 18, 1842; d. Dec. 29, 1860.

VIII. ZEPHANIAH H., b. Aug. 24, 1844; m. Apr. 3, 1871, Angie E. Newcomb, b. Oct. 6, 1849; res. Welfleet, Mass.

41

393–10. **Zephaniah**[8] **Pierce** (Solomon[7], Samuel[6], Joshua[5], Isaac[4], Azrikim[3], Ephraim[2], Michael[1]), b. July 24, 1801; m. Sept. 11, 1825, Sally Lauman. Res. Welfleet and Daxbury, Mass.

CHILDREN.

   I. EDWARD J. L., b. July 21, 1831; d. June 4, 1835.
  II. MARY J., b. Sept. 7, 1834; m. Aug. 27, 1852, James F. Graham; res. Welfleet, Mass.
 III. EDWARD J., b. June 4, 1836; d. June 4, 1838.
 IV. HOPE, b. ——; m. June 10, 1863, Joseph Graham, res. Welfleet, Mass.

393–11. **Oliver B.**[8] **Pierce** (Joshua[7], Samuel[6], Joshua[5], Isaac[4], Azrikim[2], Ephraim[2], Michael[1]), b. June 6, 1818; m. June 20, 1838, Mary A. Chipman, b. Aug. 11, 1818. He d. Oct. 7, 1883. Res. Welfleet, Mass.

CHILDREN.

    I. ELEANOR M., b. May 2, 1839; m. July 28, 1858, Francis C. Cates, b. Nov. 25, 1836; res. Welfleet, Mass. Ch., Francis S., b. June 27, 1859; d. Mar. 20, 1862; Frances E., b. June 17, 1878.
    II. CHARLES C., b. Aug. 24, 1844; d. Oct. 30, 1869.
537. III. BARNABAS H., b. Dec. 4, 1846; m. Lilla C. Newcomb.
538. IV. JAMES O., b. Sept. 23, 1849; m. Ella A. Cobb.

393–12. **Reuben**[8] **Pierce** (Thomas[7], Joshua[6], Joshua[5], Isaac[4], Azrikim[3], Ephraim[2], Michael[1]), b. 1804; m. 1826, Ruth Rich, b. 1803; d. 1865. He d. Sept. 15, 1844. Res. Princetown, Mass.

Early Sunday, September 15, 1844, occurred a disaster, that in mystery and agonizing detail paralyzed the community of Welfleet and vicinity. It was the loss of the "Commerce's" crew, and included among others, Reuben Pierce, aged 39 years. The sailors were all young men of the vicinity and highly respected, being members of the South Truro Methodist Episcopal Church. Sunday, September 15, was noticed as a beautiful day; the first charming touches of early autumn brightened the landscape; the valley lay in soft sunshine; the brown hills were lovely in repose, and the blue waters of the bay rested in quiet splendor. Such a day-picture Hubart must have realized when he wrote:

> Sweet day, so pure, so calm, so bright,
> The bridal of the earth and sky.

The "Commerce" was well known along the shore, and Monday morning, when the boats went out of the harbor they saw her lying at anchor in the roadstead off Truro shore, as is customary in fine weather. They supposed she had come in during the night, and as there was no boat, that the crew had gone home. Later in the morning, and the boat not having been seen, and none of the crew moving, one of the neighbors went to Captain Lombard's house; his wife said her husband had not been at home, and no news from them since they went away.

The vessel was then boarded. She was found carefully secured, but no signs of life. The crew had evidently left the boat. It soon transpired that the "Commerce" had been seen by several persons during Sunday, but lying abreast a high hill near the captain's house, she had not been observed by the friends. General search was made, and near noon the boat was found ashore seven miles or more south with a plank started from her bilge. More than this was never known; all else was conjecture. How a crew of ten active men, many, if not all, expert swimmers, could all be drowned in smooth water, so near the shore, probably having the usual complement of oars, thwarts, etc., how the leak occurred, and why it could not have been stopped, with many other queries, will ever remain a mystery. With Captain Lombard was found his watch, stopped at four thirty, showing the time of the accident. From time to time, during three weeks, from Barnstable to Beaver Point, a distance of thirty miles, all were found, received the sacred rites of home burial, with solemn services, and were committed dust to dust.

> Upon the breezy headland, the fishermen's graves they made;
> Where, over the daisies and clover bells, the oaken branches swayed;
> Above them the birds were singing in the cloudless skies of fall,
> And under the bank the billows were chanting their ceaseless call;
> For the foaming line was curving along the hollow shore,
> Where the same old waves were breaking, that they would ride no more.

CHILDREN.

I. JEREMIAH R., b. 1833. Ch., Willie H., b. 1861;
George N., b. 1864; Lucy E., b. 1866; Benjamin
G., b. 1869; res. Princetown, Mass.

II. MARTHA R., b. 1835.

III. JERUSHA, b. 1837 ; m. —— Dyer.

539. IV. REUBEN, b. 1838; m. Rebecca R. Smith.

V. JOSHUA R., b. 1839.

VI. BENJAMIN Y., b. 1841. Ch., Maggie E. and Fannie M.

VII. ABIGAIL Y., b. 1843; m. —— Lovett.

393–13. **Nathaniel**[8] **Pierce** (Thomas[7], Joshua[6], Joshua[5],
Isaac[4], Azrikim[3], Ephraim[2], Michael[1]), b. Sept. 14, 1791; m. Dec.
13, 1814, Martha Rich, b. Aug. 25, 1792; d. Dec. 20, 1879. He
d. Nov. 27, 1873. Res. Welfleet, Mass.

CHILDREN.

540. I. NEHEMIAH R., b. Nov. 11, 1823; m. Anna M. Allen.

II. JOANNA C., b. Nov. 13, 1828; m. July 26, 1846; m.
Oliver P. Thompson, b. May 20, 1823 ; res. Holliston, Mass., s. p.

541. III. HENRY R., b. July 30, 1817; m. Sophia Mayo.

IV. RUTH, b. Sept. 24, 1819; m. Oct. 9, 1847, Justin
Williams; d. ——; res. Truro.

V. NATHANIEL, b. Sept. 15, 1821 ; d. ——.

VI. JOSHUA R., b. Apr. 11, 1832.

393–14. **Israel**[8] **Pierce** (William[7], Joshua[6], Joshua[5], Isaac[4],
Azrikim[3], Ephraim[2], Michael[1]), b. ——; m. Deborah Rich. Res.
Welfleet, Mass.

CHILDREN.

542. I. ISRAEL R., b. ——; m. Bethiah Sweet and Rachel
Holbrook.

394. **Charles E.**[8] **Pierce** (Joseph S.[7], Nathan[6], Nathaniel[5],
Joseph[4], Azrikim[3], Ephraim[2], Michael[1]), b. May 26, 1851 ; m. Feb.

20, 1876, Ida A. Blackmer, b. Dec. 27, 1856. Res. Rehoboth, Mass.

CHILDREN.

   I. CLARENCE E., b. Sept. 10, 1877; d. Jan. 4, 1878.
  II. LENA O., b. Sept. 27, 1879.
 III. LULU A., b. June 14, 1882.
 IV. MABLE A., b. Jan. 4, 1884.

395. **George Childs**[8] **Pierce** (Childs[7], Nathan[6], Nathaniel[5], Joseph[4], Azrikim[3], Ephraim[2], Michael[1]), b. Jan. 17, 1842; m. July 3, 1865, Sarah H. Torme, b. Mar. 17, 1843. Res. 395 Broad street, Providence, R. I.

CHILDREN.

  I. CORA M., b. June 30, 1866.
 II. GEORGE A., b. Sept. 11, 1874; d. July 7, 1881.

396. **Edgar B.**[8] **Pierce** (Barnard W.[7], Aaron[6], Nathaniel[5], Joseph[4], Azrikim[3], Ephraim[2], Michael[1]), b. Oct. 10, 1842; m. Nov., 1865, Eliza R. Smith, b. Feb. 13, 1840; d. Sept. 8, 1866; m. 2nd, June 23, 1873, Mrs. Gertrude M. Smith, b. May 8, 1842. Res. New London, Conn.

CHILDREN.

   I. WINNIFRED, b. Mar. 30, 1874.
  II. GEORGIANA, b. Dec. 29, 1877.
 III. COURTTONE B., b. Mar. 4, 1885.

397. **Nelson M.**[8] **Pierce** (Jonathan W.[7], Aaron[6], Nathaniel[5], Joseph[4], Azrikim[3], Ephraim[2], Michael[1]), b. ——; m. Eliza Geers, b. ——; d. ——. He d. ——. Res. New London, Conn. Has a son and a daughter.

398. **Rufus W.**[8] **Pierce** (Jonathan W.[7], Aaron[6], Nathaniel[5], Joseph[4], Azrikim[3], Ephraim[2], Michael[1]), b. May 31, 1829; m. June 5, 1853, Sarah E. Kingsley, b. June 26, 1834. Res. Westerly, R. I.

CHILDREN.

I. SARAH, b. Aug. 31, 1854; d. Aug. 31, 1854.

II. MARY, b. Aug. 31, 1854; d. Sept. 22, 1854.

III. ADRIAN R., b. Oct. 22, 1856; m. Nov. 18, 1882, Sarah C. Austin. Ch., Grace E., b. Dec. 9, 1885; Adrian R., b. Aug. 21, 1887; res. Westerly, R. I.

IV. ADRIANA, b. Oct. 22, 1856; m. June 9, 1877, Horace M. Frazier. She d. July 3, 1886; res. Westerly, R. I. Ch., Edith, b. Oct. 13, 1881; Adriana, b. July 4, 1884; d. July 5, 1884.

399. **Horace Lanphere**[8] **Pierce** (Jonathan W.[7], Aaron[6], Nathaniel[5], Joseph[4], Azrikim[3], Ephraim[2], Michael[1]), b. Mar. 25, 1835; m. Nov. 27, 1856, Harriett Elizabeth Horton, b. May 3, 1836, in Plainfield, Conn. Res. Westerly, R. I.

CHILDREN.

543.   I. FREDERICK L., b. Oct. 8, 1857; m. Annie L. Austin.

400. **Leonard A.**[8] **Pierce** (James C.[7], Aaron[6], Nathaniel[5], Joseph[4], Azrikim[3], Ephraim[2], Michael[1]), b. Nov. 19, 1851; m. Jan. 21, 1875, Alida P. Stetson, b. June 4, 1855. Res. Taunton, Mass.

CHILDREN.

I. FREDERICK J., b. Sept. 23, 1876.

II. CORA L., b. July 18, 1878.

III. EDITH M., b. Nov. 7, 1879.

IV. FLORENCE M., b. Apr. 7, 1882.

V. RALPH S., b. Oct. 19, 1883; d. May 29, 1886.

VI. SOPHIA B., b. Oct. 4, 1885.

401. **Alonzo E.**[8] **Pierce** (Stephen[7], Asahel[6], Stephen[5], Joseph[4], Azrikim[3], Ephraim[2], Michael[1]), b. July 12, 1838; m. Sept. 20, 1865, Nellie A. White, b. Feb. 1, 1842. Res. Pawtucket, R. I.

CHILDREN.

I. ALTON L., b. Sept. 8, 1867.

II. HOWARD E., b. Nov. 26, 1870.
III. IRENE A., b. Dec. 19, 1875.

402. **Orion A.**[8] **Pierce** (Stephen[7], Asahel[6], Stephen[5], Joseph[4], Azrikim[3], Ephraim[2], Michael[1]), b. Aug. 28, 1840; m. Dec. 29, 1864, Sophia H. Orcutt, b. Oct. 9, 1843. Res. Ashland, Neb.

CHILDREN.

I. LOUISA A., b. Dec. 16, 1872.

403. **Alonzo D.**[8] **Pierce** (Alonzo[7], Asahel[6], Stephen[5], Joseph[4], Azrikim[3], Ephraim[2], Michael[1]), b. Sept. 17, 1825; m. May 9, 1854, Dulcena Nelson, b. July 30, 1829. Res. East Calais, Vt.

CHILDREN.

I. HARLEY M., b. Mar. 24, 1855; unm.; teacher, Dean Academy, Franklin, Mass.
II. INEZ M., b. June 27, 1857.

404. **Henry C.**[8] **Pierce** (Alonzo[7], Asahel[6], Stephen[5], Joseph[4], Azrikim[3], Ephraim[2], Michael[1]), b. Dec. 7, 1829; m. June 10, 1858, Margarett Riley, b. May 2, 1833. He d. June 29, 1877. Res. 45 Sycamore street, New Bedford, Mass.

CHILDREN.

I. HENRY C., b. May 16, 1859; m. Sept. 1, 1884; res. Escanaba, Mich.
II. ANNIE E., b. Apr. 8, 1862; res. New Bedford, Mass.
III. EMERANCY, b. Apr. 8, 1862; m. Feb. 16, 1882, Fred. A. Shockley; res. New Bedford, Mass.
IV. MARGARETTA, b. May 21, 1864; m. May 14, 1884, Alfred C. Whitney; res. New Bedford, Mass.
V. THIRZA D., b. May 21, 1864.·
VI. CHRISTINA, b. Apr. 15, 1871.

405. **Walter L.**[8] **Pierce** (Zepheniah G.[7], Noah[6], Stephen[5],

Joseph[4], Azrikim[3], Ephraim[2], Michael[1]), b. Oct. 20, 1855; m. Nov. 1, 1875, Dianna F. Tubas, b. Sept. 22, 1855. Res. East Calais, Vt.

CHILDREN.

I. MAUDE L., b. Aug. 5, 1877.
II. CHARLES T., b. Dec. 25, 1879.

406. **Marcus**[8] **Pierce** (Horatio[7], Noah[6], Stephen[5], Joseph[4], Azrikim[3], Ephraim[2], Michael[1]), b. July 26, 1830; m. May 1, 1855, Eliza A. Ames, b. Dec. 21, 1828. Res. Bridgewater, Mass.

CHILDREN.

I. MARCIA E., b. June 5, 1858.
II. MARCUS A., b. Feb. 11, 1860.

407. **William H.**[8] **Pierce** (Lewis D. B.[7], Noah[6], Noah[5], Joseph[4], Azrikim[3], Ephraim[2], Michael[1]), b. Feb. 2, 1840; m. Oct. 1, 1864, Ruth P. Martin, b. Nov. 22, 1846. Res. 28 Sherburne street, Providence, R. I.

CHILDREN.

I. FLORENCE B., b. Aug. 11, 1868.
II. BESSIE B., b. May 24, 1870.
III. CLARA T., b. Mar. 7, 1872.

408. **Mark A.**[8] **Pierce** (Anthony[7], Appollus[6], Noah[5], Joseph[4], Azrikim[3], Ephraim[2], Michael[1]), b. Apr. 18, 1841; m. Sept. 7, 1865, Mary E. Howland, b. Aug. 16, 1846. Res. 564 Eddy street, Providence, R. I.

CHILDREN.

I. CLARENCE A., b. Aug. 11, 1867.
II. FRANK H., b. Dec. 11, 1869.
III. EDWIN F. b. Feb. 14, 1872.
IV. LILLIAN.E., b. Nov. 22, 1885.

409. **Franklin**[8] **Pierce** (Anthony[7], Appollus[6], Noah[5], Joseph[4], Azrikim[3], Ephraim[2], Michael[1]), b. Mar. 5, 1849; m. Apr. 16, 1868,

Mary A. Smith, b. Mar. 4, 1846. Res. 564 Eddy street, Providence, R. I.

CHILDREN.

I. EARNEST A., b. Apr. 16, 1871; d. May, 1871.

II. GRACE L., b. Nov. 10, 1873; d. Oct. 23, 1880.

III. EDITH A., b. Jan. 23, 1876.

IV. HOWARD P., b. Mar. 24, 1881; d. Aug. 31, 1883.

410. **Phillip**[8] **Pierce** (Phillip[7], Wheeler[6], Wheeler[5], Mial[4], Ephraim[3], Ephraim[2], Michael[1]), b. Feb. 12, 1784; m. Mar. 29, 1807, Chloe Horton, b. June 11, 1785; d. Nov. 22, 1860. He d. June 9, 1866. Res. Savoy, Mass.

CHILDREN.

544.   I. STILLMAN, b. Apr. 12, 1808; m. Eunice Staples.

II. NANCY, b. Apr. 8, 1810; d. 1813.

III. ALMIRA, b. June 29, 1812; d. Oct. 26, 1838.

IV. PHILLIP, b. June 5, 1815; d. Oct. 21, 1857.

V. CHRISTOPHER, b. July 14, 1817; d. Nov. 11, 1835.

546.   VI. GEORGE F., b. Feb. 3, 1820; m. Anna Cain.

VII. CHLOE A., b. July 6, 1822; m. Mar. 19, 1840, Ashley Meekins.

VIII. EZRA, b. Dec. 6, 1824; d. 1828.

547.   IX. JARVIS, b. Oct. 18, 1826; m. Achsah M. Macomber.

411. **Capt. Ezra**[8] **Pierce** (Nathan[7], Nathan[6], Nathan[5], Mial[4], Ephraim[3], Ephraim[2], Michael[1]), b. 1806; m. 1827, Eliza Gurley, b. 1802; d. 1873. He d. Feb. 21, 1886. Res. Manchester, N. Y. Captain Ezra Pierce died in Manchester, N. Y., February 21, 1886, aged 79 years, 7 months and 4 days. The deceased was born in that town in 1806, and had always lived in the same house in which he died. In his death another of the land-marks, connecting the past with the present generation, has been removed. It is a notable fact that not one of the residents of the town who were early associated with him in public affairs are now living. He had held various offices in the town, being elected its supervisor in 1838, 1839, 1840, 1841, 1842, and again in 1853, 1856,

42

1857, and was justice of the peace for twenty-two years. In 1847, he was elected a Member of Assembly from Ontario county. In the several duties to which his fellow-citizens called him, he evinced sound judgment, tact and industry. In 1827, the deceased was married to Eliza Gurley, with whom he lived for many years, and whose death occurred in 1873. He leaves five children to mourn their loss, viz.: E. Jane, Clara G., Mrs. Burrus Osgood, and Mrs. Harvey N. Short, residing in Manchester, and Mrs. A. D. Arnold, residing in Kansas. The funeral services, which were appropriately and impressively conducted by Rev. M. V. Willson, were held at his home, where his relatives and friends assembled to pay him their last tribute of respect, and sympathize with his afflicted family. His kindly smiles and cordial welcome, his warm hand-grasp and cheering words are no more for us only in memory. But in the family he will be so sadly missed. His wise counsel was always cheerfully given; his parental affections, his loving care and faithful example will never be forgotten.

CHILDREN.

I. SARAH, b. Nov. 28, 1828; m. Nov. 15, 1849, Burrus Osgood, b. June 27, 1818; res. Manchester. Ch., Carlos P., b. Mar. 11, 1857; m. Jan. 22, 1889, Daisy D. Allen; Addie E., b. Jan. 6, 1859; m. Oct. 9, 1878, Joseph F. Clark; res. Manchester.

II. E. JANE, b. July 27, 1830; res. Manchester.

III. ELLEN A., b. Oct. 3, 1834; m. Sept. 18, 1861, Alanson D. Arnold, b. Feb. 27, 1834; res. Longford, Kansas. Ch., Lewis, b. Oct. 29, 1863; Hattie, b. Mar. 30, 1865; Willis, b. Oct. 7, 1867; Allen, b. Oct. 21, 1868; Robert, b. Oct. 19, 1870; Ralph, b. Apr. 21, 1873; Ray, b. Oct. 18, 1877.

IV. CAROLINE, b. Dec. 1, 1838; m. Jan. 13, 1876, Harvey N. Short, b. June 8, 1833; res. Clifton Spa, N. Y. Ch., E. Pierce, b. July 16, 1877; Stanley, b. Feb. 22, 1883.

V. CLARA G., b. Mar. 13, 1841; res. Manchester.

412. **Nathan**[8] **Pierce** (Nathan[7], Nathan[6], Nathan[5], Mial[4], Ephraim[3], Ephraim[2], Michael[1]), b. Sept. 27, 1790, in Cheshire, Mass.; m. in Manchester, N. Y., May 10, 1817, Amy Aldrich, b. May 9, 1787; d. Feb. 28, 1861. He d. Mar. 30, 1862, in Marengo, Mich.

CHILDREN.

  I. MOWRY A., b. Apr. 13, 1818; res. Manchester, Mich.
548. II. RUSSELL, b. July 11, 1828; m. Louise Hoskins.
  III. EMILY, b. Sept. 4, 1819.
549. IV. HIRAM, b. Oct. 7, 1821; m. Catherine Cassady.
  V. ADALINE, b. Sept. 26, 1823; m. —— Graham; res. Marengo, Mich.
  VI. PHEBE S., b. Nov. 5, 1825; m. Mar. 26, 1854, Peter Mulvany, b. Mar. 12, 1823, s. p. She d. Aug. 10, 1878.
  VII. AMY A., b. Oct. 27, 1830; m. Jan. 1, 1857, Peter G. Hoag, b. Feb. 20, 1829, s. p.; res. Otsego, Mich.

413. **Earl D.**[8] **Pierce** (Earl D.[7], Benjamin[6], Nathan[5], Mial[4], Ephraim[3], Ephraim[2], Michael[1]), b. Sept. 23, 1818; m. Feb. 8, 1848, Sarah B. Mauran, b. June 22, 1826. He d. Jan. 20, 1883. Res. 258 Benefit street, Providence, R. I.

CHILDREN.

  I. EDWARD D., b. Feb. 24, 1849; m. Oct. 29, 1885, Mabell V. Seagrave, b. Aug. 12, 1864, s. p.; res. 43 South Main street, Providence, R. I.
  II. LYDIA, b. Oct. 27, 1854; m. Aug., 1876, John W. Mitchell, b. Apr. 6, 1848; res. Providence, R. I. Ch., John P., b. June 4, 1880.
  III. JESSICA, b. Sept. 30, 1860.

414. **Otis**[8] **Pierce** (Pardon[7], Pardon[6], Nathan[5], Mial[4], Ephraim[3], Ephraim[2], Michael[1]), b. Oct. 4, 1796; m. in Norway, N. Y., Polly Giles, b. ——; d. Jan. 1, 1833. He d. Nov. 5, 1875. Res. Newport, N. Y.

CHILDREN.

550. 　I. AMBROSE G., b. May 8, 1820; m. Charlotte Washburn.

551. 　II. JAMES P., b. Apr. 12, 1825; m. Lucy A. Jones.

　　III. ESTHER, b. Apr. 7, 1818; m. Mar. 5, 1840, Benjamin N. Hinman, b. Mar. 10, 1813; d. Oct. 6, 1868; res. 101 West Seventh street, Oswego, N. Y. He was a farmer, justice of the peace, Presbyterian, Republican, and highly esteemed citizen. Ch., Gertrude E., b. Nov. 14, 1841; m. Andrew Ketcham; res. Bushnell's Basin, N. Y.; John E., b. Nov. 14, 1845; res. Buffalo, N. Y.; Helen J., b. Dec. 6, 1848; m. Thurston Dunham; d. July 2, 1883; Carrie E., b. Apr. 29, 1851; d. May 6, 1855; Cora A., b. Aug. 23, 1857; m. Judson Stevenson, d. July 12, 1882; Benjamin N., b. Aug. 25, 1860; m. Mina Brower; res. Hannibal, N. Y. Ch., Marguerita A. and Harry E.; E. May, b. Aug. 23, 1863; m. Edmund J. Vert; res. Cazenovia, N. Y. Ch., Harold M.

　　IV. ELIZABETH F., b. ——; m. 1846, Robert M. Cruikshank. She d. Oct. 26, 1855; res. Deerfield, N. Y. Ch., Emily, b. Oct. 28, 1852; m. May, 1872, Henry Barwell; res. Poland, N. Y. Ch., Mary E., b. Mar. 19, 1873; Henry L., b. Jan. 4, 1879; George G., b. ——; res. Poland, N. Y.

415. **Samuel S.**[8] **Pierce** (Jeremiah W.[7], Nathan[6], Nathan[5], Mial[4], Ephraim[3], Ephraim[2], Michael[1]), b. Aug. 27, 1833; m. Dec. 6, 1869, Mary G. Boyce, b. May 18, 1849. Res. Assonett Village, Freetown, Mass.

CHILDREN.

　　I. ANNIE L., b. Sept. 1, 1881.

416. **Ezra**[8] **Pierce** (Martin[7], Martin[6], Nathan[5], Mial[4], Ephraim[3], Ephraim[2], Michael[1]), b. in Rehoboth; m. Dec. 8, 1842, Joanna Horton. He d. Aug. 28, 1875. Res. Swansey, Mass.

CHILDREN.

I. ELLEN S., b. Aug. 2, 1843.
II. CHARLES E., b. Sept. 3, 1845.
III. JAMES B., b. Mar. 31, 1849.

417. **Asa T.**[8] **Pierce** (Asa[7], Peleg[6], Nathan[5], Mial[4], Ephraim[3], Ephraim[2], Michael[1]), b. Aug. 18, 1814; m. July 30, 1835, Hannah Hopkins, b. Feb. 27, 1815. Res. Munday, Mich.

CHILDREN.

I. MARTHA S., b. Apr. 29, 1837; m. Nov. 11, 1867, Mallard M. Campbell, b. June 11, 1837; d. Feb. 9, 1880; res. Munday, Mich., s. p.

552. II. NATHAN W., b. Jan. 11, 1840; m. Maggie Kinney.
III. LAURA H., b. Feb. 29, 1844; m. Mar. 23, 1869, Joseph E. Johnson, b. Aug. 15, 1836. Ch., Asa Webster, b. June 4, 1870; Joseph Frederick, b. Dec. 25, 1871; Frank H., b. Feb. 27, 1878; res. Munday, Mich.
IV. JULIANNA, b. Apr. 29, 1850; d. Feb. 16, 1852.
V. GEORGE H., b. May 16, 1852; d. Jan. 14, 1853.
VI. ASA F., b. Aug. 7, 1854; res. Munday, Mich.

418. **William B.**[8] **Pierce** (Asa[7], Peleg[6], Nathan[5], Mial[4], Ephraim[3], Ephraim[2], Michael[1]), b. Jan. 1, 1819; m. Louise G. Conant. He d. July 12, 1876. Res. ——.

CHILDREN.

I. SPENCER, b. ——.
II. MORRIS, b. ——.
III. WATSON, b. ——.
IV. SIDNEY W. G., b. ——.
V. NELLY, b. ——.

419. **Hon. Edwin C.**[8] **Pierce** (Gardner[7], Peleg[6], Nathan[5], Mial[4], Ephraim[3], Ephraim[2] Michael[1]), b. Jan. 11, 1853; m. May

19, 1881, Martha A. Collingham, b. May 22, 1853. Lawyer. Res. Providence, R. I.

Edwin Chace Pierce, son of Gardner and Elvira A. (Newman-Grace) Pierce, was born at Providence, R. I., January 11, 1853. He was educated in the public schools of his native city. The death of his father compelled him to abandon the cherished plan of pursuing a college course, and at the age of eighteen years he began the study of law in the office of E. M. Jenckes in Providence. He remained with Mr. Jenckes one year, and then passed two years as a student in the offices of Thurston, Ripley & Co., the leading law firm of Providence. Engaging in the practice of law in Providence, Mr. Pierce is still (1886) an active practitioner at the Rhode Island bar. In politics Mr. Pierce is a Republican, and in the presidential campaigns of 1876, 1880, and 1884 made many speeches in advocacy of the Republican cause in Rhode Island and other States. In 1876, 1880, and in 1884, Mr. Pierce was an earnest advocate of the nomination of James G. Blaine to the presidency, and in 1884, made speeches for Blaine and Logan at the request of the Republican National Committee. In April, 1888, he was elected to the Rhode Island Legislature. Mr. Pierce was married May 19, 1881 to Martha A. Collingham.

420. **William H.**[8] **Pierce** (Gardner[7], Peleg[6], Nathan[5], Mial[4], Ephraim[3], Ephraim[2], Michael[1]), b. Dec. 11, 1832; m. Aug. 15, 1861, Ellen M. Graves, b. Oct. 13, 1834. Res. Fall River, Mass.

CHILDREN.

I. WILLIAM W., b. Aug. 3, 1862; d. Nov. 3, 1869.
II. ETHEL J., b. Aug. 12, 1864.
III. HENRY V., b. Mar. 8, 1866; d. May 2, 1872.
IV. CLIFFORD G., b. June 12, 1868.
V. CARRIE E., b. Mar. 1, 1871.
VI. LIZZIE M., b. Dec. 10, 1873.

421. **William C.**[8] **Pierce** (Dexter[7], Peleg[6], Nathan[5], Mial[4],

Ephraim[3], Ephraim[2], Michael[1]), b. Feb. 6, 1855; m. Apr. 17, 1879, Lilla M. Bent, b. Nov. 18, 1854. Res. Worcester, Mass.

CHILDREN.

I. ALICE L., b. Sept. 11, 1880.

422. **Walter C.**[8] **Pierce** (Dexter[7], Peleg[6], Nathan[5], Mial[4], Ephraim[3], Ephraim[2], Michael[1]), b. Feb., 1855; m June 9, 1880, Mary C. Clark. b. Nov. 14, 1859. Res. 34 Ashburton street, Providence, R. I.

CHILDREN.

I. LOUISE S., b. Feb. 12, 1885.

423. **Alfred**[8] **Pierce** (Lewis[7], Preserved[6], Nathan[5], Mial[4], Ephraim[3], Ephraim[2], Michael[1]), b. May 7, 1817; m. June 10, 1841, Marietta Williams. Res. Swansey, Mass.

424. **Benjamin W.**[8] **Pierce** (Lewis[7], Preserved[6], Nathan[5], Mial[4], Ephraim[3], Ephraim[2], Michael[1]), b. Apr. 9, 1819; m. Aug. 2, 1841, Clarissa G. Carpenter, b. Sept. 3, 1818; d. Feb. 13, 1847; m. 2nd, Sept. 6, 1847, Mary A. Bragg, b. June 30, 1820. Res. Newport, R. I.

Benjamin W. Pierce was born in Swansey, April 9, 1819. His parents removed to Fall River, Mass., when he was five years of age, and a year later to New Bedford, where he remained one year, and returned to Fall River. The month before he was eight years old he went into a factory to work for fifty cents a week. He continued in that factory for ten years, without any schooling other than what he had before he went into the factory. At seventeen he first learned to write his name, and what he subsequently learned in the chirographical art, he acquired unaided. He entered as an apprentice in a printing office in Fall River in 1837. The same year he removed to Providence, where he continued in the same line of business. At twenty-two years of age he was one of the editors of the *Christian Soldier*, a weekly paper published

in Pawtucket, Mass.   In 1844, he entered upon the publication of
the *Sparkling Fountain*, a temperance paper, and waged such a
war against the rum traffic that his office was mobbed and the
type thrown into the Blackstone river.   He removed from Pawtucket to Boston in 1852, and became one of the editors of the
American Patriot, a Native American organ.   He removed to
Providence in 1856, and thence to Fall River in 1857, and was
one of a firm that started the first daily paper ever published in
that city.   The panic of that year caused the death of the paper
before it was a year old.   In 1858, he removed to Newport, as
local editor of the *Daily News*, being the first reporter ever employed in that capacity in Newport.   In 1861, he accepted a position as Newport correspondent of the Providence *Press*, which
position he held for twenty-five years.   In 1886, he commenced
the publication of the Newport *Enterprise,* an independent temperance paper, which still continues in existence.   On the 25th of
April, he celebrated his seventieth anniversary by a public enter-
tainment in Masonic Hall, Newport.   He has been prominently
identified with the temperance cause for half a century.

CHILDREN.

  I. CLARISSA P., b. Dec. 23, 1842; m. Sept., 1861,
     Robert P. Boss; res. 903 East Broadway, South
     Boston, Mass.
 II. ELIZA E., b. Apr. 3, 1857.

425. **Elisha D.**[8] **Pierce** (Preserved[7], Preserved[6], Nathan[5],
Mial[4], Ephraim[3], Ephraim[2], Michael[1]), b. Sept. 1, 1809; m. May
10, 1832, Lydia P. Potter, b. Mar. 15, 1809; d. Apr. 26, 1884.
He d. July 29, 1851.   Res. Rehoboth, Mass.

CHILDREN.

553.   I. SIDNEY W., b. Dec. 9, 1837; m. Annie F. Proctor.
      II. JULIA M., b. May 24, 1833; m. Josiah W. Graham.
          She d. Dec. 16, 1868; res. Pascoge, R. I.   Ch.,
          Elisha H., b. June 1, 1861; m. Harriett B. Taft.

III. CHARLES E., b. Nov. 6, 1835 ; d. Jan. 7, 1867.

IV. EDWARD D., b. Dec. 27, 1839; res. Lewiston, Me.

V. LUTHER S., b. Dec. 8, 1841; d. Feb. 1, 1866.

VI. LYDIA A., b. June 16, 1844; m. —— Sedgwick. She d. July 25, 1870 in Rehoboth, Mass., leaving Matthew.

VII. ELVIRA N., b. Aug. 21, 1847 ; m. —— Peterson. She d. Sept. 6, 1878.

426. **Lewis**[8] **Pierce** (Preserved[7], Preserved[6], Nathan[5], Mial[4], Ephraim[3], Ephraim[2], Michael[1]), b. June 15, 1813; m. Nov. 28, 1837, Hannah B. Chaffee, b. Oct. 14, 1810; d. Mar. 2, 1850; m. 2nd, 1851, Lucy Merchant, b. 1809; d. June 15, 1882; m. 3rd, 1884, Caroline Kent, b. 1835. Res. Pawtucket, R. I.

CHILDREN.

I. EMILY, b. Oct. 3, 1838; d. July 13, 1839.

II. LEWIS, b. Sept. 7, 1839; d. Sept. 13, 1839.

III. ADELAIDE, b. Dec. 26, 1840; res. Pawtucket, R. I.

IV. HANNAH, b. Sept. 22, 1842 ; d. Oct., 1842.

V. EDWARD, b. Dec. 11, 1844; d. Sept. 1, 1869.

VI. SUSAN M., b. Sept. 18, 1846; d. Mar. 12, 1871.

VII. LEWIS, b. Feb. 24, 1850; d. Mar. 9, 1850.

427. **Allen F.**[8] **Pierce** (Preserved[7], Preserved[6], Nathan[5], Mial[4], Ephraim[3], Ephraim[2], Michael[1]), b. May 22, 1818; m. 1846, Lydia B. Brown, b. Sept. 17, 1820. He d. ——. Res. East Providence, R. I.

CHILDREN.

I. ISABEL F., b. June 22, 1849 ; m. Nov. 29, 1871, Walter S. Cole, b. Dec. 26, 1846; res. Warren, R. I.

II. FRANK C., b. Nov. 21, 1852; unm.; res. East Providence, R. I.

III. WILLIAM B., b. June 28, 1860; unm.; res. East Providence, R. I.

43

IV. EDITH A., b. Feb. 14, 1855; m. 1873, Joseph W.
Sampson. She d. Apr. 12, 1874. Ch., Edith
A., b. Apr. 3, 1874; res. Bolton, Mass.

428. **George M.**[8] **Pierce** (Preserved[7], Preserved[6], Nathan[5],
Mial[4], Ephraim[3], Ephraim[2], Michael[1]), b. May 9, 1823; m. Sept.
21, 1845, Mary Ann Thurber, b. Sept. 15, 1826. Res. North
Swansey, Mass., and East Providence, R. I.

CHILDREN.

I. BETSEY D., b. Aug. 6, 1847; m. Aug. 27, 1871, A.
Theodore Read, b. Sept. 25, 1838; res. East
Providence, R. I.
II. GEORGIANA, b. Sept. 21, 1849; res. East Provi-
dence, R. I.
III. ELLA F., b. Mar. 30, 1853; m. May 7, 1871, John
H. Davis, b. July 23, 1848; res. Pawtucket, R. I.
Ch., Grace O., b. Oct. 1, 1871; Anna E., b. Mar.
1, 1875; George H., b. Sept. 26, 1876; Frank M., b.
Oct. 10, 1878; Mary H., b. Sept. 21, 1880; Elmer
P., b. May 20, 1884.
IV. INEZ E., b. Aug. 1, 1857; m. May 29, 1881, David
E. Peckham, b. Sept. 16, 1851. Ch., Clarence I.,
b. May 14, 1882; Roy Edward, b. May 7, 1885;
d. Aug. 21, 1885; res. East Providence, R. I.

429. **Otis**[8] **Pierce** (Martin[7], Preserved[6], Nathan[5], Mial[4],
Ephraim[3], Ephraim[2], Michael[1]), b. Mar. 12, 1827; m. Mar. 3,
1850, Judith C. C. Devoll, b. Aug. 10, 1827. Res. 1 Spruce street,
New Bedford, Mass.

CHILDREN.

554.   I. A. MARTIN, b. Mar. 14, 1852; m. Lizzie J. Macom-
ber.
II. FRANK C., b. Jan. 5, 1854; d. Jan. 12, 1879.
III. CARRIE C., b. ——; d. infant.

IV. CARRIE O., b. Feb. 28, 1862.

V. WILLIAM T., b. Dec. 23, 1865; res. Glendale, Fla.

VI. ARTHUR W., b. July 22, 1867; d. Apr. 15, 1886.

430. **Otis W.**[8] **Pierce** (Otis H.[7], Preserved[6], Nathan[5], Mial[4], Ephraim[3], Ephraim[2], Michael[1]), b. Apr. 1, 1831; m. July 9, 1854. Sarah C. Haskins, b. Feb. 2, 1835. Res. New Bedford, Mass.

CHILDREN.

I. HARRIETT E., b. Jan. 20, 1861; res. Providence, R. I.

431. **Hon. Le Grand W.**[8] **Pierce** (Hiram W.[7], Isaac[6], Nathan[5], Mial[4], Ephraim[3], Ephraim[2], Michael[1]), b. June 19, 1836; m. Nov. 14, 1867, Sarah M. Wallace, b. Feb. 6, 1844. Res. 546 Washington Boulevard, Chicago, Ill.

Le Grand Winfield Perce was born June 19, 1836, in the city of Buffalo, Erie county, N. Y., son of Hiram W. Perce and Cornelia (Ryder) Perce. He was educated in the public schools of Buffalo, and at the Wesleyan College at Lima, N. Y. He commenced the study of law, and graduated at the Albany Law School in March, 1857. Being under age at the time, he was admitted to the bar in the Supreme Court of the State of New York at the date of his graduation, his diploma, however, to date from the date of his majority in June following.

On his return to his home in Buffalo, he entered upon the practice of the law at the Erie county bar. In 1859, he went to St. Louis, Mo., with the purpose of settling there. On landing upon the levee of that city, he was met by a couple of slaves on their way to the south. The sight so impressed him, that he determined he could not live in a slave State, and although he was admitted to the bar in St. Louis, he immediately began to look for a location elsewhere in the west. Having received an offer from a law firm in Chicago, he visited that city, and finally settled there in September, 1859. He was admitted to the bar of Illinois and commenced the practice of law there. When the war broke out he tendered his services to Governor Yates, and was despatched to Cairo, with rank as captain in the State service April 21, 1861, where he served on the staff of General B. M. Prentiss until June of that year. He was not, however, regularly mustered into the service either of the State or United States, neither demanded or received pay, but acted as a volunteer. In June, 1861, having received an invitation to join Company B, Sixth Michigan Volunteers, he obtained an indefinite leave of absence from General Prentiss and joined the Sixth Michigan Volunteers at Fort Wayne, Mich., as second lieutenant of Company B, of that regiment. He was appointed first lieutenant shortly thereafter; was made captain of Company D, Sixth Michigan Volunteers, in July, 1862. He participated in all the campaigns and battles of his regiment until August, 1863, when he was appointed captain and assistant quarter-master United States Volunteers. He took part in three pitched battles and thirteen minor engagements; was brevetted major for gallant and meritorious service in the field at the first battle of Port Hudson, and at the close of the war was brevetted lieutenant-colonel and colonel for good service during the war. At the close of the war he settled at Natchez, Miss., where he again entered upon the practice of law. He was appointed Register in Bankruptcy for the Southern District of Mississippi upon the recommendation of almost the entire bar of his district. In 1868, he ran and was elected to Congress, but the State not being re-admitted to the Union, did not take his seat. He, however, was elected the next year, and took his seat in the Forty-first Congress as the representative of the sixth district of Mississippi, and was re-elected to the Forty-second Congress. In the Forty-second Congress he was chairman of the Committee on Education and Labor, and as such chairman, prepared and reported to the House the first educational bill having reference to the common schools ever passed by either house of Congress. The debate on Mr. Perce's bill lasted nearly six weeks, occupying the morning hour, and every prominent member of the house, Democratic or Republican, took part in the debate. The bill finally passed by a majority of 26. Mr. Perce was also the recognized father of the so-called Ku-Klux legislation of 1872. In 1874, Mr. Perce returned to Chicago, Ill., where he still resides, engaged in the practice of his profession.

While Mr. Perce was in Congress he introduced a bill to make Thanksgiving a legal holiday. It is a singular fact that this day was first observed in the New World on the arrival of Captain William Pierce's ship in Plymouth harbor with provisions for the Pilgrims.

CHILDREN.

I. SALLIE C., b. Nov. 18, 1868.
II. HIRAM W., b. Oct. 13, 1871.
III. FRANCES C., b. Sept. 14, 1873.
IV. MARY E., b. June 29, 1876.
V. ETHEL, b. Apr. 10, 1881.
VI. LE GRAND W., b. Mar. 9, 1885.

432. **Elbert**[8] **Pierce** (Hiram W.[7], Isaac[6], Nathan[5], Mial[4], Ephraim[3], Ephraim[2], Michael[1]), b. Aug. 21, 1831; m. June 8, 1859, Margaret A. Dickey, b. July 29, 1834. He d. Jan. 8, 1869. Res. 28 Park Place, Brooklyn, N. Y.

Elbert Pierce, for several years connected with the educational department of Messrs. Charles Scribner & Co.'s publishing house, died January 8, 1869, at his home in Brooklyn, after an illness of short duration. He was born in New York, August 21, 1831, and the family removed to Buffalo, N. Y., in 1832, where they continued to reside until the year 1857. Elbert, however, went to New York in 1850, and resided there and in Brooklyn until his death.

He was a gentleman of unusual literary ability, and of a decided active and ingenious mind. In 1851, he published through Charles Scribner "Gullivar Joe," and shortly afterward "Olla Carl, the Cooper, and his Wonderful Book." Each of these works displayed marked originality, and they enjoyed quite a wide popularity. Mr. Pierce followed these with several translations from the Swedish of Mrs. Carlen, which also had a large sale. Still later he compiled a large octavo volume which Mason Bros. published, entitled "The Battle Roll," it giving statistics of all the notable battles ever fought. Had he lived it was his intention to have compiled a supplement to this volume, embracing the battles of the Rebellion and of the Prussian War, etc. Mr. Pierce was best known, however, by the very ingenious, but simple magnetic terrestrial globe which bears his name. Exceedingly modest and unassuming and unobtrusive in his deportment, the simplicity and sincerity of his manners, made all those who knew him his firmly attached friends, and his numerous acquaintances will sympathize deeply with his family in their great loss. Eight days before his death arrangements had been made, which were not fully completed at the time of his death, whereby he became a partner in the publishing firm of Charles Scribner & Company. — [N. Y. *Sun.*

CHILDREN.

I. HENRY W., b. Feb. 27, 1861; unm.; rcs. 1030 Wilcox avenue, Chicago, Ill.

Henry W. Perce passed his childhood and youth in Brooklyn, N. Y., where he was educated. In 1880, he went to western Kansas, where he engaged in the business of cattle and sheep raising. In 1884, he came to Chicago, where he now resides. He was one of the first actual settlers in Sheridan county, Kansas. At present he is connected with the building trades, and the practice of the architectural profession.

II. CHARLES F., b. Sept. 26, 1865; res. Chicago, Ill.; reporter on the *Inter-Ocean.*

Charles F. Perce in 1881 joined his brother in Kansas. In the same year he went to the mining regions of the Rocky mountains, where he engaged in mining and metallurgical pursuits. In 1887, he came to Chicago, where he now resides. He is at present engaged in the newspaper business.

433. **Levi L.**[8] **Pierce** (Isaac[7], Isaac[6], Nathan[5], Mial[4], Ephraim[3], Ephraim[2], Michael[1]), b. Sept. 2, 1829; m. Feb. 25, 1849, Melissa A. Hopkins, b. Mar. 31, 1831. Res. Woonsocket, R. I.

CHILDREN.

I. CHARLES L. H., b. Aug. 7, 1850.
II. GEORGE W., b. Mar. 1, 1852.
III. HENRY W., b. Nov. 6, 1855; d. Aug. 18, 1886.

434. **Edwin A.**[8] **Pierce** (Isaac[7], Isaac[6], Nathan[5], Mial[4], Ephraim[3], Ephraim[2], Michael[1]), b. Feb. 18, 1832; m. June 7, 1852, Maria Illingworth, b. Sept. 9, 1832. Res. Woonsocket, R. I.

CHILDREN.

I. EARL F., b. July 11, 1853; m. Aug. 11, 1881, Jennie Talbott, b. May 7, 1862; res. s. p., Woonsocket, R. I.
II. HIRAM C., b. Aug. 31, 1855.
III. BELCORA, b. Nov. 17, 1859; m. —— Taylor, d. June 3, 1885.

435. **William F.**[8] **Pierce** (Isaac[7], Isaac[6], Nathan[5], Mial[4], Ephraim[3], Ephraim[2], Michael[1]), b. Feb. 16, 1819; m. Oct. 25, 1841, Paulina Brown, b. Dec. 20, 1829; d. Mar. 20, 1874. Res. ——.

CHILDREN.

I. WILLIAM A., b. ——; d. in infancy.
II. CHARLES L., b. June 7, 1845; m. Helen Baker. He d. Oct. 20, 1886.
III. ELLIS C., b. ——; d. in infancy.

436. **Edward M.**[8] **Pierce** (Angie[7], Isaac[6], Nathan[5], Mial[4], Ephraim[3], Ephraim[2], Michael[1]), b. Jan. 21, 1822; m. 1844, Celia J. Anthony. He d. Feb. 15, 1888. Res. Barnaby street, Fall River, Mass.

CHILDREN.

I. CAROLINE J. F., b. Mar., 1845; unm.
II. JULIA E., b. Jan., 1847; d. Oct. 21, 1868.

437. **James F.**[8] **Pierce** (Angie[7], Isaac[6], Nathan[5], Mial[4], Ephraim[3], Ephraim[2], Michael[1]), b. Aug. 26, 1826; m. July 21, 1853, Amelia L. White, b. Mar. 4, 1832. Res. Fall River, Mass.

CHILDREN.

I. EVA L., b. July 21, 1854; d. Oct. 12, 1857.
II. ELIZABETH S., b. July 17, 1855; m. July 15, 1875, Frank Borden; res. Fall River, Mass. Ch., Abbie and Gertrude.
III. CHARLES E., b. Oct. 14, 1857; d. Jan. 22, 1858.
IV. EDWARD M., b. Sept. 27, 1859; d. Feb. 5, 1861.
V. MARY A., b. Apr. 17, 1863; m. June 11, 1884, John Allen; res. Myricks, Mass. Ch., Clothier, Etta, John.
VI. CORA M., }
VII. JAMES F., } b. 1868; d. July, 1869.
VIII. ALICE S., b. May 28, 1870.

438. **Angie W.**[8] **Pierce** (Angie[7], Isaac[6], Nathan[5], Mial[4], Ephraim[3], Ephraim[2], Michael[1]), b. Nov. 5, 1853; m. Mar. 30, 1880, Mary E. Mott, b. Oct. 19, 1858; d. Jan. 28, 1883. Res. Bristol, R. I.

CHILDREN.

I. MARY A., }
II. ANGIE W., } b. May 15, 1883.

439. **Charles W.**[8] **Pierce** (Levi[7], Isaac[6], Nathan[5], Mial[4], Ephraim[3], Ephraim[2], Michael[1]), b. Jan. 12, 1833; m. Aug. 22, 1855, Emma Haddock, dau. of Squire Haddock of Columbus, Ohio, b. Feb. 5, 1837; d. Mar. 12, 1874; m. 2nd, Mrs. Anna Commons. Res. Union City, Ind.

Charles W. Pierce was born in New York city, and for several years was a clerk for his brother-in-law, Mr. Butler, of whom he learned the jeweler's trade. Soon after his marriage he moved to Indiana and located on a farm. After the death of his wife, he moved to Union City, where he now resides, engaged in the grain business. During the war he was sutler to the Forty-sixth Ohio Regiment under General Walcott. He is much respected.

CHILDREN.

I. CHARLES W., b. Sept. 13, 1858; d. Jan. 27, 1881.
II. SARAH E., b. Oct. 6, 1861; d. Aug. 24, 1865.
III. ALLIE DENMAN, b. July 6, 1864; d. July 22, 1864.
IV. EARL H., b. June   ; d. Apr. 15, 1872.
V. MARY L., b. Oct. 14, 1868.
VI. CLARENCE S., b. Dec. 9, 1870.
VII. FRANK W., b. Aug. 19, 1873.
VIII. EMMA J., b. Sept. 17, 1856; d. Aug. 19, 1867.

440. **Levi Lafayette[8] Pierce** (Levi[7], Isaac[6], Nathan[5], Mial[4], Ephraim[3], Ephraim[2], Michael[1]), b. Nov. 18, 1830; m. Sept. 1, 1855, Ellen Elizabeth Wright, b. Mar. 26, 1834. Res. Taunton, Mass.

Levi L. Pierce learned for a trade the chasing of jewelry, also learned light blacksmithing, such as window trimmings and hinges, having two trades. Levi is a good, Christian man. They have no children of their own, but adopted the youngest of his brother Charles, when he was a widower, and named him Frankie Pierce. He is now fifteen years old. Levi has worked at the chasing business in New York, in 1852, then after two or three years went back to Rehoboth on a farm, taking charge of his aunt Sarah's farm, a dear, old lady, that lived in the family for years. In 1864, he moved to Buffalo and went in partnership with his brother-in-law, James O. Robson, in the jewelry business. After a few years he went back to Rehoboth on a farm. He is now superintendent of the Taunton city farm, Taunton, Mass.

CHILDREN.

I. FRANK W., b. Aug. 19, 1873 (adopted).

441. **Earl H.[8] Pierce** (Levi[7], Isaac[6], Nathan[5], Mial[4], Ephraim[3], Ephraim[2], Michael[1]), b. Mar. 14, 1827; m. May 8, 1853, Martha

44

Maria Marr, b. Apr. 28, 1837. He d. June 5, 1859, in England, and is buried at High Gate Cemetery. Res. 267 Division street, Paterson, N. J.

Earl Horton Pierce was possessed of great musical talent, and was by profession a musical performer, and was considered one of the best of his day. In 1854, he and his brother-in-law, John William Raynor, organized a musical troupe. They traveled through the States, and in 1857, they went to Europe. They met with great success; they then made a tour of England, Ireland, Scotland and France, and played before the crowned heads, Queen Victoria and Emperor Napoleon, and the nobility. Mrs. Pierce, his widow, is living, and resides with her daughter, Mrs. Katie Lange, 267 Division street, Paterson, N. J.

CHILDREN.

I. EDWIN C., b. Feb. 17. 1854; unm.; is an architect; res. 81 Plaine street, Newark, N. J.

II. KATIE P., b. Nov. 30, 1856; m. Dec. 8, 1880, Jergan P. Lange, b. Dec. 27, 1851; res. 267 Division street, Paterson, N. J. He is a mechanical draughtsman and civil engineer. Ch., Jergan P., b. Nov. 21, 1881; Martha M., b. May 30, 1883; Edwin E., b. Oct. 29, 1884; John W., b. Aug. 16, 1886.

442. **Warren S.**[8] **Pierce** (Levi[7], Isaac[6], Nathan[5], Mial[4], Ephraim[3], Ephraim[2], Michael[1]), b. July 25, 1828; m. 1856, Eliza M. Sturdy, b. 1831; d. at Attleboro, Mass., 1865. He d. in California, 1864.

Warren S. Pierce learned the jewelry business in his young days, working at it some time, and hearing so much about the gold mines in California, he concluded to go and seek his fortune. Warren S. started for California in 1850; he was determined and persevering, depriving himself of many comforts and privileges, and enduring many hardships. He came home in 1853; not feeling satisfied he returned again to California in 1854, digging gold right along. Feeling weary of the life, and homesick, he came home to stay in 1856, but he married and taking his wife with him, he returned to California in 1857. Aleda Beatrice, their only child, was born in 1858, in California. When Aleda was almost a year old Mrs. Pierce came back to Attleboro, Warren S. remaining. He died of fever in 1864, in California. Mrs. Pierce died in 1865, in Attleboro. His death was caused by hard work and exposure in his anxiety to become rich.

CHILDREN.

I. ALEDA B., b. Jan. 27, 1858; m. Oct. 4, 1881, Herbert I. Conant ; res. 110 Botolph street, Boston, Mass.

443. **George L.**[8] **Pierce** (Waterman[7], Isaac[6], Nathan[5], Mial[4], Ephraim[3], Ephraim[2], Michael[1]), b. Sept. 9, 1837 ; m. Dec. 25, 1872, Sarah E. Cory, b. Nov. 19, 1841. Res. Providence, R. I.

CHILDREN.

I. ARCHIE LE GRAND, b. Jan. 6, 1875; d. Aug. 18, 1881.

II. WILTON CORY, b. Dec. 7, 1876; d. Oct. 12, 1879.

III. ETHEL,
IV. GRACE, } b. May 19, 1879.

V. BERTHA, b. Mar. 22, 1882.

VI. CHAUNCEY GILES, b. Apr. 9, 1881; d. May 9, 1881.

444. **Bradford B.**[8] **Pierce** (Waterman[7], Isaac[6], Nathan[5], Mial[4], Ephraim[3], Ephraim[2], Michael[1]), b. Nov. 7, 1821; m. Oct. 7, 1847, Martha K. Brown, b. Oct. 6, 1827; d. Mar. 20, 1868; m. 2nd. June 8, 1871, Susan M. Shelley, b. May 29, 1832. He d. Dec. 15, 1878. Res. 170 Broadway, Providence, R. I.

CHILDREN.

555. I. WATERMAN J., b. Aug. 29, 1848; m. Flora W. Fenner.

556. II. BRADFORD F., b. Oct. 17, 1850; m. Isabel F. Otis.
III. CLARENCE N., b. Apr. 28, 1854; m. Nov. 25, 1884,
Hannah E. Earle, s. p.; res. 26 Burnett street,
Providence, R. I.
IV. MATTIE E., b. Mar. 16, 1863; d. Aug. 25, 1863.

445. **Elisha W.**[8] **Pierce** (Waterman[7], Isaac[6], Nathan[5], Mial[4],
Ephraim[3], Ephraim[2], Michael[1]), b. Jan. 22, 1829; m. Mar. 3, 1851,
Elizabeth W. Barney, b. Mar. 17, 1829. Res. Providence, R. I.

Elisha W. Pierce was born in Rehoboth, Mass., in 1829. At
the age of twenty-one he left the paternal roof in Seekonk, Mass.,
and started for Providence, R. I., carrying with him hardly any
thing but the clothes he wore. But he went to Providence with
his mind bent on success, if such a result should be possible for
him to accomplish through hard work and plain living. He began his city life as clerk in a store, in which capacity he served
for about three years. Then anxious to try for himself he commenced business on a very small scale, working hard, and con-
ducting his business with great caution, as has ever been his way
of management. Owing to his cautious, unspeculative manner of
business life, he has assumed no risks, and contracted no debts,
unless there was a visible means of meeting his obligations.
Gradually the trade at his store increased, and with increased pa-
tronage came increased success, and if he has accomplished any
thing, it has not been through any few great strikes, but always
through hard work, careful management and perseverance.

In politics he is and always has been a staunch Republican, and
although his mode of life has been quiet and unassuming, at the
request of friends he served two terms in the Providence city
council, when he resigned, declining to accept of other honors,
which was tendered him on his resignation.

In religion he is a Free Baptist, a member of the Roger Williams Free Baptist Church of Providence, of which church his
wife and children are also members. For many years he has tried
to live with a heart grateful to God for His loving kindness and

tender mercies, shown through the many blessings He has granted to him, even through a life of unfaithful service.

CHILDREN.

I. MARY E., b. Dec. 13, 1851; m. Feb. 27, 1870, Charles E. Frost, b. Sept. 26, 1848; res. Pawtucket, R. I. Ch., Carrie E., b. June 9, 1870; Minnie E., b. Jan. 30, 1872; Charles W., b. July 15, 1875; d. Aug. 3, 1879 ; Lillian E., b. Mar. 26, 1877.

II. EDWARD E., b. Feb. 1, 1856; m. Nov. 9, 1880, Emma F. Wood, b. May 7, 1859; res. Providence, R. I.

557. III. BENJAMIN F., b. July 20, 1860; m. Sanie K. Harris.

IV. FLORENCE B., b. Jan. 10, 1862; m. June 30, 1885, Cyril R. Wood, b. Jan. 31, 1857; res. East Providence, R. I. Ch., Evelyn P., b. Feb. 11, 1886.

V. ULYSSES G. B., b. July 17, 1865; res. Pomham, R. I.

VI. ESTHER W., b. June 8, 1873.

446. **Warren R.**[8] **Pierce** (Jeremiah B.[7], Isaac[6], Nathan[5], Mial[4], Ephraim[3], Ephraim[2], Michael[1]), b. June 30, 1843 ; m. Oct. 28, 1884, Annie E. Kenyon, b. Dec. 16, 1855. Res. Providence, R. I., s. p.

Warren R. Perce, as he insists on writing his name, was born in 1843. He was graduated at Brown's University, Providence, R. I., in the class of 1865, with the highest honor, the Valedictory. The subject of this sketch studied law with Hon. Charles S. Bradley in Providence; was admitted to the Rhode Island bar October 10, 1867, and afterward was admitted to practice in the United States courts. He has ever since practiced in Providence. Being a Democrat, he has never held public office, though often nominated for various State and municipal offices, and frequently polling very heavy votes.

The spelling of the name, Perce, is the oldest known, being so spelled in the oldest book of names in the British Museum, London, and also so spelled in the list of passengers in one of the early ships to the Plymouth colony. His grandfather spelled his name Parce, sometimes Parc, and was called commonly Uncle Isaac Parce (pronounced Pass). It is said a discussion arose in his family about the spelling, and by examining the oldest stones in the family burial-ground the name Perce was found to be the oldest. Warren's father and half-uncle Hiram adopted that spelling. Another uncle adopted Pirce, the others, Pierce.

447. **Benjamin**[8] **Pierce** (Samuel[7], David[6], Nathan[5], Mial[4], Ephraim[3], Ephraim[2], Michael[1]), b. Sept. 4, 1800; m. Dec. 4, 1822, Rosanna Horton; d. Sept. 1, 1842. He d. Apr. 2, 1835. Res. Rehoboth, Mass.

CHILDREN.

I. ANDREW B., b. Jan. 13, 1825; res. Providence, R. I.
II. ELEANOR J., b. Aug. 21, 1830; m. Aug. 12, 1858, Alexander S. Arnold, b. Sept. 30, 1829; res. s. p., Valley Falls, R. I.
III. MARY A., b. Oct. 29, 1832; res. Valley Falls, R. I.
558. IV. JAMES L., b. Aug. 18, 1823; m. Mary A. Streeter.

448. **Joseph**[8] **Pierce** (Samuel[7], David[6], Nathan[5], Mial[4], Ephraim[3], Ephraim[2], Michael[1]), b. Feb. 15, 1798; m. Feb. 2, 1825, Lydia Lawton, b. Aug. 30, 1802; d. Oct. 24, 1877. He d. Mar. 24, 1881. Res. Rehoboth, Mass.

CHILDREN.

I. ELIZABETH A., b. June 21, 1841; unm.; res. Pawtucket, R. I.
559. II. ISAIAH E., b. Dec. 20, 1825; m. Mary A. Carney.
III. IRENE E., b. Jan. 24, 1831; m. William H. Hathaway; d. Jan. 15, 1884, s. p.; res. Pawtucket, R. I.
560. IV. ELLIS, b. Oct. 14, 1834; m. Annie E. Coggshall.
561. V. BENJAMIN B., b. Nov. 29, 1836; m. Julia E. Buffinton.

449. **Samuel**[8] **Pierce** (Samuel[7], David[6], Nathan[5], Mial[4], Ephraim[3], Ephraim[2], Michael[1]), b. July 12, 1787; m. Feb., 1812, Sarah Eddy, b. 1792; d. Apr. 2, 1820; m. 2nd, Oct. 29, 1820, Sally Mason, b. June 10, 1798; d. Jan. 13, 1883. Res. 240 Pine street, Providence, R. I.

CHILDREN.

I. AMY A., b. May 23, 1814; m. Apr. 11, 1836, Thomas D. Hudson; res. 10 Congdon street, Providence, R. I.

II. SARAH, b. ——; m. Henry C. Porter.

III. MARIA C., b. Jan. 17, 1813; m. Apr. 16, 1840, Joseph C. Fanning. She d. Dec. 25, 1859. Ch., Maria, b. ——; m. —— Swan; res. 226 Friendship street, Providence, R. I.; Sarah, b. ——; m. —— Lyttle; res. corner Broad and Pearl streets, Whitfield block, Providence, R. I.

562. IV. CHRISTOPHER T., b. Aug. 22, 1817; m. Eliza Fairbrother.

V. WILLIAM M., b. Jan. 3, 1822; d. Nov. 3, 1822.

VI. SARAH J., b. Mar. 26, 1823 ; d. June 20, 1824.

VII. SAMUEL, b. Nov. 7, 1824; d. Nov. 7, 1824.

VIII. JOSEPH N., b. Jan. 13, 1826; d. in California, Nov. 19, 1852.

IX. RAYMOND P., b. Dec. 13, 1827; d. June 24, 1834.

X. MARY N., b. Oct. 19, 1829; d. in Newbern, N. C., Nov. 25, 1864.

XI. SARAH, E., b. Nov. 13, 1831; res. 240 Pine street, Providence, R. I.

XII. STEPHEN M., b. Apr. 25, 1834; d. June 7, 1834.

XIII. SAMUEL R., b. May 2, 1835; res. Hilo, Hawaiian Islands.

XIV. WILLIAM P., b. Sept. 17, 1837; d. Sept. 25, 1857.

XV. ANNIE H., b. Dec. 29, 1839; m. Apr. 7, 1885, Lebbeus Bennett, b. May 22, 1829; res. s. p., 16 Elm street, Pawtucket, R. I.

450. **Holden**[8] **Pierce** (Samuel[7], David[6], Nathan[5], Mial[4], Ephraim[3], Ephraim[2], Michael[1]), b. June 22, 1789; m. Oct. 10, 1813, Mary J. Sanford, b. June 26, 1787; d. Dec. 26, 1864. He d. Apr. 8, 1857. Res. Rehoboth, Mass.

CHILDREN.

563. I. HOLDEN, b. Oct. 10, 1815; m. Mary H. Carr.
564. II. GEORGE W., b. Dec. 14, 1817; m. Lydia Perkins.
    III. LUCY P., b. Mar. 22, 1822; m. Aug. 13, 1840, Seth Lee, b. July 12, 1818; res. Wood River, Hale county, Neb., s. p.
    IV. MARIA C., b. June 4, 1827; m. Feb. 7, 1853, William A. Eddy, Jr.; res. Wood River, Neb.
    V. MARY C., b. May 26, 1824; m. Dec. 17, 1843, Benjamin L. Burdick, b. Apr., 1823; res. Portsmouth, N. H. Ch., Horace R., b. Oct. 7, 1844; ad. 1285 Broadway, room 13, New York city; Emily R., b. Nov. 28, 1846; d. Sept. 28, 1857.
    VI. EZRA, b. June 12, 1814; d. Oct. 30, 1814.
    VII. PRISCILLA C., b. Mar. 10, 1820; d. Sept. 11, 1821.

451. **James**[8] **Pierce** (Samuel[7], David[6], Nathan[5], Mial[4], Ephraim[3], Ephraim[2], Michael[1]), b. June 8, 1791; m. ——. He d. Sept., 1821, *en route* to Charleston, S. C., from Matamoras.

CHILDREN.

    I. JAMES, b. ——.
    II. ANDREW, b. ——.
    III. ELLEN, b. ——.

452. **Royal**[8] **Pierce** (Micah[7], Jobe[6], Jobe[5], Mial[4], Ephraim[3], Ephraim[2], Michael[1]), b. Jan. 19, 1803; m. Oct. 3, 1826, Mary Clark, b. Dec. 27, 1807. He d. Apr. 25, 1878. Res. Winona, Minn.

CHILDREN.

    I. FRANKLYN, b. Aug. 15, 1827; res. 488 W. No. avenue, Chicago, Ill., a dau. m. George Turkington.

II. WALLACE, b. Nov. 3, 1830; res. Winona, Minn.

III. JEMIMA, b. May 30, 1833; m. —— Bartlett; res. Winona, Minn.

VI. MARSHALL, b. Feb. 10, 1842; d. 1862.

V. EMERGENE, b. Apr. 5, 1845.

VI. CLARK M., b. Oct. 12, 1850; d. Sept. 16, 1861.

453. **William⁸ Pierce** (Micah⁷, Jobe⁶, Jobe⁵, Mial⁴, Ephraim³, Ephraim², Michael¹), b. June 28, 1807 ; m. Feb. 22, 1829, Gertrude N. Ames, b. Nov. 12, 1809 ; d. Apr. 23, 1848; m. 2nd, Nov. 22, 1848, Caroline M. Phelps, b. Nov. 30, 1811. Res. Durham, N. Y.

CHILDREN.

I. HELEN A., b. Feb. 3, 1830; m. Dec. 17, 1851, William H. Norton, b. Aug. 23, 1830; res. Durham, N. Y. Ch., Gertrude A., b. Oct. 3, 1852; m. James D. Porter; Eva L., b. Nov. 11, 1855; George N., b. July 23, 1857; m. Alida Hollis ; res. Amsterdam, N. Y.; Asher, b. Dec. 11, 1859 ; Addie E., b. Sept. 23, 1864; Clarence B., b. Sept. 10, 1866.

565. II. RODERICK G., b. Oct. 23, 1832 ; m. Olive Peck.

III. ADELAIDE L., b. Sept. 5, 1835; m. Nov. 8, 1855, William H. Post, b. May 1, 1833; res. Catskill, N. Y. Ch., William R., b. Feb. 22, 1858; m. June 10, 1885, May Cornwall, b. Mar. 13, 1861 ; res. Catskill, N. Y.

IV. GERTRUDE A., b. Apr. 23, 1842; m. Mar. 27, 1866, Silas Smith, b. Aug., 1844; res. New York city, s. p.

V. CARRIE P., b. Mar. 20, 1850; m. Oct. 28, 1873, Grove Smith, b. Dec. 2, 1845; res. Catskill, N. Y. Ch., Edwin P., b. June 8, 1876.

VI. DELIA P., b. Nov. 26, 1851; unm.

454. **Stephen V. R.**⁸ **Pierce** (Micah⁷, Jobe⁶, Jobe⁵, Mial⁴, Ephraim³, Ephraim², Michael¹), b. Jan. 1, 1809 ; m. Sept. 17,

45

1829, Maria Lockwood, b. Feb. 24, 1812. He d. Oct. 30, 1832
Res. Dunham, N. Y.

CHILDREN.

566.   I. STEPHEN W., b. Feb. 23, 1833; m. Frances O. Green.
        II. AMANDA, b. Sept. 12, 1830; d. Feb. 12, 1831.

455. **Lyman⁸ Pierce** (Micah⁷, Jobe⁶, Jobe⁵, Mial⁴, Ephraim³,
Ephraim², Michael¹), b. Sept. 17, 1817; m. Feb. 21, 1846, Cathe-
rine H. Nier, b. May 12, 1821. He d. June 13, 1885. Res.
Durham, N. Y., and Beloit, Wis.

CHILDREN.

  I. WASHINGTON, b. June 14, 1847; m. Jan., 1870,
       Mary M. Rockfeller; res. Vermillion, Kans.
 II. DELLA, b. Jan. 4, 1849; m. July 4, 1876, William
       Sternberg ; res. Sellersville, Bucks county, Pa.

456. **Phillip M.⁸ Pierce** (John M.⁷, Jobe⁶, Jobe⁵, Mial⁴,
Ephraim³, Ephraim², Michael¹), b. May 31, 1818; m. Sept. 13,
1839, Ann M. Bartlett, b. July 27, 1818; d. Oct. 4, 1876. Res.
Beloit, Wis.

CHILDREN.

  I. ANN E., b. Jan. 31, 1841 ; d. Sept. 15, 1858.
 II. EMMA E., b. Aug. 18, 1848; d. Sept. 7, 1870.

457. **Carolos M.⁸ Pierce** (John M.⁷, Jobe⁶, Jobe⁵, Mial⁴,
Ephraim³, Ephraim², Michacl¹), b. May 9, 1821; m. Feb. 15, 1843,
Catherine C. Bartlett, b. Dec. 15, 1827; d. May 18, 1879. Res.
Union Corners, Boone county, Ill.

CHILDREN.

  I. ELLGRENE C., b. Dec. 23, 1843; m. Jan. 2, 1878,
       Hattie Sprague, b. Apr. 22, 1850; res. Huron,
       So. Dak., s. p.
 II. ROSA B., b. Sept. 17, 1854; m. Sept. 3, 1878, C. F.
       Lomas, b. Aug. 20, 1856; res. Blaine, Ill., s. p.

458. **Maxon[8] Pierce** (John M.[7], Jobe[6], Jobe[5], Mial[4], Ephraim[3], Ephraim[2], Michael[1]), b. Mar. 5, 1800; m. Dec. 12, 1822, Charity Nelson, b. Apr. 14, 1804. He d. June 18, 1847. Res. Sharon, Wis.

CHILDREN.

567. I. MARK F., b. May 21, 1825; m. Harriett Wheeler and Betsey J. Potter.
II. GEORGE L., b. May 1, 1827; d. Dec. 9, 1846.
III. HANNAH E., b. Mar. 9, 1837; d. Nov. 25, 1854.

459. **Hiram[8] Pierce** (Benona[7], Jobe[6], Jobe[5], Mial[4], Ephraim[3], Ephraim[2], Michael[1]), b. Jan. 22, 1806; m. Nov. 25, 1830, Miriam Strong, b. Jan. 10, 1808; d. Mar. 31, 1882. Miriam Strong was the dau. of Noah Rockwell Strong.

Hiram Pierce was born in Durham, Greene county, N. Y., January 22, 1806; a merchant in Earlville, Delhi county, Iowa, where he was for several years a farmer, as also previously in the earlier part of his life, for some twenty years, at Blenheim, Schoharie county, N. Y. Later he moved to Chamberlain, Dakota, where he now (1889) resides.

CHILDREN.

I. PHILO PORTER, b. Aug. 13, 1831, at Blenheim, N. Y.; d. Oct. 1, 1833.
II. PHILANDER PITKIN, b. at Blenheim, Oct. 24, 1832; a merchant in Belvidere; m. May 3, 1853, Justina Cahoon of Belvidere, and had a son b. Apr., 1854; went south in 1868, and has never been heard from since.
568. III. BENONI, b. at Blenheim, Mar. 31, 1834; m. Thankful Bigsley.
IV. PHILO PORTER, b. Mar. 21, 1836; a farmer in Earlville, Iowa; m. Feb. 14, 1857, Sarah Gibbs, b. Aug. 18, 1850 (dau. of John Gibbs of Oneida, N. Y., and Elizabeth, his wife). He d. Aug. 17, 1859.

569.　　V. Calvin Wright, b. Apr. 30, 1838; m. Mary M. Fear.

　　VI. Martha Amelia, b. Mar. 30, 1840; m. Jan. 3, 1864, Franklin Eugene Wheeler, b. Feb. 1, 1836 (son of Asa and Mary Wheeler of Earlville, Iowa); a grain dealer in Earlville, Iowa. They have had one child, Etna, b. Jan. 8, 1867; d. Aug. 6, 1869.

570.　 VII. Squire William, b. Apr. 12, 1842; m. Mary J. Wheeler.

　 VIII. Laura Cornelia, b. Jan. 13, 1847; m. Dec. 25, 1866, James Seymour Reader, b. Nov. 11, 1841 (son of William and Jane Reader of North Fork, Iowa); a farmer at Earlville, Iowa. They had a child, a son unnamed, b. Feb. 10, 1869; d. Mar., 1869.

　　IX. Althæa Ophelia, b. June 28, 1848; m. May 17, 1868, Robert Healey, b. July 17, 1847 (son of John and Betsey Healey); a merchant in Earlville, Iowa.

571.　　X. Leander Llewellyn, b. May 3, 1853; m. Mary J. Walker.

460. **Lemuel D.**[8] **Pierce** (Benona[7], Jobe[6], Jobe[5], Mial[4], Ephraim[3], Ephraim[2], Michael[1]), b. Apr. 9, 1810; m. Apr. 28, 1836, Lydia Ruliffson, b. Apr. 8, 1808. Res. Henry, Dakota.

Children.

　　I. Adelia, b. June 3, 1837.
　 II. Phebia, b. Aug., 1839.
　III. Charles W., b. Mar. 25, 1842.
　IV. Willard, b. June 8, 1844.
　　V. Clinton, b. Dec. 18, 1848.
　VI. Frank B., b. Dec. 4, 1852; unm.

461. **Electus**[8] **Pierce** (Benona[7], Jobe[6], Jobe[5], Mial[4], Ephraim[3] Ephraim[2], Michael[1]), b. Jan. 13, 1829; m. Oct. 11, 1854, Clarissa

Wood, b. Dec. 27, 1834. He d. Mar. 4, 1875. Res. Jefferson, N. Y.

CHILDREN.

I. SEYMOUR J., b. Oct. 12, 1855.
II. ELVENA, b. May 18, 1857 ; m. 1881, Roscoe Bailey; res. Jefferson, N. Y.
III. ALICE, b. Sept. 12, 1858; m. Frank Foote; res. Jefferson, N. Y.
IV. EDWIN K., b. Jan. 22, 1860; m. Mina Van Duzen ; res. Jefferson, N. Y.
V. EMORY E., b. Sept. 29, 1861; m. Ella Shaver; res. Jefferson, N. Y.
VI. LOUISA R., b. May 6, 1863; m. George Franklin; res. Jefferson, N. Y.
VII. CHARLES L., b. Oct. 24, 1864.
VIII. ARTHUR E., b. July 7, 1866.
IX. NETTIE L., b. July 4, 1868.
X. MINA J., b. Feb. 27, 1870.
XI. IRENE, b. Sept. 19, 1871.
XII. EVA L., b. Aug. 11, 1873.
XIII. BENONA E., b. Nov. 19, 1875.

462. **John M.**[8] **Pierce** (Gilbert[7], Jobe[6], Jobe[5], Mial[4], Ephraim[3], Ephraim[2], Michael[1]), b. Oct. 11, 1811; m. Sept. 26, 1833, Charlotte Sickel, b. Mar. 10, 1816. Res. Ellwood, N. J.

CHILDREN.

I. NICHOLA, b. Dec. 6, 1834; m. July, 1862, Caroline Elliott; res. Egg Harbor, N. J.
II. EMMA, b. Oct. 31, 1837; m. Feb. 25, 1858, J. B. Elliott, b. Feb. 3, 1835 ; res. Sage Brook, N. Y. Ch., Frank P., b. May 30, 1860; res. Greene, N. Y.; Eddie C., b. July 28, 1862 ; res. Greene, N. Y.; Hugh C., b. Jan. 20, 1867; res. Greene, N. Y.; H. J. Earl, b. Oct. 1, 1878.
III. HATTIE, b. Nov. 23, 1839; m. 1869, W. A. Sayer; res. Ellwood, N. J.

IV. AMELIA, b. Feb. 11, 1843; m. 1869, Joseph Robinson; res. Ellwood, N. J.

V. CHARLES H., b. Mar. 26, 1851; m. 1868, Ann
Schenck; res. Ellwood, N. J.

VI. MARY C., b. Oct. 19, 1853; m. 1882, James Hard;
res. Egg Harbor, N. J.

463. **Silas G.**[8] **Pierce** (Gilbert[7], Jobe[6], Jobe[5], Mial[4], Ephraim[3],
Ephraim[2], Michael[1]), b. Feb. 4, 1818; m. Sept., 1840, Harriett
Green, b. Apr. 27, 1822; d. Aug. 18, 1853; m. 2nd, Sept., 1856,
Mariah Aldrich, b. July 28, 1827. Res. Binghamton, N. Y.

CHILDREN.

I. LODENA, b. Apr. 12, 1842; d. Feb. 24, 1856.
II. JOSEPHINE, b. Feb. 28, 1857.
III. FRED, b. Feb. 8, 1859; d. Oct. 9, 1876.
IV. GRANT, b. July 11, 1864; d. July, 1866.
V. MARK, b. Aug. 17, 1866.

464. **Jesse**[8] **Pierce** (Samuel[7], Samuel[6], Jobe[5], Mial[4], Ephraim[3],
Ephraim[2], Michael[1]), b. 1812; m. Chloe B. Martin; m. 2nd, 1841,
Charlotte Harlow, b. May 30, 1822; d. Nov. 27, 1862. Res.
Grafton, N. H.

CHILDREN.

I. LODOSKA M., b. ——.   II. JESSE F., b. ——.
III. SARAH F., b. ——.   IV. JEFFERSON H., b. ——.
V. EDWIN, b. ——.   VI. L. ALICE, b. ——.
VII. C. BELLE, b. ——.

572. VIII. MARTIN, b. Jan. 26, 1842; m. Frances H. Martin.

465. **Hiram**[8] **Pierce** (Samuel[7], Samuel[6], Jobe[5], Mial[4],
Ephraim[3], Ephraim[2], Michael[1]), b. May 12, 1803; m. Jan. 14, 1835,
Hannah Marsh, b. June 11, 1813. He d. June 8, 1870, and in
Nov., 1871, she m. Fred Strong. Res. Grafton, N. H.

CHILDREN.

I. HANNAH E., b. Dec. 30, 1838; m. Sept. 27, 1861, Eben Gove, b. Aug. 14, 1833 ; res. East Grafton, N. H. Ch., Hattie M., b. Aug. 15, 1865 ; Lizzie L., b. June 19, 1871 ; Alpheus P., b. Aug. 20, 1873.

II. MARY W., b. Feb. 14, 1842 ; m. Sept. 1, 1865, Edgar Stevens, b. Aug. 30, 1842; res. Wilkinsonville, Worcester county, Mass. Ch., Linnie M., b. Sept. 28, 1866; Arthur P., b. Apr. 14, 1870 ; Robert E., b. June 11, 1878.

III. HIRAM, b. Nov. 1, 1840; m. Ada Drew; had a son, Hiram F., b. 1875.

IV. HATTIE W., b. Nov. 25, 1843 ; m. Joseph Watson and Thomas Eichleman ; res. Alexandria, N. H.

V. MERCY, b. Mar. 31, 1845; m. Sept. 13, 1866, Alpheus Pierce Goddard (see). Ch., Hannah F., b. Sept. 18, 1867; Alpheus J., b. May 28, 1870; Jennie M., b. July 5, 1872 ; res. Freeport, Ill.

VI. OLINDA, b. Mar. 11, 1848; m. June 1, 1872, Clark G. Stiles, b. June 25, 1849. Ch., Hattie J., b. Feb. 23, 1878; res. Freeport, Ill.

VII. CELINDA, b. Mar. 11, 1848 ; m. Nov. 14, 1867, David G. Bean, b. Jan. 12, 1824; d. Sept. 7, 1871; m. 2nd, Dec., 1877, Albert W. Tucker, b. June 4, 1847; d. Apr. 9, 1879; m. 3rd, Daniel Peters, b. Nov. 4, 1851. Ch., Celinda, b. and d. Nov. 14, 1872; res. Canaan, N. H.

465-1. **Phillip**[8] **Pierce** (Samuel[7], Samuel[6], Jobe[5], Mial[4], Ephraim[3], Ephraim[2], Michael[1]), b. ——; m. Elizabeth F. Terry. He was a lawyer, res. New Bedford, Mass., where he d. Nov. 2, 1885.

CHILDREN.

573.   I. CHARLES C., b. Sept. 29, 1842 ; m. Sarah W. Dunham.

466. Seth W.[8] **Pierce** (Sylvester[7], Sylvester[6], Caleb[5], Mial[4], Ephraim[3], Ephraim[2], Michael[1]), b. ——; m. Mary Cheseborough. Res. Summerhill, Ill.

CHILDREN.

I. JAMES, b. ——; res. 2814 Eighth avenue, New York.
II. EMILY, b. ——.
III. GEORGE E., b. ——; res. Belvidere.

467. Harry H.[8] **Pierce** (Jesse[7], Caleb[6], Caleb[5], Mial[4], Ephraim[3], Ephraim[2], Michael[1]), b. May 10, 1812, in Buffalo, N. Y.; m. Jan. 10, 1856, in Alma, Mich., Elner Jane Rowland, b. Feb. 21, 1838; d. Sept. 8, 1871. He d. Apr. 28, 1881. Res. Cedar Lake, Montcalm county, Mich.

Harry Henshaw Pierce was born in the village of Hamburg, Erie county, N. Y., May 10, 1882, and emigrated to Lake county, Ind., about 1835 or 1836. He was a volunteer in the Mexican War, and served under Zachary Taylor. He died in Cedar Lake, Mich., respected and honored by his neighbors.

CHILDREN.

574. I. MYIEL J., b, Jan. 19, 1861 ; m. Elvira E. Webster.
575. II. GEORGE B., b. Feb. 19, 1868; m. Rhoda E. Cox.
III. NETTIE, b. ——; res. Ridgeway, Mich.
576. IV. ANDREW J., b. Feb. 8, 1857 ; m. Mary J. Rowland.
577. V. DUFF DE KALB, b. Mar. 7, 1859; m. Mary Agnes Wagner.

468. Simeon[8] **Pierce** (Jesse[7], Caleb[6], Caleb[5], Mial[4], Ephraim[3], Ephraim[2], Michael[1]), b. Mar. 20, 1814; m. Oct. 4, 1836, Amanda F. Pratt, b. Oct. 4, 1816; d. Dec. 19, 1861. Res. Valparaiso, Ind.

CHILDREN.

I. MELISSA E., b. Aug. 29, 1837 ; d. July 19, 1860.
II. MINERVA, b. Nov. 3, 1841 ; m. June 4, 1868, Reuben Quartermass, s. p. ; res. Port Hutchinson, Kans.
III. CLARISSA, b. July 16, 1844 ; d. Apr. 10, 1866.

469. David C.[8] **Pierce** (Jesse[7], Caleb[6], Caleb[5], Mial[4], Ephraim[3],

Ephraim[2], Michael[1]), b. Apr. 3, 1820; m. Oct. 15, 1843, Sallie E.
Lindsay, b. Nov. 3, 1826. Res. Moline, Kans.

CHILDREN.

I. DEXTER L., b. June 6, 1846; m. Feb. 28, 1878. Res.
Wichita, Kans.
II. FLORA A., b. Jan. 23, 1849; m. 1869, C. Binyon ; res.
Crown Point, Ind.
III. NELSON C., b. Feb. 24, 1856; d. May 26, 1857.
IV. NELLIE M., b. Mar. 9, 1858; m. S. B. Hemenway; res.
Arkansas City, Kans.
V. DAVID C., b. Nov. 26, 1860; m, 1881; res. Moline,
Kans.
VI. DANIEL J., b. Sept. 11, 1868; res. Moline, Kans.

470. **Seneca[8] Pierce** (Levi[7], Caleb[6], Caleb[5], Mial[4], Ephraim[3],
Ephraim[2], Michael[1]), b. Aug. 22, 1809; m. Nov. 15, 1829, Lucy
Pitcher, b. July 3, 1811; d. Mar. 2, 1876. He d. Mar. 19, 1874.
Res. North East, Pa.

CHILDREN.

578.   I. DEXTER, b. Jan. 3, 1831 ; m. Eliza A. Newton.
II. ELLEN, b. June 5, 1833 ; d. Dec. 2, 1833.
III. LABAN, b. June 5, 1835; res. Clifton, Dakota.
IV. MARTHA, b. June 16, 1838; m. —— Ireland; res.
Dakota.
V. LUCY A., b. May 29, 1840 ; m. E. Moulthrop ; res. North
East, Pa.
VI. MARIETTA, b. Oct. 25, 1841 ; m. —— Ainsworth, and
d. 1880.
VII. WILLIAM W., b. Oct. 27, 1842; res. Erie, Pa.
579. VIII. JAMES K., b. Feb. 25, 1845 ; m. Lucy F. Smith.
IX. SARAH L., b. Mar. 3, 1848; m. S. Morse ; res. North
East, Pa.
X. JOHN, b. Aug. 28, 1850; res. Peru, Ind.
XI. HARRIETT E., b. June 30, 1853; m. F. Wells ; res.
North East, Pa.
XII. BENJAMIN F., b. ——; res. Oakland, Cal.
46

471. **Dr. Amos M.**[8] **Pierce** (Amos[7], Shuball[6], Joshua[5], Mial[4], Ephraim[3], Ephraim[2], Michael[1]), b. Nov. 17, 1818; m. Harriett N. Frost, b. 1829. He d. Jan. 30, 1885. Res. Bennington, Vt., and Morris, Ill.

CHILDREN.

I. WILLIAM A., b. May 22, 1851; m. Mar. 10, 1881; M. D.; res. Osceola, Ind.

II. FRANK F., b. July 14, 1853; m. 1878; res. Osceola, Ind.

III. FREDERIC, b. Sept. 21, 1856; d. Aug. 11, 1859.

IV. GEORGIE, b. Oct. 11, 1859; d. Oct. 8, 1860.

V. HATTIE G., b. 1861; res. Morris, Ill.

VI. JENNIE MAY, b. 1866; res. Morris, Ill.

472. **Hiram**[8] **Pierce** (Mason[7], Shuball[6], Joshua[5], Mial[4], Ephraim[3], Ephraim[2], Michael[1]), b. Apr. 13, 1803; m. May 18, 1823. He d. Apr. 13, 1883. Res. Colton, N. Y.

Hiram Pierce was born in 1803. In 1827, he moved to Colton, St. Lawrence county, N. Y. He was prominent in business circles, and a successful merchant and manufacturer. In his last years he devoted himself to farming and passed his days in quiet. At one time he owned a saw-mill, and had a starch factory. For many years he held the office of justice of the peace.

473. **Hon. James M.**[8] **Pierce** (Jabez M.[7], Henry[6], Joshua[5], Mial[4], Ephraim[3], Ephraim[2], Michael[1]), b. July 12, 1821; m. 1882, Mrs. (Bancroft) Palmer. He d. 1887, s. p. Res. San Diego, Cal.

James M. Pierce, a pioneer citizen and one of the most prominent and enterprising business men of this city, died yesterday forenoon after an illness of less than a month. While it was generally known that he was ill, the citizens were scarcely prepared to hear of his death, and expressions of regret and sorrow were heard on all sides. The immediate cause of his death was apoplexy, brought on by strain from a fall he received while examining the work on the Pierce-Morse building about three weeks ago. In falling the deceased struck in such a manner that his spine was injured, and a few days ago paralysis set in and he lost the entire control of his lower extremities. The deceased was one of the most public spirited citizens, and his name is connected with a majority of the enterprises that have brought this city into prominence. He was benevolent almost to a fault, giving in a quiet and unostentatious manner that endeared him to all. The funeral will take place this afternoon from the South-west Institute building on Florence Heights.

James M. Pierce was born in Providence, R. I., sixty-five years ago, and spent his earlier years in his native town. During the gold fever in 1852, Mr. Pierce, then a young man, determined to try his fortune in the new country, and taking passage from New York, he came around Cape Horn. Instead of going to the mines, the young man saw an opportunity in San Francisco to make money in a slower but surer way, and opened a general forwarding and commission store, handling freight and goods for miners. A few years subsequent saw him in San José, where he resided for several years, and then removed to Oregon. In the latter State he entered into business and was unusually successful, retiring in 1869, with a fortune. Then he came to this city, which he made his home up to the time of his death.

He was elected to the Assembly from this county in 1875, as a Republican, over Wallace Leach, Democrat. He had at different times served on the board of supervisors, and as a city trustee, and in 1877 and 1878, he was president of the Chamber of Commerce. He was one of the founders of the old Bank of San Diego, the first bank established in the city, and was at the time of his death, vice-president of the Consolidated National Bank, and president of the County Savings Bank. He was one of the founders of the San Diego Benevolent Association, and with his wife, founded the South-west Institute. He built the Central market, and with E. W. Morse, was engaged in the erection of the magnificent block, now nearly completed, on the corner of Sixth and F streets. He was an active member of the Society for Improving and Beautifying San Diego. He was also a prominent member of the Masonic Order and of the Odd Fellows. The deceased was married about four or five years ago, to Mrs. Palmer, a sister of Hubert H. Bancroft, the historian, who survives him. [San Diego paper.]

474. **John H.**[8] **Pierce** (Jabez M.[7], Henry[6], Joshua[5], Mial[4], Ephraim[3], Ephraim[2], Michael[1]), b. Oct. 2, 1827; m. Oct. 2, 1851, Esther J. Ryder, b. May 19, 1834. Res. 40 Grosvenor street, Providence, R. I.

CHILDREN.

I. FRANK E., b. Oct. 19, 1853; res. 17 and 19 Chardon street, Boston, Mass.

II. MARY J., b. July 3, 1856; m. 1877, Charles E. Hall; res. East Providence, R. I.

III. HENRIETTA L., b. Nov. 26, 1862.

IV. JAMES M., b. Mar. 13, 1866.

V. ANNIE L., b. June 28, 1872; d. Oct. 23, 1876.

475. **Mason R.**[8] **Pierce** (Nathaniel R.[7], Barnard[6], Joshua[5], Mial[4], Ephraim[3], Ephraim[2], Michael[1]), b. Mar. 27, 1817; m. June 20, 1838, Betsey S. Hall, b. Mar. 1, 1814; d. Mar. 7, 1863; m. 2nd, Apr. 14, 1864, Mary R. Bagley. Res. 221 East One Hundred and Twenty-sixth street, New York.

Mason R. Pierce was the son of Nathaniel R. and Mary Pierce of Rehoboth, county of Bristol, Mass. He was born in Dighton, Mass. (where his parents temporarily resided), March 27, 1817. When at the age of four years, while his parents were engaged out of doors, he arose from the trundle-bed, and seeing breakfast prepared on the table, he made fast to a piece of boiled pork, and made tracks for his grandfather's, which was about a quarter of a mile away, across the fields. On the return of the parents for breakfast, they were greeted with surprise at the absence of their boy, also the meat portion of their breakfast. This caused a vigilant search, which resulted in finding the boy hiding under the bed at his grandfather's. The pork was not accounted for, but his refusal of breakfast gave evidence he was not hungry. The grandfather, being so well pleased at the joke, offered to give the boy four cents a day to come over and help him work his farm. The boy's parents, to carry out this joke, were careful to send him to his grandfather every fair day. At the close of the year his father made out a bill of his time, which he presented to his grandfather. This was promptly paid and a receipt exchanged.

The grandfather then agreed to give the boy five cents per day for the next year; this agreement was agreeably carried out by both parties. At the age of six years his father made him generally useful on and about his own farm, in which he continued until his fourteenth year.

When twelve years of age, his father gave him the privilege of planting two rows of potatoes for his own benefit, around a cornfield next to the wall, to make room for the horse and plow to be worked without treading down the corn in hoeing time. In the fall when the potatoes were dug, they measured eight bushels, and sold for 12½ cents a bushel. He sold them in exchange for a New Testament, to use as a school book; this book was used in school by him, and later on by his four children. It is now kept by him as a keepsake in his library. His advantages of education was limited to six weeks of district school in the winter of each year. When he was thirteen years of age he attended a district school in Swansey, two and a half miles from his home, for a period of four weeks; also a district school in Warren, R. I., for three months. At fourteen years of age, he went to work in a cotton mill in Attleboro, Mass., for J. C. Dodge & Co., at $2 per week wages. From the 1st of December, 1831, until March, 1832, he drove horses from the gravel pit, to the dump and back, in the building of the Boston and Providence railroad, for $2.50 per day. At sixteen years, he engaged as an apprentice to the " mason trade," with his uncle, Bradford S. Pierce, in New Bedford, Mass. The arrangement with his uncle was to serve five years, and attend evening school each winter. His first year he was to receive $5; the second year, $20; the third year, $25; the fourth year, $35; the fifth and last year, $65, and board. At the expiration of the fifth year, in settlement, he came out $18 in debt to his uncle, $9 to his father, $4 to his oldest sister, making in all $31. He continued to work for his uncle for $1.50 per day. His first earnings he used to cancel his indebtedness. When nineteen years of age, he was baptized and made a member of the Christian Church of New Bedford, Mass. On June 20, 1838, he married a wife in Cumberland, R. I., Miss Betsey S. Hall. In September following they went to house-keeping in New Bedford, Mass. In December of the same year they moved to Rehoboth, to carry out a contract made with his father to build for him a farm house. On April 26, 1839, they were favored with a pair of twins (*double blessedness*), a daughter and son, who were named Cilecia E. and Cilecius M. Pierce. The daughter died May 6, 1839, aged ten days. In the spring of 1841, they moved to Providence, R. I., where he was engaged with Messrs. Tallman, Bucklin, Gillmore & Hunt, in building eighteen brick school-houses for the city; also a great deal of other work. In 1842, he built himself a stone cottage, located on South street in said city of Providence. He joined the church of that city by affiliation, and superintended a Sabbath-school for two years, where their third child, a son, was born on August 23, 1842, and was named Bradford D. Pierce. In the year 1844, they moved to Cumberland, near Lonsdale, on the Blackstone river, where he took charge of building extensive bleaching works in Lonsdale village, for Messrs. Brown & Ives. On August 3, 1844, their fourth child, a daughter, was born, and named Georgietta N. Pierce. He continued working for the same firm, repairing and improving the mills at Albion, Mansville, Woonsocket, and all along the Blackstone river. In 1846, he contracted to build a private residence for Isaac B. Davis, in the city of Worcester, Mass. Together with other work in and about the said city of Worcester, he built himself a stone cottage, which he sold later to Dr. Green of that city; it was located on John street.

In 1848, he engaged with the Boston and Providence Railroad Company to construct depot buildings, bridges and culverts at East Attleboro, Mansfield, Foxboro and Canton. He moved his family to East Attleboro, where his fifth child, a son, was born on September 5, 1848, and was named Shepard H. Pierce. In 1849, he moved his family to Mansfield, where he had built a cottage for himself, where the Taunton and New Bedford branch railroad forms a junction with the Boston and Providence railroad.

On the 11th of August, 1851, he left his business in charge of his cousin, Asa B. Pierce, and took passage in the steamer "Georgia" at New York for California; after a very rough passage, and a stop at Jamaica for repairs, he arrived at Chagres on the 27th of the same month; from thence he and some six hundred others (Mrs. Jesse Fremont, wife of Colonel Fremont, being one of the party, *en route* to meet her husband, who was then pioneering in California), embarked in small boats for Cruses; these boats being propelled by the natives of Chagres, and Jamaica creoles. Each boat carried twelve persons, besides the propellers. They were two and a half days going to Cruses, where they all took passage, by mule and foot trains, for Panama, where they arrived all muddy, hungry and tired. All the mules had to be abandoned on the first day out, on account of mud, and each person had to pick his or her way as best they could through the miserable and forsaken country of uncivilization. They arrived one day too late to connect with steamer for San Francisco, and a delay of twelve days, in waiting for steamer to cross the Pacific to their destination, which was reached in eighteen days, on the steamer "Oregon," which plied between Panama and San Francisco, and carried the United States mail, which arrived on the 1st day of October, 1851, in San Francisco. In the afternoon of the same day, he commenced work, laying brick, on the American Theater, which was then being erected. When that was finished he went to work on the Jenny Lind Theater, putting on the plaster and stucco finish, after which he took steamer for Sacramento, and from there joined a wagon-train for the mining regions, in the mountains. They stopped at Drytown, Sutters Creek, Jackson and Mocalomy Hill. In Calaveres county, after a general survey of the situation he started a bake-shop and eating ranche, also trading-post at Sutters Creek. In connection with an express line to San Francisco, bought and sold gold dust, miner's wearing apparel, mining tools, all kinds of provisions, newspapers, novels, etc., expressing letters, papers, etc., to and from San Francisco. He followed this line of business with great success for some twelve months, when the government stationed a post route, which interfered with his expressage. Private enterprise created opposition which suggested to him it was best to quit while the play was good; suiting the action to the word, he sold out his whole business, and with a neighbor, they packed a pair of mules with the proper utensils and started on a prospecting tour in search of rich " gold digging." After roughing it for about four weeks they returned and divided the purse of $90, which they had collected while away. He then disposed of the mule and utensils, taking the mail-coach for Sacramento *en route* to San Francisco. At said city he contracted for building some brick stores and dwelling. He then took passage in steamer " Unicorn " to Panama; from thence to Cruses (on foot), there taking the railroad train to Aspinwall; from thence by steamer " Northern Light" to New York city, thence by rail to his home in Mansfield, Mass. In the spring of 1853, he and his nephew, G. H. Butterworth, purchased a cotton mill in Mansfield, where they manufactured printing goods for William H. Reynolds, commission merchant of Providence, R. I. In the fall of 1856, their mill was burned, incurring heavy loss. In 1856, he entered into a contract with Mr. Gardner Chilson of Mansfield, to build an iron foundry, machine shop and other buildings near the junction of the Taunton branch railroad with the Boston and Providence railroad station at Mansfield.

In 1857, he contracted with the Union Straw Works Company of Foxboro, Mass., for all the mason work in the construction of their extensive buildings and water fountain. He also built the town house and fences in the Foxboro common, with iron rail and stone posts for the town. And took charge of erecting buildings, setting engines, pumps, boilers, and the sinking of a shaft to 125 feet deep in search for anthracite coal in the town of Mansfield, Mass., for the Mansfield Mining Company.

In 1858 and 1859, he and his uncle Bradford S. Pierce of New

Bedford, Mass., took out patents for improvements in molds and machinery for the manufacture of cement drain and sewer pipe, artificial stone, etc., which diverted his time and talent to another field of labor, which called for building machinery, traveling to introduce and license the patents, start companies in the manufacture of cement pipe, both drain and sewer, building material, etc., through the United States, from Maine to California.

In 1861 and 1862, he contracted with the Central Park commissioners for the entire drainage and sewerage of the park, and much other work in and about the city of New York. On March 7, 1863, his wife died, and on the 16th of the following April he went to Havana, Cuba, to introduce a general system of sewerage in that city. While there he was taken sick with yellow fever, which confined him two weeks, after which he returned to New York city. On August 4, 1864, he married his second wife, Mrs. Mary L. Bagley of New York. They traveled in the interest of their patents to all of the important cities and towns in the United States, also attending many of the State and county agricultural fairs. They spent the entire season of the World's fair at Philadelphia in 1876, exhibiting, etc. His wife exhibited in the Woman's Pavilion, and in the Horticultural Hall some of her newly-improved flower stands, end window gardens, for which she received a special diploma. In May, 1880, they settled down to housekeeping at their present residence, No. 221 East One Hundred and Twenty-sixth street, New York city. He belongs to the order of F. and A. M., Masonic Lodge, No. 106 of the city and State of New York.

He is a life member of the American Institute of New York city; President of the Cement Pipe Machine Patents Association of New Bedford, Mass.; Republican in politics; fair-dealing and universal justice constitutes his religion. The present he appreciates, the past he cannot recall, the future is yet unborn. Not to do to others those things which he would not that others should do to him, is his motto. He is conversant with the Scriptures, and the works of the most of the eminent theological writers. He gives Moses great credit for shrewdness, while telling to the Jews the story of God's creation of every thing out of nothing, in omitting to explain the origin of the water which he claimed God moved upon when thus engaged in the great work of the creation. It probably did not occur to him at this early period, 2,493 years after the creation of Adam, that much of the component parts of water were animal, which, at its death, formed the earth, and which in its contraction created heat and gas that often exploded when coming in contact with water, heaving up mountains, opening channels for the guidance of rivers, creating earthquakes, and by their internal convulsions causing a general disarrangement of the earth's surface. And he believes that, because Joshua, 2,916 years after Adam, did not discover that the sun did neither rise, set, nor move, is evidence that his knowledge of astronomy was limited, or he might have conceived the idea that the sun was a great electric light caused by the rapid motion of the earth in its revolutions, casting off its electrical force to a central point aad reflecting back its rays to earth, supplying a genial temperature necessary to make the conditions which creates all animal and vegetable life. He places no reliance on any religious faith, creed, superstition or miracles, as all such are void of proof of the fact. His practice is individual responsibility and proper action in this his earthly life, trusting to the powers that be for further results. He will be seventy-two years old on the 27th day of March, 1889.

CHILDREN.

I. CILECIA C., b. Apr. 26, 1839; d. May 6, 1839.
580. II. MACON C., b. Apr. 26, 1839; m. Harriett E. Corney.
581. III. BRADFORD D., b. Aug. 23, 1842; m. Ellen F. Downey.
IV. GEORGETTE A., b. Aug. 3, 1844; m. Frank Leavitt; res. Mansfield, Mass.
V. SHEPARD H., b. Sept. 23, 1848; res. Hotel Brunswick, Kansas City, Mo.

476. **Abraham**[8] **Pierce** (Jeremiah[7], Barnard[6], Joshua[5], Mial[4], Ephraim[3], Ephraim[2], Michael[1]), b. Feb. 1, 1828; m. Nov. 5, 1849, Harriett E. Freeman, b. Oct. 25, 1833. Res. Rehoboth and East Attleboro, Mass.

CHILDREN.

I. ELLA M., b. Sept. 5, 1850; d. Apr. 2, 1852.
II. JENNIE M., b. Oct. 4, 1852; m. Jan. 7, 1875, William H. Wilmarth, s. p.; res. Attleboro, Mass.
III. LILLIAN A., b. Sept. 24, 1854; m. Jan. 3, 1883, A. W. Hills; res. Attleboro, Mass. Ch., Alice M., b. Apr. 9, 1885.

47

IV. GEORGE A., b. July 18, 1864; m. Dec. 17, 1885,
Frances A. Brooks, b. Sept. 19, 1863; res. s. p.,
Attleboro, Mass.

V. HARRIETT E., b. May 29, 1867.

VI. HENRY M., b. Dec. 7, 1873.

476½. **Galen**[8] **Pierce** (Jeremiah[7], Barnard[6], Joshua[5], Mial[4],
Ephraim[3], Ephraim[2], Michael[1]), b. July 18, 1824; m. Apr. 13,
1847, Phebe A. G. Barney; d. May 29, 1880. Res. East Providence, R. I.

CHILDREN.

I. EUGENIA E., b. Feb. 27, 1848; m. May 14, 1872,
Stephen S. Rich, b. Mar. 11, 1846; res. East Providence, R. I. Ch., Phebe E., b. Mar. 21, 1873;
Davis W., b. June 21, 1874; Alfred P., b. Nov.
14, 1875; d. Sept. 30, 1877; Stephen J., b. Nov.
15, 1876; Grace M., b. Feb. 20, 1878; Lyra E., b.
Mar. 26, 1879; Leah V., b. Mar. 26, 1879; d. July
25, 1879; Arthur G., b. Sept. 2, 1881; Adin B., b.
Jan. 24, 1885.

II. ALFRED G., b. Apr. 25, 1853; d. Oct. 2, 1853.

582.   III. WALTER B., b. Nov. 5, 1855; m. Emma Andrews.

IV. GALEN F., b. Mar. 30, 1865.

477. **Charles M.**[8] **Pierce** (Charles M.[7], Barnard[6], Joshua[5],
Mial[4], Ephraim[3], Ephraim[2], Michael[1]), b. July 26, 1823; m. Mar.
11, 1851, Sarah A. Durfee, b. Dec. 27, 1826; d. Oct. 6, 1855; m.
2nd, Nov. 28, 1860, Amanda E. Hill, b. Aug. 7, 1836. He d.
Sept. 12, 1875. Res. 731 Country street, New Bedford, Mass.

CHILDREN.

I. FRANK C., b. Jan. 12, 1852.

II. ANNIE C., b. Aug. 23, 1861; m. Herbert Howland.
He d. July 6, 1885, leaving one child, Grace E.

III. WILLIAM C., b. Nov. 21, 1863.

IV. MARY A. H., b. July 21, 1865.

V. EMILY H., b. Sept. 1, 1867.
VI. ALBERT B., b. Dec. 25, 1869.
VII. ELIZABETH S., b. Sept. 30, 1871.

478. **Warren G.**[8] **Pierce** (Charles M.[7], Barnard[6], Joshua[5], Mial[4], Ephraim[3], Ephraim[2], Michael[1]), b. Apr. 25, 1832; m. Nov. 23, 1855, Mary M. Manchester. Res. 121 Hillman street, New Bedford, Mass.

CHILDREN.

I. LELAND C., b. Sept. 21, 1860; res. 121 Hillman street, New Bedford, Mass.
II. ARTHUR M., b. Apr. 22, 1865; res. 121 Hillman street, New Bedford, Mass.

479. **Asa B.**[8] **Pierce** (Barnard[7], Barnard[6], Joshua[5], Mial[4], Ephraim[3], Ephraim[2], Michael[1]), b. Dec. 30, 1826; m. Sept. 22, 1850, Angenette Harden, b. Mar. 2, 1824. Res. 147 Elm street, New Bedford, Mass.

CHILDREN.

583.   I. FRANK E., b. Dec. 26, 1851; m. Helen Williams.
II. DORA G., b. Oct. 14, 1853; m. Jan. 9, 1874, Charles Williams. She d. May 9, 1878; res. New Bedford, Mass. Ch., Dora, b. Dec., 1877.
III. ELLA B., b. Oct. 11, 1855; d. May 3, 1863.

480. **Ira C.**[8] **Pierce** (Barnard[7], Barnard[6], Joshua[5], Mial[4], Ephraim[3], Ephraim[2], Michael[1]), b. Sept. 11, 1823; m. Aug. 9, 1849, Susan H. Soule, b. 1820; d. July 6, 1856; m. 2nd, July 15, 1858, Catherine Burbank, b. Jan. 26, 1836. Res. Hyde Park, Mass.

CHILDREN.

I. ELINOR F., b. Jan. 23, 1850; d. Apr. 23, 1852.
II. WILLIAM, b. Nov. 3, 1853; d. May 12, 1854.
III. ABIGAIL H., b. Mar. 3, 1855; d. Sept. 30, 1855.

IV. ARTHUR H., b. Feb. 3, 1859; d. Aug. 29, 1859.
V. SUSAN H., b. May 5, 1861.
VI. ELINOR L., b. Dec. 12, 1865.

481. **Andrew G.**[8] **Pierce** (Otis N.[7], Barnard[6], Joshua[5], Mial[4], Ephraim[3], Ephraim[2], Michael[1]), b. Aug. 9, 1829; m. July 17, 1854, Caroline L. Hillman, b. June 16, 1832. Res. 103 Spring street, New Bedford, Mass.

CHILDREN.

I. EDWARD T., b. May 24, 1855.
II. MARY B., b. Feb. 3, 1858.
III. ANDREW G., b. Mar. 28, 1864.
IV. LOUISA C., b. Apr. 2, 1866.
V. ALBERT R., b. Jan. 26, 1869.
VI. HARVEY L., b. Mar. 23, 1872; d. Jan. 19, 1873.
VII. ELSIE H., b. May 21, 1874.

482. **Erskine H.**[8] **Pierce** (Bradford S.[7], Barnard[6], Joshua[5], Mial[4], Ephraim[3], Ephraim[2], Michael[1]), b. Dec. 17, 1849; m. Feb. 18, 1873, Henrietta M. Fisher, b. Jan. 3, 1851. Res. 52 Fifth street, New Bedford, Mass.

CHILDREN.

I. SYLVIA C., b. July 27, 1878.

483. **Crawford S.**[8] **Pierce** (Bradford S.[7], Barnard[6], Joshua[5], Mial[4], Ephraim[3], Ephraim[2], Michael[1]), b. Sept. 10, 1847; m. Nov. 18, 1869, Elizabeth Delano, b. Mar. 7, 1847. Res. 9 Bedford street, New Bedford, Mass.

CHILDREN.

I. EDWARD E., b. Dec. 18, 1870.
II. LIZZIE D., b. Aug. 9, 1872.
III. ALICE L., b. July 1, 1875; d. Oct. 21, 1882.
IV. CLIFTON B., b. Apr. 12, 1878.

484. **Mason**[8] **Pierce** (William[7], Joshua[6], Joshua[5], Mial[4], Ephraim[3], Ephraim[2], Michael[1]), b. ——; m. Susan Lewis, b. 1810; d. July 10, 1866; m. 2nd, June 6, 1870, Ann D. Paine. Res. Bristol, R. I.

CHILDREN.

    I. ALONZO N., b. ——.

485. **Alfred**[8] **Pierce** (William[7], Joshua[6], Joshua[5], Mial[4], Ephraim[3], Ephraim[2], Michael[1]), b. ——; m. May 24, 1841, Alvira Horton. Res. Bristol, R. I.

CHILDREN.

    I. SERAPHINE B., b. ——; m. Dec. 25, 1861, William F. Paull; res. Bristol, R. I.
    II. ELLA F., b. Aug. 28, 1853; d. Apr. 28, 1855.
    III. ELLA P., b. ——; m. June 1, 1878, Lucien E. Chadwick; res. Bristol, R. I.

486. **Frank H.**[8] **Pierce** (Joshua[7], Joshua[6], Joshua[5], Mial[4], Ephraim[3], Ephraim[2], Michael[1]), b. May 29, 1848; m. Nov. 11, 1879, Hannah J. Halton, b. Aug. 29, 1852. Res. South Rehoboth, Mass.

CHILDREN.

    I. HOWARD F., b. June 19, 1882; d. Mar. 24, 1883.
    II. ELMER K., b. Mar. 27, 1884.
    III. FLORENCE M., b. Mar. 4, 1886.

487. **Joshua**[8] **Pierce** (Joshua[7], Joshua[6], Joshua[5], Mial[4], Ephraim[3], Ephraim[2], Michael[1]), b. Dec. 27, 1826; m. Jan. 12, 1853, Mary A. Lamb, b. Apr., 1825; d. s. p., Jan. 16, 1872; m. 2nd, Mar. 19, 1874, Mrs. Sarah (Booth) Joslyn, b. Mar. 25, 1845, s. p. Res. 110 Thurbers avenue, Providence, R. I.

Joshua Pierce was born in Rehoboth, Mass., in 1826. He resided there until 1845, when he moved to Providence, R. I., to reside and learned the mason's trade. He followed his trade for thirty-two years, and in 1876 erected a residence at 110 Thurbers avenue, where he resides.   He is at the present time engaged in the grocery business.

488. **Wheaton**[8] **Pierce** (Joshua[7], Joshua[6], Joshua[5], Mial[4], Ephraim[3], Ephraim[2], Michael[1]), b. June 1, 1832; m. Sept. 10, 1857, Hannah M. Sollett.   He was killed, June 6, 1864, at Cold Harbor, Va.   Res. Rehoboth, Mass.

CHILDREN.

I. EUDORA A., b. Apr. 13, 1860.
II. GEORGE W., b. Feb. 22, 1858; res. Nebraska.

489. **Charles M.**[8] **Pierce** (Joshua[7], Joshua[6], Joshua[5], Mial[4], Ephraim[3], Ephraim[2], Michael[1]), b. Mar. 18, 1834; m. Mar., 1861, Alma Holly; m. 2nd, 1866, Harriett Whipple.   Res. Greenville, Conn.

CHILDREN.

I. LEONARD, b. 1862.
II. LEWIS, b. 1868.

490. **David B.**[8] **Pierce** (Joshua[7], Joshua[6], Joshua[5], Mial[4], Ephraim[3], Ephraim[2], Michael[1]), b. Mar. 24, 1834; m. June 11, 1863, Elsia A. Adams, b. Oct. 11, 1844.   Res. Greenville, Conn.

CHILDREN.

I. DANIEL O., b. Mar. 23, 1865; d. Dec. 24, 1865.
II. DANIEL O., b. Nov. 16, 1867.

491. **Wilson D.**[8] **Pierce** (Joshua[7], Joshua[6], Joshua[5], Mial[4], Ephraim[3], Ephraim[2], Michael[1]), b. July 22, 1842; m. Apr. 14, 1867, Alazada Horton.   Res. North Dighton, Mass.

CHILDREN.

I. HERBERT W., b. Feb. 14, 1870.

II. LEONARD W., b. Apr. 9, 1878.
III. NATHAN F., b. July 8, 1880.
IV. HERALD L., b. Oct. 15, 1885.

492. **Martin R.**[8] **Pierce** (Leonard[7], Joshua[6], Joshua[5], Mial[4], Ephraim[3], Ephraim[2], Michael[1]), b. May 3, 1807; m. Nov. 15, 1829, Nancy Bartlett, b. Aug. 15, 1807; d. Sept. 1, 1835; m. 2nd, Mar. 6, 1836, Emily M. Graham, b. Mar. 16, 1818. Res. Honeoye Falls, N. Y.

CHILDREN.

584. I. FRANCIS M., b. July 29, 1830; m. Malvina Sumner.
585. II. BYRON, b. Sept. 30, 1832; m. Sarah Ann Simpson.
586. III. MARTIN, b. Dec. 3, 1837; m. Mollie Richie.
587. IV. SEYMOUR, b. May 10, 1840; m. Lottie Garfield.
    V. EMILY L., b. June 21, 1841; m. Sept. 11, 1866, John R. Briggs, b. July 31, 1839; d. June 23, 1875; res. Honeoye Falls, N. Y. Ch., Ella P., b. June 25, 1867; Lewis G., b. Nov. 26, 1868; John R., b. Nov. 11, 1869; d. July 19, 1870; Lena M., b. Dec. 13, 1873.
    VI. MARIA T., b. Nov. 29, 1845; m. May 12, 1870, James M. Pride, b. July 13, 1842; res. Honeoye Falls, N. Y. Ch., E. Raymond, b. Oct. 2, 1874.
    VII. FANNY O., b. Sept. 24, 1853; m. Dec. 31, 1873, Delbert Adams, b. June 19, 1849; res. Honeoye Falls, N. Y. Ch., Guy, b. Feb. 26, 1878; d. Oct. 9, 1884.
    VIII. ELLA W., b. Oct. 25, 1857; m. June 28, 1881, Edmund Clayton Smith, b. June 19, 1857, s. p.; res. Honeoye Falls, N. Y.
    IX. LEWIS G., b. May 5, 1843; d. July 5, 1850.
    X. JAMES C., b. Apr. 9, 1851; d. Sept. 15, 1851.

493. **Obadiah**[8] **Pierce** (David[7], Obadiah[6], David[5], David[4], Ephraim[3], Ephraim[2], Michael[1]), b. Mar. 5, 1833; m. June 27,

1855, Betsey G. Stilwell, b. Feb. 26, 1837. Res. Fall River, Mass.

CHILDREN.

I. LOUISA B., b. Jan. 28, 1863.
II. CHARLES D., b. Jan. 3, 1865; d. Mar. 10, 1884.
III. GEORGE F., b. Dec. 9, 1873; d. Jan. 22, 1883.

494. **Herbert S.**[8] **Pierce** (James L.[7], Obadiah[6], David[5], David[4], Ephraim[3], Ephraim[2], Michael[1]), b. Apr. 18, 1852; m. July, 1876, Annette Blanchard, b. Dec. 25, 1857; d. June 3, 1885; m. 2nd, July 29, 1886, Jennie Cory Howland, b. Nov. 5, 1862; add. 237 South Water street, New Bedford, Mass.

CHILDREN.

I. GRACE B., b. June 15, 1881.

495. **James M.**[8] **Pierce** (Dexter[7], Obadiah[6], David[5], David[4], Ephraim[3], Ephraim[2], Michael[1]), b. June 28, 1840; m. Oct. 14, 1873, Catherine R. Warner, b. June 28, 1838. Res. Warwick Neck, R. I.

CHILDREN.

I. WILLIAM W., b. Nov. 19, 1875.
II. JAMES D., b. Dec. 19, 1876.

496. **Dexter L.**[8] **Pierce** (Dexter[7], Obadiah[6], David[5], David[4], Ephraim[3], Ephraim[2], Michael[1]), b. Apr. 7, 1846; m. Jan. 18, 1877, Clara E. Henshaw, b. Feb. 16, 1851. Res. 150 Cranston street, Providence, R. I.

CHILDREN.

I. CLARA I., b. Jan. 25, 1878.
II. BESSIE H., b. Nov. 18, 1880.
III. EARL D., b. Nov. 6, 1882.

497. **Isaac N.**[8] **Pierce** (Isaac[7], David[6], David[5], David[4], Ephraim[3], Ephraim[2], Michael[1]), b. May 27, 1843; m. Nov., 1870,

Harriett L. Barnes, b. 1846; d. 1877; m. 2nd, Nov. 19, 1884, Minnie L. Thomas, b. Nov. 29, 1861. Res. East Douglass and Springfield, Mass.

CHILDREN.

I. FAVLIN M., b. Sept. 10, 1885.

498. **Charles S.**[8] **Pierce** (Isaac[7], David[6], David[5], David[4], Ephraim[3], Ephraim[2], Michael[1]), b. June 4, 1856; m. Feb. 22, 1883, Irene G. Marble. Res. Somerset, Mass.

CHILDREN.

I. CLAYTON S., b. Nov., 1883; d. Sept., 1884.

499. **Lorenzo**[8] **Pierce** (Clothier[7], David[6], David[5], David[4], Ephraim[3], Ephraim[2], Michael[1]), b. July 20, 1817; m. Mary R. Gifford, b. ——. He d. July 11, 1873. Res. New Bedford, Mass.

CHILDREN.

I. WILLIAM, b. ——; add. room 9, Rickstone's block, New Bedford, Mass.

501. **John W.**[8] **Pierce** (Clothier[7], David[6], David[5], David[4], Ephraim[3], Ephraim[2], Michael[1]), b. May 19, 1819; m. May 22, 1843, Corrinna C. Purinton of Somerset. She d. Sept., 1846; m. 2nd, Sept. 30, 1847, Chloe Pierce, b. Dec. 8, 1823. Res. 44 Fifth street, New Bedford, Mass.

CHILDREN.

I. MINERVA A., b. July 9, 1848; d. unm. Oct. 5, 1888.
II. FRANK, b. Feb. 10, 1850; d. in Boston, Nov. 19, 1887, a merchant.
III. EDWARD E., b. Dec. 5, 1856; d. Dec. 29, 1863.
IV. EDWARD, b. Sept. 4, 1866. His profession is medicine. He is now (1889) at the Michigan University at Ann Arbor.

48

502. **William C.**[8] **Pierce** (Clothier[7], David[6], David[5], David[4], Ephraim[3], Ephraim[2], Michael[1]), b. July 31, 1821; m. May 24, 1848, Julia Almy Slocum, b. Mar. 14, 1824. She res. 34 Seventh street, New Bedford, Mass. He d. Apr. 12, 1859, s. p.

503. **Thomas R.**[8] **Pierce** (David[7], David[6], David[5], David[4], Ephraim[3], Ephraim[2], Michael[1]), b. Sept. 16, 1827 ; m. Jan. 1, 1851, Lucy B. Fuller, b. Feb. 12, 1832. Res. 112 Fifth street, New Bedford, Mass.

CHILDREN.

    I. MARIA J., b. Oct. 30, 1851 ; m. Oct. 31, 1871, Charles
       F. Borden ; res. 112 Fifth street, New Bedford,
       Mass.

504. **Lavello I.**[8] **Pierce** (Lloyd N.[7], David[6], David[5], David[4], Ephraim[3], Ephraim[2], Michael[1]), b. Dec. 14, 1850; m. Oct. 8, 1874, Addie B. Sherman, b. Feb. 6, 1855; d. July 8, 1881; m. 2nd, Dec. 8, 1885, Sarah A. Mahan, b. Feb. 28, 1862. Res. Palatka, Fla.

CHILDREN.

    I. WILLIAM L., b. May 16, 1876; res. 122 Acushnet
       avenue, New Bedford, Mass.
    II. ARTHUR M., b. June 2, 1877 ; d. Dec. 18, 1879.
    III. GEORGE I., b. Sept. 11, 1879; d. Mar., 1881.

505. **Benjamin W.**[8] **Pierce** (Asa[7], John[6], Jonathan[5], David[4], Ephraim[3], Ephraim[2], Michael[1]), b. Aug. 13, 1821 ; m. Sept. 30, 1857, Abbie A. W. Kempton, b. Mar. 30, 1821 ; d. Feb. 2, 1885. He d. Sept. 20, 1878. Res. New Bedford, Mass.

CHILDREN.

    I. CHARLES F., b. Mar. 19, 1859; res. 59 Spring street,
       New Bedford, Mass.
588. II. ELISHA KEMPTON, b. Feb. 22, 1862 ; m. Mary C.
       Lasus.

III. FREDERICK C., b. Jan. 6, 1868; res. 19 Mill street, New Bedford, Mass.

506. **Asa C.**[8] **Pierce** (Asa[7], John[6], Jonathan[5], David[4], Ephraim[3], Ephraim[2], Michael[1]), b. Oct. 16, 1823, m. Elizabeth Church, b. May, 1858; m. 2nd, Apr. 29, 1863, Felicia H. Church, b. May 30, 1828. Res. 42 Fifth street, New Bedford, Mass.

CHILDREN.

I. ANNIE, b. Apr. 27, 1858; m. Frank M. Bisbee; res. New Bedford, Mass.

507. **Charles Henry**[8] **Pierce** (Asa[7], John[6], Jonathan[5], David[4], Ephraim[3], Ephraim[2], Michael[1]), b. Oct. 23, 1835; m. June 13, 1861, Charlotte Hinckley Smith, b. Nov. 24, 1839. Res. corner Maple and Ash streets, New Bedford, Mass.

CHILDREN.

I. WILLIAM T., b. Mar. 16, 1862; res. Shullsburgh, Wis.; unm.
II. ARTHUR, b. May 31, 1863; d. Aug. 5, 1863.
III. HARRIETT D., b. Mar. 17, 1866; m. Sept. 25, 1888, Benjamin H. Anthony; res. 3 Maple street; he is connected with the *Standard*.
IV. MARGARET S., b. Aug. 14, 1867.
V. CHARLOTTA, b. Nov. 24, 1872.

508. **Allen F.**[8] **Pierce** (Abel F.[7], Comfort[6], Comfort[5], John[4], John[3], Ephraim[2], Michael[1]), b. Sept. 3, 1824; m. Lydia ——. Res. Rehoboth, Mass.

CHILDREN.

I. ISABEL F., b. June 22, 1849.
II. FRANCIS C., b. Nov. 21, 1852.

509. **Chauncey B.**[8] **Pierce** (Abel F.[7], Comfort[6], Comfort[5], John[4], John[3], Ephraim[2], Michael[1]), b. June 21, 1826; m. Ellen M. ——. Res. Rehoboth, Mass.

CHILDREN.

I. AURELIA J., b. Aug. 12, 1851.

510. **Col. John H.**[9] **Pierce** (John J.[8], John J.[7], Benjamin[6], Benjamin[5], Benjamin[4], Benjamin[3], Benjamin[2], Michael[1]), b. Feb. 29, 1848; m. Nov. 22, 1871, Marie E. R. De Belisle, b. May 16, 1856. Res. Oak Park, Ill., and Plantsville, Conn.

The Boston *Globe* recently published the following article in relation to Colonel John H. Pierce:

A thousand miles an hour? May one breakfast in New York and lunch in London?

Nothing less, we assure you, when the theories of Colonel John H. Pierce are put in practice.

The story which a *Globe* reporter heard from the lips of the inventor was like a tale from the Arabian Nights or a conception of Jules Verne. Listening to his enthusiastic utterances one could readily believe that it was no visionary scheme of a Colonel Sellers, but the carefully thought-out plan of a man of no little ability.

When the reporter came upon the little manufacturing village of Plantsville, on the New Haven and Northampton railroad, it did not impress him with the idea that it was the home of an inventive genius, who is prepared to astonish the world with the magnitude of his scheme. Plantsville has about fifteen hundred inhabitants, and is the counterpart of hundreds of other places in New England. Evidently the natives are not all aware that one of the men who walks their streets carries under his hat so much of which they never dreamed in their wildest imagination. The first two men could not tell who he was; the third pointed out his boarding-place.

The colonel proved a good man to interview. He lost no time. He has been a newspaper man himself. Models, patents, scientific papers and drawings were scattered about his apartments. Colonel Pierce said that as yet little was known outside his room of his plan for connecting this continent with the old world by means of pneumatic tubes. Some statement of a brief nature has been made to a local paper; only within a day, almost, has it been developed to its present stage. In response to a request to give the facts the inventor was all enthusiasm, but spoke with care and precision, and with the air of a man who knew whereof he affirmed.

"Yes, I believe my plan is a practical one. This country can be connected with Europe by means of pneumatic tubes of large proportions. When the theories are reduced to practice they may be modified to some extent, but I assure you the time is coming—it may not be at once, but it is certain. You know the general public were, for a long time, sceptical about the sub-marine telegraph," said the colonel, smiling.

"How would they be laid and operated?"

"After the manner of the cables, as I will hereafter explain. We will be obliged to have them laid exactly straight, or as near straight as the surface of the globe will permit. They will be operated by currents of air, but in principles quite different in some respects from those governing the small lines now in use; the general principles remain the same. Of course, the tubes will always be in couples, with currents of air driven through them, the current in one tube always moving in an opposite direction from the other.

"In speaking of it I have usually taken for illustration the heaviest cannon. Suppose the orifice were still larger, or a car in place of the charge, the tube of the gun indefinitely continuous, and finally suppose the speed only governed by the rapidity with which the air can be forced through."

"Will it not be difficult to force currents of air the distance you contemplate?"

"Oh, no. The speed of this current can be made as great as desired, and with scarcely any limit, by simply using a great number of steam fans on the principle of those used in blast furnaces."

"How will they be stopped — speed be checked?"

"On half tubes of the proper length. As a tube approaches its terminus, branches or arteries for the passage of air currents only can connect with the companion tube, and thus the force be communicated from one to another. This is something of importance, and its utility will be proved of value for the conservation of power on short lines."

"These facts are of interest, but what the public most wishes to learn is about the utility of the scheme as a means of transit. How will it be constructed and run — and how will it save time," suggested the reporter.

"I have just reached the point. The tubes must be large enough to admit of pasengers, of course, yet small as possible. I would have individuals sit tandem, one ahead of the other, you see. Friction? That would be prevented by ball bearings — necessary appliances. The motion would hardly be perceptible to the passengers. It is hard to speculate upon the speed attainable. One hundred miles an hour would be the easiest thing in the world. One thousand miles an hour is not impossible with polished steel surface for tube lining, and exterior friction we could provide for. The speed, owing to the curvature of the earth's surface, will tend to overcome all weight, and make the pressure greatest on the upper portion of the tube, when running at maximum speed. Think of going to London in such a way and in such time as that.

" Yet it is no wild theory. A cannon ball, for instance, would pierce the air, but a car such as I describe would not; in fact, it would not move as fast as the air surrounding it.

" This method of transit possesses advantages over the railways. Temperature within the tube can be regulated perfectly by currents of air, heated or cooled. No jar will wear out the nerves of the passenger, or contact wear the car. There cannot possibly be collisions. No loss of power through exhaust, as with the locomotive. No army of employees to keep it in repair. No expensive purchase of right of way, or construction of tunnels, bridges, etc. One who carefully considers the subject cannot fail to see the advantages. Simplicity and economy are apparent."

" Earthquakes, do you say ? I have thought of that. I do not think danger is to be apprehended from that score. One point that worried me a great deal was how to prevent parting, but that has been solved. You are right in supposing the expense of laying such a line would be considerable, but not as much as will be at first imagined. It will cost less than the sum for which a railroad can be laid and equipped."

Colonel Pierce said that it would not cost a very large sum to build an experimental line for a short distance, say a few miles. He looks to get capitalists interested in his plans sufficiently to put in the necessary funds to do this. The plan proposed would be an expensive one, however. It would be necessary to partially manufacture it as laid. Iron would be first used, and the pipe in sections as long as could be conveniently handled. When put together a wire netting would be wove around it. This would have to be continuous. Another netting outside these two, prepared in a similar way, and others still around these, until sufficiently strong to maintain the tubing beyond the possibility of parting. The whole should be filled with one of the many cheap gummy substances that would protect from water.

His plan has been submitted in its details to several experts, and has met with approval. The great question with the inventor at the present time is to get the necessary funds to carry forward the work, for he is a man of comparatively little capital. He feels confident that in the end he will receive the recognition and encouragement which his work deserves.

Colonel Pierce is a man with an interesting personal history. He comes of good, old New England stock, though he was born in Waltham, in the Province of Quebec. When he was eleven years of age his parents moved to Illinois. They were cultivated people, and educated their boy at home. He had but four years of schooling. In 1862, he enlisted in the Eleventh Illinois Cavalry, and the Ninth United States Veteran Volunteers, and saw three years of active service. It will be remembered that this was Bob Ingersoll's regiment. Pierce is one of the youngest veterans in the country, being but thirty-nine years of age. He was only fourteen when he enlisted, but was large of his age. He enlisted three times and was rejected twice because of his youth. He served in the line, and is perhaps the youngest veteran in the country who served in this capacity. Others younger were musicians. When he enlisted he was five feet three inches in height; when he was discharged he had grown to five feet nine inches.

He won his title of " colonel " from the fact that he was lieutenant-colonel of the Moraska cavalry, a regiment formed at the time of the uprising in the Black Hills, but which saw little active service.

Colonel Pierce has made a reputation as a newspaper man. He was for ten years on the Omaha *Bee.* Over the signature of " Ranger " he made the Black Hills famous, being the first to write them up. He spent some time on the staff of the Chicago *Inter-Ocean*, and represented them at the railway exposition at the Santa Fe Tertio Millennial and New Orleans Exposition. Many newspaper men will remember him from the fact that he was secretary of the Press Association at the latter exposition. At one time he published a literary magazine.

Two years ago he came east. Interest excited at expositions led him to study mechanics. The result has been several valuable inventions that afford him, to-day, considerable income from royalties. They are upon various articles manufactured by the Peck, Stow & Wilcox Company, one of whose numerous factories is located in Plantsville. These inventions and the necessary detail take up much of his time. What leisure he can spare is devoted to the development of his pet scheme — the cherished idea of his life. He is a man of fine presence, and when talking on his favorite topic his face lights up with enthusiasm, and he impresses the spectator as a man not only in earnest, but in love with his subject. Whether his scheme is a feasible one only time will tell, but one thing is very sure, it is certain to cause no little talk.

CHILDREN.

I. EDGAR B., b. Oct. 18, 1872.
II. MARY W., b. Nov. 29, 1880.
III. COUNCIL B., b. Apr. 22, 1883.

511. **John W.**[9] **Pierce** (Isaac W.[8], Isaac W.[7], Isaac[6], Daniel[5], Clothier[4], Clothier[3], John[2], Michael[1]), b. Sept. 19, 1862; m. Nov. 11, 1882, Christina Hendrickson, b. ——. Res. Loa, Pinti county, Utah.

512. **Charles E. D.**[9] **Pierce** (Charles H.[8], Squier[7], Squier[6], Azrikim[5], Samuel[4], Azrikim[3], Ephraim[2], Michael[1]), b. June 4, 1841; m. Oct. 30, 1864, Eliza L. Metcalf, b. Dec. 18, 1844. Res. Fall River, Mass.; P. O. box 224.

CHILDREN.

I. ELIZA M., b. Sept. 29, 1866.
II. OWEN M., b. July 17, 1868.
III. CHARLES D., b. July 5, 1870.
IV. GEORGE H., b. July 30, 1872.
V. NORMAN B., b. Feb. 6, 1875; d. Oct. 10, 1875.
VI. ROBINSON M., b. July 12, 1876.

513. **Beriah N.**[9] **Pierce** (Alonzo[8], Nathan[7], Joseph[6], Azrikim[5], Samuel[4], Azrikim[3], Ephraim[2], Michael[1]), b. Nov. 18, 1835; m. May 26, 1859, M. Kate Cormac, b. May 29, 1842. Res. Indianapolis, Ind.

Beriah N. Pierce, son of Alonzo Pierce, born November 18, 1835; educated for the legal profession, commenced practice in 1859, and was the same year married at Warsaw, N. Y., to M. Kate Cormac. He continued the practice of law in Western New York and St. Louis, Mo., until 1873, when he removed to Corning, Iowa, where he devoted his entire time and attention to the advancement of the poultry business as an industry, traveling from State to State, assisting in organizing associations, acting as expert, sketching and engraving various new and useful breeds for illustration and publication, until his services were in demand from the Atlantic to the Pacific ocean, and from the Gulf of Mexico to the great lakes. He now travels annually, in the thorough-bred poultry interest alone, from 15,000 to 30,000 miles. He has been a witness to the increase of the business from a nominal one to that with an annual yield equal to the great corn crop, and superior to the yearly output of the gold and silver mines of the United States.

In 1883, he established at Indianapolis, Ind., a monthly magazine devoted to the thorough-bred poultry business and kindred subjects, known as the *Fanciers' Gazette,* which has reached an extended circulation in all the States and Territories of the United States, and Provinces of Canada. He is now the editor of the same, and his sons, Edward A. and Burt N., are interested with him in publishing it, together with specialty engraving.

CHILDREN.

I. EDWARD A., b. at Warsaw, N. Y., Apr. 16, 1864.
II. BURT N., b. at Warsaw, N. Y., Apr. 14, 1867.
III. WILLIAM CORMAC, b. at Corning, Iowa, May 31, 1873.
IV. CLAYTON BELKNAP, b. at Corning, Iowa, Aug. 25, 1881.

514. **Melford A.**[9] **Pierce** (Alonzo[8], Nathan[7], Joseph[6], Azrikim[5], Samuel[4], Azrikim[3], Ephraim[2], Michael[1]), b. Sept. 17, 1842; m. Aug. 17, 1869, Hattie Dwight, b. 1852. Res. Corning, Iowa.

CHILDREN.

I. ALBERT B., b. Aug. 25, 1870.
II. EVERETT B., b. May 25, 1878.
III. LUCY W., b. Jan. 26, 1884.

515. **Fred H.**[9] **Pierce** (Allan[8], Nathan[7], Joseph[6], Azrikim[5], Samuel[4], Azrikim[3], Ephraim[2], Michael[1]), b. July 8, 1858; m. Feb. 28, 1885, Ada N. Stevens. Res. Warsaw, N. Y.

49

CHILDREN.

I. FRED, b. May 9, 1886.

516. **Elmer E.**[9] **Pierce** (Allan[8], Nathan[7], Joseph[6], Azrikim[5], Samuel[4], Azrikim[3], Ephraim[2], Michael[1]), b. Oct. 6, 1861; m. May 25, 1885, Florence Bacon, b. Dec., 1864. Res. Frankton, Falk county, Dakota.

CHILDREN.

I. ALLEN W., b. Mar. 26, 1887.

517. **Andrew J.**[9] **Pierce** (Andrew T.[8], Azrikim[7], Joseph[6], Azrikim[5], Samuel[4], Azrikim[3], Ephraim[2], Michael[1]), b. Feb. 1, 1844; m. Jan. 18, 1866, Elizabeth S. Winman, b. Jan. 9, 1842; d. Oct. 24, 1874. Res. Hortonville, Mass.

CHILDREN.

I. CHARLES L., b. Oct. 29, 1866.
II. ABBEY M., b. Jan. 29, 1869; d. July 25, 1869.

518. **Nathan F.**[9] **Pierce** (Andrew T.[8], Azrikim[7], Joseph[6], Azrikim[5], Samuel[4], Azrikim[3], Ephraim[2], Michael[1]), b. July 12, 1846; m. Dec. 23, 1873; Hattie E. Whitmarsh, b. Nov. 21, 1857. Res. 157 South street, Providence, R. I.

CHILDREN.

I. GEORGIANA M., b. Sept. 22, 1874.
II. WALTER E., b. Dec. 5, 1876.

519. **William H.**[9] **Pierce** (Andrew T.[8], Azrikim[7], Joseph[6], Azrikim[5], Samuel[4], Azrikim[3], Ephraim[2], Michael[1]), b. Apr. 7, 1858; m. Mar. 18, 1880, Martha S. Douglass, b. Apr. 2, 1855. Res. Hortonville, Mass.

CHILDREN.

I. CARRIE M., b. Nov. 20, 1882.

520. **Silas A.**[9] **Pierce** (Andrew T.[8], Azrikim[7], Joseph[6], Azrikim[5], Samuel[4], Azrikim[3], Ephraim[2], Michael[1]), b. Jan. 27, 1860; m. Dec. 14, 1880, Sarah F. Baker, b. Sept. 14, 1860. Res. Hortonville, Mass.

CHILDREN.

I. ADDIE B., b. Jan. 2, 1883.
II. JOHN B., b. Feb. 15, 1886.
III. IOLA E., b. June 26, 1888.

521. **William F.**[9] **Pierce** (Frederick P.[8], Daniel[7], Joseph[6], Azrikim[5], Samuel[4], Azrikim[3], Ephraim[2], Michael[1]), b. May 25, 1848; m. Nov. 1, 1868, Eliza J. Brown, b. Aug. 25, 1848. Res. 114 Orms street, Providence, R. I.

CHILDREN.

I. EMMA F. T., b. July 8, 1870; d. July 31, 1870.
II. HENRY A., b. July 31, 1871; d. July 31, 1871.
III. DE WITT C., b. May 5, 1873.
IV. CHESTER A., b. Aug. 12, 1875.
V. LOUIS B., b. Sept. 8, 1877 ; d. Sept. 24, 1877.
VI. EDITH VAN M., b. Oct. 7, 1882; d. Nov. 13, 1883.
VII. EMMA M., b. Apr. 7, 1884.

522. **Charles L.**[9] **Pierce** (Frederick P.[8], Daniel[7], Joseph[6], Azrikim[5], Samuel[4], Azrikim[3], Ephraim[2], Michael[1]), b. Apr. 28, 1853; m. May 16, 1877, Nellie R. Newcomb, b. Apr. 22, 1856. Res. Providence, R. I.

CHILDREN.

I. IDA M., b. Feb. 6, 1880.

523. **Ashmun**[9] **Pierce** (Samuel[8], Nathaniel[7], Samuel[6], Joshua[5], Isaac[4], Azrikim[3], Ephraim[2], Michael[1]), b. Mar. 13, 1816; m. Oct. 13, 1844, Elizabeth Mansfield. Res. Orrington, Me., s. p.

524. **John W.**[9] **Pierce** (Samuel[8], Nathaniel[7], Samuel[6], Joshua[5], Isaac[4], Azrikim[3], Ephraim[2], Michael[1]), b. Oct. 16, 1825; m. 1857,

Lucinda Forbes, b. 1832; d. Nov. 19, 1858.   He d. Oct. 31, 1857.
Res. Orrington, Me.

CHILDREN.

I. JOHN, b. 1858; d. 1858.

525. **Nathaniel⁹ Pierce** (Isaac⁸, Nathaniel⁷, Samuel⁶, Joshua⁵,
Isaac⁴, Azrikim³, Ephraim², Michael¹), b. Jan. 30, 1802; m. Mar.
11, 1824, Dorcas Godfrey, b. 1799; d. Apr. 10, 1845; m, 2nd, July
20, 1846, Calista Shepherd, d. Sept. 13, 1849; m. 3rd, May 14,
1850, Mary H. Young, b. June 24, 1817.   He d. June 9, 1885.
Res. Ellsworth, Me.

CHILDREN.

I. ELIZA A., b. May 16, 1825; m. John Wooderson. She
   d. Feb. 10, 1853; res. Bangor, Me. A son, George
   F., res. in Stockton, Cal.

II. CHARLES W., b. Oct. 17, 1826; m. Mary L. Hanson;
   res. Wells Beach, Me.   Has a son, Charles H.

III. SARAH S., b. Oct. 3, 1828; d. Feb. 19 1850.

IV. MARY A., b. July 4, 1831; d. Mar. 2, 1832.

V. NATHANIEL A., b. Oct. 3, 1833; d. Oct. 31, 1834.

589.   VI. HENRY A., b. Dec. 30, 1834; m. Arabella D. Young.

VII. SUSAN H., b. Sept. 24, 1836; m. May 21, 1855, Wil-
   liam Seavey.   She d. May 26, 1839; res. Bangor,
   Me.   Ch., Gertrude; m. George Moody; res.
   Bangor.

VIII. THOMAS E., b. Aug. 15, 1838; d. Apr. 8, 1841.

IX. GEORGE F., b. Dec. 21, 1840; d. Apr. 10, 1844.

X. CLARA S., b. Jan. 14, 1848; m. May 21, 1873, Edward M. Potter, Jr.; res. Brunswick, Me.

XI. EDSON H., b. Dec. 8, 1851; m. Dec. 24, 1882, Eliza L.
   Booker.   Has a son, Edson N.; res. Stockton, Cal.

526. **Simeon⁹ Pierce** (Isaac⁸, Nathaniel⁷, Samuel⁶, Joshua⁵,
Isaac⁴, Azrikim³, Ephraim², Michael¹), b. Oct. 22, 1803; m. Dec.
25, 1823, Sarah D. Dean, b. Dec. 29, 1804; d. May 5, 1853.   He
d. in Hyde Park, Mass., Aug. 13, 1870.   Res. Orrington, Me.

CHILDREN.

590.   I. SIMEON O., b. July 8, 1823; m. Sarah J. McGuire.
591.   II. JOHN D., b. Aug. 9, 1826; m. Martha Tomlinson.
     III. SARAH D., b. July 26, 1828.
    IV. MARY A., b. July 26, 1830; m. June 16, 1846, Clark
        Gullifer, b. 1816; d. Dec., 1864. She d. May 4,
        1877. Ch., Archeia, Frank and Clara, d. in in-
        fancy; Flora E., b. Nov. 5, 1851; m. May 4, 1871,
        John W. Murray; d. Feb. 5, 1877; Edgar C., b.
        Dec. 4, 1856; m. 1883; Alice J., b. Oct. 31, 1864;
        m. June 4, 1883, Frank D. Smith; res. Adrian,
        Mich.
      V. RANSOM N., b. Oct. 29, 1832.
    VI. SUSAN A., b. July 16, 1835.
   VII. NEWAMAN N., b. June 1, 1837.
  VIII. JANE L., b. Oct. 4, 1839.
    IX. EMMA C., b. Mar. 28, 1842.
     X. CHARLES W., b. July 14, 1844.
    XI. FRANKLIN S., b. ——.

527. **Capt. Allan B.**[9] **Pierce** (Nathaniel[8], Nathaniel[7], Samuel[6], Joshua[5], Isaac[4], Azrikim[3], Ephraim[2], Michael[1]), b. Apr. 1,
1821; m. Nov. 29, 1846, Charlotte Osgood, b. Aug. 25, 1822.
Res. Orrington, Me.

Capt. Allan Burr Pierce was a short, heavy man with piercing
black eyes; master of his profession. A sea captain, succeeding
perfectly in a financial venture. A man quick tempered, but
with a heart easily touched even in his excited moments.

CHILDREN.

    I. ARTHUR A., b. May 9, 1848; m. Nov., 1873; res.
       Orrington, Me.
   II. HELEN F., b. Dec. 7, 1855.

528. **Capt. George F.**[9] **Pierce** (Nathaniel[8], Nathaniel[7], Samuel[6], Joshua[5], Isaac[4], Azrikim[3], Ephraim[2], Michael[1]), b. Jan. 6,

1820; m. Oct. 14, 1846, Lucy A. Eldridge, b. July 27, 1826. Res. Orrington, Me.

Capt. George F. Pierce was a straightforward, honorable man, tall and straight with the usual black hair and eyes of the family. A sea-faring man, who in a short time became captain of a large vessel. He was engaged mostly in the West India trade, gaining a large property.

CHILDREN.

I. GEORGIE A., b. Feb. 3, 1851.

529. **Capt. Harding R.**[9] **Pierce** (Nathaniel[8], Nathaniel[7], Samuel[6], Joshua[5], Isaac[4], Azrikim[3], Ephraim[2], Michael[1]), b. Feb. 7, 1807; m. Jan. 1, 1838, Abbie R. Smith, b. July 20, 1824. He d. Sept. 5, 1877. Res. Orrington, Me.

Capt. Harding R. Pierce, who was born in 1807, like the remainder of the family, early went to sea, but soon returned to his father's house, and took the homestead, following agriculture the remainder of his days. He was the most calm and even-tempered of the brothers, a tall man with dark hair and eyes.

CHILDREN.

I. SELINA A., b. May 14, 1843; m. Capt. Albert N. Harding; d. June 8, 1871 ; m. 2nd, Dec. 12, 1875, Capt. Henry C. Kendall, b. Apr. 6, 1830; res. Orrington, Me. Ch., Albert P., b. Apr. 18, 1869; d. Nov. 27, 1869; Percy H., b. June 25, 1877; d. June 8, 1878; Mellen B., b. Dec. 3, 1879; Harold W., b. Mar. 1, 1883; d. Nov. 11, 1886.

II. ELLEN B., b. Apr. 22, 1847; m. Dec. 21, 1879, —— Harding.

530. **Capt. David**[9] **Pierce** (Nathaniel[8], Nathaniel[7], Samuel[6], Joshua[5], Isaac[4], Azrikim[3], Ephraim[2], Michael[1]), b. Sept. 13, 1808; m. Mary Crockett. Res. Hampden, Me.

Capt. David Pierce was a short, thick set man with coal-black hair and eyes. Like his ancestors, he followed the sea, and rose from common seaman to master of several large vessels. He amassed a good property. On one of his trips he was hurt on a burning steamer, the " Potomac," which was burned off Portland, Me., from the effects of which he died.

CHILDREN.

    I. FLORENCE B., b. Sept. 13, 1857; d. unm.

    II. AGUS E., b. Sept. 14, 1853.

    III. ALICE S., b. May 14, 1851; m. Dec. 20, 1872, George H. Fraiser; res. s. p., Wakefield, Mass.

592.   IV. MARCUS, b. June 29, 1843; m. Annie E. Hopkins.

    V. WARREN N., b. Sept. 9, 1845; m. Sept. 20, 1873, Mrs. Warren Case, b. Sept. 10, 1843; res. s. p., Bangor.

    VI. JEREMIAH FRENCH, b. June 30, 1847; m. June 30, 1877, Belle Proctor; res. s. p., Norwich, Conn.

    VII. WILLIS, b. Mar. 21, 1849. He was killed in the rebellion while serving as ensign in the navy.

    VIII. ALBERT B., b. Sept. 18, 1859; m. June 10, 1883, Hattie Brown. He d. s. p., June, 1885; res. Norwich, Conn.

    IX. HELEN A., b. Apr. 18, 1837; m. Feb. 4, 1863, Mark Folsom; res. Wakefield, Mass. Ch., Annie E., b. Dec. 10, 1869; d. 1875; Lillian H., b. Apr. 10, 1863; Walter B., b. Feb. 10, 1865; Martin W., b. Apr. 10, 1867; William B., b. Apr. 4, 1869.

    X. ANNIE F., b. July 24, 1841; m. June 19, 1867, Capt. Howard C. Case. She d. June 29, 1869, s. p.

    XI. ISABELLE A., b. Nov. 7, 1847; unm.

531. **Capt. Nathaniel H.[9] Pierce** (Nathaniel[8], Nathaniel[7], Samuel[6], Joshua[5], Isaac[4], Azrikim[3], Ephraim[2], Michael[1]), b. Sept. 30, 1822; m. Sarah Bartlett. Res. Brewer Village, Me.

Capt. Nathaniel Howes Pierce, the youngest of the sons, was a small-sized man, with light blue eyes and fair hair, a gentleman in every sense, with a perfect disposition.   He was a shipmaster by profession.

CHILDREN.

    I. GERTRUDE B., b. Apr. 5, 1858; m. Oct. 30, 1877, G. Clifford Brastow, b. Jan. 31, 1851; d. Dec. 18, 1882; res. Brewer, Me. Ch., Frank C., b. Aug. 25, 1878.

593.   II. WALTER H., b. June 12, 1855; m. Harriett L. Grant.

532. **Capt. Daniel W.**[9] **Pierce** (David[8], Nathaniel[7], Samuel[6], Joshua[5], Isaac[4], Azrikim[3], Ephraim[2], Michael[1]), b. Jan. 29, 1817; m. 1845, Deborah B. Snow, b. Feb. 22, 1809; d. Mar. 23, 1884, s. p. Res. South Orrington, Me.

533. **Capt. Horace W.**[9] **Pierce** (David[8], Nathaniel[7], Samuel[6], Joshua[5], Isaac[4], Azrikim[3], Ephraim[2], Michael[1]), b. July 11, 1828; m. Apr. 27, 1854, Elizabeth J. Bartlett, b. Jan. 20, 1835. Res. South Orrington, Me.

CHILDREN.

    I. FRED H., b. June 23, 1859; m. Apr. 14, 1886, Ida E. Mitchell; res. New York city.

    II. EUGENE M., b. Dec. 19, 1865; res. Bartlett, Ramsay county, Dakota.

534. **Reuben S.**[9] **Pierce** (David[8], Nathaniel[7], Samuel[6], Joshua[5], Isaac[4], Azrikim[3], Ephraim[2], Michael[1]), b. Oct. 10, 1821; m. Oct. 19, 1844, Mercy T. Eldridge. He d. Feb. 17, 1852. Res. South Orrington, Me.

CHILDREN.

    I. WILLIAM S., b. Sept. 21, 1845.

    II. CLARA A., b. Dec. 23, 1849; m. Nov. 22, 1875, Loren N. Downs; res. Boston, Mass. Ch., Winnifred E., b. July 17, 1878.

    III. REUBEN S., b. Feb. 17, 1852.

535. **Thomas G.**[9] **Pierce** (Thomas N.[8], Samuel[7], Samuel[6], Joshua[5], Isaac[4], Azrikim[3], Ephraim[2] Michael[1]), b. Sept. 12, 1832; m. June 17, 1852, Mary A. Fales, b. Mar. 29, 1832. Res. West Foxboro, Mass.

CHILDREN.

I. CARRIE F., b. Aug. 27, 1856; m. Dec. 12, 1880, Frank A. Comey, b. Sept. 17, 1855; res. Attleboro, Mass. Ch., Alberta, b. Apr. 21, 1880.
II. NELLIE M, b. May 1, 1860; d. Dec. 27, 1863.
III. MYRTIE M., b. May 2, 1866; m. July 4, 1886, William H. White, b. Apr. 8, 1864; res. s. p., Attleboro, Mass.
IV. ETTA A., b. Apr. 7, 1868.

536. **Elisha**[9] **Pierce** (Samuel[8], David[7], Samuel[6], Joshua[5], Isaac[4], Azrikim[3], Ephraim[2], Michael[1]), b. Jan. 18, 1826; m. Dec. 27, 1863, Mary S. Gallup, b. May 16, 1842. Res. West Medford, Mass.

CHILDREN.

I. ELISHA G., b. Dec. 30, 1867.

537. **Barnabas H.**[9] **Pierce** (Oliver B.[8], Joshua[7], Samuel[6], Joshua[5], Isaac[4], Azrikim[3], Ephraim[2], Michael[1]), b. Dec. 4, 1846; m. Nov. 25, 1874, Lilla C. Newcomb, b. July 11, 1853. Res. Welfleet, Mass.

CHILDREN.

I. ARTHUR W., b. Sept. 17, 1877.
II. EDWARD E., b. May 5, 1879; d. June 2, 1881.

538. **James O.**[9] **Pierce** (Oliver B.[8], Joshua[7], Samuel[6], Joshua[5], Isaac[4], Azrikim[3], Ephraim[2], Michael[1]), b. Sept. 23, 1849; m. May 23, 1874, Ella A. Cobb, b. Mar. 26, 1850. Res. Welfleet, Mass.

CHILDREN.

I. CHARLES C., b. ——; II. NELLIE F., b. ——.

539. **Reuben [9] Pierce** (Reuben[8], Thomas[7], Joshua[6], Joshua[5], Isaac[4], Azrikim[3], Ephraim[2], Michael[1]), b. 1838; m. Jan. 6, 1856, Rebecca R. Smith, b. Oct. 11, 1840. He d. Apr. 10, 1865. Res. Provincetown, Mass.

CHILDREN.

    I. ANNA F., b. 1858; m. —— Baker.
    II. ALMIRA N., b. 1860; m. —— Fisher.
   III. RUTH A., b. Aug. 2, 1862.
   IV. ETTA, b. July 17, 1864.
    V. EDWARD F., b. Feb. 26, 1865; m. Apr. 11, 1884, Hannah H. Fisher, b. Mar. 13, 1867; res. Falmouth, Mass.

540. **Nehemiah R.[9] Pierce** (Nathaniel[8], Thomas[7], Joshua[6], Joshua[5], Isaac[4], Azrikim[3], Ephraim[2], Michael[1]), b. Nov. 11, 1823; m. Dec. 7, 1852, Anna M. Allen, b. Apr. 18, 1827. He is president of the Citizens' Bank. Res. Dysart, Iowa.

CHILDREN.

594.   I. THOMAS A., b. Aug. 31, 1855; m. Cora B. Keith.
595.   II. WENDELL P., b. May 23, 1860; m. Tinna Brown.
   III. ABBIE A., b. Nov. 7, 1861.
   IV. RUTH E., b. Aug. 14, 1863; m. June 7, 1883, Royal Matthews, b. Oct. 3, 1859; res. Davenport, Iowa. Ch., Leigh, b. Oct. 28, 1884.

541. **Henry R.[9] Pierce** (Nathaniel[8], Thomas[7], Joshua[6], Joshua[5], Isaac[4], Azrikim[3], Ephraim[2], Michael[1]), b. July 30, 1817; m. Feb. 24, 1836, Sophia Mayo. He d. Nov. 24, 1875. Res. Provincetown, Mass., and Union Prairie, Iowa.

CHILDREN.

    I. HENRY R., b. Feb. 20, 1839; d. Sept. 18, 1839.
    II. MARTHA A., b. Mar. 21, 1841; d. May 6, 1863.
   III. SARAH P., b. Sept. 30, 1843; m. July 28, 1868, C. E. Parker.

Sarah Phillips, the third child and the second daughter, was also born in Provincetown, Mass., the 30th of September, 1843. She was married to C. E. Parker, at Holliston, Mass., July 28, 1868. They have since resided there, and Mr. Parker has been agent of the Boston and Albany railroad for several years. He has held the position during all this time, and has enjoyed the confidence of both the officials of the road and the community in which he lives. Three children have been born to them, but have all gone across the great river to the hereafter. Nannie M. was born May 8, 1875, and died November 8, 1878; Jennie was born November 18, 1879, and died August 16, 1880; Josie M., the twin of Jennie, died May 28, 1880. The three children were born in Holliston, and were buried in Jay, Me., the home of Mr. Parker's parents.

    IV. SOPHIA, b. Dec. 31, 1845; d. Apr. 1, 1846.

    V. ISAAC N., b. Jan. 8, 1848; d. June 14, 1849.

    VI. SOPHIA, b. Apr. 9, 1851; d. Aug. 19, 1851.

    VII. HENRY, b. Apr. 9, 1851; d. Oct. 31, 1851.

    VIII. FRANKLIN, b. Aug. 29, 1853; d. Sept. 12, 1853.

596.   IX. WALTER C., b. Nov. 17, 1856; m. Hattie A. Howes.

    X. NANNIE, b. Nov. 8, 1858; d. Mar. 19, 1872.

    XI. DEBORAH, b. Mar. 31, 1860; m. Aug. 10, 1880, Eert U. Iwwerks. Ch., Eert U., b. Apr. 1, 1883; res. Sioux City, Iowa.

    XII. JESSIE F., b. Aug. 31, 1861; res. Holliston, Mass.

    XIII. MARTHA A., b. Apr. 21, 1863; m. Sept. 18, 1883, Rev. L. E. Taylor; res. Putney, Vt.

542. **Israel R.**[9] **Pierce** (Israel[8], William[7], Joshua[6], Joshua[5], Isaac[4], Azrikim[3], Ephraim[2], Michael[1]), b. ——; m. Dec. 6, 1827, Bethiah Swett, b. Aug. 1, 1808; d. July 27, 1869; m. 2nd, May 30, 1870, Rachel Holbrook. Res. Welfleet, Mass.

CHILDREN.

    I. ISRAEL, b. Oct. 6, 1828; m. Apr. 23, 1851, Emma Collins. He d. June 19, 1859; res. Welfleet, Mass.

II. JAMES F., b. Jan. 1, 1831; m. Dec. 26, 1852, Adeline
B. Hawes; res. Portland, Me.

597. III. BENJAMIN H. S., b. Sept. 10, 1832; m. Ruth G. Freeman.

598. IV. WARREN E., b. Sept. 20, 1834; m. Anna Hopkins.

V. ALONZO L., b. Mar. 15, 1836; m. Nov. 17, 1870, Almera
A. Chase; res. Welfleet, Mass.

VI. JOHN S., b. Nov. 28, 1837; m. May 13, 1855, Lucy Neal
res. Boston.

VII. BETHIAH R., b. Aug. 6, 1839; d. Apr. 15, 1841.

VIII. DEBORAH R., b. Aug. 21, 1841; m. May 17, 1864, John
W. Freeman, b. July 28, 1878; res. Welfleet, Mass.

IX. WILLIAM P., b. Apr. 18, 1843; m. Mar. 16, 1868, Ella
Hawthorne; res. Portland, Me.

X. BETHIAH S., b. Nov. 3, 1844; d. Jan. 27, 1855.

XI. GEORGE A., b. July 28, 1846; drowned Mar. 6, 1866.

XII. EDWARD W., b. June 24, 1848; m. Nov. 5, 1869, Mary
Lecount; res. Welfleet, Mass.

XIII. MELZER G., b. ——.

XIV. SYLVANUS R., b. Apr., 1853; m. Aug. 16, 1874, Mary
Anderson; res. Welfleet, Mass.

543. **Frederick Leander[9] Pierce** (Horace L.[8], Jonathan
W.[7], Aaron[6], Nathaniel[5], Joseph[4], Azrikim[3], Ephraim[2], Michael[1]),
b. Oct. 8, 1857; m. Oct. 8, 1879, Annie Laurie Austin, b. Mar.
21, 1861. Res. Westerly, R. I.

CHILDREN.

I. FREDERIC GORHAM, b. Feb. 14, 1884.

544. **Stillman[9] Pierce** (Phillip[8], Phillip[7], Wheeler[6], Wheeler[5],
Mial[4], Ephraim[3], Ephraim[2], Michael[1]), b. Apr. 12, 1808; m. June
15, 1834, Eunice Staples, b. Aug. 7, 1810. Res. Savoy, Mass.

CHILDREN.

I. SAMUEL L., b. ——.

546. **George F.[9] Pierce** (Phillip[8], Phillip[7], Wheeler[6], Wheeler[5],
Mial[4], Ephraim[3], Ephraim[2], Michael[1]), b. Feb. 3, 1820; m. Sept.
12, 1850, Anna Cain, b. May 23, 1821. Res. Savoy, Mass.

CHILDREN.

I. WILLARD H., b. July 15, 1858.

547. **Jarvis⁹ Pierce** (Phillip⁸, Phillip⁷, Wheeler⁶, Wheeler⁵, Mial⁴, Ephraim³, Ephraim², Michael¹), b. Oct. 18, 1826; m. Sept. 25, 1856, Achsah M. Macomber, b. May 2, 1836. Res. Savoy, Mass., and Cedarville, Kans.

CHILDREN.

I. ALICE, b. Mar. 26, 1858; m. Sept. 26, 1880, William L. Stanborough, b. May 20, 1861. Ch., Flora M., b. June 30, 1881, d. June 30, 1881 ; Achsah M., b. July 10, 1882; Robert S., b. Jan. 28, 1884; Albert M., b. May 20, 1885 ; Luther B., b. Nov. 29, 1887 ; res. Haydenville, De Kalb county, Mo.
II. LEWIS W., b. Mar. 4, 1862 ; unm.
III. IDA M., b. May 21, 1868.

548. **Russell⁹ Pierce** (Nathan⁸, Nathan⁷, Nathan⁶, Nathan⁵, Mial⁴, Ephraim³, Ephraim², Michael¹), b. in Manchester, N. Y., July 11, 1828; m. in Marengo, Mich., Nov. 13, 1866, Louise Hoskins, b. May 11, 1839. Res. Cresco, Calhoun county, Mich.

CHILDREN.

I. MARIAN, b. Sept. 7, 1867.
II. WILLIAM H., b. Oct. 30, 1869.
III. ELLA L., b. Nov. 30, 1872.
IV. IDA, b. June 2, 1876.

549. **Hiram⁹ Pierce** (Nathan⁸, Nathan⁷, Nathan⁶, Nathan⁵, Mial⁴, Ephraim³, Ephraim², Michael¹), b. Oct. 7, 1821; m. Dec. 4, 1848, Catherine Cassidy, b. 1828. Res. Sylvan and Chelsea, Mich.

CHILDREN.

I. MARY A., b. Oct. 4, 1849.
II. ANNETT L., b. Nov. 6, 1850; m. Nov. 10, 1875, Adial C. Prudden ; res. Fulton, Mich.

III. AMEY A., b. Nov. 29, 1852; m. Sept. 3, 1879, Thomas
E. Guthrie; res. Fulton, Mich.
IV. SUSIE, b. Oct. 18, 1854; m. Nov. 26, 1876, Alfred R.
Congdon; res. Chelsea, Mich.
V. ALMA J., b. Sept. 16, 1856.
VI. LILLY I., b. Dec. 8, 1858.
VII. HERMAN, b. Jan. 26, 1861; m. Oct. 14, 1888, Minnie
Dancer; res. Chelsea, Mich.
VIII. SHERMAN, b. May 8, 1863.
IX. RALPH H., b. Sept. 29, 1865.
X. JOHN R., b. Mar. 18, 1868.
XI. MAX M., b. Oct. 9, 1872.

550. **Ambrose G.**[9] **Pierce** (Otis[8], Pardon[7], Pardon[6], Nathan[5],
Mial[4], Ephraim[3], Ephraim[2], Michael[1]), b. May 8, 1820; m. Mar.
30, 1844, Charlotte Washburn, b. Jan. 30, 1827. Res. North Hannibal, Oswego county, N. Y.

CHILDREN.

I. ELIZABETH E., b. Oct. 3, 1845; d. Aug. 19, 1847.
II. EMILY F., b. Oct. 18, 1848; m. Feb. 6, 1872, John A.
Cox. She d. May 18, 1877; res. Hannibal, N. Y.
III. PARDON E., b. Dec. 19, 1850; d. Sept. 19, 1855.
IV. FLORA E., b. Mar. 17, 1853; m. Mar. 28, 1875, William
J. Bradt; res. North Hannibal, N. Y.
V. OTIS E., b. Apr. 15, 1856; d. Sept. 11, 1887.
VI. JEANETTE E., b. Oct. 21, 1858; d. Aug. 25, 1881.
VII. CHARLOTTE E., b. Apr. 17, 1861; m. Mar. 31, 1886,
Robert S. Lindsay; res, North Hannibal, N. Y.
VIII. EDWIN A., b. Dec. 14, 1863; res. North Hannibal,
N. Y.
IX. ROBERT E., b. Jan. 6, 1867; res. Tacoma, W. T.
X. CHARLES E., b. July 25, 1869; d. Oct. 2, 1881.

551. **James P.**[9] **Pierce** (Otis[8], Pardon[7], Pardon[6], Nathan[5],
Mial[4], Ephraim[3], Ephraim[2], Michael[1]), b. Apr. 12, 1825; m. Feb.
12, 1843, Lucy A. Jones, b. ――――. Res. Newport, N. Y.

CHILDREN.

I. MILLARD N., b. Aug. 6, 1850; m. Nov. 18, 1870, Kate
Waterman, s. p.; res. Newport, N. Y.

599.   II. FRANK E., b. July 12, 1859; m. Jane Harris.

552. **Rev. Nathan W.**[9] **Pierce** (Asa T.[8], Asa[7], Peleg[6],
Nathan[5], Mial[4], Ephraim[3], Ephraim[2], Michael[1]), b. Jan. 11, 1840;
m. Sept. 4, 1865, Maggie Kinney, b. Apr. 23, 1842. Res.
Williamston, Mich.

Rev. Nathan W. Pierce of Williamston writes as follows :

" I was raised from early infancy in the wilds of Michigan. My
early advantages were very limited. At the age of eighteen (in
March, 1858), I gave my heart to God, and joined the Methodist
Episcopal Church. In September, 1864, I was received into the
Detroit Annual Conference of the above-named Church. I have
taken work in connection with the same each year since. I am
just six feet high; spare built; but health good. I expect to blow
the Gospel trumpet of a free salvation to the best of my ability
while I live. I expect to die and go up to glory shouting victory,
where I hope to meet all of the Pierce family. When your history is complete let me know, for I want a copy."

CHILDREN.

I. MATILDA H., b. Oct. 15, 1866.
II. ALBERT R., b. July 14, 1869.
III. ALICE G., b. Oct. 15, 1871.
IV. JARED F. W., b. Mar. 14, 1877.

553. **Sidney W.**[9] **Pierce** (Elisha[8], Preserved[7], Preserved[6],
Nathan[5], Mial[4], Ephraim[3], Ephraim[2], Michael[1]), b. Dec. 9, 1837 ;
m. May 9, 1861, Annie F. Proctor, b. Aug. 18, 1836. Res. No.
16 Fifield avenue, Providence, R. I.

CHILDREN.

I. LUTHER S., b. Oct. 25, 1866; d. June 11, 1867.
II. LUETTA S., b. Feb. 6, 1868.

554. **Dr. A. Martin[9] Pierce** (Otis[8], Martin[7], Preserved[6], Nathan[5], Mial[4], Ephraim[3], Ephraim[2], Michael[1]), b. Mar. 14, 1852; m. Oct. 17, 1878, Lizzie J. Macomber, b. Dec. 10, 1853. Res. New Bedford, Mass.

Dr. Pierce was born in New Bedford and always resided there. He attended the public schools and graduated from the High School in 1870; then entered the office of Dr. E. P. Abbé, the leading physician of New Bedford, as a student of medicine. Graduated from the College of Physicians and Surgeons of New York. Before graduating he passed a competitive examination for the position of assistant physician and surgeon to Charity Hospital, Blackwell's Island. He was connected with the hospital from December, 1872, to October 1, 1874. He then took charge of the small-pox hospital, Blackwell's Island, and was there for two months. January 1, 1875, he began private practice in New Bedford, and was associated with Dr. Abbé from that time until July, 1882. Since then he has been alone. In 1878 and 1879 he was physician to the poor department of the city. He joined the Massachusetts Medical Society in 1875, and was secretary of the county society for a number of years. At present he is one of the visiting physicians and surgeons of St. Luke's Hospital of New Bedford, and president of the New Bedford Society for Medical Improvement.

CHILDREN.

    I. EDWARD A., b. Aug. 4, 1879.
   II. ELIZABETH, b. Jan. 20, 1883.
  III. ALICE, b. Aug. 21, 1884.

555. **Waterman J.[9] Pierce** (Bradford B.[8], Waterman[7], Isaac[6], Nathan[5], Mial[4], Ephraim[3], Ephraim[2], Michael[1]), b. Aug. 29, 1848; m. Nov. 22, 1876, Flora W. Fenner. Res. 28 Exchange Place, Providence, R. I.

CHILDREN.

    I. OLIVER P., b. Dec. 22, 1877.
   II. WATERMAN J., b. Sept. 28, 1879.

556. **Bradford F.**[9] **Pierce** (Bradford B.[8], Waterman[7], Isaac[6], Nathan[5], Mial[4], Ephraim[3], Ephraim[2], Michael[1]), b. Oct. 17, 1850; m. Jan., 1871, Isabel F. Otis, b. June 24, 1850. Res. Scituate, R. I.

CHILDREN.

I. MARTHA K., b. May 16, 1872.
II. BRADFORD F., b. Oct. 16, 1874.
III. ARTHUR H., b. Feb. 6, 1879.
IV. EARLE B., b. July 6, 1883.

557. **Benjamin F.**[9] **Pierce** (Elisha W.[8], Waterman[7], Isaac[6], Nathan[5], Mial[4], Ephraim[3], Ephraim[2], Michael[1]), b. July 20, 1860; m. Dec. 14, 1880, Sunie K. Harris, b. June 11, 1859. Res. Providence, R. I.

CHILDREN.

I. BENNIE K., b. Nov 9, 1884.

558. **James L.**[9] **Pierce** (Benjamin[8], Samuel[7], David[6], Nathan[5], Mial[4], Ephraim[3], Ephraim[2], Michael[1]), b. Aug. 18, 1823; m. July 31, 1845, Mary A. Streeter, b. Mar. 9, 1826. Res. 101 Harrison street, Providence, R. I.

CHILDREN.

I. EMILY F., b. Mar. 13, 1853; m. Samuel A. Otis; res. Providence, R. I.
II. JAMES B., b. Mar. 19, 1857; d. May 5, 1857.
III. ARNOLD S., b. June 13, 1862.

559. **Isaiah E.**[9] **Pierce** (Joseph[8], Samuel[7], David[6], Nathan[5], Mial[4], Ephraim[3], Ephraim[2], Michael[1]), b. Dec. 20, 1825; m. Sept. 14, 1853, Mary A. Carney, b. June 17, 1829. Res. 5 North Bend street, Pawtucket, R. I.

CHILDREN.

I. LYDIA E., b. Feb. 22, 1855; m. Dec. 26, 1881, James H. Whitaker; res. 40 Seventh street, Lowell, Mass.
II. BERTHA A., b. Jan. 9, 1859.

51

III. AMELIA J., b. Oct. 6, 1860; m. Apr. 29, 1885, Oscar A. Jilson; res. 5 North Bend street, Pawtucket, R. I.

IV. OSCAR A. J., b. ——.

V. EDWARD L., b. Sept. 1, 1862; m. June 8, 1886, Hattie F. Matthews; res. Denver street, Pawtucket, R. I.

VI. ELIZABETH L., b. Feb. 7, 1865.

VII. ELSIE G., b. Sept. 16, 1868.

VIII. JOSEPH C., b. Aug. 18, 1866.

IX. JAMES, b. Nov. 20, 1870.

X. MARYETTE A., b. Nov. 8, 1856; d. Nov. 14, 1869.

560. **Ellis⁹ Pierce** (Joseph⁸, Samuel⁷, David⁶, Nathan⁵, Mial⁴, Ephraim³, Ephraim², Michael¹), b. Oct. 14, 1834; m. May 21, 1856, Annie E. Coggshall, b. July 13, 1838; d. June 9, 1871. Res. 10 South street, Pawtucket, R. I.

CHILDREN.

I. IDA S., b. Ang. 8, 1857; m. Apr. 29, 1885, Frank E. Crawford, b. Mar., 1858. She d. May, 1887, s. p.; res. Pawtucket, R. I. A Pawtucket paper has this of Mrs. Crawford's death :

The host of friends of Mr. Frank F. Crawford will be deeply grieved to learn that his wife died last night. The deceased suffered from consumption, and, although she had been gradually failing of late, and the end was known to be not far away, yet her death was, in a measure, of a sudden nature. She was out riding Sunday, and it is thought that the excessive heat of the day tended to shorten her lease of life. She was in the thirtieth year of her age, and had been married about two years. She was the daughter of Ellis Pierce, and for a number of years she had been a member of the First Baptist Church. She was a devout Christian, a faithful wife, and was possessed of many traits that endeared her to her acquaintances. Two years ago she was made a happy bride at the altar, and to-day the same bridal robes cling about her form, cold in death. But there are none of the usual mourning surroundings.

There is nothing to be seen that would remind one of the awful truth. The remains are not inclosed in a long, narrow and sombre-looking crape-bedecked box, but recline easily and naturally upon a sofa, almost hidden with flowers, resting partly upon the left side and facing the entrance. She has the appearance of sleeping quietly after a tiresome bridal journey, and would awake in a moment. Around and about the sofa there are deep beds of floral pieces, which are offerings of love and respect from the relatives and friends of the deceased, among whom she was a universal favorite. The funeral was held at the house, yesterday afternoon, the services being conducted by Rev. Dr. Bullen, assisted by Rev. J. J. Woolley. The date of burial has not yet been decided upon.

II. EMILY J., b. May 13, 1859; d. Sept. 4, 1880.

III. JOSEPH P., b. July 11, 1861 ; d. Dec. 27, 1861.

IV. ANNIE L., b. Dec. 24, 1862; m. May 15, 1885, William L. Chatterton, b. Dec. 21, 1860; res. s. p., Pawtucket, R. I.

561. **Benjamin B.**[9] **Pierce** (Joseph[8], Samuel[7], David[6], Nathan[5], Mial[4], Ephraim[3], Ephraim[2], Michael[1]), b. Nov. 29, 1836 ; m. Jan. 3, 1866, Julia E. Buffington, b. June 25, 1845. He d. Nov. 9, 1885. Res. 7 Walcott street, Providence, R. I.

CHILDREN.

I. BYRON W., b. Dec. 5, 1866.

II. AMERY W., b. July 22, 1872.

III. JULIA I., b. Oct. 29, 1874.

IV. RUTH A., b. July 9, 1877.

V. EMILY J., b. Dec. 2, 1880.

VI. JOSEPHINE P., b. Mar. 1, 1882.

VII. ESTHER B., b. Apr. 25, 1886.

562. **Christopher T.**[9] **Pierce** (Samuel[8], Samuel[7], David[6], Nathan[5], Mial[4], Ephraim[3], Ephraim[2], Michael[1]), b. Aug. 22, 1817; m. Aug. 6, 1840, Eliza Fairbrother. He d. May 27, 1867.

CHILDREN.

I. CHARLES T., b. ——; formerly resided in Wichita, Kans.

II. NELLIE, b. ——.

563. **Holden[9] Pierce** (Holden[8], Samuel[7], David[6], Nathan[5], Mial[4], Ephraim[3], Ephraim[2], Michael[1]), b. Oct. 10, 1815; m. Nov. 1, 1842, Mary H. Carr, b. Feb. 10, 1825; d. Feb. 7, 1885. Res. Rehoboth, Mass.

Holden Pierce was born in Rehoboth, Mass. He enlisted for the war, and was a member of Company B, Ninth Regiment of Rhode Island Volunteers. He was wounded in the first battle of Fredericksburg, a spent minnie ball entering his cheek, under the eye, near the nose, and was not extracted until after he had been in the hospital at Portsmouth Grove, R. I., three months. He then pulled it from his throat, it having worked down there. Regaining his health sufficiently he was ordered back to his regiment, and the first battle he was engaged in was at Spottsylvania Court-House, where he was again wounded in the shoulder, which disabled him for life. He was again sent to Portsmouth Grove hospital, where he remained until December, 1864, when he was pronounced unfit for service in consequence of his wounds, and honorably discharged. If he had understood the matter he would not have accepted his discharge, for he enlisted for the war and was not obliged to accept his papers, and if he had not, he would have been entitled to pay during the war and a full pension. Whereas now he has only received half pension up to the present time, and he has never been able to do any thing for his own support, or that of his family. He is as deserving as any soldier, as he was very faithful in the performance of every duty, and never was known to find any fault under any circumstance. No soldier ever suffered more that lived. His wife died very suddenly in 1885.

CHILDREN.

I. SARAH E., b. Sept. 11, 1843; d. July 1, 1844,

II. ELLA F., b. Aug. 11, 1845; m. Nov. 3, 1864, Charles

H. Utton, b. July 12, 1840; m. 2nd, Sept. 11, 1883,
Ezbon O. Cook, b. Mar. 18, 1847; res. 16 Lawn avenue, Pawtucket, R. I. Ch., Jessie O., b. July 18,
1884; Fred T., b. Mar. 30, 1866; res. Central Falls;
John H., b. Sept. 11, 1867; res. Eston, Mass.

III. MALVINA F., b. Nov. 27, 1847; m. July 25, 1866,
Charles D. Kinney, b. Sept. 18, 1842; res. Reho-
both, Mass. Ch., Thomas H., b. July 25, 1867;
Mary H. B., b. Aug. 2, 1869; Ada B., b. Sept. 6, 1871;
Josephine P., b. Dec. 10, 1873; Sarah M., b. Dec.,
1875; Louise D., b. Sept. 28, 1879; Abby C., b.
Sept. 13, 1881.

IV. HANNAH, b. June 3, 1850; m. June 30, 1867, Rufus T.
Slocum, b. Jan. 4, 1849; res. South Scituate, R. I.
Ch., James E., b. Sept. 17, 1868; Benjamin H., b.
Oct. 29, 1870; Minnie E., b. Oct. 12, 1872; d. 1874;
Fannie M., b. Mar. 12, 1875; Rufus S., b. Nov. 21,
1879; Arthur M., b. Mar. 5, 1881; Annie E., b. Nov.
5, 1883; John N., b. Jan. 26, 1886.

V. JAMES H., b. May 31, 1857; unm.; res. Pawtucket,
R. I.

VI. ANSON B., b. July 5, 1852, d. Sept. 27, 1853.

VII. ABBY C., b. Feb. 26, 1854; d. Sept. 18, 1855.

VIII. JOSEPHINE H., b. Mar. 12, 1866; d. Feb. 7, 1873.

564. **George W.**[9] **Pierce** (Holden[8], Samuel[7], David[6], Nathan[5],
Mial[4], Ephraim[3], Ephraim[2], Michael[1]), b. Dec. 14, 1817; m. Sept.
4, 1839, Lydia Perkins, b. Aug. 20, 1820. Res. Lawrence, Kans.
George W. Pierce was born in Rehoboth, Mass. For a time
after his marriage he resided in Rhode Island, and was one of the
first to emigrate from Providence, R. I., to Kansas, and was in
great danger of his life at the time of the border warfare, and suffered great loss by them. They burned his shop and fired his
house with a determination to destroy it, but by the presence of
mind of his wife it was saved. She was admirably fitted for the
wife of a pioneer. His oldest son was in the war, and the hus-
bands of his sister Lee's two daughters were also in the war, doing
very good service for their country.

CHILDREN.

I. FRANCES, b. Jan. 7, 1841 ; m. 1862, Milton Hay. She
d. s. p., Jan. 14, 1864; res. Kanwaka, Kans.

600.　II. LEONARD S., b. Oct. 27, 1842 ; m. Sarah Holinbury.

III. EMELINE, b. Apr. 14, 1845; m. Aug. 19, 1866, Harry
Leonard. She d. Oct. 23, 1883; res. Lawrence,
Kans. Ch., Herbert, b. Aug. 29, 1867; d. Sept. 16,
1868; Albert H., b. June 19, 1869; Eugene L., b
Aug. 8, 1873; Ernest A., b. Dec. 18, 1876; d. Nov.
30, 1879.

IV. ELIZABETH, b. July 29, 1847 ; d. Oct. 14, 1851.

V. MARYETTA, b. Mar. 19, 1849 ; d. Sept. 21, 1851.

VI. JAMES H., b. Jan. 18, 1851 ; d. July 29, 1879.

VII. GEORGE A., b. Feb. 23, 1854; res. Ottawa, Kans.

VIII. CHARLES F., b. Nov. 29, 1855.

601.　IX. WILLIAM JAMES, b. Dec. 3, 1860 ; m. Estella Chapman.

565. **Roderick G.**[9] **Pierce** (William[8], Micah[7], Jobe[6] Jobe[5],
Mial[4], Ephraim[3], Ephraim[2], Michael[1]), b. Oct. 23, 1832; m. Mar.
5, 1856, Olive Peck, b. Dec. 13, 1836.　Res. New York city, N. Y.

CHILDREN.

I. NELLIE E., b. June 16, 1861.

II. EDWARD R., b. June 21, 1870.

566. **Stephen W.**[9] **Pierce** (Stephen V. R.[8], Micah[7], Jobe[6],
Jobe[5], Mial[4], Ephraim[3], Ephraim[2], Michael[1]), b. Feb. 23, 1833 ;
m. Jan. 1, 1852, Frances O. Green, b. Mar. 7, 1835.　Res. Ashland, Mass.

CHILDREN.

I. JULIA E., b. Dec. 30, 1852.

567. **Mark F.**[9] **Pierce** (Maxon[8], John M.[7], Jobe[6], Jobe[5], Mial[4],
Ephraim[3], Ephraim[2], Michael[1]), b. May 21, 1825; m. June 13,
1847, Harriett Wheeler, b. Feb. 14, 1828; d. Mar. 30, 1859; m.
2nd, June 24, 1860, Betsey J. Potter, b. Apr. 14, 1827.　Res. Big
Foot Prairie, McHenry county, Ill.

CHILDREN.

I. MAHALA E., b. Aug. 13, 1848 ; m. Jan. 1, 1868, John B. Stevens ; res. Big Foot Prairie.

II. GEORGE W., b. Nov. 17, 1854; m. Oct. 21, 1874, Anna Muffate ; res. Big Foot Prairie.

III. MAXON W., b. Feb. 29, 1856; m. Feb. 27, 1878, Flora Treat ; res. Big Foot Prairie.

IV. AMES M., b. Dec. 28, 1864.

V. ALMA J., b. May 1, 1866.

568. **Benoni**[9] **Pierce** (Hiram[8], Benona[7], Jobe[6], Jobe[5], Mial[4], Ephraim[3], Ephraim[2], Michael[1]), b. Mar. 31, 1834; m. Apr., 1859, Thankful Theresa Bixby, b. Mar. 12, 1842 (dau. of Dr. Moses Bixby of Lena, Ill., and Abigail Bixby). Res. Earlville, Iowa.

CHILDREN.

I. A son unnamed, b. Mar. 16, 1861.

II. HERMAN LORENZO, b. Dec. 23, 1862.

III. ALMER EUGENE, b. Aug. 10, 1864; d. Apr., 1867.

IV. MARY ANGIE, b. Mar. 31, 1868.

569. **Calvin W.**[9] **Pierce** (Hiram[8], Benona[7], Jobe[6], Jobe[5], Mial[4], Ephraim[3], Ephraim[2], Michael[1]), b. Apr. 30, 1838; m. Nov. 1, 1862, Mary Martha Fear, b. Apr. 7, 1844 (dau. of John Terry Fear and Electa, his wife), a grain buyer in Waterloo, Iowa.

CHILDREN.

I. A son unnamed, b. Sept. 11, 1863; d. Sept. 27, 1863.

II. ELMER PERRY, b. Oct. 4, 1864.

III. LOTTIE, b. Dec. 20, 1866 ; d. Apr. 19, 1867.

IV. WILLIE DELOS, b. Feb. 2, 1868.

V. HENRY C., b. Sept. 27, 1878.

570. **Squire William**[9] **Pierce** (Hiram[8], Benona[7], Jobe[6], Jobe[5], Mial[4], Ephraim[3] Ephraim[2], Michael[1]), b. Apr. 12, 1842; m. Sept. 18, 1863, Mary Jane Wheeler, b. Aug. 9, 1844 (dau. of Asa and Mary Wheeler of Earlville, Iowa); a grain dealer in Jessup, Buchanan county, Iowa.

CHILDREN.

I. ETTIE, b. Dec., 1864.
II. FANNY, b. Apr. 18, 1868; d. Aug. 17, 1869.

571. **Leander L.**[9] **Pierce** (Hiram[8], Benona[7], Jobe[6], Jobe[5], Mial[4], Ephraim[3], Ephraim[2], Michael[1]), b. May 3, 1853; m. June 24, 1875, Mary J. Walker, b. Oct. 5, 1855. Res. Chamberlin, Dakota.

CHILDREN.

I. LULA B., b. July 23, 1877.
II. HOWARD A., b. Aug. 23, 1880.

572. **Martin**[9] **Pierce** (Jesse[8], Samuel[7], Samuel[6], Jobe[5], Mial[4], Ephraim[3], Ephraim[2], Michael[1]), b. Jan. 26, 1842; m. in Concord, N. H., Frances H. Martin, b. Jan. 23, 1845. Res. Grafton, N. H.

CHILDREN.

I. ALLAN L., b. July 29, 1868.
II. MATTIE V., b. July 1, 1882.

573. **Charles C.**[9] **Pierce** (Phillip[8], Samuel[7], Samuel[6], Jobe[5], Mial[4], Ephraim[3], Ephraim[2], Michael[1]), b. Sept. 29, 1842; m. Apr. 21, 1870, Sarah W. Dunham, b. June, 1843. Res. Freeport, Ill.

CHILDREN.

I. PHILLIP A., b. Apr., 1877.
II. MALCOLM, b. July, 1882.
III. GARRY, b. Nov., 1885.

574. **Myiel J.**[9] **Pierce** (Harry H.[8], Jesse[7], Caleb[6], Caleb[5], Mial[4], Ephraim[3], Ephraim[2], Michael[1]), b. at Merrilville, Ind., Jan. 29, 1861; m. Oct. 29, 1880, Elvira M. Webster, b. Apr. 19, 1863. He is a Seven Day Adventist, and a Democrat. Res. Cedar Lake, Mich.

CHILDREN.

I. ERNEST L., b. Feb. 12, 1882.
II. CHAUNCEY L., b. Dec. 31, 1884.
III. LEWIS S., b. Apr. 2, 1886.
IV. HARRY H., b. Apr. 5, 1888.

575. **George B.**[9] **Pierce** (Harry H.[8], Jesse[7], Caleb[6], Caleb[5], Mial[4], Ephraim[3], Ephraim[2], Michael[1]), b. at Arcada, Mich., Feb. 19, 1861; m. July 4, 1887, Rhoda E. Cox, b. July 6, 1868. He is an Adventist, and a Republican. Res. Cedar Lake, Mich.

CHILDREN.

I. BASIL A., b. Apr. 15, 1888.

576. **Andrew J.**[9] **Pierce** (Harry H.[8], Jesse[7], Caleb[6], Caleb[5], Mial[4], Ephraim[3], Ephraim[2], Michael[1]), b. Feb. 8, 1857; m. Nov. 17, 1876, Mary J. Rowland, b. Dec. 7, 1856. Res. Ithaca, Mich.

CHILDREN.

I. SIMEON H., b. Sept. 7, 1877.
II. MYIEL J., b. June 13, 1879.
III. EMMIT A., b. Sept. 30, 1881.
IV. DANIEL B., b. Oct. 21, 1883.
V. WALTER H., b. July 8, 1885.

577. **Duff De Kalb**[9] **Pierce** (Harry H.[8], Jesse[7], Caleb[6], Caleb[5], Mial[4], Ephraim[3], Ephraim[2], Michael[1]), b. Mar. 7, 1859; m. June 23, 1884, Mary Agnes Wagner, b. July 19, 1868. He is a lumber manufacturer, and a Republican. Res. Cedar Lake, Mich.

CHILDREN.

I. NAMA LOUISE, b. Mar. 24, 1885.

578. **Dexter**[9] **Pierce** (Seneca[8], Levi[7], Caleb[6], Caleb[5], Mial[4], Ephraim[3], Ephraim[2], Michael[1]), b. June 3, 1831; m. Oct. 18, 1853, Eliza A. Newton, b. Feb. 16, 1824. Res. ——, N. Y.

52

CHILDREN.

602.   I. WILLIAM F., b. Jan. 16, 1855; m. Maria H. Akers.
603.   II. CHARLES D., b. July 16, 1859; m. Ella N. Bartholomew.

579. **James K.**[9] **Pierce** (Seneca[8], Levi[7], Caleb[6], Caleb[5], Mial[4], Ephraim[3], Ephraim[2], Michael[1]), b. Feb. 25, 1845; m. Feb. 26, 1866, Lucy F. Smith, b. Jan. 20, 1844. Res. Manchester, Iowa.

CHILDREN.

I. LENORA MAY, b. Feb. 27, 1874 ; d. Nov. 21, 1874.

580. **Macon C.**[9] **Pierce** (Mason R.[8], Nathaniel R.[7], Barnard[6], Joshua[5], Mial[4], Ephraim[3], Ephraim[2], Michael[1]), b. Apr. 26, 1839; m. July 3, 1856, Harriett E. Corney, b. Mar. 23, 1838. Res. South Norwalk, Conn.

CHILDREN.

I. FRED W., b. July 10, 1857 ; res. Foxboro, Mass.
II. WARREN C., b. July 13, 1859; m. 1880; d. Oct. 21, 1883, leaving a daughter, Mary W., in Attleboro, Mass.

581. **Bradford D.**[9] **Pierce** (Mason R.[8], Nathaniel R.[7], Barnard[6], Joshua[5], Mial[4], Ephraim[3], Ephraim[2], Michael[1]), b. Aug. 23, 1842; m. Mar. 10, 1860, Ellen F. Downey, b. May 10, 1842. Res. Bridgeport, Conn.

CHILDREN.

I. MASON B., b. Dec. 24, 1860 ; d. Jan. 31, 1865.
II. ELEANOR R., b. Sept. 10, 1862; d. Mar. 1, 1865.
III. BRADFORD DE W., b. Dec. 26, 1865.

582. **Walter B.**[9] **Pierce** (Galen[8], Jeremiah[7], Barnard[6], Joshua[5], Mial[4], Ephraim[3], Ephraim[2], Michael[1]), b. Nov. 5, 1855 ; m. Oct. 10, 1880, Emma Andrews, b. July 22, 1858. Res. East Providence, R. I.

CHILDREN.

I. GERTRUDE E., b. Dec. 13, 1884.

583. **Frank E.**[9] **Pierce** (Asa B. , Barnard[7], Barnard[6], Joshua[5], Mial[4], Ephraim[3], Ephraim[2], Michael[1]), b. Dec. 26, 1851 ; m. Apr. 27, 1879, Helen Williams, b. Oct. 31, 1858. Res. New Bedford, Mass., and 261 West One Hundred and Twenty-fifth street, New York city.

CHILDREN.

I. DORA A., b. Apr. 24, 1880.
II. FRED E., b. July 21, 1881.
III. ELLA M., b, Dec. 24, 1882.

584. **Francis M.**[9] **Pierce** (Martin R.[8], Leonard[7], Joshua[6], Joshua[5], Mial[4], Ephraim[3], Ephraim[2], Michael[1]), b. July 29, 1830; m. Dec. 21, 1858, Malvina P. Somers, b. June 27, 1829. Res. Honeoye Falls, N. Y.

CHILDREN.

I. FRANK M., b. Dec. 1, 1859; m. Jan. 31, 1879, Jennie A. Ayres, b. Jan. 6, 1860, s. p. ; res. 141 Twenty-sixth street, Chicago, Ill.
II. NELLIE C., b. Mar. 27, 1861 ; m. Mar. 12, 1884, William C. Dolbeer, b. Apr. 22, 1858 ; res. Mendon, N. Y. Ch., Charles P., b. Apr. 5, 1886.
III. FRED S., b. Aug. 21, 1862 ; res. 372 West Taylor street, Chicago, Ill.
IV. CLARA B., b. Aug. 31, 1864.

585. **Byron**[9] **Pierce** (Martin R.[8], Leonard[7], Joshua[6], Joshua[5], Mial[4], Ephraim[3], Ephraim[2], Michael[1]), b. Sept. 30, 1832; m. Feb. 14, 1860, Sarah A. Simpson, b. May 5, 1832; d. May 11, 1873. Res. Alpine, Mich.

CHILDREN.

I. SEYMOUR S., b. July 8, 1861 ; res. Grand Rapids, Mich.

586. **Martin**[9] **Pierce** (Martin R.[8], Leonard[7], Joshua[6], Joshua[5], Mial[4], Ephraim[3], Ephraim[2], Michael[1]), b. Dec. 3, 1837; m. Nov. 15, 1866, Mollie Richie, b. Feb. 20, 1845. Res. Honeoye Falls, N. Y.

CHILDREN.

I. CHARLES R., b. Aug. 26, 1869.

587. **Seymour⁹ Pierce** (Martin R.⁸, Leonard⁷, Joshua⁶, Joshua⁵, Mial⁴, Ephraim³, Ephraim², Michael¹), b. May 10, 1840; m. Nov. 7, 1866, Lottie Garfield, b. Sept. 30, 1843. Res. Honeoye Falls, N. Y.

CHILDREN.

I. JESSIE G., b. Mar. 14, 1869.

588. **Elisha K.⁹ Pierce** (Benjamin W.⁸, Asa⁷, John⁶, Jonathan⁵, David⁴, Ephraim³, Ephraim², Michael¹), b. Feb. 22, 1862; m. Nov. 26, 1883, Mary C. Lasus, b. Apr., 1861. Res. 19 Hill street, New Bedford, Mass.

CHILDREN.

I. ALICE D., b. Sept. 26, 1886.

589. **Henry A.¹⁰ Pierce** (Nathaniel⁹, Isaac⁸, Nathaniel⁷, Samuel⁶, Joshua⁵, Isaac⁴, Azrikim³, Ephraim², Michael¹), b. Dec. 30, 1834; m. Jan. 1, 1857, Arabella D. Young. Res. Ellsworth, Me.

CHILDREN.

I. HESTER M., b. Aug. 8, 1858; m. July 3, 1881, Fred W. Brown, a lawyer ; res. Belfast.
II. HENRY N., b. May 29, 1861.
III. LAURA S., b. Apr. 28, 1867.
IV. MARY E., b. Feb. 13, 1869.
V. ROBERT W., b. Mar. 9, 1871.
VI. FANNY B., b. Feb. 19, 1877.
VII. LOUISE W., b. June 15, 1879; d. Jan. 29, 1884.

590. **Simeon O.¹⁰ Pierce** (Simeon⁹, Isaac⁸, Nathaniel⁷, Samuel⁶, Joshua⁵, Isaac⁴, Azrikim³, Ephraim², Michael¹), b. July 8, 1823; m. June 11, 1857, Sarah J. McGuire, b. May 9, 1837. He d. Oct. 25, 1886. Res. Shingle Springs, California.

CHILDREN.

604.   I. GEORGE E., b. May 8, 1858; m. Jennie M. Lovless.
      II. FRANK B., b. June 19, 1868; d. Nov. 9, 1877.
605.   III. WILLIAM O., b. May 11, 1860; m. Jennie Burns.

591. **John D.**[10] **Pierce** (Simeon[9], Isaac[8], Nathaniel[7], Samuel[6], Joshua[5], Isaac[4], Azrikim[3], Ephraim[2], Michael[1]), b. Aug. 9, 1826; m. Dec. 23, 1847, Martha Tomlinson, b. Mar. 26, 1828. Res. Bangor, Me.

CHILDREN.

    I. HENRY O., b. Jan. 1, 1849; m. Laura T. Foster; res. Bangor.
   II. ELLA M., b. Oct. 22, 1851; m. Joseph A. Bicknell.
  III. ANNA L., b. Mar. 9, 1864; m. July 28, 1865.

592. **Captain Marcus**[10] **Pierce** (David[9], Nathaniel[8], Nathaniel[7], Samuel[6], Joshua[5], Isaac[4], Azrikim[3], Ephraim[2], Michael[1]), b. June 29, 1843; m. Mar. 10, 1870, Annie E. Hopkins, b. Aug., 1846. Res. Hampden, Me.

Captain Marcus Pierce was born in 1843; he is now (1888) captain of the steamer " Katahdin " of the Boston and Bangor Steamship Company.

CHILDREN.

    I. WILLIS G., b. Apr. 5, 1877.
   II. HOWARD M., b. Apr. 28, 1879.

593. **Walter H.**[10] **Pierce** (Nathaniel H.[9], Nathaniel[8], Nathaniel[7], Samuel[6], Joshua[5], Isaac[4], Azrikim[3], Ephraim[2], Michael[1]), b. June 12, 1855; m. Oct. 15, 1878, Harriett L. Grant, b. Feb. 25, 1855. Res. West Everett, Mass.

CHILDREN.

    I. CLIFFORD H., b. July 17, 1882.

594. **Thomas A.**[10] **Pierce** (Nehemiah R.[9], Nathaniel[8], Thomas[7], Joshua[6], Joshua[5], Isaac[4], Azrikim[3], Ephraim[2], Michael[1]), b. Aug. 31, 1855; m. Aug. 31, 1882, Cora B. Keith, b. Aug. 31, 1859; d. Feb. 19, 1885. Res. Vinton, Iowa.

CHILDREN.

I. CORA A., b. Sept. 10, 1883.

595. **Wendell P.**[10] **Pierce** (Nehemiah R.[9], Nathaniel[8], Thomas[7], Joshua[6], Joshua[5], Isaac[4], Azrikim[3], Ephraim[2], Michael[1]), b. May 23, 1860; m. Feb. 21, 1884, Tinna Brown, b. Apr. 24, 1858; d. Feb. 1, 1885. Res. Dysart, Iowa.

CHILDREN.

I. TINNA W., b. Jan. 20, 1885.

596. **Walter C.**[10] **Pierce** (Henry R.[9], Nathaniel[8], Thomas[7], Joshua[6], Joshua[5], Isaac[4], Azrikim[3], Ephraim[2], Michael[1]), b. Nov. 17, 1856; m. Nov. 28, 1878, Hattie A. Howe. Res. Waukon, Iowa.

CHILDREN.

I. JESSIE M., b. Aug. 10, 1879.
II. LUTHER H., b. Apr. 20, 1881.
III. DORA B., b. Dec. 17, 1883.

597. **Benjamin H. S.**[10] **Pierce** (Isaac R.[9], Israel[8], William[7], Joshua[6], Joshua[5], Isaac[4], Azrikim[3], Ephraim[2], Michael[1]), b. Sept. 10, 1832; m. May 23, 1855, Ruth G. Freeman, b. Mar. 16, 1836. Res. Welfleet, Mass.

CHILDREN.

I. WILLIAM C., b. Sept. 10, 1863.
II. EUNICE A., b. Apr. 6, 1857; d. June 17, 1868.
III. LILLIA F., b. Nov. 3, 1867; m. Sept. 23, 1883, Chester E. Newcomb; res. Welfleet, Mass.
IV. BERTHA S., b. Apr. 7, 1870.
V. CARRESSA W., b. Oct. 27, 1875.
VI. HERBERT, b. Oct. 1, 1860.

598. **Warren E.**[10] **Pierce** (Isaac R.[9], Israel[8], William[7], Joshua[6], Joshua[5], Isaac[4], Azrikim[3], Ephraim[2], Michael[1]), b. Sept. 20, 1834; m. Apr. 8, 1858, Anna Hopkins, b. Apr. 27, 1836. Res. Welfleet, Mass.

CHILDREN.

I. ABBOTT L., b. Oct. 27, 1860.

II. LINDA A., b. Mar. 17, 1863; m. May 11, 1886, Thomas F. Holbrook; res. 117 Walnut street, Fall River, Mass.

III. WARREN L., b. July 31, 1865.

IV. GEORGE A., b. Aug. 6, 1867; d. July 19, 1868.

V. GEORGE A., b. July 3, 1870.

VI. NELLIE E., b. July 9, 1873.

VII. EDMUND H., b. Dec. 1, 1876.

599. **Frank E.**[10] **Pierce** (James P.[9], Otis[8], Pardon[7], Pardon[6], Nathan[5], Mial[4], Ephraim[3], Ephraim[2], Michael[1]), b. July 12, 1859; m. Nov., 1883, Jane Harris, b. ——. Res. Newport, N. Y.

CHILDREN.

I. BASIL A., b. ——.

600. **Leonard S.**[10] **Pierce** (George W.[9], Holden[8], Samuel[7], David[6], Nathan[5], Mial[4], Ephraim[3], Ephraim[2], Michael[1]), b. Oct. 27, 1842; m. Dec. 25, 1865, Sarah Holinbury, b. Jan. 13, 1847. Res. Lawrence, Kans.

CHILDREN.

I. ROSA, b. Jan. 8, 1876.

II. JENNIE, b. Mar. 1, 1878; d. Oct. 17, 1881.

III. LEONARD G., b. Jan. 6, 1880.

IV. OLIVER, b. Mar. 3, 1882.

601. **William James**[10] **Pierce** (George W.[9], Holden[8], Samuel[7], David[6], Nathan[5], Mial[4], Ephraim[3], Ephraim[2], Michael[1]), b. Dec. 3, 1860; m. Feb. 15, 1881, Estella Chapman. Res. Lawrence, Kans.

CHILDREN.

I. FRANK W., b. Dec. 10, 1881.

II. GEORGE E., b. Sept. 27, 1885.

602. **William F.**[10] **Pierce** (Dexter[9], Seneca[8], Levi[7], Caleb[6], Caleb[5], Mial[4], Ephraim[3], Ephraim[2], Michael[1]), b. Jan. 16, 1855; m.

June 25, 1878, Maria H. Akers, b. June 10, 1856. Add. 971
Broadway, Oakland, Cal.

CHILDREN.

  I. MABEL L., b. Aug. 30, 1879.
  II. HAZEL E., b. June 22, 1883.

603. **Hon. Charles D.**[10] **Pierce** (Dexter[9], Seneca[8], Levi[7],
Caleb[6], Caleb[5], Mial[4], Ephraim[3], Ephraim[2], Michael[1]), b. July 16,
1859; m. May 14, 1885, Ella N. Bartholomew, b. June 15, 1858.
Add. 971 Broadway, Oakland, Cal.

The young, level-headed and popular mayor of the city of Oakland has gained this highly honorable position as a representative
of the business men and industrial classes of this municipality.
He came to California at the age of fifteen years, finished his education in the Santa Barbara College, and by his own exertions
established in conjunction with his brother, Frank Pierce, the
house of Pierce & Co., hardware merchants. He has always taken
a deep interest in the welfare of his constituents, and his sterling
integrity and reliability as a business man have given him a
popularity among the sons of toil, and an official position seldom
gained by a man under thirty years of age. He has been a leading and active member of the Oakland Board of Trade, and was
selected by the merchants of this city to act as one of the members of the Freeholders' Commission to frame a city charter.
His brilliant career forcibly illustrates the triumphs of peace.
Official position has been given without asking and against his
express desire. He has been closely identified with the growth
and development of Oakland, a city of homes and manufactures;
believes in her future greatness, and is never so happy as when he
is advancing her interests. In the F. and A. M. he has been sig-
nally honored. He is a member of Oakland Commandery,
No. 11, Knights Templar, 32° in Scottish Rite Masonry, member
of the Grand Consistory of California, and promoted to the Court
of Honor of Washington, D. C., from which body he holds an
official patent. Surrounded by an interesting family, honored
and esteemed by his neighbors, there seems to be a bright future
for him in keeping with the success he has attained in the past.

604. **George E.**[11] **Pierce** (Simeon O.[10], Simeon[9], Isaac[8],
Nathaniel[7], Samuel[6], Joshua[5], Isaac[4], Azrikim[3], Ephraim[2], Mi-

chael[1]), b. May 8, 1858; m. June 11, 1881, Jennie M. Lovless, b. May 8, 1866. Res. Shingle Springs, Cal.

CHILDREN.

I. ROSS E., b. July 14, 1882.
II. HUGH O., b. Sept. 5, 1883.
III. GUY, b. Dec. 25, 1885.

605. **William O.**[11] **Pierce** (Simeon O.[10], Simeon[9], Isaac[8], Nathaniel[7], Samuel[6], Joshua[5], Isaac[4], Azrikim[3], Ephraim[2], Michael[1]), b. May 11, 1860; m. Jan., 1884, Jennie Burns, b. 1862. Res. Shingle Springs, Cal.

CHILDREN.

I. SIMEON O., b. Jan., 1885.
II. CLYDE, b. Feb., 1886.

53

INDEX.

NAMES OTHER THAN PIERCE.

56

www.ingramcontent.com/pod-product-compliance
Lightning Source LLC
Chambersburg PA
CBHW050557270326
41926CB00012B/2093